Walkoffs, Last Licks, and Final Outs

Walkoffs, Last Licks, and Final Outs

Baseball's Grand (and not-so-grand) Finales

Bill Chuck
and
Jim Kaplan

Foreword by
Jon Miller

ACTA SPORTS

WALKOFFS, LAST LICKS, AND FINAL OUTS
Baseball's Grand (and not-so-grand) Finales
by Bill Chuck and Jim Kaplan
Foreword by Jon Miller

Edited by L.C. Fiore
Cover design by Tom A. Wright
Interior design and typesetting by Desktop Edit Shop, Inc.

Published by: ACTA Sports
              5559 W. Howard Street
              Skokie, IL 60077
              (800) 397-2282
              info@actasports.com
              www.actasports.com

Statistics appearing within the text courtesy of Baseball-Reference.com.

Boxscores, career lines and linescores courtesy of Retrosheet.org. The information used here was obtained free of charge from and is copyrighted by Retrosheet. Interested parties may contact Retrosheet at www.retrosheet.org.

Ballpark specs courtesy of Ballparks.com and BallparksOfBaseball.com.

Photographs courtesy of the National Baseball Hall of Fame, with the exception of "Cal Ripken, Jr." ©Sam Friedman. Used by permission.

Portions of this book previously appeared in Billy-Ball.com, *Bill Mazeroski's Baseball 2001,* and MSNBC.com.

Library of Congress Number: 2007941426

ISBN: 978-0-87946-342-7

Printed in the United States of America by Versa Press

Year: 15 14 13 12 11 10 09 08

Printing: 10 9 8 7 6 5 4 3 2 1

Table of Contents

Foreword

Red Sox Nation embraced a San Francisco Giant with a loud, long ovation in June of 2007 at Fenway. It would seem a rather unlikely occurrence from such a large gathering of Red Sox lovers, until you realize the object of their affection was the former Red Sox post-season hero, Dave Roberts.

I had the great pleasure to broadcast the 2004 American League Championship Series for ESPN Radio. In Game 4, with the Yankees leading the series three games to none, and leading the game by a run in the ninth—and with the great Mariano Rivera on the mound no less—Roberts entered the game as a pinch runner.

At that fateful moment, my mind flashed back to an oft-repeated, little observed pre-game ritual at Dodger Stadium during the previous three seasons: Hours before game time—before batting practice even—there was Roberts in the batting cage and on the basepaths working with the legendary Maury Wills, perhaps the greatest base stealer of all-time.

In this treasure of a book, *Walkoffs, Last Licks, and Final Outs: Baseball's Grand (and not-so-grand) Finales*, you'll learn the inside story of how Roberts achieved the most important stolen base in Red Sox history (remember the stakes: If he stole the bag, the Sox were still alive; if he failed, the season was all but over). That steal would ultimately lead to the Sox' historic comeback in the ALCS and first World Series win in 86 seasons.

By the way, on that June evening last season, Roberts—now wearing the black and orange of the Giants—after many doffs of his cap, acknowledging the roar of the Fenway Faithful—stepped in the box, rapped out a base hit, and started a two-run Giants rally that quickly turned all that Fenway love into a far-distant memory.

Memories are the constant companion of a baseball broadcaster and a baseball fan. Seeing Roberts at Fenway last season took me back to memories of Rivera and Wills but also of David Ortiz (who won that memorable Game 4 with a 12th-inning home run), and, of course, Curt Schilling pitching Game 6 at Yankee Stadium with the now-famous "bloody sock."

My ESPN Sunday Night Baseball partner Joe Morgan and I—about to start our 19th season in the SNB booth together—both prefer being in a ballpark to almost any other place. We share a love for the game but are also inevitably reminded of games and moments that linger indelibly in our minds.

However, there is one story Joe never mentioned to me: his last major league at-bat. Happily, that moment is recounted within these pages (fittingly, for a future Hall of Famer, Joe hit a double).

We all remember the Iron Man, Cal Ripken, Jr., breaking Lou Gehrig's consecutive games-played record in 1995. Herein you'll encounter the story of the night "The Streak" ended.

Less remembered, but nonetheless touched upon in this book, is the night Cal's consecutive innings streak ended (he had played every inning of every game for more than five seasons!). I remember that night well, and a momentous night it was.

It was September 14, 1987, at the old Exhibition Stadium in Toronto. Cal's Orioles were taking one of the worst beatings in franchise history. By the eighth inning, the Blue Jays led, 17-3. The Jays had done it by hitting an all-time major league record nine home runs! A great night for the Blue Jays, a momentous achievement, and a historic night for the ages…at least, it was…until…

…the Orioles took the field in the last of the eighth, without Cal! Ron Washington (now managing the Texas Rangers) had taken over for Ripken at shortstop. After playing every inning of every game for 904 straight games, Ripken was out (removed from the game by his dad, Cal Sr., then the Orioles' manager).

As we all contemplated the odd sight of the Orioles on the field without Ripken, Fred McGriff walloped yet another Blue Jays Big Fly! Wow! It was Toronto's 10th of the game, a record that still stands twenty-one years later (the previous record had been eight).

Orioles catcher Terry Kennedy was asked after the game why, with all the homeruns flying all over the park, no Blue Jay hitters were hit or even brushed back.

Kennedy said, "If they had taken liberties, leaning out over the plate and clobbering pitches they shouldn't have, we would have sent them a message. But every home run they hit was on a fat pitch. In fact, there were so many fat pitches tonight I'm shocked they only hit ten!"

But the headlines in Baltimore and Washington the next day were not about the historic homer barrage but rather about Ripken's one-inning absence: "Ripken's Innings Streak Ends" screamed the bold print at the top of the page (followed by a fine-print whisper: "O's lose").

One of the thrills for me as a radio/TV play-by-play man for the Giants (my job during the week), is running into former Giants greats such as Willie Mays and Willie McCovey at beautiful AT&T Park in San Francisco. What thrills those two Hall of Famers provided a young Giants fan such as me.

All Giants fans remember precisely where they were and what they were doing when, in Game 7, Willie McCovey hit the line drive right at Bobby Richardson for the final out of the 1962 World Series (I was an eleven-year-old sitting in the dentist's chair in Castro Valley, California).

I remember legendary cartoonist Charles Schulz drawing a Peanuts comic strip soon after, where Charlie Brown cried out in anguish "Why couldn't McCovey's ball have been just two feet higher!?"

That World Series, and it was a classic between the Yankees and the Giants, is recounted within. I love the anecdote from Don Larsen—the former Yankee and author of the only perfect game in World Series history—who recalled being the winning pitcher in Game 4 for the Giants in 1962 "…on My Day". Sure enough, on the sixth anniversary of his 1956 Perfect Game at Yankee Stadium, Larsen was back at The Stadium to beat the Yankees (by recording only one out, in the sixth inning, and this time he wasn't perfect, issuing a walk to one of the two batters he faced).

Baseball is there every day, whenever you would like to enjoy it, whenever you might need it to help escape the toils and strains of real life. While you enjoy today's game, it inevitably stirs memories of other days and nights spent with the game.

If that's you, this is your book. Enjoy!

Jon Miller
Play-by-play Announcer ESPN Sunday Night Baseball, 19th year
Play-by-play Announcer, San Francisco Giants, 12th year
Play-by-play Announcer, Major League Baseball, since 1974

Introduction

I love baseball. I watch games from Opening Day through to the end of the season. So it was no surprise that on a beautiful Saturday on October 6, 2001, I was at home watching baseball on television. It was especially difficult saying goodbye to that season, as baseball seemed to provide the salve the country needed after September 11. It was once again, as America's game has always been, a great unifier.

The game on television had no meaning to the standings; the Red Sox were finishing in second, once again, to you-know-who, and would end their season with an uninspired 82-79 record, 13½ games out of first. Their hosts that day at Camden Yards were the Baltimore Orioles, who would finish the season with a depressing 63-98-1 record.

Yet I was watching this game—every inning, every pitch—to the very end. I can't be certain, but I venture to guess that most of the 48,807 fans stayed to the end of the game too, even though the Sox would win 5-1 (and it was never really a contest). And when Red Sox reliever Ugueth Urbina blew that final 3-2 fastball past Orioles left fielder Brady Anderson for the final out, the disappointment of a crowd that had been screaming only moments before was palpable. And when Urbina "pulled the trigger" to celebrate this meaningless strikeout, my feelings were also mixed with anger.

You see, waiting in the on-deck circle was Cal Ripken, Jr., who remains both a baseball and American icon. The crowd that had been shouting "We want Cal!" now stood and cheered the future Hall of Famer as he walked back to the dugout for the last time in his career. I couldn't help but think how Urbina had disrespected his sport by not throwing a pitch so wide that Anderson would have walked and the fans and baseball and the world would have had one last chance to stand and cheer for Ripken as he stood at the plate. It seemed so empty for him to retire while waiting in the on-deck circle.

I think of that moment frequently. I have watched playing careers come and go, stadiums close, teams move, streaks end, comebacks materialize, and players walk off after a homer. That Ripken moment, though, was the genesis for this book.

This book is not about statistics, the lifeblood of baseball: It's about the stories behind the moments, big and small, that make baseball special. That's the heart and soul of the game. The book is a book about the famous, like Cal Ripken, Jr., and the everyday player, like Joe Pignatano—a journeyman catcher who in five years in the big leagues played with four teams in five cities. In Piggy's last season, 1962, he played with the hapless yet endearing New York Mets, who finished their inaugural year with a record of 40-120. Their final game, in what would be Pignatano's final game, was played on September 30, 1962, in front of 3,960 fans at Wrigley Field against the Chicago Cubs.

In the 8th inning, Sammy Drake and Richie Ashburn both singled off Bob Buhl. For Drake and Ashburn (a future Hall of Famer), these would be their last at-bats in the major leagues. The next batter hit a broken-bat shot to the right of second base for what appeared to be a base hit—at least to Drake and Ashburn. Cubs second baseman Kenny Hubbs (whose last game would be a year minus one day from then) casually caught the ball and tossed it to future Hall of Famer Ernie Banks at first (his final game would be September 26, 1971) to double up Ashburn. Banks then tossed it to shortstop Andre Rodgers at second for the third out. Joe Pignatano, in his last time at-bat in the major leagues, had hit into a triple play.

Writing a book of this nature can either be an enormous chore or an enormous pleasure depending on whom you are working with. I opted to make sure it would be the latter. I contacted my friend Jim Kaplan, who is a gifted baseball writer and editor, and asked if he would like to "come out and play." If there is anyone who would appreciate a final moment it's Jim, because he has written brilliantly about Bill Mazeroski, whose walk-off homer for the 1960 World Champion Pittsburgh Pirates is among all of sports' greatest moments.

We tried to collect the unusual and the interesting and shed new light on the memorable. The great thing about baseball is that it will always produce indelible moments; in the future, we will always do our best not to leave these moments stranded in the on-deck circle.

Pennant Races

Bobby Thomson kissing the bat that made baseball history in 1951.

1908

On October 8, 1908, the Chicago Cubs beat the New York Giants, 4-2, in the replay of a September 23 game that had ended in a disputed 1-1 tie. The Cubs' Mordecai (Three Finger) Brown relieved Jack Pfiester in the first inning and out-dueled Christy Mathewson to clinch the National League pennant.

The September 23 face-off was one of the most controversial games in baseball history. The Giants appeared to have won, 2-1, when Al Bridwell singled home Harry McCormick from third with two outs in the home ninth. However, alert Cub second baseman Johnny Evers noticed that Fred Merkle, the pinch runner on first, neglected to touch second base and instead headed into the clubhouse once the "winning" run had scored. Evers procured a ball and stepped on second base for the force even while Giants fans surged around him. That evening, first base umpire Hank O'Day ruled that the run didn't count: Officially, the game ended in a 1-1 tie. One day later, National League President Henry Pulliam upheld O'Day's decision, and the game was replayed once the Cubs and Giants finished the regular season tied for first place.

In the aftermath, the offending Merkle, all of nineteen years old at the time, earned the nickname Bonehead, which he would carry for the remainder of his career.

Chicago Cubs vs. New York Giants

National League Pennant
Wednesday, September 23, 1908
Polo Grounds III

BATTING

Chicago Cubs	AB	R	H	RBI
Hayden rf	4	0	0	0
Evers 2b	4	0	1	0
Schulte lf	4	0	0	0
Chance 1b	4	0	1	0
Steinfeldt 3b	2	0	1	0
Hofman cf	3	0	1	0
Tinker ss	3	1	1	0
Kling c	3	0	1	0
Pfiester p	3	0	0	0
Totals	30	1	5	1

FIELDING
DP: 2. Tinkers-Chance. 1. Evers-Chance.
E: Steinfeldt, Tinker 2

BATTING
SH: Steinfeldt (1, off Mathewson)
Team LOB: 3

New York Giants	AB	R	H	RBI
Herzog 2b	3	1	1	0
Bresnahan c	3	0	0	0
Donlin rf	4	0	1	1
Seymour cf	4	0	1	0
Devlin 3b	4	0	2	0
McCormick lf	3	0	0	0
Merkle 1b	3	0	1	0
Bridwell ss	4	0	0	0
Mathewson p	3	0	0	0
Totals	31	1	6	1

FIELDING
DP: 1. Mathewson-Bridwell-Merkle

BATTING
SH: Bresnahan (1, off Pfiester)
HBP: McCormick (1, by Pfiester)

PITCHING

Chicago Cubs	IP	H	R	ER	BB	SO
Pfiester	9	6	1	0	2	0

New York Giants	IP	H	R	ER	BB	SO
Mathewson	9	5	1	1	0	9

Umpires: Hank O'Day, Bob Emslie

Time of Game: 1:30 **Attendance:** 20,000

Team	1	2	3	4	5	6	7	8	9	R	H	E
CHI N	0	0	0	1	0	0	0	0	0	1	5	3
NY N	0	0	0	0	1	0	0	0	0	1	6	0

1938

On September 28, 1938, the Chicago Cubs and the Pittsburgh Pirates squared off in Wrigley Field for the National League pennant. With the game tied 5-5, and with the sun setting in the ninth inning, the umpires ruled the game would have to be determined or it would have to be called on account of darkness. With two outs in the bottom of the inning, Gabby Hartnett came to bat representing the Cubs' last chance. On an 0-2 pitch, he hit a pennant-winning home run into the gathering darkness over the left field wall that came to be known as the "Homer in the Gloamin.'" The blow inspired a lot of purple prose, but John Carmichael of the Chicago *Daily News* possessed the decency to write, "We surrender to inadequacy."

Chicago Cubs vs. Pittsburgh Pirates

National League Pennant
Wednesday, September 28, 1938
Wrigley Field

Team	1	2	3	4	5	6	7	8	9	R	H
PIT N	0	0	0	0	0	3	0	2	0	5	10
CHI N	0	1	0	0	0	2	0	2	1	6	12

1940 — Detroit Tigers vs. Cleveland Indians

Sometimes it pays to be the right guy at the right time in the right place. For example, Floyd Giebell on September 27, 1940, had appeared in all of one game for the Detroit Tigers when they asked him to be a human sacrifice and pitch against Bob Feller of the Cleveland Indians in the opener of a four-game series. This would allow Detroit to save Bobo Newsom, Schoolboy Rowe and Tommy Bridges in the event they were needed to clinch the pennant later in the series. Tigers manager Del Baker made a wise choice: Feller pitched a three-hitter and gave up just two runs, but Giebell pitched a six-hit shutout and the Tigers clinched the pennant. It was Giebell's last major league win.

American League Pennant
Friday, September 27, 1940
Cleveland Stadium

Team	1	2	3	4	5	6	7	8	9	R	H
DET A	0	0	0	2	0	0	0	0	0	2	3
CLE A	0	0	0	0	0	0	0	0	0	0	6

1946 — St. Louis Cardinals vs. Brooklyn Dodgers

On October 3, 1946, the St. Louis Cardinals beat the Brooklyn Dodgers 8-4, clinching the National League pennant in the finale of baseball's first three-game playoff. The Cardinals led 8-1 going into the bottom of the ninth inning when the Dodgers knocked out Cards starting pitcher Murry Dickson and promptly loaded the bases with one out against Harry (The Cat) Brecheen. But Brecheen struck out Eddie Stanky and pinch hitter Howie Schultz, erasing dreams of a pennant for hopeful Dodger fans.

National League Pennant
Thursday, October 3, 1946
Ebbets Field

Team	1	2	3	4	5	6	7	8	9	R	H
STL N	0	2	0	0	3	0	1	2	0	8	13
BRO N	1	0	0	0	0	0	0	0	3	4	6

1948 — Cleveland Indians vs. Boston Red Sox

Cleveland and Boston ended the 1948 season tied for first place—both teams were 96-58. On October 4, the Indians beat the Red Sox 8-3, in a one-game playoff (the American League's first), clinching the pennant. Rookie knuckleballer Gene Bearden (20-7) bested the surprise Red Sox starter, 36-year-old Denny Galehouse (8-8). The Indians' shortstop-manager Lou Boudreau hit two home runs and two singles for the victors.

The Red Sox' loss prevented what would have been the only all-Boston World Series against the National League Boston Braves, but enabled the Tribe to win their first World Championship since 1920 and their last World Championship to date. Boston manager Joe McCarthy's decision to use Galehouse over the well-rested Mel Parnell (15-8) and Ellis Kinder (10-7) adorns the Hall of Shame inside every Red Sox fan's heart.

American League
Tiebreaker
Monday, October 4, 1948
Fenway Park

Team	1	2	3	4	5	6	7	8	9	R	H
CLE A	1	0	0	4	1	0	0	1	1	8	13
BOS A	1	0	0	0	0	2	0	0	0	3	5

When Casey Stengel began managing the New York Yankees in 1949, he was already sixty years old. But Stengel led his team down to the wire against their archrivals, the Boston Red Sox.

Heading into their final two games of the season, at Yankee Stadium, the Yankees trailed the Sox by one game. In the penultimate showdown, the Yankees' Allie Reynolds faced 25-game winner Mel Parnell. Boston's Magic Number was two, meaning one Red Sox victory plus one Yankee loss would send the Sox into the World Series.

Boston scored a run in the first inning and then three more in the third on a scratch single and five walks. The last two walks were granted by Yankee reliever-extraordinaire Joe Page, who walked home two runs by issuing free passes to Al Zarilla and Billy Goodman. But the Yankees scored twice in the fourth and twice again in the fifth to tie the game at 4-4. Pennant races are filled with unexpected heroes, and one Yankee version stood up with two outs in the bottom of the eighth: Long John Lindell, a 6-foot 4½-inch, 217-pound reserve outfielder, came to the plate batting all of .239. But he deposited a fastball into the left field stands for his sixth home run of the season and gave the Yankees a 5-4 win. Despite his early wildness, Page surrendered only one hit in 6⅔ innings of relief.

The scene was set for a winner-take-all finale on Sunday, October 2, before 68,055 New York fans. Boston's Ellis Kinder (23-5) faced the Yankees' Vic Raschi (20-10). Yankee leadoff batter Phil Rizzuto lined a triple down the left field line. The next batter, Tommy (Old Reliable) Henrich, hit a grounder to second baseman Bobby Doerr, who was playing back. Doerr took the out at first while Rizzuto scored. The game remained 1-0 until the bottom of the eighth.

Boston manager Joe McCarthy brought in Mel Parnell, who had nothing left from the day before. He was greeted by Henrich's fourth homer of the season. (Old Reliable was well-named.) After Parnell gave up a single to Yogi Berra, Marse Joe pulled him for the infrequently-used veteran Tex Hughson. The move looked brilliant when Joe DiMaggio banged into a double play, but things changed in a New York minute. Lindell singled, Billy Johnson singled, and Cliff Mapes walked to load the bases. The new hero of the moment, Jerry Coleman, hit a looping fly to right. Zeke Zarilla rushed in at breakneck speed, but the ball fell in front of him and all three runners scored before Coleman was thrown out trying to stretch his double into a triple.

The Yanks were now on top 5-0, heading to the ninth, with Vic Raschi on the mound. Johnny Pesky fouled out, but Ted Williams walked and Vern Stephens singled. Bobby Doerr then lifted a long drive to center field. Joltin' Joe DiMaggio had been "Ailin' Joe" for three weeks with a viral infection: He simply did not have the speed to track down the ball. It dropped for a two-run triple, cutting the Yankee lead to 5-2. Rather than risk any further damage, DiMaggio came trotting in. Cliff Mapes moved to center, with Hank Bauer switching from left to right and Gene Woodling from right to left. Zarilla immediately tested Mapes with a short fly to center that Mapes easily handled, but Goodman singled home Doerr to make it 5-3 with the tying run coming to the plate.

At-bat: Red Sox catcher Birdie Tebbetts, a .270 hitter with limited power. No match for Raschi, he hit a twisting foul pop behind first base that Henrich caught to give the Yankees their sixteenth American League Championship. A bloop by Jerry Coleman had sent Ted Williams and the Red Sox home for the winter.

"Williams never forgave me," Coleman said during his Hall of Fame induction. "Ted used to give me hell. I said, 'Ted, let me tell you something. You're out in left field in Yankee Stadium, it's shady and bright and you can't see anything. What you saw was the cover of that ball. The core is still in orbit somewhere.'"

American League Tiebreaker
Sunday, October 2, 1949
Yankee Stadium

Team	1	2	3	4	5	6	7	8	9	R	H
BOS A	0	0	0	0	0	0	0	0	3	3	5
NY A	1	0	0	0	0	0	0	4	x	5	9

On September 18, 1950, the Associated Press reported: "The Phillies, their first pennant in thirty-five years virtually in their grasp, today announced a precedent-shattering plan for distribution and sale of World Series tickets." When the story was published on September 19, Philadelphia led the Brooklyn Dodgers by nine games with fifteen left to play.

So how does this story find itself in a chapter about fabulous finishes? Because those 1950 Whiz Kids were still, after all, the Philadelphia Phillies.

On September 19, Hank Sauer's 30th home run and a two-hit pitching performance by Frank Hiller gave the Chicago Cubs a 1-0 victory over the Phillies, thwarting Robin Roberts' effort to become Philadelphia's first 20-game winner since 1917. Meanwhile, the Boston Braves edged the St. Louis Cardinals 8-7, and the Dodgers swept a doubleheader from the Pirates 14-3 and 3-2.

September 19, 1950:

Team	Record	GB
Philadelphia	87-55	—
Boston	79 -60	6½
Brooklyn	78-61	7½

On September 20, the Phils defeated the Cubs, 9-6; Jim Konstanty picked up his 16th win in relief. The Braves lost to the Cards 1-0, and the Dodgers won 7-2 over the Pirates.

September 20:

Team	Record	GB
Philadelphia	88-55	—
Boston	79-61	7½
Brooklyn	79-61	7½

On September 21, the Phillies, who had a good mix of youngsters like pitching star Robin Roberts, center fielder Richie Ashburn, Granny Hamner, Willie Jones, Del Ennis and Curt Simmons, and veterans like Andy Seminick, Dick Sisler and Eddie Waitkus, had an off day. Both the Braves (behind Warren Spahn, who became the National League's first 21-game winner) and the Dodgers won.

None of the three teams played on September 22, but there was good news for Philadelphia: Rookie pitcher Bubba Church, who had been hit in the face by a Ted Kluszewski line drive on September 10, rejoined the team. Overall, Church went 8-6 with a 2.73 ERA and allowed only 113 hits in 142 innings. The bad news was that star southpaw Simmons was now in the military, a member of Pennsylvania's Twenty-Eighth Division for the rest of the season.

September 21-22:

Team	Record	GB
Philadelphia	88-55	—
Boston	80-61	7
Brooklyn	80-61	7

On September 23, the New York Giants edged the Braves 4-3 in 10 innings, while the Dodgers beat the Phillies, 3-2.

September 23:

Team	Record	GB
Philadelphia	88-56	—
Brooklyn	81-61	6
Boston	80-62	7

On Sunday, September 24, the Braves lost, but the Dodgers demolished the Phillies, 11-0.

September 24:

Team	Record	GB
Philadelphia	88-57	—
Brooklyn	82-61	5
Boston	80-63	7

On September 25, Philadelphia beat the Braves in the first game of a doubleheader 12-4, getting 18 hits behind Ken Heintzelman. The Phils lost the second game 5-3 with Konstanty making his then-record-tying 70th appearance and taking the loss. The Dodgers also split a doubleheader, winning 3-2 and losing 4-3 to the Giants.

September 25:

Team	Record	GB
Philadelphia	89-58	—
Brooklyn	83-62	5
Boston	81-64	7

On September 26, the Phils scored three in the

eighth to finish off the Braves, 8-7. The Dodgers beat the Giants, 8-4.

September 26:

Team	Record	GB
Philadelphia	90-58	—
Brooklyn	84-62	5
Boston	81-65	8

On September 27, the Phils had a doubleheader with the Giants. In the 10th inning of the first game, Giants right fielder Del Ennis fielded Alvin Dark's single and fired home, but baserunner Monte Irvin crashed into catcher Andy Seminick and knocked him out cold. Irvin scored; the Phils lost, 8-7. Then Jim Hearn shut out the Phillies 5-0 in Game 2. Joseph M. Sheehan of the New York *Times* wrote, "The Phillies, having the very deuce of a time wrapping up a pennant generally conceded to them for weeks, yesterday derived their only satisfaction from the scoreboard's news that the Dodgers had lost the second game of their doubleheader with the Braves."

September 27:

Team	Record	GB
Philadelphia	90-60	—
Brooklyn	85-63	4

It wasn't much better for the Phils on September 28, when they dropped another twinbill to the Giants. The score was 3-1 in each game. Meanwhile, the Dodgers and Braves split a doubleheader.

September 28:

Team	Record	GB
Philadelphia	90-62	—
Brooklyn	86-64	3

The Phillies had September 29 off, but they could still back into the pennant because the Dodgers had another doubleheader with the Braves. The Dodgers won the first 7-5; the second game they won, 7-6. Meanwhile, over in the American League, the Yankees clinched and waited to see who their opponent would be.

September 29:

Team	Record	GB
Philadelphia	90-62	—
Brooklyn	88-64	2

Two games remained in the season, and as the baseball gods often arrange these things, the Phillies were playing the Dodgers. "That's the way it ought it be," said Sawyer. "We'd rather win it on our own anyway. You can't expect the other fellow to help you out."

In Lake Success, New York, delegates to the Political and Security Committee of the General Assembly of the United Nations were heatedly debating the growing crisis in Korea. Next door, in the delegates lounge, a large crowd of representatives good-naturedly debated the Phillies-Dodgers game being viewed on television.

The Dodgers silenced the debate before 23,879 at Ebbets Field: They defeated the Phillies, 7-3. There was one day left to the season.

September 30:

Team	Record	GB
Philadelphia	90-63	—
Brooklyn	89-64	1

October 1, 1950. If the Phillies won, they would capture their first pennant in thirty-five years; if Brooklyn won, it would force a best-of-three playoff. Nineteen-game winner Robin Roberts made his third start in five days for the Phils, with Don Newcombe going for Brooklyn. On September 6, Newk had shut out the Phils in the first game of a doubleheader and come back to start the second game as well, going seven innings.

Just like the season, the final game would go down to the wire before 35,073 fans at Ebbets Field. Brooklyn scored when Pee Wee Reese hit a drive off the in-play screen over the right field wall and raced around the bases for an inside-the-park home run. For their part—despite knocking Newk around a little bit—the Phillies only managed to put one run on the scoreboard too.

In the bottom of the ninth, Cal Abrams walked on a 3-2 fastball. Reese attempted two bunts before singling to left center, sending Abrams to second. Even though the powerful Duke Snider was at the plate, everybody expected the Duke of Flatbush to bunt the runners into scoring position; after all, he did have six sacrifices that season. But Snider swung away and lined a single to center. Richie Ashburn—one of the best defensive center fielders in baseball history—was playing shallow and charged the ball.

Although there were no outs, third base coach Milt Stock waved Abrams home. Ashburn's throw to catcher Stan Lopata was perfect, and Abrams was tagged out at the plate. The Dodgers' Jackie Robinson then drew an intentional walk, but Carl Furillo fouled out to first and Gil Hodges flew out to right, sending the game into extra innings tied, 1-1.

Roberts led off the 10th with a single up the middle. Eddie Waitkus dropped in a popfly single, and the Phils had runners on first and second. The next batter, Ashburn, tried to move them up with a bunt, but Roberts was thrown out at third. Dick Sisler, who already had three singles, was the next batter. On a 1-2 pitch, Sisler chipped one over the left field wall 348 feet away and the Phillies won by the final score of 4-1. For the Dodgers, Stock's decision to send Abrams home made for a long winter's journey into spring.

October 1:

Team	Record	GB
Philadelphia	91-63	—
Brooklyn	89-65	2

1951 _____ Brooklyn Dodgers vs. Philadelphia Phillies

On September 30, 1951, the last day of the regular season, the Dodgers needed to beat the Phillies to tie the New York Giants for the National League pennant. Preacher Roe (22-3) started for the Dodgers, but by the bottom of the third inning the Phils led, 6-1. The Dodgers cut the deficit to 6-5 going into the bottom of the fifth, but the Phils retaliated with two runs of their own to extend their lead, 8-5.

The Dodgers scored three times in the top of the eighth behind a two-run double by Rube Walker and an RBI single by Carl Furillo. The score remained 8-8 through the 12th inning. Thanks to a game-saving catch by Jackie Robinson—snaring a bases-loaded line drive in the 13th inning—the score remained tied.

Until Robinson took Robin Roberts deep in the top of the fourteenth. Then, despite giving up a lead-off single to Richie Ashburn in the bottom of the inning, reliever Bud Podbielan held the Phils in check and the Dodgers won 9-8, sending them to face the Giants in a three-game playoff.

National League Pennant
Sunday, September 30, 1951
Shibe Park

Team	1	2	3	4	5	6	7	8	9	10	11	12	13	14	R	H
BRO N	0	0	1	1	3	0	0	3	0	0	0	0	0	1	9	17
PHI N	0	4	2	0	2	0	0	0	0	0	0	0	0	0	8	15

1951 _____ New York Giants vs. Brooklyn Dodgers

On October 3, 1951, the New York Giants' Bobby Thomson hit The Shot Heard 'Round the World—a three-run, ninth inning home run off Ralph Branca that gave the Giants a 5-4 victory over the rival Brooklyn Dodgers, clinching the National League pennant in the finale of the best-of-three playoff. Ballyhooed beyond belief, the achievement turned a modest Scottish immigrant into a cultural icon.

Some sudden celebrities grow spoiled by the attention and embittered by the demands on their time. But while approaching the 50th anniversary of The Shot, as Thomson endured banquets, interviews and appearances, he was more amused than overwhelmed by the fuss—and grateful for the celebrity that allowed him to do good works.

Baseball has had other comparable moments, but

Sports Illustrated named Thomson's blow the second-greatest sporting achievement of the twentieth century, trailing only the U.S. hockey team's Olympic victory over the Soviet Union on February 22, 1980. "It's a good thing I wasn't first," Thomson said when we caught up with him at his home late in 2000, adding, "The hockey team had national significance."

But Thomson's feat may have had greater impact on individuals. People still trade stories about what they were doing when Thomson teed off. In the U.S. Postal Service's tribute to the 1950s, The Shot earned a stamp alongside Luci & Desi, school integration, and Rock 'n' Roll.

"Let me show you something," Thomson said, bouncing off the couch. "Whoopsie, got a little arthritis in the knee, but it's okay when I get up."

Among his many charitable activities, he was

running the Bobby Thomson Celebrity Golf Outing for The Arthritis Foundation. Thomson returned from his office with two copies of *Underworld*, a Don DeLillo novel that opens with a long chapter about "The Shot." One of the book covers—a Greek translation—features Thomson's likeness on the cover. A note from DeLillo warned Thomson, "Don't make any plans for next October 3 [2001]…You'll probably find yourself in the White House eating sushi with Bush or Gore."

"People tell me three things touched them," Thomson said, shaking his head and smiling. "President Kennedy's assassination, Pearl Harbor, and my homer."

How did he become a figure as outsized as a balloon in the Macy's Day Parade? "The great rivalry of the New York teams, the New York media, and Russ Hodges' description of the game on the radio," he said. Thomson described The Shot with such affection that he seemed to find new insights with each telling.

In 1951, the three New York teams—the Dodgers, Giants and Yankees—dominated baseball and baseball dominated sport. As heated National League rivals, the Giants and Dodgers wouldn't speak to one another. Their antagonism reached a peak in 1951 when the Giants, trailing by 13 games on August 12, rallied to tie the Bums by season's end. The teams split the first two games of a best-of-three playoff. In Game 3 at the Polo Grounds, the Dodgers took a 4-1 lead into the last of the ninth. Cameramen set up in the Dodger clubhouse. Thomson, then the Giants' twenty-seven-year-old third baseman, had never been so miserable as he contemplated watching his hated crosstown rivals in the World Series.

What followed, though, taught him to never, ever give up. With Dodger ace Don Newcombe on the mound, Alvin Dark and Don Mueller nosed groundballs through the infield. Monte Irvin followed with a popout. When the next batter, Whitey Lockman, doubled to left, Dark scored, Mueller advanced to third, and Thomson's turn to bat came with the Dodgers' lead cut to 4-2.

But Thomson wasn't concentrating on hitting. Mueller had injured an ankle sliding into third base, and Thomson joined his teammates down the line.

"I'm feeling for the poor guy. It took my mind completely off the game," he said. "When they carried him off, our manager, Leo Durocher, told me, 'Bobby, if you ever hit one, hit one now.' I thought, 'Leo, you're out of your mind.'

"I had to walk ninety feet to the plate. People ask me what the crowd was like. I was the only guy in the ballpark. I started to psyche myself up, which I had never done before: 'Get up there and give yourself a chance to hit. Wait and watch.' It was a Ted Williams kind of thinking—fundamentals. Then I'm calling myself a son of a bitch all the way down the line. All kinds of crazy stuff."

Thomson noted that right-hander Ralph Branca had replaced Don Newcombe on the mound. Branca threw the first pitch down the middle. Thomson took it.

"The guys were telling me later that they wanted to kill me," he said of his teammates.

Then Branca threw one high and inside, trying to set up Thomson for a third pitch over the outside corner. Thomson jumped all over it. The ball screamed toward the left field stands. Thomson thought, "Upper deck," because the overhang at the Polo Grounds—an inviting target—extended past the lower grandstand. Branca was saying, "Sink, sink." The ball started to drop, and Thomson thought, "Base hit."

But the ball disappeared into the lower stands and a tableau in American culture unfolded: On the field, while the Giants charged toward home plate, Thomson loped around the bases, huffing and puffing—probably hyperventilating, he later thought. All the Dodgers left the field except second baseman Jackie Robinson, who watched to see if Thomson touched every base. The Dodgers on the bench, who had estimated their pennant-winning shares at $5,000 a man, were sick at heart. In the press section, Giants announcer Russ Hodges made arguably the most celebrated call in sports history:

There's a long fly. It's gonna be…I believe…The Giants win the pennant! Bobby hit that ball into the lower deck of the leftfield stands. The Giants win the pennant, and they're going crazy! They're going crazy! I don't believe it, I don't believe it, I will not believe it!

Thomson saw his life changed forever. "Perry Como had a fifteen-minute, early-evening TV show. The guy said to me, 'Bobby, we'd love to have you on. We'll give you five-hundred bucks.'

"'I'd really like to share this moment with my family,' I said.

"The guy said, 'We'll give you one-thousand bucks.'

"The old Scottish came out in me. I said, 'For one-thousand bucks, my family can wait,' and I did it."

Thomson was marked, all right. The media adopted "Shot Heard 'Round the World" from Ralph Waldo Emerson's Revolutionary War reference in "The Concord Hymn" (1837). When Thomson arrived at Yankee Stadium the next day, a fan thrust a ball into his hand—The ball, the fan claimed—and wanted two free tickets to the Series opener. Thomson asked the clubhouse attendant for tickets, and the guy laughed. Eight or nine other balls sat in Thomson's locker.

The Yankees beat the Giants four games to two in the World Series. Thomson had two more good seasons with New York, was traded to Milwaukee, and broke his ankle during spring training of 1954. A kid named Hank Aaron was waiting to replace him.

Thomson retired from baseball in 1960 with a .270 batting average and 264 homers over 15 seasons. The transition to life outside sport is difficult for many athletes, but for Thomson and his late wife Winkie, it was relatively simple.

"We had moved into this house in 1958 and we got so wrapped up in our first home I didn't look forward to leaving for spring training," Thomson said. He spent thirty-five years as a successful paper-product salesman, an accomplishment he swears gave him as much pleasure as anything in baseball.

He joined the Optimists, coached Little League, served as a councilman and evolved into a regular suburban schmoozer: just another guy at the barbecue. When we met him, he was living alone but had kids, grandchildren and a girlfriend nearby, and he wasn't lonely.

The Shot has always been with him. "I remember one day crossing Third Avenue," he said, "and this guy going the other way points at me, 'I still hate you.' I turned around and he was looking back at me, laughing. At golf meetings and the A&P, people want to tell me where they were. You never get used to it. But let's face it: It's fun to be remembered."

And profitable, too. Thomson and his longtime friend Ralph Branca (recovered from his untimely gopher ball) make appearances at card, memorabilia and autograph shows.

"Peanuts compared to some of these guys today," Thomson said.

But Thomson felt enriched in other ways too. Beaming, he produced a front-page story from the October 27, 1989, Wall Street *Journal* entitled, "This 50-year-old Sees His Idol as Last of the Sports Heroes." A transit association executive named Albert Engelken, who watched The Shot as a twelve year old and idolized Thomson ever since, was about to turn fifty. Unbeknownst to him, his wife Betsy and Thomson arranged for a meeting. Suddenly, Thomson was standing by Engelken's car at exit 10 off the New Jersey Turnpike.

When his nonplussed new friend asked why he took time to accommodate someone he never met, Thomson said, "You know, Albert, if you have the chance in life to make someone this happy, you have an obligation to do it."

Thanks to the *Journal*, those undeniably generous, incredibly important words were soon shot…'round the world.

National League Tiebreaker—Game 3
Wednesday, October 3, 1951
Polo Grounds V

	1	2	3	4	5	6	7	8	9	R	H
BRO N	1	0	0	0	0	0	0	3	0	4	8
NY N	0	0	0	0	0	0	1	0	4	5	8

Bobby Thomson, OF/3B, 1946-1960

G	AB	R	H	2B	3B	HR	RBI	BB	IBB	SO	HBP	SH	SF	XI	ROE	GDP	SB	CS	AVG	OBP	SLG	BFW
1779	6305	903	1705	267	74	264	1026	559	23i	804	34	36	23i	0i	29i1	63	38	22i	.270	.332	.462	-0.3

On September 29, 1959, the Dodgers beat the Braves two games to none, winning the best-of-three playoff for the National League pennant. L.A. won Game 2, 6-5, in the 12th inning, having overcome a 5-2 deficit in the ninth. Dodger Gil Hodges scored the winning run when second baseman Felix Mantilla fielded Carl Furillo's grounder and threw it away.

National League Tiebreaker—
Game 2
Tuesday, September 29, 1959
LA Memorial Coliseum

Team	1	2	3	4	5	6	7	8	9	10	11	12	R	H	E
MIL N	2	1	0	0	1	0	0	1	0	0	0	0	5	10	2
LA N	1	0	0	1	0	0	0	0	3	0	0	1	6	15	2

1962 ___ San Francisco Giants vs. Los Angeles Dodgers

Although by now both teams had moved to the west coast, history was set to repeat itself. October 3, 1962—eleven years to the day after the 1951 Dodger-Giant playoff finale. Alvin Dark, the Giants' shortstop in 1951, was now the Giants' manager. Leo Durocher, the Dodgers' manager in 1951, was now a Dodger coach. Willie Mays was still the Giants' center fielder and Johnny Podres was still the Dodgers' pitcher. And just as in 1951, the Giants would overcome a 4-2 deficit in the ninth inning to win the National League pennant.

In the top of the ninth, batting for Giants pitcher Don Larsen, Matty Alou coaxed a walk from pitcher Ed Roebuck. The next batter, Harvey Kuenn, hit into a forceout at second, but an ailing Willie McCovey (batting for Chuck Hiller) reached on a walk before being replaced by pinch runner Ernie Bowman. Felipe Alou followed with a walk and Mays reached on an infield hit that scored Kuenn from third. Roebuck was finally yanked for reliever Stan Williams, whereupon Orlando Cepeda hit a sacrifice fly that scored Bowman while Felipe Alou scooted to third. The score was now tied, 4-4. A wild pitch from Williams moved Mays to second and an intentional walk issued to Ed Bailey loaded the bases. Williams then walked Jim Davenport to score Felipe Alou with the go-ahead run.

Only now did Dodger manager Walt Alston replace Williams with Ron Perranoski, but it was too little, too late. Jose Pagan reached on an error by Larry Burright (with Mays scoring) before the Dodgers could get out of the inning. They now trailed, 6-4, and they went down quietly in the ninth.

While the 1951 debacle left Dodger fans dumbfounded, the 1962 collapse bequeathed nothing but anger and outrage. In the winter-long postmortems, critics wondered how Alston, among other things, could have left Roebuck in to start the ninth and waited so long before summoning closer Perranoski. As for the Giants, their fate was also eerily similar to 1951: They lost the World Series, again to the New York Yankees, this time in seven games.

National League Tiebreaker—Game 3
Wednesday, October 3, 1962
Dodger Stadium

BATTING

San Francisco Giants	AB	R	H	RBI	BB	SO	PO	A
Kuenn lf	5	1	2	1	0	0	2	0
Hiller 2b	3	0	1	0	0	0	4	1
McCovey ph	0	0	0	0	1	0	0	0
Bowman pr,2b	0	1	0	0	0	0	0	0
F. Alou rf	4	1	1	0	1	0	4	0
Mays cf	3	1	1	1	2	0	3	0
Cepeda 1b	4	0	1	1	0	0	8	0
Bailey c	4	0	2	0	1	0	3	0
Davenport 3b	4	0	1	1	1	0	2	4
Pagan ss	5	1	2	0	0	0	1	1
Marichal p	2	1	1	0	0	0	0	0
Larsen p	0	0	0	0	0	0	0	1
M. Alou ph	1	0	1	0	0	0	0	0
Nieman ph	1	0	0	0	0	1	0	0
Pierce p	0	0	0	0	0	0	0	0
Totals	36	6	13	4	6	1	27	7

FIELDING -
E: Bailey (6), Pagan (21), Marichal (4).
BATTING -
2B: Hiller (22,off Roebuck).
SH: Hiller (8,off Podres); Marichal (7,off Podres).
SF: Cepeda (7,off Williams).
IBB: Mays 2 (11,by Podres,by Roebuck); Bailey (5,by Williams).
Team LOB: 12.

Los Angeles Dodgers	AB	R	H	RBI	BB	SO	PO	A
Wills ss	5	1	4	0	0	0	3	6
Gilliam 2b,3b	5	0	0	0	0	0	3	1
Snider lf	3	2	2	0	0	0	2	1
Burright 2b	1	0	0	0	0	0	3	2
Walls ph	1	0	0	0	0	0	0	0
T. Davis 3b,lf	3	1	2	2	1	0	1	1
Moon 1b	3	0	0	0	0	0	8	0
Fairly 1b,rf	0	0	0	0	0	0	2	0
Howard rf	4	0	0	1	0	1	0	0
Harkness 1b	0	0	0	0	0	0	0	0
Roseboro c	3	0	0	1	1	1	3	1
W. Davis cf	3	0	0	0	1	0	2	0
Podres p	2	0	0	0	0	1	0	2
Roebuck p	2	0	0	0	0	0	0	0
Williams p	0	0	0	0	0	0	0	0
Perranoski p	0	0	0	0	0	0	0	0
Totals	35	4	8	3	3	3	27	14

FIELDING -
DP: 3. Gilliam-Wills-Moon, Wills-Moon, Wills-Burright-Fairly.
E: Gilliam (20), Burright (15), Roseboro (14), Podres (6).
BATTING -
2B: Snider (11,off Marichal).
HR: T. Davis (27,6th inning off Marichal 1 on 0 out).
SH: Fairly (11,off Larsen).
IBB: Roseboro (11,by Larsen); W. Davis (10,by Larsen).
Team LOB: 8.

BASERUNNING -
SB: Wills 3 (104,2nd base off Marichal/Bailey 2,3rd base off Marichal/Bailey);
T. Davis (18,3rd base off Larsen/Bailey).

PITCHING

San Francisco Giants	IP	H	R	ER	BB	SO	HR
Marichal	7	8	4	3	1	2	1
Larsen W(5-4)	1	0	0	0	2	1	0
Pierce SV(1)	1	0	0	0	0	0	0
Totals	9	8	4	3	3	3	1

IBB: Larsen 2 (7,Roseboro,W. Davis).

Los Angeles Dodgers	IP	H	R	ER	BB	SO	HR
Podres	5	9	2	1	1	0	0
Roebuck L(10-2)	3.1	4	4	3	3	0	0
Williams	0.1	0	0	0	2	0	0
Perranoski	0.1	0	0	0	0	1	0
Totals	9	13	6	4	6	1	0

Podres faced 3 batters in the 6th inning
WP: Williams (7).
IBB: Podres (14,Mays); Roebuck (6,Mays); Williams (11,Bailey).

Umpires: Dusty Boggess, Augie Donatelli, Jocko Conlan, Al Barlick

Time of Game: 3:00 **Attendance:** 45693

	1	2	3	4	5	6	7	8	9	R	H	E
SF N	0	0	2	0	0	0	0	0	4	6	13	3
LA N	0	0	0	1	0	2	1	0	0	4	8	4

During the 2007 season, the one in which the New York Mets collapsed like the walls of Jericho, the beneficiaries were the Philadelphia Phillies, whose fans that year had the dubious distinction of celebrating the team's 10,000th loss. The collapse and milestone were mentioned frequently in the not-so-grand closing days of the Mets' season. Baseball fans were reminded time and again of perhaps the ten worst losses in Phillies history: those that that occurred in succession from September 21 to September 30, 1964.

In the days prior to division winners and wild cards, the Phils were ensconced in first place in the National League and preparing to face the Yankees in the World Series. They held a six-and-a-half game lead with twelve games to play.

The Phils were led on the mound by a strong one-two combination of Jim Bunning and Chris Short, while Dennis Bennett and Art Mahaffey solidified the back end of the rotation. In the bullpen, the Phils' were blessed with two top relievers: Jack Baldschun and Ed Roebuck.

Their offense was formidable, led by their star rookie third baseman slugger Richie Allen and the veteran outfielder Johnny Callison, who had won the All-Star Game that year, at the shiny new Shea Stadium in New York, with a walk-off homer.

The supporting cast of Tony Gonzalez, Tony Taylor, Cookie Rojas, and Bobby Wine provided decent offense and solid defense. But more than all those pieces, they were led by Gene Mauch, a man many described as a managerial genius.

"We executed better than any team in the league," Bunning said, reflecting on Mauch's managerial skill. "Moving base runners, turning the double play…we seemed to do everything perfectly."

For much of the season they played brilliantly. By September 20 they held a 6½-game lead on second-place Cincinnati with only 12 games remaining. The front office printed World Series tickets and programs. Nobody ever expected to hear the cry, "Stop the presses!"

September 21, 1964 – The Reds were in town for the start of a three game series that should have finished them off. Art Mahaffey was on the mound for Philadelphia, facing the not-so-immortal John Tsitouris. With the score tied at zero and one out in the top of the sixth inning, the even-less-immortal back-up infielder Chico Ruiz singled and advanced to third on a Vada Pinson single. Pinson was thrown out at second trying to advance on the hit.

As Mahaffey went into his windup against the immortal Frank Robinson, Ruiz broke for home. If author Malcolm Gladwell were a sportswriter, he would have referred to this moment as "the tipping point," because from the moment Ruiz took off with his team's best hitter at the plate, the Phillies were never the same. Mahaffey threw a wild pitch, Ruiz scored, and the Reds won, 1-0.

Ray Kelly of the Philadelphia *Evening Bulletin* wrote, "It's one of those things that simply isn't done. Nobody tries to steal home with a slugging great like Frank Robinson at the plate. Not in the sixth inning of a scoreless game."

The lead was now 5½ games over the Reds, 6 games over the St. Louis Cardinals, and 7 games over the San Francisco Giants.

September 22, 1964 – Chris Short couldn't complete the 5th inning as Jim O'Toole and the Reds won handily, 9-2.

The lead was now 4½ games over the Reds, 5 games over the Cardinals, and 6 games over the Giants. There were 10 games to go.

September 23, 1964 – The Reds completed the sweep at Shibe Park by scoring four times in the 7th inning to defeat Dennis Bennett and the Phils, 6-4.

The lead was now 3½ games over the Reds, 5 games over the Cardinals, and 5 games over the Giants. There were 9 games to go.

September 24, 1964 – The Phillies hosted the Milwaukee Braves, a powerful-hitting team led by Hank Aaron, Eddie Mathews, Joe Torre, Rico Carty, and Felipe Alou. But the Braves were just over .500 due to the sorry state of their pitching staff. Nonetheless, it was the Braves' Wade Blasingame who outpitched Phillies ace Jim Bunning that night, and the Phils lost their fourth straight, 5-3. Meanwhile, the Cardinals swept a doubleheader from the Pirates in Pittsburgh with Bob Gibson and Ray Sadecki picking up the wins.

The lead was now 3 games over the Reds, 3½ games over the Cardinals, and 4½ games over the Giants. As a frame of reference, we can tell you that the Milwaukee Braves had already been eliminated because they were 10 games out and there were 8 games to go.

September 25, 1964 – The Reds swept a doubleheader from the Mets. The Giants topped the Chicago Cubs and the Cardinals defeated the Pirates once again. The Phillies' Chris Short held a 1-0 lead through six innings but couldn't hold off the Braves bats in the 7th and 8th when Milwaukee took a 3-1 lead. But in the bottom of the 8th Callison hit a two-run homer and the game went into extra innings.

In the top of the 10th, Joe Torre hit a two-run homer off Bobby Locke, but Dick Allen countered with a two-run shot of his own off Bob Sadowski in the bottom of the inning. John Boozer was the fifth Phillies pitcher used and the two runs he gave up in the 12th were the difference as Milwaukee won, 7-5.

The lead was now 1½ games over the Reds, 2½ games over the Cardinals, and 3½ games over the Giants. There were 7 games to go.

September 26, 1964 – The Reds' John Tsitouris was victorious again, defeating the Mets. Curt Simmons led the Cardinals over the Pirates, and the Phillies had Bobby Shantz on the mound defending a 4-3 lead against the Braves in the ninth. But Hank Aaron led off with a single. Mauch sent in Danny Cater to play left because he had a stronger arm than Cookie Rojas. Eddie Mathews singled to right. Frank Bolling pinch hit for Wade Blasingame and grounded to Ruben Amaro at short. Amaro flipped the ball to Tony Taylor…who dropped the ball. The bases, now loaded, were quickly cleared when Rico Carty tripled on what baseball historian John Shiffert described as Shantz' "only bad pitch as a Phillie." In the bottom of the ninth, the pitching-poor Braves brought in a forty-three-year old lefty who hadn't pitched in thirteen days. But Warren Spahn retired the Phils one-two-three and picked up the save.

The Phillies' lead was now a half game over the Reds, 1½ games over the Cardinals, and 3 games over the Giants. There were 6 games to go.

September 27, 1964 – The Giants had a Sunday doubleheader at Wrigley Field. They lost the first game, 4-2. The second game was a great match-up, scoreless through seven, but the Chicago Cubs finally scored four in the eighth off of Juan Marichal (20-8). Larry Jackson (23-10) gave up just one run in the ninth and the Giants lost the doubleheader.

The Reds were in New York for a doubleheader and they won their eighth and ninth straight as the Mets lost their 104th and 105th games of the season.

The Cardinals were in Pittsburgh and Roger Craig, an escapee from the Mets, combined with Barney Schultz to shut out the Bucs. The Cardinals had won five in a row.

The good news for the Phillies was that their bats woke up: Johnny Callison hit three homers. The bad news? Jim Bunning, pitching on two days' rest, had nothing. The Braves won, 14-8. It was their seventh-straight loss.

After the games that day, the Reds were in first place. The Phils trailed by a game. The Cards were in third place, one and a half games back. The Giants were now four and a half behind.

September 28, 1964 – The Phillies moved on to St. Louis and once again Chris Short was on the mound; Mauch had given him two days' rest. Bob Gibson pitched for the Cardinals and was Gibson-like. The Cards won, 5-1. The Phils had lost eight straight, the Cardinals had won six straight, and the Reds and their nine-game winning streak took the night off.

The first-place Reds now led St. Louis by one, the Phillies by 1½ and the Giants by 4½.

September 29, 1964 – It was another day, another loss for the Phils…and another win for the Cards. The Phils started the hurting Dennis Bennett, who gave up five hits and three runs when he was mercifully relieved after getting just four outs. The fourth starter, Art Mahaffey, who was or wasn't injured (depending on whose side you believe), was one of five Phillies relievers that night. It didn't matter. St. Louis won their seventh straight, 4-2. The Phils had now dropped nine in a row.

The big news was that Bob Friend stopped the Reds' winning streak as the Pirates won, 2-0.

The Cardinals and Reds were now tied for first. The Phillies were a game and a half back. The Giants were three and a half back. There were four games to play.

September 30, 1964 – Some may call it the rarified air of first place, others may attribute it to pressure, but the Reds lost that night in 16 heart-breaking innings, 1-0. The Giants won in twelve innings. The Phillies lost in nine.

It was indeed Jim Bunning's turn again (didn't he just pitch three days ago?). The Cards held an 8-0 lead after four innings. They won, 8-5. The Cardinals had won a remarkable eight straight games. The Phillies had lost an even more remarkable ten straight. Gene Mauch had been compelled to start pitchers Chris Short and Jim Bunning six times in those 10 games, all losses.

The Cardinals were now in first place alone by one game over the Reds and 2½ games over the Phillies.

October 1, 1964 – The Reds broke their losing streak by defeating the Pirates, 5-4. They now trailed the Cards by a mere half game with the Phillies coming to town.

October 2, 1964 – Maybe the Phillies were due. Chris Short was back on the mound, working on short rest. He pitched well, giving up just one earned run, but the Phils' trailed 3-0 heading into the eighth inning. The Reds had the formidable Jim O'Toole on the mound, but finally the Phils did something they hadn't done in recent memory…they strung some hits together and scored four times. Excluding the game in which they lost 14-8 to the Braves, the Phils averaged under three runs of offense over their ten-game losing streak. Apparently, they needed four runs, because as far as the Reds were concerned they broke out of their slump at the worst possible time. The Phillies won, 4-3.

Meanwhile, the Cardinals were sitting pretty. They were in first place and facing the horrible Mets. But baseball can be an evil, mean-spirited game designed to make you pay. Little Al Jackson defeated Bob Gibson, 1-0. (They were due as well.) The Cardinals' winning streak was over and the Mets, the forty-games-behind New York Mets, had won a big game.

The Cardinals maintained their half-game lead over the Reds, but the Phillies remained alive, just 1½ games back.

October 3, 1964 – The Reds were off the day before the season ended but that didn't make it a bad day. The Mets had done it again. They clobbered the Cardinals, 15-5. The Cards and Reds were now tied for first place. The Phillies had an off day as well and they were now just one game back.

October 4, 1964 – It didn't take Einstein to figure this one out: The Phillies needed to beat the Reds again and the Mets had to somehow find a way to defeat the Cardinals. If the Mets swept the series, the season would end in a three-way tie. But only half the plan worked.

With the pennant on the line for the Reds and the Phillies, Jim Bunning (yes, again) came through and defeated John Tsitouris and the Reds, 10-0. Both teams had records of 92-70.

In St. Louis, Curt Simmons was back on the mound trying to fend off the Mets. He couldn't do it. Simmons pitched 4⅓ innings, giving up three runs. When he left the game the Cards were losing, 3-2. After pitching eight innings on Friday night, into the game came Bob Gibson in relief. That was pretty much that. The Cardinals won 11-5 and won the pennant by one game over the Phils and Reds.

U.S. Senator Jim Bunning told the NY *Post* in 2007, "The one thing we never got in '64 was the one performance, the one big hit, the one huge pitching performance that could have stopped the bleeding."

The Cardinals were a great team in 1964 and they went on to defeat the New York Yankees in the World Series, but this great ending was not about the team that won; it was about the Phillies and a mighty collapse that affected an entire city and community of fans for a generation.

Rarely has a race been as heated as the American League pennant race of 1967. And rarely has one man had a bigger effect on the result than Carl Yastrzemski of the Boston Red Sox.

Through the games of Thursday, September 28, the standings stood as follows:

Team	Record	GB
Minnesota	91-69	—
Detroit	89-69	1
Boston	90-70	1
Chicago	89-70	1½

The final weekend began Friday when the Chicago White Sox were eliminated from the pennant race by losing to Washington, 1-0. A California vs. Detroit doubleheader was rained out, and neither Minnesota nor Boston was scheduled.

Boston's Impossible Dream became a realistic possibility on Saturday, September 30, when the Red Sox topped Minnesota 6-4 in a game where the lead changed hands three times. Playing before 32,909 Fenway Park fans—including Vice President Hubert H. Humphrey, Massachusetts Senator Edward M. Kennedy, and many little boys perched on top of the billboards—Jose Santiago gave Boston seven strong innings and both George Scott and Carl Yastrzemski hit homers. Yaz' was a three-run blast that made the final difference; vying for a Triple Crown (3-for-4, 4 RBI), he was heating up just at the right moment. When Detroit split two games with California, the standings through September 30 read:

Team	Record	GB
Boston	91-70	—
Minnesota	91-70	—
Detroit	90-70	½

And so the season boiled down to October 1, with Boston meeting Minnesota and Detroit playing a doubleheader with California. Sunday loomed sunny. The Red Sox (who had finished a half game out of 10th place in 1966 and in the second division nine times running) trotted out 21-game-winner Jim Lonborg against the Twins' 20-game-winner Dean Chance. Lonborg, whose steady hands later made him a dentist, looked composed in the pregame clubhouse. Chance resembled nothing so much as a deer caught in the headlights.

Nonetheless, the Twins took a 2-0 lead on first and third-inning errors by Scott and Yastrzemski respectively, while the Fenway Park crowd of 35,773 squirmed in their seats. But in the home half of the sixth, Lonborg led off with a bunt single.

"He fooled everybody in the park, including me, the pitcher and the third baseman," Boston's rookie Red Sox manager Dick Williams marveled to reporters.

Singles by Jerry Adair and Dalton Jones loaded the bases. Then Yastrzemski, who already had two hits for the afternoon and four hits in a row stretching back to Saturday, singled home two runs to tie the score. The Red Sox took the lead when Ken Harrelson grounded to shortstop Zoilo Versalles, who threw home—too late to nail Jones. It was only 3-2, but the Twins' rookie manager Cal Ermer made a fateful decision by jerking Chance for Al Worthington.

With Scott squaring around to bunt, Worthington uncorked a wild pitch. Yastrzemski moved to third and Harrelson's pinch runner, Jose Tartabull, went to second. On another wild pitch, Yastrzemski scored and Tartabull headed to third. After Scott struck out, Rico Petrocelli walked and Reggie Smith singled off first baseman Harmon Killebrew's glove to make it 5-2.

Behind Yastrzemski's 4-for-4 performance, Lonborg held on to throw a seven-hit complete game and win, 5-3. When shortstop Petrocelli squeezed Rich Rollins' popup for the final out, fans stormed the field, scaled the screen behind home plate, tried to dismantle the scoreboard, and nearly disrobed Lonborg.

"This is the happiest day of my life," Red Sox owner Thomas A. Yawkey told reporters at the scene.

The players agreed; they slobbered one another with shaving cream and poured beer on everyone foolish enough to come near. Why not champagne? Because the Tigers had won the opener of their doubleheader and they would force a playoff if they won the nightcap. But once the Angels beat the Tigers (and their eight desperate pitchers) 8-5, champagne flowed all over New England.

There was much to celebrate. The greatest rags-to-riches story of any pennant chase; Lonborg's Cy Young season; and Yaz' Triple Crown finish. It could only be the stuff impossible dreams are made of.

In the opening game of baseball's first American League Championship Series, October 4, 1969, the Baltimore Orioles and Minnesota Twins were tied 3-3 going into the last of the 12th inning. The Orioles' Mark Belanger led off with an infield hit, advanced to second on Andy Etchebarren's sacrifice bunt, moved to third on Don Buford's groundout, and scored on Paul Blair's bunt single for a 4-3 victory.

The next day, Minnesota's Dave Boswell and Baltimore's Dave McNally pitched scoreless ball through 10 innings. After working the 11th, McNally sat down with a three-hit, 11-strikeout shutout still intact. In the bottom of the inning, Boog Powell walked and moved to second on Brooks Robinson's sacrifice bunt. Dave Johnson was intentionally walked. After Mark Belanger fouled out to third, Ron Perranoski came in to face pinch hitter Curt Motton, who singled to right to score Powell with the winning run.

A day later, the Orioles beat the Twins 11-2 to win the best-of-five series, 3-0.

American League Championship Series—Game 2
Sunday, October 5, 1969
Memorial Stadium

Team	1	2	3	4	5	6	7	8	9	10	11	R	H	E
MIN A	0	0	0	0	0	0	0	0	0	0	0	0	3	1
BAL A	0	0	0	0	0	0	0	0	0	0	1	1	8	0

In Game 1 of the 1972 American League Championship Series on October 7, Mickey Lolich of the Detroit Tigers faced Catfish Hunter of the Athletics at Oakland-Alameda County Coliseum. Hunter gave up one run in the second while Lolich allowed one run in the third. The score was tied 1-1 heading into extra innings. In the top of the 11th, Al Kaline hit a home run off Rollie Fingers to give Detroit a 2-1 lead. In the bottom of the inning, Sal Bando singled and was replaced by pinch runner Blue Moon Odom. Then Mike Epstein singled to put runners on first and second, and Mike Hegan entered the game to run for Epstein.

Relief pitcher Chuck Seelbach came in to face Gene Tenace, who forced Odom at third on a bunt attempt. Then rookie Gonzalo Marquez (who went 5-for-8 during the postseason) singled to right, driving home Hegan with the tying run. When right fielder Al Kaline's throw to third hit Tenace and bounded away, Tenace bounced up and darted home with the winning run.

American League Championship Series—Game 1
Sunday, October 7, 1972
Oakland-Alameda County Coliseum

BATTING

Detroit Tigers	AB	R	H	RBI	BB	SO	PO	A
McAuliffe 2b	5	0	0	0	0	2	3	4
Kaline rf	5	1	1	1	0	0	3	0
Sims c	5	0	1	0	0	0	3	0
Cash 1b	4	1	1	1	1	0	12	0
Horton lf	3	0	0	0	0	1	3	0
G. Brown ph	1	0	0	0	0	0	0	0
Stanley lf	1	0	0	0	0	0	1	0
Northrup cf	3	0	1	0	1	0	4	0
Rodriguez 3b	4	0	0	0	0	1	1	5
Brinkman ss	4	0	2	0	0	0	1	1
Lolich p	4	0	0	0	0	1	0	2
Seelbach p	0	0	0	0	0	0	0	0
Totals	39	2	6	2	2	4	31	12

FIELDING -
DP: 2. Rodriguez-McAuliffe, Rodriguez-McAuliffe-Cash.
E: McAuliffe (1), Kaline (1).

BATTING -
2B: Brinkman 2 (2,off Hunter,off Fingers); Sims (1,off Hunter).
HR: Cash (1,2nd inning off Hunter 0 on 0 out); Kaline (1,11th inning off Fingers 0 on 0 out).
Team LOB: 6.

Oakland Athletics	AB	R	H	RBI	BB	SO	PO	A
Campaneris ss	4	1	0	0	1	0	3	6
Alou rf	5	0	1	0	0	0	0	0
Rudi lf	4	0	1	1	0	1	5	0
Jackson cf	5	0	2	0	0	1	4	0
Bando 3b	4	0	2	0	0	0	2	5
Odom pr	0	0	0	0	0	0	0	0
Epstein 1b	3	0	2	0	2	0	14	0
Hegan pr	0	1	0	0	0	0	0	0
Tenace c	5	1	0	0	0	1	4	0
Green 2b	0	0	0	0	0	0	1	0
Mangual ph	1	0	0	0	0	0	0	0
Kubiak 2b	2	0	1	0	0	0	0	5
Hendrick ph	1	0	0	0	0	0	0	0
Maxvill 2b	0	0	0	0	0	0	0	1
Marquez ph	1	0	1	1	0	0	0	0
Hunter p	3	0	1	0	0	0	0	0
Blue p	0	0	0	0	0	0	0	0
Fingers p	1	0	0	0	0	0	0	0
Totals	39	3	11	2	3	3	33	17

FIELDING -
DP: 1. Kubiak-Campaneris-Epstein.
E: Kubiak (1).

BATTING -
SH: Bando (1,off Lolich).
SF: Rudi (1,off Lolich).
Team LOB: 10.

PITCHING

Detroit Tigers	IP	H	R	ER	BB	SO	HR
Lolich L(0-1)	10	10	3	2	3	3	0
Seelbach	0.1	1	0	0	0	0	0
Totals	10.1	11	3	2	3	3	0

Lolich faced 2 batters in the 11th inning

Oakland Athletics	IP	H	R	ER	BB	SO	HR
Hunter	8	4	1	1	2	4	1
Blue	0	0	0	0	0	0	0
Fingers W(1-0)	3	2	1	1	0	0	1
Totals	11	6	2	2	2	4	2

Hunter faced 1 batter in the 9th inning
Blue faced 1 batter in the 9th inning

Umpires: Red Flaherty, Nestor Chylak, John Rice, Don Denkinger, Larry Barnett, Art Frantz

Time of Game: 3:00   **Attendance:** 29566

	1	2	3	4	5	6	7	8	9	10	11	R	H	E
DET A	0	1	0	0	0	0	0	0	0	0	1	2	6	2
OAK A	0	0	1	0	0	0	0	0	0	0	2	3	11	1

With the National League Championship Series tied at two games apiece, the Pittsburgh Pirates held a slim 2-1 lead heading into the ninth inning of Game 5. Cincinnati Reds catcher Johnny Bench immediately greeted reliever Dave Giusti with a game-tying, solo home run. Giusti was soon chased from the game after surrendering singles to Tony Perez (replaced by pinch runner George Foster) and Denis Menke. Bob Moose, who started and lost Game 2, entered the game for Guisti and eliminated Cesar Geronimo on a fly-out to right (Foster advanced to third). The next batter, Darrel Chaney, popped out to the shortstop. But with everyone in Riverfront Stadium bracing for extra innings and Hal McRae at the plate, Moose uncorked a walk-off wild pitch and Foster scored the pennant-winning run.

National League Championship Series—Game 5
Wednesday, October 11, 1972
Riverfront Stadium

BATTING

Pittsburgh Pirates	AB	R	H	RBI	BB	SO	PO	A
Stennett lf	4	0	1	0	0	0	1	0
Oliver cf	3	0	0	0	0	1	1	0
Clemente rf	3	0	1	0	1	1	3	0
Stargell 1b	4	0	0	0	0	2	12	0
Robertson 1b	0	0	0	0	0	0	1	0
Sanguillen c	4	2	2	0	0	0	5	0
Hebner 3b	4	1	2	0	0	0	0	2
Cash 2b	4	0	2	0	0	2	2	5
Alley ss	4	0	0	0	0	1	1	1
Blass p	3	0	0	0	0	2	0	3
Hernandez p	0	0	0	0	0	0	0	0
Giusti p	0	0	0	0	0	0	0	0
Moose p	0	0	0	0	0	0	0	0
Totals	33	3	8	2	1	7	26	11

BATTING -
2B: Hebner (1,off Gullett).
SH: Oliver (1,off Hall).
IBB: Clemente (1,by Hall).
Team LOB: 5.

Cincinnati Reds	AB	R	H	RBI	BB	SO	PO	A
Rose lf	3	0	1	1	0	1	3	0
Morgan 2b	4	0	0	0	0	0	2	3
Tolan cf	4	0	0	0	1	2	0	0
Bench c	4	1	2	1	0	0	7	1
Perez 1b	4	0	1	0	0	2	8	1
Foster pr	0	1	0	0	0	0	0	0
Menke 3b	3	0	1	0	1	0	1	4
Geronimo rf	4	1	1	1	0	0	2	0
Chaney ss	4	1	1	0	0	1	1	1
Gullett p	0	0	0	0	0	0	0	0
Borbon p	0	0	0	0	0	0	1	0
Uhlaender ph	1	0	0	0	0	0	0	0
Hall p	0	0	0	0	0	0	0	0
Hague ph	0	0	0	0	1	0	0	0
Concepcion pr	0	0	0	0	0	0	0	0
Carroll p	0	0	0	0	0	0	0	0
McRae ph	0	0	0	0	0	0	0	0
Totals	31	4	7	3	2	5	27	10

FIELDING -
DP: 1. Morgan-Chaney-Perez.
E: Chaney (3).

BATTING -
2B: Rose (4,off Blass).
HR: Geronimo (1,5th inning off Blass 0 on 0 out); Bench (1,9th inning off Giusti 0 on 0 out).
SH: Gullett (1,off Blass); Rose (1,off Blass).
Team LOB: 5.

PITCHING

Pittsburgh Pirates	IP	H	R	ER	BB	SO	HR
Blass	7.1	4	2	2	2	4	1
Hernandez	0.2	0	0	0	0	1	0
Giusti L(0-1)	0	3	2	2	0	0	1
Moose	0.2	0	0	0	0	0	0
Totals	8.2	7	4	4	2	5	2

Giusti faced 3 batters in the 9th inning
WP: Moose (1).

Cincinnati Reds	IP	H	R	ER	BB	SO	HR
Gullett	3	6	3	3	0	2	0
Borbon	2	1	0	0	0	1	0
Hall	3	1	0	0	1	4	0
Carroll W(1-1)	1	0	0	0	0	0	0
Totals	9	8	3	3	1	7	0

Gullett faced 2 batters in the 4th inning
WP: Gullett (1).
IBB: Hall (1,Clemente).

Umpires: Augie Donatelli, John Kibler, Harry Wendelstedt, Ken Burkhart, Doug Harvey, Bill Williams

Time of Game: 2:19 **Attendance:** 41887

	1	2	3	4	5	6	7	8	9	R	H	E
PIT N	0	2	0	1	0	0	0	0	0	3	8	0
CIN N	0	0	1	0	1	0	0	0	2	4	7	1

1973 — Oakland A's vs. Baltimore Orioles

In pivotal Game 3 of the 1973 American League Championship Series, Mike Cuellar of the Baltimore Orioles squared off against Ken Holtzman of the Oakland Athletics for a classic pitcher's duel. The Orioles only had three hits off Holtzman before Bert Campaneris' 11th-inning, leadoff, walk-off home run gave Oakland the 2-1 win. The A's won the Series three games to two.

**American League
Championship Series—Game 3
Tuesday, October 9, 1973
Oakland-Alameda
County Coliseum**

	1	2	3	4	5	6	7	8	9	10	11	R	H	E
BAL A	0	1	0	0	0	0	0	0	0	0	0	1	3	0
OAK A	0	0	0	0	0	0	0	1	0	0	1	2	4	3

1976 — New York Yankees vs. Kansas City Royals

After the first two games were split in Kansas City and the next two were split in New York, a memorable Game 5 was played at Yankee Stadium before 56,821 fans on October 14, 1976. The Royals scored two first-inning runs, and the Yanks responded with two runs of their own in the bottom of the inning. Buck Martinez put the Royals ahead with a run-scoring single in the second, but the Yankees scored twice to take a 4-3 lead in the third. They scored another pair in the sixth inning to make it 6-3. In the top of the eighth, the Royals' Al Cowens singled and pitcher Grant Jackson was summoned to replace starting pitcher Ed Figueroa. Pinch hitting for Tom Poquette, Jim Wohlford followed with a single before George Brett homered to tie the game at six.

After the Yanks went 1-2-3 in the bottom of the eighth, pitcher Dick Tidrow worked his way out of a first-and-second, two-out jam thanks to a disputed call on a force at second base. The game headed into the bottom of the ninth still tied.

The exigent circumstances: The Royals longed to reach the Fall Classic in only their eighth year of existence, while the Yankees hadn't reached the World Series since 1964. Royals manager Whitey Herzog brought in fireballer Mark Littell to face fastball-hitting Chris Chambliss. Littell had surrendered only one home run all season, but Chambliss put his first pitch over the right-center field fence for a pennant-winning, walk-off homer. Chambliss had to battle his way around the bases, running around, over and through the throngs that burst onto the field to celebrate.

Chambliss didn't touch home plate until much later, when he was escorted off the field by New York's Finest.

**American League Championship
Series—Game 5
Thursday, October 14, 1976
Yankee Stadium**

	1	2	3	4	5	6	7	8	9	R	H	E
KC A	2	1	0	0	0	0	0	3	0	6	11	1
NY A	2	0	2	0	0	2	0	0	1	7	11	1

O n October 2, 1978, the Yankees clinched the American League East title and beat the Red Sox 5-4 on Bucky Dent's improbable three-run, go-ahead home run off Mike Torrez that barely cleared the Green Monster in Fenway Park. Winning pitcher Ron Guidry (25-3) went on to win the Cy Young Award, and it was little consolation to Boston fans when their own Jim Rice was named Most Valuable Player. The Yankees and Red Sox owned baseball's best records at game time; it was as if they had played the seventh game of the World Series. The Yankees eventually won the Fall Classic four games to two over the Los Angeles Dodgers.

American League Tiebreaker
Monday, October 2, 1978
Fenway Park

BATTING

New York Yankees	AB	R	H	RBI	BB	SO	PO	A
Rivers cf	2	1	1	0	2	0	2	0
Blair ph,cf	1	0	1	0	0	0	0	0
Munson c	5	0	1	1	0	3	7	1
Piniella rf	4	0	1	0	0	0	4	0
Jackson dh	4	1	1	1	0	0	0	0
Nettles 3b	4	0	0	0	0	1	1	3
Chambliss 1b	4	1	1	0	0	0	8	0
White lf	3	1	1	0	1	1	4	0
Thomasson lf	0	0	0	0	0	0	1	0
Doyle 2b	2	0	0	0	0	0	0	0
Spencer ph	1	0	0	0	0	0	0	0
Stanley 2b	1	0	0	0	0	0	0	0
Dent ss	4	1	1	3	0	1	0	2
Guidry p	0	0	0	0	0	0	0	1
Gossage p	0	0	0	0	0	0	0	0
Totals	35	5	8	5	3	6	27	7

FIELDING -
PB: Munson (8).

BATTING -
2B: Rivers (25,off Torrez); Munson (27,off Stanley).
HR: Dent (5,7th inning off Torrez 2 on 2 out); Jackson (27,8th inning off Stanley 0 on 0 out).
Team LOB: 6.

BASERUNNING -
SB: Rivers 2 (25,2nd base off Torrez/Fisk,2nd base off Stanley/Fisk).

Boston Red Sox	AB	R	H	RBI	BB	SO	PO	A
Burleson ss	4	1	1	0	1	1	4	2
Remy 2b	4	1	2	0	0	0	2	5
Rice rf	5	0	1	1	0	1	4	0
Yastrzemski lf	5	2	2	2	0	1	2	0
Fisk c	3	0	1	0	1	0	5	1
Lynn cf	4	0	1	1	0	0	1	0
Hobson dh	4	0	1	0	0	1	0	0
Scott 1b	4	0	2	0	0	2	8	0
Brohamer 3b	1	0	0	0	0	0	1	1
Bailey ph	1	0	0	0	0	1	0	0
Duffy 3b	0	0	0	0	0	0	0	0
Evans ph	1	0	0	0	0	0	0	0
Torrez p	0	0	0	0	0	0	0	0
Stanley p	0	0	0	0	0	0	0	0
Hassler p	0	0	0	0	0	0	0	0
Drago p	0	0	0	0	0	0	0	0
Totals	36	4	11	4	2	7	27	9

BATTING -
2B: Scott (16,off Guidry); Burleson (32,off Guidry); Remy (24,off Gossage).
HR: Yastrzemski (17,2nd inning off Guidry 0 on 0 out).
SH: Brohamer (4,off Guidry); Remy (14,off Guidry).
IBB: Fisk (6,by Guidry).
Team LOB: 9.

PITCHING

New York Yankees	IP	H	R	ER	BB	SO	HR
Guidry W(25-3)	6.1	6	2	2	1	5	1
Gossage SV(27)	2.2	5	2	2	1	2	0
Totals	9	11	4	4	2	7	1

IBB: Guidry (1,Fisk).

Boston Red Sox	IP	H	R	ER	BB	SO	HR
Torrez L(16-13)	6.2	5	4	4	3	4	1
Stanley	0.1	2	1	1	0	0	1
Hassler	1.2	1	0	0	0	2	0
Drago	0.1	0	0	0	0	0	0
Totals	9	8	5	5	3	6	2

Stanley faced 1 batter in the 8th inning

Umpires: Don Denkinger, Jim Evans, Al Clark, Steve Palermo

Time of Game: 2:52 **Attendance:** 32925

	1	2	3	4	5	6	7	8	9	R	H	E
NY A	0	0	0	0	0	0	4	1	0	5	8	0
BOS A	0	1	0	0	0	1	0	2	0	4	11	0

1980   Houston Astros vs. Philadelphia Phillies

After the Philadelphia Phillies won Game 1 of the 1980 National League Championship Series 3-1, the Houston Astros struck back and won Game 2, 7-4, in ten innings. No less than seven players—Terry Puhl, Enos Cabell, Joe Morgan, Cesar Cedeno, Dave Bergman, Rafael Landestoy and Jose Cruz—contributed to Houston's four-run 10th inning.

In Game 3 the Astros beat the Phillies 1-0 in 11 innings on Morgan's triple and Denny Walling's sacrifice fly. The Phillies won Game 4 in 10 innings 5-3 on a single by Pete Rose and doubles by Greg Luzinski and Manny Trillo. Finally, Philadelphia won Game 5, 8-7, on 10th-inning doubles by Del Unser and Garry Maddox.

Four of the five games went into extra innings.

National League Championship Series

Game 1
Tuesday, October 7, 1980
Veterans Stadium

	1	2	3	4	5	6	7	8	9	R	H	E
HOU N	0	0	1	0	0	0	0	0	0	1	7	0
PHI N	0	0	0	0	0	2	1	0	x	3	8	1

Game 2
Wednesday, October 8, 1980
Veterans Stadium

	1	2	3	4	5	6	7	8	9	10	R	H	E
HOU N	0	0	1	0	0	0	1	1	0	4	7	8	1
PHI N	0	0	0	2	0	0	0	1	0	1	4	14	2

Game 3
Friday, October 10, 1980
Astrodome

	1	2	3	4	5	6	7	8	9	10	11	R	H	E
PHI N	0	0	0	0	0	0	0	0	0	0	0	0	7	1
HOU N	0	0	0	0	0	0	0	0	0	0	1	1	6	1

Game 4
Saturday, October 11, 1980
Astrodome

	1	2	3	4	5	6	7	8	9	10	R	H	E
PHI N	0	0	0	0	0	0	0	3	0	2	5	13	0
HOU N	0	0	0	1	1	0	0	0	1	0	3	5	1

Game 5
Sunday, October 12, 1980
Astrodome

	1	2	3	4	5	6	7	8	9	10	R	H	E
PHI N	0	2	0	0	0	0	0	5	0	1	8	13	2
HOU N	1	0	0	0	0	1	3	2	0	0	7	14	0

1985   St. Louis Cardinals vs. Los Angeles Dodgers

In Game 5 of the 1985 National League Championship Series, the St. Louis Cardinals and the Los Angeles Dodgers were tied at two games apiece and two runs apiece as they headed into the ninth inning. Dodger right-hander Tom Niedenfuer nixed Willie McGee on a popup and then faced switch-hitter Ozzie Smith. Batting from the left side of the plate, the Wizard did something he had never done before as a lefty: Smith slammed a Niedenfuer fastball into the right field stands for a walk-off, 3-2 victory.

Jack Buck made the call:

Smith corks one into right, down the line! It may go! Go crazy, folks, go crazy! It's a home run and the Cardinals have won the game by a score of 3-2 on a home run by the Wizard!

National League
Championship Series—Game 5
Monday, October 14, 1985
Busch Stadium II

	1	2	3	4	5	6	7	8	9	R	H	E
LA N	0	0	0	2	0	0	0	0	0	2	5	1
STL N	2	0	0	0	0	0	0	0	1	3	5	1

I n Game 5 of the 1986 American League Championship Series, the California Angels led the
Boston Red Sox three games to one. Closer Donnie Moore was ready to clinch the pennant for the
Angels, and entered the game to protect a 5-4 lead
with a runner on first and two outs in the ninth inning. Moore threw a split-fingered fastball that Dave

Henderson blasted into the left field stands to put the
Red Sox up by one. The Angels tied the score in their
half of the inning but lost 7-6 on Henderson's sacrifice fly (off Moore again) in the eleventh. The deflated
Angels lost the next two games and the Red Sox went
on to win the ALCS in seven games. Moore never
recovered his form. He committed suicide in 1988.

American League Championship Series—Game 5
Sunday, October 12, 1986
Anaheim Stadium

	1	2	3	4	5	6	7	8	9	10	11	R	H	E
BOS A	0	2	0	0	0	0	0	0	4	0	1	7	12	0
CAL A	0	0	1	0	0	2	2	0	1	0	0	6	13	0

Donnie Moore, RP, 1975-1988

G	GS	CG	SHO	GF	SV	IP	H	BFP	HR	R	ER	BB	IB	SO	SH	SF	WP	HBP	BK	2B	3B	GDP	ROE	W	L	ERA	PW
416	4	0	0	229	89	655	698	2793	53	308	267	186	49	416	48	26	22	8	14	99	19	52	49	43	40	3.67	6.2

1986_____ New York Mets vs. Houston Astros

Even though the New York Mets led the Houston Astros three games to two in the 1986 National League Championship Series, they felt a sense of desperation going into Game 6 at the Astrodome. Facing them in Game 7 would be Astro ace Mike Scott, who beat them in Game 1, 1-0, on a five-hitter in which he struck out 14 men; he beat them again in Game 4, 3-1. The Mets most likely needed to win Game 6 if they were going to the World Series.

The Astros scored three first-inning runs off Bobby Ojeda. This was a large margin in a series where only one game was decided by as many as two runs. Houston starter Bob Knepper maintained the shutout into the ninth, but Lenny Dykstra led off with a triple and scored on a single by Mookie Wilson. After Kevin Mitchell grounded out, Keith Hernandez doubled home Wilson to make it 3-2, and Knepper gave way to closer Dave Smith, who had failed in Game 3. Though he'd saved 33 games for the Astros, Smith couldn't find the plate with a strobe light. He walked Gary Carter and Darryl Strawberry to load the bases, and after Ray Knight took a pitch that Smith felt should have been called strike three, Knight tied the game with a sacrifice fly. That's how it stayed, 3-3, as the two 1962 expansion rivals moved into extra innings.

The game remained tied into the 14th, with Roger McDowell completing five innings of one-hit relief for the Mets. The Astros' Smith gave way to Larry Andersen, who gave way to Aurelio Lopez, and afternoon gave way to evening. In the top of the 14th, Carter singled off Lopez; Strawberry walked; Knight forced Carter at third on a failed sacrifice; and Wally Backman singled home Strawberry before Lopez could shut the door. The Mets led 4-3 and threatened to end Houston's season.

But with one out in their half of the 14th, the Astros tied the score when Billy Hatcher's long fly off Jesse Orosco hit the foul pole down the left field line (Hatcher had hit only six homers during the regular season). There was no scoring in the 15th before one of baseball's most dramatic denouements occurred in the 16th inning. After Strawberry doubled, Knight's single drove him home while Knight took second on the throw to the plate. With the score 5-4, star-crossed Astros pitcher Jeff Calhoun replaced Lopez. Calhoun threw a wild pitch and Knight advanced to third; Calhoun walked Backman before unleashing a second wild pitch that scored Knight and moved Backman to second. Dykstra singled, driving home Backman to give the Mets an apparently impregnable 7-4 lead with the Astros down to

National League Championship Series—Game 6
Wednesday, October 15, 1986
Astrodome

BATTING

New York Mets	AB	R	H	RBI	BB	SO	PO	A
Wilson cf,lf	7	1	1	1	1	2	2	0
Mitchell lf	4	0	0	0	0	1	2	0
Elster ss	3	0	0	0	0	1	2	2
Hernandez 1b	7	1	1	1	0	2	20	6
Carter c	5	0	2	0	2	0	9	2
Strawberry rf	5	2	1	0	2	1	0	0
Knight 3b	6	1	1	2	0	1	1	7
Teufel 2b	3	0	1	0	0	0	0	5
Backman ph,2b	2	1	1	1	2	0	1	2
Santana ss	3	0	1	0	0	0	4	1
Heep ph	1	0	0	0	0	1	0	0
McDowell p	1	0	0	0	0	0	2	2
Johnson ph	1	0	0	0	0	0	0	0
Orosco p	0	0	0	0	0	0	1	0
Ojeda p	1	0	0	0	0	0	1	2
Mazzilli ph	1	0	0	0	0	1	0	0
Aguilera p	1	0	0	0	0	1	0	0
Dykstra ph,cf	4	1	2	1	1	0	1	0
Totals	54	7	11	6	8	11	48	30

BATTING -
2B: Hernandez (1,off Knepper); Strawberry (1,off Lopez).
3B: Dykstra (1,off Knepper).
SH: Orosco (1,off Calhoun).
SF: Knight (1,off Smith).
IBB: Backman (1,by Smith); Dykstra (1,by Lopez).
Team LOB: 9.

Houston Astros	AB	R	H	RBI	BB	SO	PO	A
Doran 2b	7	1	2	0	0	1	1	6
Hatcher cf	7	2	3	2	0	0	2	0
Garner 3b	3	1	1	1	0	1	0	5
Walling ph,3b	4	0	0	0	0	0	2	2
Davis 1b	7	1	3	2	0	1	21	0
Bass rf	6	0	1	0	1	2	3	0
Cruz lf	6	0	1	1	0	1	1	0
Ashby c	6	0	0	0	0	0	12	1
Thon ss	3	0	0	0	0	0	3	3
Reynolds ph,ss	3	0	0	0	0	2	3	3
Knepper p	2	0	0	0	1	1	0	2
Smith p	0	0	0	0	0	0	0	0
Puhl ph	1	0	0	0	0	0	0	0
Andersen p	0	0	0	0	0	0	0	1
Pankovits ph	1	0	0	0	0	0	0	0
Lopez p	0	0	0	0	0	0	0	1
Calhoun p	0	0	0	0	0	0	0	0
Lopes ph	0	1	0	0	1	0	0	0
Totals	56	6	11	6	3	9	48	24

FIELDING -
DP: 2. Thon-Davis, Doran-Reynolds-Davis.
E: Bass (1).

BATTING -
2B: Garner (1,off Ojeda); Davis (1,off Aguilera).
HR: Hatcher (1,14th inning off Orosco 0 on 1 out).
Team LOB: 5.

BASERUNNING -
SB: Doran (2,2nd base off Ojeda/Carter).
CS: Bass 2 (3,Home by Ojeda/Carter,2nd base by McDowell/Carter).

PITCHING

New York Mets	IP	H	R	ER	BB	SO	HR
Ojeda	5	5	3	3	2	1	0
Aguilera	3	1	0	0	0	1	0
McDowell	5	1	0	0	1	2	0
Orosco W(3-0)	3	4	3	3	1	5	1
Totals	16	11	6	6	3	9	1

Houston Astros	IP	H	R	ER	BB	SO	HR
Knepper	8.1	5	3	3	1	6	0
Smith	1.2	0	0	0	3	2	0
Andersen	3	0	0	0	1	1	0
Lopez L(0-1)	2	5	3	3	2	2	0
Calhoun	1	1	1	1	1	0	0
Totals	16	11	7	7	8	11	0

Lopez faced 2 batters in the 16th inning
WP: Calhoun 2 (2).
IBB: Smith (1,Backman); Lopez (3,Dykstra).

Umpires: Fred Brocklander, Doug Harvey, Lee Weyer, Frank Pulli, Dutch Rennert, Joe West

Time of Game: 4:42 **Attendance:** 45718

	1 2 3	4 5 6	7 8 9	10 11 12	13 14 15	16	R	H	E
NY N	0 0 0	0 0 0	0 0 3	0 0 0	0 1 0	3	7	11	0
HOU N	3 0 0	0 0 0	0 0 0	0 0 0	0 1 0	2	6	11	1

their final three outs.

The 45,718 in attendance stayed in their seats. With one out in the Astros' half of the 16th, Davey Lopes batted for Calhoun and walked. Successive singles by Bill Doran and Billy Hatcher scored a run to make it 7-5. The Mets gathered on the mound to give Orosco a breather. A fastball-slider pitcher, he was throwing nothing but tepid heat. As first baseman Keith Hernandez told the New York *Times*' George Vecsey, "I said, 'Kid [catcher Gary Carter's nickname], if you call another fastball, I'm going to come to home plate and we're going to have to fight.' Kid told me: 'We're not going to fight.'"

Orosco threw nothing but breaking balls from that point on. After getting Denny Walling to force Hatcher at second, he yielded a Glenn Davis single to center, narrowing the lead to 7-6 and putting runners on first and second with two outs. Finally, Orosco struck out Kevin Bass on a 3-2 pitch to end the game.

"I was scared to death," Mets manager Dave Johnson said. "I was scared they were going to come back, one more time."

The game set an LCS-record for innings and time: 16 innings and four hours and forty-two minutes. At 7:48 P.M., the Astros were on their way home; the Mets were the National League champions and on their way to beating the Boston Red Sox in the World Series. It was little consolation to the Astros that Mike Scott became the first National League player on a losing team to win the NLCS Most Valuable Player Award.

The Pittsburgh Pirates led the Atlanta Braves 2-0 as Game 7 of the 1992 National League Championship Series went into the bottom of the ninth inning. Terry Pendleton led off with a double and advanced to third when David Justice reached on an infield error by second baseman Jose Lind. Sid Bream walked to load the bases, ousting Pittsburgh starter Stan Belinda in favor of Doug Drabek. Ron Gant hit a sacrifice fly to bring the Braves within one, 2-1. Damon Berryhill walked to load the bases. When Brian Hunter popped out to short, the Braves were down to their last out. Pinch hitting for pitcher Jeff Reardon, Francisco Cabrera, who had all of 10 at-bats during the season, singled to left. After Justice scored the tying run, Bream famously slid home ahead of Barry Bonds' throw for the series-winner. The crowd of 51,975 at Atlanta-Fulton County Stadium went wild; Pittsburgh has never recovered.

National League Championship Series—Game 7
Wednesday, October 14, 1992
Atlanta-Fulton County Stadium

BATTING

Pittsburgh Pirates	AB	R	H	RBI	BB	SO	PO	A
Cole rf	2	1	0	0	1	0	1	0
McClendon ph,rf	0	0	0	0	2	0	0	0
Espy pr,rf	0	0	0	0	0	0	0	0
Bell ss	4	1	1	0	1	1	1	1
Van Slyke cf	4	0	2	1	0	0	2	0
Bonds lf	3	0	1	0	1	0	4	0
Merced 1b	3	0	0	1	0	0	10	0
King 3b	4	0	1	0	0	0	2	2
LaValliere c	4	0	1	0	0	2	5	0
Lind 2b	4	0	1	0	0	0	1	4
Drabek p	3	0	0	0	0	2	0	0
Belinda p	0	0	0	0	0	0	0	0
Totals	31	2	7	2	5	5	26	7

FIELDING -
DP: 1. King.
E: Lind (2).

BATTING -
2B: Van Slyke (3,off Smoltz); Lind (2,off Smoltz); Bell (2,off Smoltz); King (4,off Avery).
SH: Drabek (1,off Stanton).
SF: Merced (1,off Smoltz).
IBB: Bonds (1,by Smoltz); McClendon (1,by Stanton).
Team LOB: 9.

Atlanta Braves	AB	R	H	RBI	BB	SO	PO	A
Nixon cf	4	0	1	0	0	0	2	0
Blauser ss	4	0	0	0	0	2	0	1
Pendleton 3b	4	1	1	0	0	0	1	3
Justice rf	4	1	0	0	0	1	6	1
Bream 1b	3	1	1	0	1	0	4	1
Gant lf	2	0	0	1	1	1	4	0
Berryhill c	3	0	1	0	1	0	8	0
Lemke 2b	2	0	1	0	0	0	1	1
L. Smith ph	1	0	0	0	0	0	0	0
Belliard 2b	0	0	0	0	0	0	1	0
Hunter ph	1	0	0	0	0	0	1	0
Smoltz p	1	0	0	0	0	0	0	0
Treadway ph	1	0	1	0	0	0	0	0
Stanton p	0	0	0	0	0	0	0	0
P. Smith p	0	0	0	0	0	0	0	0
Avery p	0	0	0	0	0	0	0	0
Sanders ph	1	0	0	0	0	0	1	0
Reardon p	0	0	0	0	0	0	0	0
Cabrera ph	1	0	1	2	0	0	0	0
Totals	32	3	7	3	3	5	27	7

BATTING -
2B: Berryhill (1,off Drabek); Bream (3,off Drabek); Pendleton (2,off Drabek).
SF: Gant (1,off Belinda).
Team LOB: 7.

PITCHING

Pittsburgh Pirates	IP	H	R	ER	BB	SO	HR
Drabek L(0-3)	8	6	3	1	2	5	0
Belinda	0.2	1	0	0	1	0	0
Totals	8.2	7	3	1	3	5	0

Drabek faced 3 batters in the 9th inning

Atlanta Braves	IP	H	R	ER	BB	SO	HR
Smoltz	6	4	2	2	2	4	0
Stanton	0.2	1	0	0	1	0	0
P. Smith	0	0	0	0	1	0	0
Avery	1.1	2	0	0	0	0	0
Reardon W(1-0)	1	0	0	0	1	1	0
Totals	9	7	2	2	5	5	0

WP: Reardon (1).
IBB: Smoltz (2,Bonds); Stanton (1,McClendon).

Umpires: John McSherry, Randy Marsh, Steve Rippley, Gary Darling, Gerry Davis, Ed Montague

Time of Game: 3:22   **Attendance:** 51975

	1	2	3		4	5	6		7	8	9		R	H	E
PIT N	1	0	0		0	0	1		0	0	0		2	7	1
ATL N	0	0	0		0	0	0		0	0	3		3	7	0

There may be no great races anymore. Now teams play all season for division titles, not pennants. And if the two best teams in a league play in the same division, it doesn't matter who wins the division because the second-place team will qualify for the postseason as a wild card entry.

The last real division race of consequence? The 1993 National League West. This was the final season in which each league had two divisions, there was no wild card, and only two teams in each league made the postseason. In other words, a team needed to win their division…or go home.

The teams with the best records in baseball were the Atlanta Braves and the San Francisco Giants, both—despite the geographical uncertainty—in the NL West. Going into the final games of October 3, the Giants and Braves were tied with records of 103-58. It would have been even more perfect if they'd played one another that day, but the schedule gods pitted the Braves at home against the Colorado Rockies and the Giants against their ancient tormentors in Los Angeles, the Dodgers.

The Braves had more left in their tanks than the Giants had in theirs: Bobby Cox started Tom Glavine (21-6), who beat the Rockies 5-3 with scoreless relief from Steve Bedrosian and Greg McMichael. Frank Robinson, the manager for the Giants, had to use Salomon Torrez (3-4), who lasted just 3⅓ innings, giving up five hits, five walks and three runs. The Dodgers went on to win, 12-1.

National League West—1993

Team Name	G	W	L	T	PCT	GB	RS	RA
Atlanta Braves	162	104	58	0	.642	-	767	559
San Francisco Giants	162	103	59	0	.636	1.0	808	636
Houston Astros	162	85	77	0	.525	19.0	716	630
Los Angeles Dodgers	162	81	81	0	.500	23.0	675	662
Cincinnati Reds	162	73	89	0	.451	31.0	722	785
Colorado Rockies	162	67	95	0	.414	37.0	758	967
San Diego Padres	162	61	101	0	.377	43.0	679	772

This was the year of the "Refuse to Lose" Seattle Mariners, who ended the 1995 season tied with the California Angels atop the American League West. In a one-game playoff for the division title, the Mariners' Randy Johnson faced the Angels' Mark Langston. On May 25, 1989, the Mariners had picked up Johnson in a multi-player trade with the Expos for…Mark Langston. Free-agent Langston then signed with California after the '89 season.

Vince Coleman singled home a run in the fourth to give Johnson and the Mariners a 1-0 lead. Johnson only allowed three hits while striking out 12, leading the Mariners to a 9-1 win, advancing them into the postseason for the first time in their nineteen-year history.

American League West Tiebreaker
Monday, October 2, 1995
Kingdome

	1	2	3	4	5	6	7	8	9	R	H	E
CAL A	0	0	0	0	0	0	0	0	1	1	3	1
SEA A	0	0	0	0	1	0	4	4	x	9	12	0

1995 ___ Seattle Mariners vs. New York Yankees

The American League Division Series had already been unforgettable. The New York Yankees seemed to have the series in hand when they won the first two games at home 9-6 and 7-5, the latter on Jim Leyritz' home run in the 15th inning. When the series shifted to Seattle, the Mariners won Game 3, 7-4, behind Randy Johnson, and Game 4, 11-8, on Edgar Martinez' grand slam.

In Game 5, the Yankees took a 4-2 lead heading into the bottom of the eighth inning, but Ken Griffey, Jr. hit a one-out homer off starter David Cone to cut the lead to one. One out later, Tino Martinez walked. Jay Buhner singled him to second. Alex Diaz walked and then Cone walked Doug Strange to force home the tying run. The score remained tied through the ninth and 10th innings. But in the top of the 11th, the Yankees' Randy Velarde singled home a run off Johnson, who was pitching in relief on one day's rest and finally began to weaken in his third inning of work.

The Yankees were also down to a relieving starter, Jack McDowell, who had come in for rookie Mariano Rivera in the ninth inning. Joey Cora beat out a bunt single to lead off the 11th, and Griffey, Jr. singled to center, sending Cora to third. Could one swing of the bat save an entire franchise? They think so in Seattle: Edgar Martinez doubled home both runners to win the series. "The Double," as Mariners fans still call it, may have saved baseball in Seattle by regenerating interest in the team and sparking enthusiasm for a new stadium (Safeco Field) that was subsequently built in 1999.

American League Division Series—Game 5
Sunday, October 8, 1995
Kingdome

BATTING

New York Yankees	AB	R	H	RBI	BB	SO	PO	A
Boggs 3b	5	0	0	0	0	3	0	0
Leyritz ph,c	1	0	0	0	0	1	0	0
B. Williams cf	2	2	0	0	4	1	2	0
O'Neill rf	5	2	1	2	1	1	3	0
Sierra dh	4	0	0	0	1	2	0	0
Mattingly 1b	5	0	1	2	0	1	3	2
James lf	2	0	0	0	1	0	1	0
G. Williams pr,lf	1	0	0	0	0	1	0	0
Stanley c	4	0	1	0	1	0	12	0
Kelly pr,2b	1	0	0	0	0	0	0	0
Fernandez ss	4	0	2	0	0	0	5	2
Velarde 2b,3b	4	0	1	1	1	2	4	1
Cone p	0	0	0	0	0	0	0	0
Rivera p	0	0	0	0	0	0	0	0
McDowell p	0	0	0	0	0	0	0	0
Totals	37	5	6	5	10	12	30	5

BATTING -
2B: Fernandez 2 (2,off Benes,off Charlton); Mattingly (4,off Benes).
HR: O'Neill (3,4th inning off Benes 1 on 1 out).
SH: Fernandez (1,off Johnson).
IBB: James (1,by Benes); B. Williams (1,by Johnson).
Team LOB: 10.

Seattle Mariners	AB	R	H	RBI	BB	SO	PO	A
Coleman lf	6	0	1	0	0	0	6	0
Cora 2b	5	2	2	1	0	0	3	0
Griffey cf	5	2	2	1	1	1	2	0
E. Martinez dh	6	0	3	2	0	1	0	0
T. Martinez 1b	3	1	2	0	1	1	4	1
Rodriguez pr,ss	1	1	0	0	0	0	0	0
Buhner rf	5	0	3	1	0	2	1	0
Sojo ss	2	0	0	0	0	1	1	1
Newson ph	1	0	0	0	0	1	0	0
Fermin ss	0	0	0	0	0	0	0	1
Diaz ph	0	0	0	0	1	0	0	0
Widger c	1	0	0	0	0	1	7	0
Wilson c	3	0	1	0	0	2	8	0
Strange ph,3b	1	0	0	1	1	0	0	0
Blowers 3b,1b	5	0	1	0	0	2	2	2
Benes p	0	0	0	0	0	0	1	0
Charlton p	0	0	0	0	0	0	0	0
Johnson p	0	0	0	0	0	0	0	0
Totals	44	6	15	6	4	12	33	5

FIELDING -
DP: 1. Sojo-T. Martinez.

BATTING -
2B: T. Martinez (1,off Cone); E. Martinez 2 (3,off Cone,off McDowell).
HR: Cora (1,3rd inning off Cone 0 on 2 out); Griffey (5,8th inning off Cone 0 on 1 out).
SH: Cora (3,off Rivera).
IBB: Griffey (1,by Rivera).
Team LOB: 13.

PITCHING

New York Yankees	IP	H	R	ER	BB	SO	HR
Cone	7.2	9	4	4	3	9	2
Rivera	0.2	1	0	0	1	1	0
McDowell L(0-2)	1.2	5	2	2	0	2	0
Totals	10	15	6	6	4	12	2

McDowell faced 3 batters in the 11th inning
WP: Cone 2 (2).
IBB: Rivera (1,Griffey).

Seattle Mariners	IP	H	R	ER	BB	SO	HR
Benes	6.2	4	4	4	6	5	1
Charlton	1.1	1	0	0	2	1	0
Johnson W(2-0)	3	1	1	1	2	6	0
Totals	11	6	5	5	10	12	1

Charlton faced 2 batters in the 9th inning
IBB: Benes (1,James); Johnson (1,B. Williams).

Umpires: Jim Evans, Dan Morrison, Tim Welke, John Hirschbeck, Joe Brinkman, Rocky Roe

Time of Game: 4:19 **Attendance:** 57411

	1	2	3	4	5	6	7	8	9	10	11	R	H	E
NY A	0	0	0	2	0	2	0	0	0	0	1	5	6	0
SEA A	0	0	1	1	0	0	0	2	0	0	2	6	15	0

New York Mets vs. Cincinnati Reds

fter the New York Mets and the Cincinnati Reds finished the regular season tied at 96-66, the Mets won a one-game playoff 5-0 on a two-hitter by Al Leiter to secure the National League wild card.

National League Wild Card Tiebreaker
Monday, October 4, 1999
Cinergy Field

	1	2	3	4	5	6	7	8	9	R	H	E
NY N	2	0	1	0	1	1	0	0	0	5	9	0
CIN N	0	0	0	0	0	0	0	0	0	0	2	0

National League Championship Series—Game 5
Sunday, October 17, 1999
Shea Stadium

BATTING

Atlanta Braves	AB	R	H	RBI	BB	SO	PO	A
Williams lf	7	0	1	0	1	1	2	0
Boone 2b	3	1	1	0	0	1	0	3
Nixon pr	0	0	0	0	0	0	0	0
Lockhart 2b	4	0	2	1	0	1	1	3
C. Jones 3b	6	1	3	1	2	2	2	1
Jordan rf	7	0	2	1	1	3	4	0
Klesko 1b	2	0	0	0	1	0	8	1
Hunter ph,1b	3	0	0	0	1	0	7	0
A. Jones cf	5	0	0	0	1	2	2	0
Perez c	4	0	2	0	1	1	7	0
Battle pr	0	0	0	0	0	0	0	0
Myers c	1	0	0	0	1	1	7	0
Weiss ss	6	1	2	0	1	1	2	7
Maddux p	3	0	0	0	0	3	1	0
Hernandez ph	1	0	0	0	0	1	0	0
Mulholland p	0	0	0	0	0	0	0	0
Guillen ph	1	0	0	0	0	0	0	0
Remlinger p	0	0	0	0	0	0	0	0
Springer p	0	0	0	0	0	0	0	0
Fabregas ph	1	0	0	0	0	1	0	0
Rocker p	0	0	0	0	0	0	0	0
McGlinchy p	1	0	0	0	0	1	0	1
Totals	55	3	13	3	10	19	43	16

FIELDING -
DP: 2. Weiss-Klesko, Lockhart-Weiss-Hunter.
E: Klesko 2 (2).

BATTING -
2B: Perez (2,off Yoshii); Boone (1,off Yoshii); C. Jones 2 (2,off Yoshii,off Dotel); Williams (1,off Hershiser); Weiss (2,off Mahomes).
3B: Lockhart (1,off Dotel).
SH: A. Jones (1,off Hershiser).
HBP: Boone (1,by Hershiser).
IBB: C. Jones 2 (3,by Hershiser,by Dotel); Perez (1,by Hershiser); Jordan (2,by Wendell); Williams (1,by Mahomes).
Team LOB: 19.

BASERUNNING -
SB: Nixon (1,2nd base off Wendell/Piazza); Battle (1,2nd base off Benitez/Piazza); Weiss (2,2nd base off Dotel/Pratt).
CS: Klesko (1,Home by Hershiser/Piazza).

New York Mets	AB	R	H	RBI	BB	SO	PO	A
Henderson lf	5	1	1	0	0	1	2	0
Rogers p	0	0	0	0	0	0	0	0
Bonilla ph	1	0	0	0	0	1	0	0
Dotel p	0	0	0	0	0	0	0	0
M. Franco ph	0	0	0	0	1	0	0	0
Cedeno pr	0	1	0	0	0	0	0	0
Alfonzo 2b	6	0	1	0	0	2	2	4
Olerud 1b	6	1	2	2	1	0	11	1
Piazza c	6	0	1	0	0	3	17	1
Pratt c	0	0	0	1	1	0	4	0
Ventura 3b	7	0	2	1	0	1	0	7
Mora rf,cf,rf	6	0	1	0	0	2	3	1
Hamilton cf	3	0	2	0	0	0	2	0
Agbayani ph,rf,lf	1	0	0	0	2	0	1	0
Ordonez ss	6	0	0	0	0	0	1	2
Yoshii p	1	0	0	0	0	1	0	0
Hershiser p	1	0	0	0	0	0	2	0
Wendell p	0	0	0	0	0	0	0	0
Cook p	0	0	0	0	0	0	0	0
Mahomes p	1	0	0	0	0	1	0	0
J. Franco p	0	0	0	0	0	0	0	0
Benitez p	0	0	0	0	0	0	0	0
Dunston ph,cf	3	1	1	0	0	1	0	0
Totals	53	4	11	4	5	13	45	16

FIELDING -
DP: 2. Piazza-Ventura-Hershiser, Ventura-Alfonzo-Olerud.
E: Olerud (2).

BATTING -
2B: Hamilton (1,off Maddux).
HR: Olerud (2,1st inning off Maddux 1 on 1 out).
SH: Alfonzo (1,off McGlinchy).
IBB: Olerud (1,by McGlinchy).
Team LOB: 12.

BASERUNNING -
SB: Agbayani (1,2nd base off McGlinchy/Myers); Dunston (1,2nd base off McGlinchy/Myers).

PITCHING

Atlanta Braves	IP	H	R	ER	BB	SO	HR
Maddux	7	7	2	2	0	5	1
Mulholland	2	1	0	0	0	2	0
Remlinger	2	1	0	0	0	2	0
Springer	1	0	0	0	1	1	0
Rocker	1.1	0	0	0	0	0	0
McGlinchy L(0-1)	1	2	2	2	4	1	0
Totals	14.1	11	4	4	5	13	1

IBB: McGlinchy (1,Olerud).

New York Mets	IP	H	R	ER	BB	SO	HR
Yoshii	3	4	2	2	1	3	0
Hershiser	3.1	1	0	0	3	5	0
Wendell	0.1	0	0	0	1	1	0
Cook	0	0	0	0	0	0	0
Mahomes	1	1	0	0	2	1	0
J. Franco	1.1	1	0	0	0	2	0
Benitez	1	1	0	0	0	1	0
Rogers	2	1	0	0	1	1	0
Dotel W(1-0)	3	4	1	1	2	5	0
Totals	15	13	3	3	10	19	0

Yoshii faced 4 batters in the 4th inning
HBP: Hershiser (1,Boone).
IBB: Hershiser 2 (2,C. Jones,Perez); Wendell (1,Jordan); Mahomes (1,Williams); Dotel (1,C. Jones).

Umpires: Jerry Layne, Jerry Crawford, Ed Montague, Jeff Kellogg, Charlie Reliford, Ed Rapuano

Time of Game: 5:46   **Attendance:** 55723

	1 2 3	4 5 6	7 8 9	10 11 12	13 14 15	R	H	E
ATL N	0 0 0	2 0 0	0 0 0	0 0 0	0 0 1	3	13	2
NY N	2 0 0	0 0 0	0 0 0	0 0 0	0 0 2	4	11	1

The Atlanta Braves won the first three games before the New York Mets took Game 4 of the National League Championship Series. Then a Shea Stadium crowd witnessed a game for the ages. Well actually, the game *took* ages, and by the time it was over both managers Bobby Valentine and Bobby Cox had aged a bit.

The Mets scored twice in the first inning off Greg Maddux on a John Olerud home run, but the Braves scored a pair in the fourth off Masato Yoshii. The score remained 2-2 until the 15th inning, when the Braves' Keith Lockhart tripled to drive home Walt Weiss.

In the bottom of the inning, the Mets' Shawon Dunston led off with a single against Kevin McGlinchy, the sixth Atlanta pitcher used. Matt Franco walked, Edgar Alfonzo sacrificed them both into scoring position, and John Olerud was intentionally walked to load the bases. Todd Pratt walked, scoring the tying the run, but there was drama still ahead: Robin Ventura hit a massive drive over the right-center field fence for a walk-off, grand-slam single. Yes, single. It would have been a homer, but Ventura was mobbed by his celebrating teammates before he reached second base and never completed his trip around the bases. After five hours and forty-six minutes of play, Ventura was credited with one of the greatest singles in playoff history.

"As long as I got to first base, I just don't care," he said.

You won't find his name listed on Baseball-Reference.com, but we can tell you there isn't a Cubs fan around who can't tell you the name of the guy who helped cost the Chicago Cubs a trip to the World Series on October 14, 2003:

Steve Bartman.

With all due respect to Leonard Bernstein:

Bartman, say it loud and the wound is oozing.

Say it soft and it's still like losing,

Bartman, Cubs fans never stop saying: "Bartman!"

Now we know all of this is unfair, but let's remember the circumstances. Game 6 of the National League Championship Series and the Cubbies were a mere five outs from the Promised Land: their first World Series appearance since 1945. They led 3-0 over the Florida Marlins in the eighth inning. With one out and Florida's Juan Pierre on second base, Luis Castillo hit a flyball down the left field line that drifted into foul territory. Cubs left fielder Moises Alou drifted over and over…closer to the stands…and leapt for the ball.

And now, with all due respect to Ernest Thayer:

Oh, somewhere in this favored land the sun is shining bright,

The band is playing somewhere, and somewhere hearts are light,

And somewhere men are laughing, and little children crawl;

But there is no joy at Wrigley—Steve Bartman tips the ball.

Poor Steve Bartman. He was a lifelong Cubs fan and all he did was try to catch a ball that was drifting and drifting into the stands. His eyes were on the ball and he couldn't see that the ball was also drifting and drifting into the glove of Alou.

Given a second chance, a new lease on life, Castillo drew a walk and Pierre advanced to third off the shaken Cubs' pitcher, Mark Prior. Ivan Rodriguez singled home Pierre; Alex Gonzalez erred on Miguel Cabrera's grounder to load the bases; and Derrek Lee unloaded the bases, driving home two runs and chasing Prior from the game.

In came Kyle Farnsworth, who intentionally walked Mike Lowell. Jeff Conine's sacrifice fly plated one and moved the other two runners into scoring position. Todd Hollingsworth was intentionally passed to load 'em up again. This time it was Mike Mordecai's chance to unload the bases and he did so with a bases-clearing double.

Mike Remlinger relieved Farnsworth, and Pierre (at-bat for the second time that inning) relieved Mordecai from standing on second base too long by hitting a run-scoring single. Finally, Castillo popped out to second and the side was retired.

Now in case you lost track, the Marlins scored 8 runs on 5 hits, one error, and one Bartman.

The Marlins went on to win this game as well as Game 7. They also went on to win the World Series… all because of Steve Bartman.

Doesn't sound right, does it? Well, it shouldn't.

National League Championship Series Game 6
Tuesday, October 14, 2003
Wrigley Field

	1	2	3		4	5	6		7	8	9		R	H	E
FLA N	0	0	0		0	0	0		0	8	0		8	9	0
CHI N	1	0	0		0	0	1		1	0	0		3	10	2

The finale of the 2003 American League Championship Series will always be known as "The Day Grady Little Lost His Job." But it was so much more.

With the New York Yankees and the Boston Red Sox tied at three games apiece, the Sox chased Roger Clemens and took a 5-2 lead into the eighth inning at Yankee Stadium. Boston starter Pedro Martinez had been roughed up for three hits and a run in the seventh, and Sox diehards from Eastport to Block Island were shocked to see him take the mound in the eighth. "Take Pedro out!" grannies in Lewiston, Maine, must have screamed, hurling their afghans at the screen. In fact, Pedro said later that he told Little after the seventh inning, "I said, 'Get the guys ready in case I get in trouble.'"

The hubbub subsided somewhat when Martinez got Nick Johnson to popout to short. But Derek Jeter then doubled. "Take Pedro out!" fishermen in Oak Bluffs, Massachusetts, muttered into their beers. Yankee centerfielder Bernie Williams singled Jeter home to make it 5-3. "Take Pedro out!" artists in Brattleboro, Vermont, grumbled, throwing paint onto their canvases in disgust. Little came running out to the mound to talk to Martínez. "He asked me if I had any bullets in my tank," Martínez said. "I said I had enough." When Yankees Hideki Matsui and Jorge Posada added run-scoring doubles to tie the score, Little finally trudged to the mound to remove Martinez. Sox fans everywhere agreed: He had unquestionably waited too long.

But the game wasn't over. Reliever Alan Embree replaced Martinez and coaxed Jason Giambi to fly out to center. Mike Timlin replaced Embree and walked two men—one intentionally—before getting Alfonso Soriano to ground into a forceout and end the inning.

It was anyone's game. Mariano Rivera, the most productive of postseason relievers, took the mound for the Yankees—and gave the Red Sox their chances. In the ninth, Boston's Damian Jackson stood on second with two outs, and Todd Walker ripped the ball—right into the glove of second baseman Soriano. In the 10th, David Ortiz doubled with two outs, but his pinch runner, Gabe Kapler, was stranded when Kevin Millar popped up. Meanwhile, Timlin retired the Yankees 1-2-3 in the ninth. The Red Sox summoned Tim Wakefield to pitch the tenth. The knuckleballer had won twice during the series and was vying for ALCS Most Valuable Player. He retired the Yankees in order. And then Rivera had to pitch a third inning, no easy task for a closer not accustomed to pitching more than an inning each outing. He got through the Red Sox half of the 11th and was surely headed for the showers. Things didn't look so bad.

Aaron Boone, who had pinch run for Ruben Sierra in the eighth and stayed in the game to play third base, led off against Wakefield in the 11th. The redoubtable Wakefield threw his patented knuckler; Boone blasted it to oblivion; and suddenly the Yankees were celebrating another trip to the World Series. For their part, the Bostononians walked off the field with visions of Enos Slaughter, Bucky "Freakin'" Dent, and other old nemeses that had haunted the Red Sox Nation for a century.

In the offseason, Grady Little was fired. Aaron Boone violated his contract with the Yankees by playing basketball; he tore up his knee and was released. All those head-shaking New England Calvinists just knew the "Curse of the Bambino" would follow them to their graves. They were so downtrodden, they couldn't even say, "Wait 'til next year."

Maybe that's why next year finally provided the balm.

American League Championship Series Game 7 Thursday, October 16, 2003 Yankee Stadium

	1	2	3	4	5	6	7	8	9	10	11	R	H	E
BOS A	0	3	0	1	0	0	0	1	0	0	0	5	11	0
NY A	0	0	0	0	1	0	1	3	0	0	1	6	11	1

2004__ Boston Red Sox vs. New York Yankees

For all the postseason gloom that has soured their team's history, the Boston Red Sox have been a blessed team. They've had unquestionably one of the best players in baseball history (Babe Ruth), unquestionably one of the best hitters (Ted Williams), and unquestionably one of the best pitchers (fans can choose between Lefty Grove and Roger Clemens). In 2004, Red Sox glory came to include the most important stolen base in baseball history.

The Hub nine were down to their last inning of the 2004 American League Championship Series. The New York Yankees led the series three games to none and led Game 4, 4-3, with Sox-killer Mariano Rivera on the mound. But Rivera committed a cardinal sin and walked the leadoff hitter, Kevin Millar.

As the Fenway Park faithful began to stir, Dave Roberts was sent in to run for Millar. Third base coach Dale Sveum signaled "bunt" to the batter, but Roberts waved his arms and told first base coach Lynn Jones, "I'm stealing the base." The bunt sign was abandoned.

Roberts never thought about failing. "That goes back to what Maury Wills told me," he later explained to a San Francisco *Chronicle* writer. Roberts was referring to the old Dodger base-stealer, who stole 586 bases in his career and had a career success rate of 74%. "He said it doesn't matter who's catching or who's pitching. Just worry about getting a good jump. He's the one who told me there is going to be some point in my life where everybody in the ballpark knows I'm going to steal a base, and you have to steal it. You can't be afraid to take that chance.

"If it wasn't for him, I wouldn't have had the courage to do that."

Roberts planned to wait one pitch in order to get loose, but Rivera threw over to first several times, giving Roberts a chance to settle in. On the first pitch to Bill Mueller, Roberts took off. The Yankees were prepared. Rivera got the pitch home in a speedy 1.25 seconds; catcher Jorge Posada threw to second in a speedy 1.75 seconds; Roberts slid headfirst; and shortstop Derek Jeter's tag was just late. Now there was a man on second with nobody out. As Roberts stood up and dusted himself off, one could almost feel the weight of history shifting. The British had surrendered at Saratoga; Pickett's Charge had failed miserably; the lads had stormed Omaha Beach and made their way up the embankment. It did not take a starry-eyed optimist to see the crest of the hill and the easy route down.

When the members of this younger generation of Red

American League Championship Series—Game 4
Sunday, October 17, 2004
Fenway Park

BATTING

New York Yankees	AB	R	H	RBI	BB	SO	PO	A
Jeter ss	4	1	1	0	1	0	2	3
Rodriguez 3b	5	1	1	2	1	1	0	1
Sheffield rf	5	0	0	0	1	1	2	0
Matsui lf	5	1	2	0	1	1	4	0
Williams cf	6	0	1	1	0	1	2	0
Posada c	4	1	2	0	2	0	10	0
Sierra dh	6	0	2	0	0	1	0	0
Clark 1b	6	0	2	1	0	1	7	2
Cairo 2b	4	0	1	0	1	1	5	2
Hernandez p	0	0	0	0	0	0	0	0
Sturtze p	0	0	0	0	0	0	0	0
Rivera p	0	0	0	0	0	0	1	1
Gordon p	0	0	0	0	0	0	0	0
Quantrill p	0	0	0	0	0	0	0	0
Totals	45	4	12	4	7	7	33	10

FIELDING -
DP: 1. Jeter-Cairo-Clark.
E: Clark (1).

BATTING -
2B: Matsui (5,off Lowe).
3B: Matsui (1,off Lowe).
HR: Rodriguez (2,3rd inning off Lowe 1 on 2 out).
SH: Cairo (1,off Lowe); Jeter (1,off Embree).
IBB: Sheffield (1,by Embree).
Team LOB: 14.

Boston Red Sox	AB	R	H	RBI	BB	SO	PO	A
Damon cf	5	1	0	0	1	0	4	0
Cabrera ss	6	1	1	1	0	2	3	2
Ramirez lf	3	1	2	0	3	1	3	0
Ortiz dh	5	1	2	4	1	1	0	0
Varitek c	5	0	0	0	0	3	9	1
Nixon rf	5	0	0	0	0	0	2	0
Millar 1b	2	0	1	0	2	0	9	1
Roberts pr	0	1	0	0	0	0	0	0
Reese 2b	1	0	0	0	0	1	0	0
Mueller 3b	5	1	2	1	0	0	1	4
Bellhorn 2b	2	0	0	0	1	2	2	4
Mientkiewicz ph,1b	1	0	0	0	0	0	2	0
Lowe p	0	0	0	0	0	0	1	2
Timlin p	0	0	0	0	0	0	0	0
Foulke p	0	0	0	0	0	0	0	0
Embree p	0	0	0	0	0	0	0	1
Myers p	0	0	0	0	0	0	0	0
Leskanic p	0	0	0	0	0	0	0	1
Totals	40	6	8	6	8	10	36	16

BATTING -
HR: Ortiz (1,12th inning off Quantrill 1 on 0 out).
SH: Mientkiewicz (1,off Rivera).
Team LOB: 10.

BASERUNNING -
SB: Roberts (1,2nd base off Rivera/Posada); Damon (1,2nd base off Gordon/Posada).

PITCHING

New York Yankees	IP	H	R	ER	BB	SO	HR
Hernandez	5	3	3	3	5	6	0
Sturtze	2	1	0	0	1	0	0
Rivera	2	2	1	1	2	2	0
Gordon	2	0	0	0	1	1	0
Quantrill L(0-1)	0	2	2	2	0	0	1
Totals	11	8	6	6	8	10	1

Quantrill faced 2 batters in the 12th inning

Boston Red Sox	IP	H	R	ER	BB	SO	HR
Lowe	5.1	6	3	3	0	3	1
Timlin	1	3	1	1	3	0	0
Foulke	2.2	0	0	0	2	3	0
Embree	1.2	2	0	0	1	0	0
Myers	0	0	0	0	1	0	0
Leskanic W(1-0)	1.1	1	0	0	0	1	0
Totals	12	12	4	4	7	7	1

WP: Timlin (1).

IBB: Embree (1,Sheffield).

Umpires: Jim Joyce, Jeff Kellogg, Joe West, Randy Marsh, Jeff Nelson, John Hirschbeck.

Time of Game: 5:02 **Attendance:** 34826

	1	2	3	4	5	6	7	8	9	10	11	12	R	H	E
NY A	0	0	2	0	0	2	0	0	0	0	0	0	4	12	1
BOS A	0	0	0	0	3	0	0	0	1	0	0	2	6	8	0

Sox fans are all doddering grandparents, they will still remember what happened next.

Once Roberts made his way to second, Red Sox Nation knew their team would become the first to rally from three games down in a postseason series and go all the way. Bill Mueller singled Roberts home, and the game went into extra innings. The Yankees loaded the bases in the 11th, and placed a man in scoring position in the 12th, but somehow the tide had turned. Come the last of the 12th, Manny Ramirez singled. Then up stepped one of the most popular players in Red Sox history, David Ortiz. Big Papi hit the ball way into the stands, his second walk-off homer that postseason, and suddenly the Sox were back in it. In Game 5, the Yankees led 4-2. The Soxsies tied it up and went into extra innings, thrills and chills, and Ortiz won it with a walk-off single in the fourteenth. You can't imagine the joy, the elation throughout New England, maybe the world. It wasn't just that the Sox had won, which would have been enough. And it wasn't just that the Yankees had lost (that too would have been sufficient). It was that the Red Sox beat the Yankees; Main Street beat Wall Street; David beat Goliath.

If it were possible to get better, it did in Game 6. The Red Sox' Curt Schilling, pitching despite a quasi-surgically repaired ankle and blood literally soaking through his sock, bested the Yankees, 4-2. By then the die was cast. Never mind that it was Game 7 in Yankee Stadium. The Yankees had lost the game before it started and by the time it ended they had officially lost, 10-3.

The St. Louis Cardinals, facing the Red Sox in the World Series, had no chance against this team of destiny. The Red Sox beat them four straight.

The next season on Opening Day, the franchise invited many Red Sox greats back for the hoisting of the World Series banner in Fenway Park. Roberts was playing for San Diego by then, but he took the day off in order to make a curtain call. He received the loudest ovation of anyone.

Red Sox manager Terry Francona said, "Roberts' steal was the most thrilling event I've ever been associated with. I doubt we could have done all that without him."

Dave Roberts, OF, 1999-2006

G	AB	R	H	2B	3B	HR	RBI	BB	IBB	SO	HBP	SH	SF	XI	ROE	GDP	SB	CS	AVG	OBP	SLG	BFW
666	2204	358	594	76	42	21	181	245	6	278	16	36	17	1	31	19	207	50	.270	.344	.371	-1.7

LAST LICK

Most everyone remembers the 2004 postseason and Curt Schilling's bloody sock. But many fans forget that there were two "Curts" on that pitching staff, and the other Curt had an important role as well. Curt Leskanic appeared in 32 regular-season games for the 2004 Boston Red Sox and he appeared in Games 1, 3 and 4 in the famous American League Championship Series against the New York Yankees. In Game 4, an arm-weary Leskanic recorded the last four Yankee outs, enabling David Ortiz to hit his walk-off home run. That night, Leskanic picked up the win in what would be his last major league appearance.

The Houston Astros were eliminated from the playoffs by the Atlanta Braves in 1997, 1999 and 2001, but on October 9, 2005, leading two games to one in the best-of-five National League Division Series, Houston hoped to bounce the Braves for the second consecutive year and advance to a re-match with the St. Louis Cardinals in the National League Championship Series.

The Braves took a 4-0 lead in the top of the third when Adam LaRoche hit a grand slam to right-center off Brandon Backe. Atlanta stretched the lead to 5-0 in the fifth and still led 6-1 heading into the bottom of the eighth. But with one out, the Astros loaded the bases for their slugger, Lance Berkman. Sometimes a game can change on one pitch; just ask Braves reliever Kyle Farnsworth, who gave up Berkman's grand slam, making the score 6-5. But this alone does not make a grand finale—a two-out, game-tying, ninth-inning home run by Houston catcher Brad Ausmus makes this game bookworthy.

The Astros went into orbit. The score remained tied through the 11th, 12th, 13th, 14th (fans in attendance celebrated a second seventh-inning stretch), 15th, 16th, 17th…

In the game's second bottom of the ninth inning (ostensibly the 18th inning), pitcher Roger Clemens—of all people—led off. The losing pitcher as the starter in Game 2, Clemens was pressed into relief duty for just the second time in his career. He had thrown

three one-hit innings; he also owned a .160 career batting average. Swinging mightily, Clemens struck out. Next up: Chris Burke, who entered the game in the 10th inning as a pinch runner for Lance Berkman and who had already played both center field and left field. In two plate appearances Burke had so far flied out and walked. What else was there for him to do but deposit a Joey Devine pitch into the left field stands for a 7-6 Astros victory and a second trip to the NLCS against the Cardinals?

The defensive star of the game was Shaun Dean, a name you will never find on Baseball-Reference.com. A comptroller at Joslin Construction, Dean caught both Berkman's grand slam and Burke's series-winning homer from his seat in the stands.

"I never caught one in a game before," said Dean, twenty-five, of Porter, Texas. Dean presented the balls to a representative of the Hall of Fame on that Friday, and in exchange the Astros gave him four box seats for one of their games against St. Louis in the NLCS.

National League Division Series— Game 4
Sunday, October 9, 2005
Minute Maid Park
Time of Game: 5:50

	1 2 3	4 5 6	7 8 9	10 11 12	13 14 15	16 17 18	R	H	E
ATL N	0 0 4	0 1 0	0 1 0	0 0 0	0 0 0	0 0 0	6	13	0
HOU N	0 0 0	0 1 0	0 4 1	0 0 0	0 0 0	0 0 1	7	10	1

Perhaps it's unfair that we don't attribute to the Philadelphia Phillies the amazing run that enabled them to capture the National League East on the final day of the 2007 season. But honestly, while the Phillies played great ball, this was more about the implosion of the New York Mets than the play of any other team.

The Mets held a seven-game lead over the Phillies with 17 games remaining. What more does a team need? Well, it turns out they needed an eight-game lead with 16 games remaining.

How does a team blow such a lead? The Mets had the perfect storm—they stopped hitting, pitching and fielding (committing 21 errors in these 17 games). They mis-ran the bases, when they ran at all. Their starters barely started and their bullpen (5.27 ERA over the final 17 games) didn't finish; the pitching staff had a 5.96 ERA over the final 17 games, while the Phils had a 3.44 over the same period. Pep talks from their reserved manager Willie Randolph made little difference.

The pattern had been building throughout the season. In April, the Mets' team ERA was 2.96; in May, 3.69; in June, 4.20; July, 4.50; August, 4.93; and in September, when it mattered most, 5.11. But even so…the Mets went an unbelievable 5-12 (while the Phils went 13-4) and in the process became the first major league team to fail to finish in first place after owning a lead of seven games or more with 17 remaining. New York, which had that margin on Sept. 12, also matched the largest lead blown in September.

The Mets played .294 ball down the stretch. Had they played just .411 baseball they would have won it. But as the Seattle *Times*' Larry Stone brilliantly said of the Mets' manager, "Randolph drove the Mets down the stretch at Mauch 1 speed." This was a reference to the great collapse of 1964 when Gene Mauch's Phils had a 6½-game lead with 12 to play. Those Phils lost 10 straight to finish second to the St. Louis Cardinals.

Hope still sprang eternal heading into the final three games of the season. The Mets and the Phillies were tied for first. They were even tied for first after New York lost 7-4 to the Marlins on Friday night, but won 13-0 on Saturday.

The Mets had their 300-game winner, Tom Glavine, ready to pitch them to victory (or at least a playoff) on that final Sunday. But Glavine lasted just one-third of an inning, surrendering seven runs on five hits. It was Glavine's fourth-straight loss.

Glavine chuckled when he answered a question from a New York *Times* reporter who asked if this was his worst finale. "I've had 20 years and won one World Series," he said. "That means 19 seasons didn't end the way I wanted."

Randolph looked at the reporters surrounding him after the final indignity and said he spoke to his players after the game. "I told my players this is a life lesson in baseball and in how to become champions. And, when you get to that road, you have to seize it because you never know when it's going to come again."

The baseball gods are funny aren't they? As Phil Sheridan wrote in the October 1, Philadelphia *Inquirer*, "If you're from Philadelphia, the ominous thunderhead of 1964 hangs over you, casting a permanent shadow of nagging doubt in your sports psyche. But if you were too young to see or to remember that infamous collapse, watching these Mets has given you a feel for what it must have been like."

National League East: September 12, 2007

Team	Record	GB
New York Mets	83-62	-
Philadelphia	76-69	7.0
Atlanta	74-72	9.5
Washington	65-81	18.5
Florida	63-83	20.5

National League East: October 1, 2007

Team	Record	GB
Philadelphia	89-73	-
New York Mets	88-74	1.0
Atlanta	84-78	5.0
Washington	73-89	16.0
Florida	71-91	18.0

As all the attention of the baseball world seemed to be focused on the great New York Mets' collapse of 2007, the Colorado Rockies forgot how to lose. There were as many as four teams scrambling around the National League West in September of 2007 hoping for a division victory or a wild-card berth.

The Los Angeles Dodgers dropped out the madness first, leaving the shocking Arizona Diamondbacks (who would make the postseason despite defying any Pythagorean or Bill Jamesian Theorem by scoring fewer runs than they gave up); the pitching-rich San Diego Padres (led by Jake Peavy, who would lead the league in wins, strikeouts and ERA); and the perennial NL West doormats, the Colorado Rockies.

Mixed into this gumbo were the truly-cursed Chicago Cubs and the consistently-mediocre Milwaukee Brewers, both from the Central Division and battling for the division crown and perhaps a wild-card spot. Meanwhile, the Mets and Phils, fighting for rights to the NL East, both also had a shot at ending up as the wild-card participant.

Sound complex? On the morning of Friday, September 28, with the season ending Sunday, September 30, here were the scenarios:

- If the Mets tied for the wild-card lead, they would host Arizona and San Diego but play at Colorado. Arizona went 0-4 in wild-card coin flips and would be on the road at Colorado, Philadelphia and San Diego.
- Coin flips held Sept. 7 determined New York would visit Philadelphia if they tied for the NL East.
- In the NL West, Colorado and San Diego would be at Arizona, and Colorado would be at San Diego.
- In the wild-card race, Philadelphia would be at Colorado and San Diego, and San Diego would be at Colorado.
- If there were a tie in the NL Central, Milwaukee would play at Chicago.

And what if they all tied? What if the Phillies, Mets, Diamondbacks, Rockies and Padres finished with the same record?

- That would have created ties in the NL East, the NL West, and the wild-card race, requiring four

days of tiebreaker games to determine postseason berths.

- The NL East: The Phillies would play the Mets on Monday at Citizens Bank Park.
- In the West, the team with the best head-to-head record against the others would choose whether it preferred one tiebreaker road game or two home games. (Presumably, the team with the choice would take one road game.) Monday's winner would then host the club with the bye on Tuesday for the NL West title.
- Starting Wednesday, the three teams that failed to win division titles would be involved in a two-day, two-game tiebreaker to determine the wild-card winner.

So how did this mess shake itself out? With great irony. On Saturday, September 29, the Padres were one strike away from winning a third-consecutive playoff berth. Potential Hall-of-Famer Trevor Hoffman was on the mound facing the Brewers. Hoffman threw his killer change-up, the batter swung…and lined it into the right field corner for a triple, driving home the tying run. The Brewers won it, 4-3, in the 11th inning.

The Brewers batter who had the key hit in the ninth? Tony Gwynn Jr., son of the greatest Padre in history.

But the Padres still might have reached the playoffs, without a play-in, had they only beat the Brewers on that final Sunday. The Brewers had been eliminated on Friday night, but they hammered San Diego regardless, 11-6.

In the meantime, Colorado held on for a 4-3 victory over NL West champion Arizona to force a play-in game. The fact that a play-in included the Rockies was shocking if one examined the standings of September 15:

National League West: September 15, 2007

West	Record	GB
Arizona	83-66	-
San Diego	80-67	2.0
Los Angeles	79-69	3.5
Colorado	76-72	6.0
San Francisco	66-82	16.5

Colorado was 44-44 before the All-Star break, but since then had gone 46-29. But that wasn't the key number. Colorado lost only once after September 16…talk about grand finales. What happened? To start with, in September, the Rockies' Matt Holliday hit .367 with 12 homers, 30 RBI and 29 runs scored; the Rockies' Brad Hawpe hit .467 with 20 RBI in the last 11 games; the Rockies' Todd Helton hit .386 in the final 14 games with three homers and 13 RBI; and the Rockies' bullpen had a 2.49 ERA, holding opponents to a .212 batting average.

On October 1, it all came down to game number 163, and it took an extraordinary ending to bring this extra-regular season game to conclusion. The Rockies jumped out to a quick 3-0 lead over Jake Peavy after two innings, but they quickly learned that would not suffice as the Padres sent 10 players to bat against Josh Fogg in the third and scored five times, thanks in large part to Adrian Gonzalez, who blasted a grand slam.

Todd Helton responded with a homer in the bottom of the third. After single runs in the fifth and sixth, Colorado held a 6-5 lead. But as Tracy Ringolsby of the Rocky Mountain *News* wrote, "Nothing has come easy for the Rockies. No sense starting now."

Brian Giles drove home a run for the Padres, and that was enough to send the extra game into extra innings. The 6-6 score stayed the same but the tension mounted as the game entered the 13th inning. (An unlucky inning for both teams.) Jorge Julio, the ninth of ten Rockies pitchers, came on to start the inning. He walked Giles, and then gave up a Scott Hairston two-run homer. After one more single, Ramon Ortiz entered the game and retired the Padres in order.

Trevor Hoffman was called on for the bottom of the 13th; the great closer sought redemption. Unfortunately, he's still looking. Kazuo Matsui and Troy Tulowitzki hit back-to-back doubles against baseball's all-time saves leader and just like that it was 7-6 Padres.

Up stepped Matt Holliday. With one triple off the scoreboard in right, he accomplished four things.

First, he tied the game. Second, he put the winning run on third with no one out. Third, by going 2 for 6, Holliday won the NL batting title (.340) over Atlanta's Chipper Jones (.337). Fourth, by driving home the tying run he also won the league RBI crown with 137, one more than Philadelphia's Ryan Howard.

The score was 7-7, there was no one out and a runner on third, and Todd Helton batted against Hoffman. He was intentionally passed. Jamey Carroll, who pinch ran for Garrett Atkins in the seventh and stayed in at third base, came to the plate. With the infield in and the outfield shallow, Carroll hit a liner to Brian Giles in right. The throw appeared to beat Holliday to the plate, but catcher Michael Barrett couldn't handle it and Holliday barreled in headfirst for the winning run. To many observers it appeared as if he never touched the plate and should have been out when Barrett recovered the ball and tagged the dazed and bleeding Holliday. But the umpires saw it differently and the Rockies (90-73), who had been in fourth place and 6½ games back in the NL West on Sept. 16, had finally overtaken San Diego (89-74) to become the wild-card team and make their first postseason appearance since 1995.

"You can't draw it up any better than that," Rockies manager Clint Hurdle told reporters after the game. "You don't think that someone drawing this up doesn't have a sense of drama…a sense of humor?"

After winning 14 of their final 15 regular season games, the Rockies then swept Philadelphia in the NL Division Series and Arizona in the NL Championship Series before they themselves were swept by the Boston Red Sox in the World Series.

National League West: October 1, 2007:

West	Record	GB
Arizona	90-72	-
Colorado	90-73	0.5
San Diego	89-74	1.5
Los Angeles	82-80	8.0
San Francisco	71-91	19.0

World Series

Kirk Gibson celebrates his walk-off home run in 1988.

The ultimate of all ultimate grand finales is Game 7 of the World Series. From the shaping of the rosters in the off-season through spring training, the long grind of the regular season, the hurdles of the post-season, and six World Series games, there can be only one survivor. Which raises certain questions:

1. How could thirty-five World Series—more than one-third the total—go to the grandest of finales, the winner-take-all Game 7?
2. How could only five of those games be blowouts?
3. And how could the rest give us such delicious storylines: twelve one-run games, nine shutouts, five cliffhangers that ended with walk-off hits, and a smorgasbord of heroes, goats, good and bad defensive plays, good and bad baserunning, good and bad managing, rookie sensations, bad bounces, and punishment from the weather?

Using RetroSheet.org, Gabriel Schechter, a research associate at the National Baseball Hall of Fame & Museum, provides the following summary of all World Series endings from 1903-2006:

- Thirteen times, the Series ended with a swinging strike three
- The Series ended with double plays twice, in 1921 and 1947
- The Series ended with line-drive outs five times
- The Series ended with groundball outs 35 times
- The Series ended with flyballs or popups 34 times
- The home team ended eleven Series with a walk-off run: 1912, 1924, 1927, 1929, 1935, 1953, 1960, 1991, 1993, 1997 and 2001

As Thomas Boswell wrote in the Washington *Post*, "...baseball has consistently suspended disbelief in October."

Chicago Cubs vs. Detroit Tigers

World Series—Game 1
Tuesday, October 8, 1907
Westside Grounds

With the Detroit Tigers leading the Chicago Cubs 3-1 in Game 1 of the 1907 World Series, Detroit's Wild Bill Donovan looked unbeatable heading into the ninth inning. But Frank Chance singled to right and Harry Steinfeldt was hit by a pitch. Johnny Kling popped up on a bunt attempt, but Johnny Evers loaded the bases when third baseman Bill Coughlin bobbled a grounder. Wildfire Schulte grounded to the pitcher, which drove home one run and cut the lead to 3-2. Then pinch hitter Del Howard struck out on an outside pitch, but the ball eluded catcher Boss Schmidt. Howard reached first and Steinfeldt scored the tying run. The Tigers prevented any additional runs, but the game was called after 12 innings by darkness with the score knotted, 3-3. One could say that Schmidt, who allowed seven stolen bases and committed two errors in the opener in addition to the passed ball, was fit to be tied; the Cubs won the next four straight games, claiming the first of back-to-back World Series championships—their last of the twentieth century.

BATTING

Detroit Tigers	AB	R	H	RBI	BB	SO	PO	A
Jones lf	5	1	3	0	1	0	3	1
Schaefer 2b	6	1	1	0	0	0	7	4
Crawford cf	5	1	3	2	0	1	1	0
Cobb rf	5	0	0	0	0	0	0	0
Rossman 1b	3	0	0	1	1	0	9	3
Coughlin 3b	5	0	0	0	0	0	2	1
Schmidt c	5	0	2	0	0	0	13	2
O'Leary ss	4	0	0	0	0	1	0	3
Donovan p	5	0	0	0	0	3	2	2
Totals	43	3	9	3	2	7	36	15

FIELDING -
DP: 1. Schaefer-Rossman.
E: Coughlin (1), Schmidt 2 (2).

BATTING -
SH: O'Leary (1,off Overall).
SF: Rossman (1,off Overall).
Team LOB: 8.

BASERUNNING -
SB: Jones 2 (2,2nd base off Overall/Kling 2).
CS: Schaefer (1,2nd base by Overall/Kling).

Chicago Cubs	AB	R	H	RBI	BB	SO	PO	A
Slagle cf	6	0	2	0	0	0	2	0
Sheckard lf	5	0	1	0	0	2	2	0
Chance 1b	4	2	1	0	2	2	15	0
Steinfeldt 3b	3	1	1	0	0	0	1	3
Kling c	4	0	2	1	1	1	7	5
Evers 2b,ss	4	0	2	0	0	0	4	2
Schulte rf	5	0	1	1	0	1	2	0
Tinker ss	3	0	0	0	0	3	3	5
Howard ph	1	0	0	0	0	1	0	0
Zimmerman 2b	1	0	0	0	0	1	0	2
Overall p	3	0	0	0	0	1	0	3
Moran ph	0	0	0	0	0	0	0	0
Reulbach p	2	0	0	0	0	0	0	0
Totals	41	3	10	2	3	12	36	20

FIELDING -
DP: 1. Evers-Tinker.
E: Steinfeldt (1), Kling (1), Evers 2 (2), Tinker (1).

BATTING -
SH: Evers (1,off Donovan); Steinfeldt (1,off Donovan).
HBP: Steinfeldt (1,by Donovan); Sheckard (1,by Donovan).
Team LOB: 9.

BASERUNNING -
SB: Sheckard (1,2nd base off Donovan/Schmidt); Evers (1,2nd base off Donovan/Schmidt);
Steinfeldt (1,2nd base off Donovan/Schmidt); Howard (1,2nd base off Donovan/Schmidt);
Slagle 2 (2,2nd base off Donovan/Schmidt,3rd base off Donovan/Schmidt);
Chance (1,2nd base off Donovan/Schmidt).
CS: Slagle (1,2nd base by Donovan/Schmidt); Evers (1,Home by Donovan/Schmidt).

PITCHING

Detroit Tigers	IP	H	R	ER	BB	SO	HR
Donovan	12	10	3	1	3	12	0

HBP: Donovan 2 (2,Steinfeldt,Sheckard).

Chicago Cubs	IP	H	R	ER	BB	SO	HR
Overall	9	9	3	1	2	5	0
Reulbach	3	0	0	0	0	2	0
Totals	12	9	3	1	2	7	0

Umpires: Hank O'Day, Jack Sheridan

Time of Game: 2:40 **Attendance:** 24377

	1	2	3	4	5	6	7	8	9	10	11	12	R	H	E
DET A	0	0	0	0	0	0	0	3	0	0	0	0	3	9	3
CHI N	0	0	0	1	0	0	0	0	2	0	0	0	3	10	5

1908   Detroit Tigers vs. Chicago Cubs

The Chicago Cubs' Orval Overall became the only World Series pitcher to strike out four batters in one inning: He struck out four Detroit Tigers in the first inning of Game 5 of the 1908 World Series. After leadoff batter Matty McIntyre walked, Charley O'Leary struck out, Sam Crawford singled, Ty Cobb struck out, and Claude Rossman struck out but reached on the wild pitch. Finally, Germany Schaefer struck out for the fourth K of the inning—a record that still stands today.

World Series—Game 5
Wednesday, October 14, 1908
Bennett Park

	1	2	3	4	5	6	7	8	9	R	H	E
CHI N	1	0	0	0	1	0	0	0	0	2	10	0
DET A	0	0	0	0	0	0	0	0	0	0	3	0

1908   Detroit Tigers vs. Chicago Cubs (Part II)

Boss Schmidt was best known for his boxing skills. Reportedly, he twice knocked out Ty Cobb. The 1907 World Series went to the Chicago Cubs, four games to nothing, with one tie. In the final out of the final game, Schmidt batted for catcher Jimmy Archer and popped out to shortstop.

The following season brought the same two teams together with similar results: The Cubs won in five games. Once again, in the final inning of the final game, the final batter was Schmidt, who topped a ball in front of the plate that catcher Johnny Kling threw to Frank Chance for the final out of the Series. Schmidt is the only player to make the last out in two consecutive World Series.

Boss Schmidt, C, 1906-1911

G	AB	R	H	2B	3B	HR	RBI	BB	HBP	SH	SB	AVG	OBP	SLG	BFW
477	1480	137	360	41	22	3	124	36	18	58	23	.243	.270	.307	0.6

1909   Pittsburgh Pirates vs. Detroit Tigers

In a memorable season, Washington Senators pitchers Bob Groom and Walter Johnson each lost at least 25 games—a feat still unprecedented—and the Cleveland Indians' Neal Ball made the first unassisted triple play. But John Heydler, interim president of the National League, had his mind on something else. He suggested that Pittsburgh Pirates manager Fred Clarke start rookie Babe Adams in the opener against the Detroit Tigers. Adams had gone 12-3 with a microscopic 1.11 ERA in his first full season, but he'd started just 12 times.

"I understand Camnitz is out for us," Heydler said in reference to Howie Camnitz (25-6), who had muscle and throat problems but actually did compete in the Series. "I don't know who you'll pitch tomorrow, but a few weeks ago I saw Dolly Gray make the Tigers throw their bats away. Now Gray pitches just like Adams does, only I think Babe is a bit faster and has a sharper break on his fastball. Why don't you start Babe Adams?"

Clarke complied, and the twenty-seven-year-old right-hander won Game 1, 4-1, over Detroit's 29-game winner George Mullin. Adams won Game 5, 8-4, on a raw, cold day in Pittsburgh. Finally, he was asked to pitch Game 7 on two days' rest.

"Back home on the farm, my father once told me never to start anything I can't finish," Adams said. Starting and finishing, he beat Detroit 8-0 with his third six-hitter in nine days.

Heydler must have known something: Adams won 194 games in nineteen years.

Babe Adams, P, 1906-1926

G	GS	CG	SHO	GF	SV	IP	H	BFP	HR	R	ER	BB	IB	SO	SH	WP	HBP	BK	2B	3B	GDP	ROE	W	L	ERA	PW
482	354	206	44	89	15	2995.1	2841	11947	68	1129	917	430	i	1036i	244	26	47	2	68i	33i	19i	34	194i	140	2.76	17.7

The Philadelphia Athletics and the New York Giants split the first two games of the 1911 World Series, and Game 3 went into extra innings tied 1-1 after Frank (Home Run) Baker hit a ninth-inning tater off Giants pitcher Christy Mathewson. It was then time for the gifts to be bestowed: With one out in the 11th inning and Philadelphia's Eddie Collins on first, Baker reached on an infield single. When Giants third baseman Buck Herzog threw wildly on the play for his third error of the game, Collins and Baker advanced to third and second. On the next play, shortstop Art Fletcher fumbled Danny Murphy's grounder, Collins scored, and Baker reached third. Harry Davis scored Baker with a single before the three-hit, two-run, two-error half-inning ended. The Giants scored one in their half when Beals Becker, making his major league debut, pinch hit for Christy Mathewson and reached on an error by Collins; Herzog scored. But Becker was caught stealing second base, and Philadelphia won, 3-2.

World Series—Game 3
Wednesday, October 14, 1911
Polo Grounds V

	1	2	3		4	5	6		7	8	9		10	11		R	H	E
PHI A	0	0	0		0	0	0		0	0	1		0	2		3	9	1
NY N	0	0	1		0	0	0		0	0	0		0	1		2	3	5

Sixty-two years after he dropped a flyball in the final inning of the 1912 World Series, the New York *Times* ran the following headline above Fred Snodgrass' obituary: "Fred Snodgrass, 86, Dead; Ballplayer Muffed 1912 Fly."

But did Snodgrass deserve to be called "goat?" With the New York Giants leading the Boston Red Sox 2-1 after 9½ innings, Snodgrass did indeed drop Clyde Engel's easy flyball to center, putting a man on second with no one out. But historians agree that Snodgrass then made a circus catch to rob Harry Hooper of a double, but which allowed Engle to advance to third. Suppose Snodgrass did what he was really supposed to do, which was catch the first ball and miss the second: Either way there would have been a runner in scoring position with one out.

But what followed mattered even more. Steve Yerkes, a .252 hitter, worked Hall of Fame pitcher Christy Mathewson for a walk. When Tris Speaker lofted a harmless foul between home plate and first base, the stories vary. Some say Mathewson called "Chief!" to instruct catcher Chief Meyers to go for the ball. More historians blame first baseman Fred (Bonehead) Merkle, who stood like a drugstore Indian instead of pursuing the popup. In any case, the ball dropped in and Speaker had new life. He celebrated by driving in Engle with a single and took second on the throw home, while Yerkes raced to third. After Duffy Lewis was intentionally walked, Larry Gardner hit a sacrifice fly to win the game.

So who was the goat? Certainly not Snodgrass. Mathewson for walking the unthreatening Yerkes while "trying to get him to bat at bad balls," as he later admitted himself? Merkle or Bender for failing to catch the foul? ("That was the play which really broke our backs," said Mathewson later.) Maybe the Giants as a team should take the blame, or maybe the Red Sox should take the credit. After the game, people were praising little-used Red Sox pinch hitter Olaf Henriksen for tying the game with a double in the eighth inning, as well as winning pitcher Smokey Joe Wood for saving a run with a barehanded stop in the 10th. Had history remembered it differently, there might have been a hero instead of a goat.

World Series—Game 8
Wednesday, October 16, 1912
Fenway Park

BATTING

New York Giants	AB	R	H	RBI	BB	SO	PO	A
Devore rf	3	1	1	0	2	0	3	1
Doyle 2b	5	0	0	0	0	0	1	5
Snodgrass cf	4	0	1	0	1	0	4	1
Murray lf	5	1	2	1	0	0	3	0
Merkle 1b	5	0	1	1	0	1	10	0
Herzog 3b	5	0	2	0	0	1	2	1
Meyers c	3	0	0	0	1	0	4	1
Fletcher ss	3	0	1	0	0	1	2	3
McCormick ph	1	0	0	0	0	0	0	0
Shafer ss	0	0	0	0	0	0	0	0
Mathewson p	4	0	1	0	0	1	0	3
Totals	**38**	**2**	**9**	**2**	**4**	**4**	**29**	**15**

FIELDING -
E: Doyle (5), Snodgrass (1).

BATTING -
2B: Murray 2 (4,off Bedient,off Wood); Herzog (4,off Bedient).
SH: Meyers (1,off Bedient).
Team LOB: 11.

BASERUNNING -
SB: Devore (4,2nd base off Bedient/Cady).
CS: Snodgrass (3,2nd base by Bedient/Cady); Meyers (1,3rd base by Bedient/Cady); Devore (2,2nd base by Bedient/Cady).

Boston Red Sox	AB	R	H	RBI	BB	SO	PO	A
Hooper rf	5	0	0	0	0	0	4	0
Yerkes 2b	4	1	1	0	1	1	0	3
Speaker cf	4	0	2	1	0	1	2	0
Lewis lf	4	0	0	1	1	1	0	0
Gardner 3b	3	0	1	1	0	1	0	4
Stahl 1b	4	1	2	0	0	1	15	0
Wagner ss	3	0	1	0	1	0	3	5
Cady c	4	0	0	0	0	0	5	3
Bedient p	2	0	0	0	0	0	0	1
Henriksen ph	1	0	1	1	0	0	0	0
Wood p	0	0	0	0	0	0	0	2
Engle ph	1	1	0	0	2	0	0	0
Totals	**35**	**3**	**8**	**3**	**5**	**4**	**30**	**18**

FIELDING -
E: Speaker (2), Gardner 2 (3), Wagner (3).

BATTING -
2B: Gardner (2,off Mathewson); Henriksen (1,off Mathewson); Stahl 2 (2,off Mathewson).
SF: Gardner (1,off Mathewson).
IBB: Lewis (1,by Mathewson).
Team LOB: 9.

PITCHING

New York Giants	IP	H	R	ER	BB	SO	HR
Mathewson L(0-2)	9.2	8	3	1	5	4	0

IBB: Mathewson (1,Lewis).

Boston Red Sox	IP	H	R	ER	BB	SO	HR
Bedient	7	6	1	1	3	2	0
Wood W(3-1)	3	3	1	1	1	2	0
Totals	**10**	**9**	**2**	**2**	**4**	**4**	**0**

Umpires: Silk O'Loughlin, Cy Rigler, Bill Klem, Billy Evans

Time of Game: 2:37   **Attendance:** 17034

	1	2	3		4	5	6		7	8	9	10		R	H	E
NY N	0	0	1		0	0	0		0	0	0	1		2	9	2
BOS A	0	0	0		0	0	0		1	0	0	2		3	8	4

Fred Snodgrass, OF, 1908-1916

G	AB	R	H	2B	3B	HR	RBI	BB	IBB	SO	HBP	SH	XI	ROE	GDP	SB	CS	AVG	OBP	SLG	BFW
923	3101	453	852	143	42	11	351	386	0i	359i	65	106	0i	16i	5i	215	56i	.275	.367	.359	0.9

1914 — Boston Braves vs. Philadelphia Athletics

A last-place team in mid-July, the "Miracle" Boston Braves won 34 of their last 44 games to take the National League pennant. In the World Series, they were underdogs against the American League Champion Philadelphia Athletics. Yet the Braves won Game 1, 7-1, and Game 2, 1-0, on Bill James' two-hit shutout over Hall of Fame pitcher Eddie Plank. The series shifted to Fenway Park, which the Braves were borrowing from the Red Sox in lieu of the shabby South End Grounds they called home. The A's took Game 3 into extra innings and seemed to win it with a two-run home run in the 10th inning, but the Braves countered with a pair of their own on a homer and a sacrifice fly.

In the last of the 12th, the Braves' Hank Gowdy led off with a double and was replaced by pinch runner Les Mann. After an intentional pass was issued to Larry Gilbert, Herbie Moran bunted to A's pitcher Bullet Joe Bush, who threw wildly to third and allowed Mann to score the winning run.

The A's learned in four quick games that every miracle that season belonged to the Braves.

World Series—Game 3
Monday, October 12, 1914
Fenway Park

	1	2	3	4	5	6	7	8	9	10	11	12	R	H	E
PHI A	1	0	0	1	0	0	0	0	0	2	0	0	4	8	2
BOS N	0	1	0	1	0	0	0	0	0	2	0	1	5	9	1

1916 — Boston Red Sox vs. Brooklyn Robins

Twenty-one-year-old Babe Ruth of the Boston Red Sox and Sherry Smith of the Brooklyn Robins (later, the Dodgers) staged the greatest extended pitching duel in World Series history.

In Game 2 at Braves Field, Brooklyn scored a run in the first when Hy Myers' drive to right-center went for an inside-the-park home run after Harry Hooper and Tilly Walker both fell down chasing it. Boston countered in the third on Everett Scott's triple and Ruth's RBI grounder, but after that it was goose eggs into extra innings.

Tension mounted as the defensive wizardry escalated. Hooper threw out Smith trying to stretch a double in the third inning; Myers robbed Hooper of a hit with a shoestring catch in the sixth and threw out Hal Janvrin at the plate in the ninth. With the Red Sox threatening again in the 10th on Scott's single and Pinch Thomas' sacrifice, Hooper singled off third baseman Mike Mowrey's glove, but Mowrey nipped Scott rounding third by firing to shortstop Ivy Olson. In the 13th, Boston left fielder Duffy Lewis made a great running catch with two outs to prevent Mowrey from scoring. Boston catcher Thomas threw out a man trying to steal, and Brooklyn catcher Otto Miller picked a runner off first. All the while, Ruth and Smith helped their own causes—Ruth with two putouts and four assists, Smith with one putout and six assists.

Finally, in the home half of the 14th, Dick Hobitzell walked for the fourth time; Duffy Lewis sacrificed him to second; and pinch runner Mike McNally, making his major league debut, scored the game-winning run on a pinch-hit single by Del Gainer off Sherry Smith.

This 14-inning game took only two hours and thirty-two minutes. And 47,373 fans lapped up what authors Richard M. Cohen and David S. Neft called, "the most tenacious pitching duel in Series history."

World Series—Game 2
Monday, October 9, 1916
Braves Field

	1	2	3	4	5	6	7	8	9	10	11	12	13	14	R	H	E
BRO N	1	0	0	0	0	0	0	0	0	0	0	0	0	0	1	6	2
BOS A	0	0	1	0	0	0	0	0	0	0	0	0	0	1	2	7	1

Cleveland second baseman Bill Wambsganss recorded the only unassisted triple play in World Series history. On a hit-and-run play Wamby caught Clarence Mitchell's sharp line drive just to the right of second base. He stepped on second to double up Pete Kilduff, and tagged Otto Miller coming from first. In Ring Lardner's words, "It was the first time in World Series' history that a man named Wambsganss had ever made a triple play assisted by consonants only."

World Series—Game 5
Sunday, October 10, 1920
Dunn Field

	1	2	3	4	5	6	7	8	9	R	H	E
BRO N	0	0	0	0	0	0	0	0	1	1	13	1
CLE A	4	0	0	3	1	0	0	0	x	8	12	2

Bill Wambsganss, 2B, 1914-1926

G	AB	R	H	2B	3B	HR	RBI	BB	SO	HBP	SH	SB	CS	AVG	OBP	SLG	BFW
1491	5237	710	1359	215	59	7	520	490	357	47	323	142	74i	.259	.328	.327	-9.8

LAST LICK

In 1921, the New York Giants beat the New York Yankees five games to three, in the last World Series played under the best-of-nine format.

1924_ Washington Senators vs. New York Giants

The season had two bonuses. While Rogers Hornsby led the National League by batting .424 (the highest regular-season average in the modern era) stranger things were happening in the Junior Circuit. Described as "First in war, first in peace, last in the American League" by Charley Dryden, sports editor of the San Francisco *Chronicle*, the Washington Senators finally finished in first place when Walter Johnson led the American League with 23 wins and a 2.72 ERA. In addition, Senators Joe Judge, Sam Rice, and Goose Goslin all hit better than .320. But player-manager Bucky Harris had his hands full against the New York Giants, who repeated as National League champs with a lineup boasting six future Hall of Famers.

When the Giants pulled ahead three games to two, the smug denizens of the press sat nodding sagely like dipping oil field pumping jacks. But Harris delivered a two-run single, and the pesky Senators won Game 6, 2-1. Then Harris surprised everyone by picking Curly Ogden, a right-hander who had started just four games all season, to pitch Game 7. Giants manager John McGraw must have wondered what Harris had in mind.

With the Giants loading up on left-handed batters, Harris planned to use Ogden for just a few batters before switching to left-hander George Mogridge, who had gone 16-11. Once Ogden struck out Freddie Lindstrom on three pitches and walked Frankie Frisch, Harris made the change. Mogridge got out the two lefties, Ross Youngs and George (Highpockets) Kelly, to end the inning.

Harris opened the scoring with a fourth-inning home run. In the sixth, the Giants finally came to life. Youngs walked, and Kelly singled him to third. With the left-handed Bill Terry up, McGraw played the sometimes overrated "percentages" and pinch hit right-hander Irish Meusel. To counter, Harris yanked Mogridge for Firpo Marberry, one of baseball's earliest relief specialists, who had saved 15 games. Meusel's sacrifice fly scored a run; Wilson singled Kelly to third; and errors by Judge and Ossie Bluege sent two more runs across the plate. With the Giants leading 3-1, all was well with the oddsmakers.

But Harris and his offense weren't through. Facing Virgil Barnes in the eighth, the Senators' Nemo Leibold batted for Tommy Taylor (a reader here may reach for his or her baseball almanac) and doubled to left. Catcher Muddy Ruel, 0-for-18 in the Series, squeezed out an infield single, sending Leibold to third. Rookie Bennie Tate pinch hit for Marberry and walked. After Earl McNeeley flied to short left, the

BATTING

New York Giants	AB	R	H	RBI	BB	SO	PO	A
Lindstrom 3b	5	0	1	0	0	2	0	3
Frisch 2b	5	0	2	0	1	1	3	4
Youngs rf,lf,rf	2	1	0	0	4	1	2	0
Kelly cf,1b	6	1	1	0	0	2	8	2
Terry 1b	2	0	0	0	0	1	6	1
Meusel ph,lf,rf,lf	3	0	1	1	0	0	1	0
Wilson lf,cf	5	1	1	0	1	2	4	0
Jackson ss	6	0	0	0	0	1	1	4
Gowdy c	6	0	1	0	0	0	8	0
Barnes p	4	0	0	0	0	2	1	2
Nehf p	0	0	0	0	0	0	0	0
McQuillan p	0	0	0	0	0	0	0	0
Groh ph	1	0	1	0	0	0	0	0
Southworth pr	0	0	0	0	0	0	0	0
Bentley p	0	0	0	0	0	0	0	0
Totals	45	3	8	1	6	12	34	16

FIELDING -
DP: 2. Kelly-Jackson, Jackson-Frisch-Kelly.
E: Jackson (3), Gowdy (1).

BATTING -
2B: Lindstrom (2,off Mogridge).
3B: Frisch (1,off Johnson).
SH: Lindstrom (1,off Johnson).
SF: Meusel (1,off Marberry).
IBB: Youngs 2 (2,by Johnson 2).
Team LOB: 14.

BASERUNNING -
SB: Youngs (1,2nd base off Johnson/Ruel).

Washington Senators	AB	R	H	RBI	BB	SO	PO	A
McNeely cf	6	0	1	1	0	1	4	0
Harris 2b	5	1	3	3	0	1	4	1
Rice rf	5	0	0	0	0	0	2	0
Goslin lf	5	0	2	0	0	1	3	0
Judge 1b	4	0	1	0	1	0	11	1
Bluege ss	5	0	0	0	0	0	1	7
Taylor 3b	2	0	0	0	0	2	0	3
Leibold ph	1	1	1	0	0	0	0	0
Miller 3b	2	0	0	0	0	0	1	1
Ruel c	5	2	2	0	0	0	13	0
Ogden p	0	0	0	0	0	0	0	0
Mogridge p	1	0	0	0	0	1	0	0
Marberry p	1	0	0	0	0	0	1	0
Tate ph	0	0	0	0	1	0	0	0
Shirley pr	0	0	0	0	0	0	0	0
Johnson p	2	0	0	0	0	0	0	1
Totals	44	4	10	4	2	7	36	14

FIELDING -
DP: 1. Johnson-Bluege-Judge.
E: Judge (1), Bluege 2 (3), Taylor (1).

BATTING -
2B: Leibold (1,off Barnes); Goslin (1,off Bentley); Ruel (1,off Bentley); McNeely (3,off Bentley).
HR: Harris (2,4th inning off Barnes 0 on 1 out).
IBB: Judge (1,by Bentley).
Team LOB: 8.

PITCHING

New York Giants	IP	H	R	ER	BB	SO	HR
Barnes	7.2	6	3	1	1	6	1
Nehf	0.2	1	0	0	0	0	0
McQuillan	1.2	0	0	0	0	1	0
Bentley L(1-2)	1.1	3	1	0	1	0	0
Totals	11.1	10	4	3	2	7	1

IBB: Bentley (1,Judge).

Washington Senators	IP	H	R	ER	BB	SO	HR
Ogden	0.1	0	0	0	1	1	0
Mogridge	4.2	4	2	1	1	3	0
Marberry	3	1	1	0	1	3	0
Johnson W(1-2)	4	3	0	0	3	5	0
Totals	12	8	3	1	6	12	0

Mogridge faced 2 batters in the 6th inning
IBB: Johnson 2 (3,Youngs 2).

Umpires: Bill Dinneen, Ernie Quigley, Tommy Connolly, Bill Klem

Time of Game: 3:00 **Attendance:** 31667

	1	2	3	4	5	6	7	8	9	10	11	12	R	H	E
NY N	0	0	0	0	0	3	0	0	0	0	0	0	3	8	3
WAS A	0	0	0	1	0	0	0	2	0	0	0	1	4	10	4

runners holding, Harris singled over Lindstrom's head to drive in two runs and tie the score. Reliever Art Nehf got the Giants out of the inning.

In came Walter Johnson, who had lost both of his starts in the Series. At thirty-six years old, he might have been pitching in his last Series game. He was old, and he was struggling.

With runners on first and third and one out in the ninth, the Big Train struck out future Hall of Famer Kelly on three pitches and coaxed Meusel to ground out. Johnson cruised through the 10th. With a runner on second and one out in the 11th, he struck out Frisch, deliberately walked Youngs, and struck out Kelly. Johnson sailed through the 12th, allowing one hit.

The old man had struck out five batters in four innings. In the home half of the 12th, the Senators' Ruel popped up behind home plate, but catcher Hank Gowdy threw off his mask and tripped over it, allowing the ball to drop. (Somewhere the Marx brothers were laughing.) Ruel doubled to left. That brought Johnson to the plate, and Harris never considered batting for him. The bench was bare, Johnson was a good hitter (.283 in 1924), and he was once more pitching at his best. Could he win his own game? Johnson's grounder to short was booted by Travis Jackson, with Ruel holding on second. But the fun was surely over when McNeeley hit a made-to-order double-play grounder to third.

Not in this World Series. Not in this Game 7. Not when a kid skipper gets timely hits and outthinks one of the most successful managers in baseball history. Not when a tired old pitcher summons whatever it was that made him a first-ballot Hall of Famer. Not when the fates had a catcher stepping on his mask and a Hall-of-Fame shortstop making an untimely error. McNeeley's grounder took a strange bounce to career over Lindstrom's head into left, and Ruel crossed the plate to give the Washington Senators, suddenly first in baseball, a 4-3 win.

"For just long enough…the Old Master was the Johnson of old, the 'Kansas Cyclone,' sweeping the proud champions of the National League to their bitterest defeat," Bill Corum wrote in the New York *Times*.

Afterward, Commissioner Kennesaw Mountain Landis told sportswriter Fred Lieb that Landis had just seen the best of baseball. In *The Seventh Game: The 35 World Series That Have Gone the Distance*, Barry Levenson rated the 1924 finale the best Game 7 ever.

The Washington Senators made the World Series for the second straight season in 1925. Despite starting 6-14, the Pittsburgh Pirates won the National League by 8½ games over the second place New York Giants, behind future Hall of Famers Kiki Cuyler (.357 with 26 triples and 41 stolen bases), Max Carey (.343 with 46 steals) and Pie Traynor (.320). The Bucs led the league in runs, hits, doubles, triples, walks, RBI, stolen bases, batting average and slugging percentage.

With Walter Johnson out-pitching Lee Meadows, the Senators took Game 1, 4-1. Pittsburgh won Game 2, but the Senators took Games 3 and 4, the latter behind a six-hit shutout by Johnson, to build up a three-games-to-one lead that had never been overcome in Series history. Undaunted, the Pirates took Games 5 and 6.

Washington still had Johnson, who at age thirty-seven finished the season 20-7 and won both his Series starts. The Pirates trotted out Vic Aldridge, who had gone 15-7 and also won two Series games.

Pitching on two days' rest, Aldridge gave up four first-inning runs on two hits, three walks, and two wild pitches in just one-third of an inning before he was relieved by Johnny Morrison. Johnson allowed three runs in the third, but Washington increased its lead to 6-3 with two runs off Morrison in the fourth. It started raining in the fifth inning, when the Pirates cut the lead to two after back-to-back doubles by Carey and Cuyler.

By the seventh inning, the rain was still falling, and Walter Johnson was still on the mound. Pirate Eddie Moore reached on a two-base error by the American League's Most Valuable Player that season, Roger Peckinpaugh, who dropped his pop fly. Carey, who went 4-for-5 with three doubles in Game 7 and hit .458 in the Series, doubled home Moore. Third baseman Pie Traynor tripled home Carey with the tying run, but was thrown out at the plate trying to stretch his triple into an inside-the-park home run. The inning ended with the score tied, 6-6.

In the top of the eighth, Peckinpaugh homered to give Washington what proved to be a fleeting 7-6 lead. In the bottom of the inning, catcher Earl Smith doubled with two outs. A pinch runner, Emil Yde, scored the tying run on pinch hitter Carson Bigbee's

double. Moore walked and Carey loaded the bases by reaching on another error by Peckinpaugh, this one on a routine groundball that he fielded but threw wildly to second. Peckinpaugh made one error in Game 1, two in Game 2, one in Game 3, another in Game 5, one in Game 6, and now two in Game 7. This error proved devastating when Kiki Cuyler hit a two-run double for the Pirates' eighth double of the day and their 15th hit of the long, wet afternoon off Walter Johnson.

Heading into the ninth with a 9-7 lead, the Pirates made a surprise choice and brought in relief pitcher Red Oldham, who had appeared in only 11 games during the season. In his first Series appearance, he struck out eventual Hall of Fame center fielder Sam Rice, who led all batters in the series with 12 hits, on a called third strike. Another future Hall of Famer, player-manager Bucky Harris, lined out hard to second. With two outs and nobody on base, Oldham faced his third consecutive future Hall of Famer, Goose Goslin.

Blessed with a large proboscis that produced the nickname Goose while he was in the minor leagues, Goslin used to joke that he would have "hit .500 if he could have seen over his nose." Up to that point in the series, he had hit three home runs, just as he had done the prior year against the Giants, and had driven in six and scored six. Alas, he took a called third strike, the only called third strike to end a World Series, and the Pirates became the first team to rally from a 3-1 Series deficit to win a best-of-seven series.

The banner headline on the front page of the Pittsburgh *Post* the next day read, "PIRATES WIN WORLD CHAMPIONSHIP IN GREATEST SERIES GAME EVER PLAYED." Oldham played one last year for the Pirates, his last as a major leaguer, and finished his career with a record of 39-48. It was the only inning he ever pitched in the World Series.

World Series—Game 7
Thursday, October 15, 1925
Forbes Field

	1	2	3	4	5	6	7	8	9	R	H	E
WAS A	4	0	0	2	0	0	0	1	0	7	7	2
PIT N	0	0	3	0	1	0	2	3	x	9	15	3

World Series—Game 7
Sunday, October 10, 1926
Yankee Stadium

S ome call Babe Ruth the goat of the 1926 World Series. Two New York Yankee errors contributed to the St. Louis Cardinals' three-run fourth inning; Tommy Thevenow's leaping catch prevented a Yankee run; and the Cardinals' Pete Alexander struck out Tony Lazzeri with the bases loaded in the seventh, all of which added up to a 3-2 Cardinal lead in the ninth.

Still pitching, Alexander got Earle Combs and Joe Dugan on grounders to third. The Babe, who had homered and walked three times, worked Alexander for another freebie. With Bob Meusel at the plate and Lou Gehrig on deck, Ruth, who always had a flair for the dramatic, took off for second. In a trice, sure-armed catcher Bob O'Farrell threw him out to end the Series.

It was unexpected for Ruth to steal, but was it unwise? Although he'd pitched an exhausting complete game the day before, Alexander retired all six of the batters prior to Ruth. The Babe felt he could jumpstart a rally if he reached scoring position. It's not widely known, but Ruth was a good and intelligent baserunner who stole home 10 times in his career. This was the only time the World Series ended on a caught-stealing.

BATTING

St. Louis Cardinals	AB	R	H	RBI	BB	SO	PO	A
Holm cf	5	0	0	0	0	0	2	0
Southworth rf	4	0	0	0	0	0	0	0
Hornsby 2b	4	0	2	0	0	0	4	1
Bottomley 1b	3	1	1	0	0	0	14	0
L. Bell 3b	4	1	0	0	0	0	0	4
Hafey lf	4	1	2	0	0	1	3	0
O'Farrell c	3	0	1	1	0	0	3	2
Thevenow ss	4	0	2	2	0	1	1	3
Haines p	2	0	1	0	0	1	0	4
Alexander p	1	0	0	0	0	0	0	0
Totals	34	3	8	3	0	2	27	14

BATTING -
SH: Haines (1,off Hoyt); Bottomley (1,off Pennock).
SF: O'Farrell (1,off Hoyt).
Team LOB: 7.

BASERUNNING -
CS: Hafey (1,2nd base by Hoyt/Severeid).

New York Yankees	AB	R	H	RBI	BB	SO	PO	A
Combs cf	5	0	2	0	0	0	2	0
Koenig ss	4	0	0	0	0	0	2	3
Ruth rf	1	1	1	1	4	0	2	0
Meusel lf	4	0	1	0	0	0	3	0
Gehrig 1b	2	0	0	0	2	0	11	0
Lazzeri 2b	4	0	0	0	0	3	3	1
Dugan 3b	4	1	2	0	0	0	1	3
Severeid c	3	0	2	1	0	0	3	1
Adams pr	0	0	0	0	0	0	0	0
Collins c	1	0	0	0	0	0	0	0
Hoyt p	2	0	0	0	0	0	0	1
Paschal ph	1	0	0	0	0	0	0	0
Pennock p	1	0	0	0	0	0	0	1
Totals	32	2	8	2	6	3	27	10

FIELDING -
E: Koenig (4), Meusel (1), Dugan (1).

BATTING -
2B: Severeid (1,off Haines).
HR: Ruth (4,3rd inning off Haines 0 on 2 out).
SH: Koenig (1,off Haines).
IBB: Ruth (1,by Haines).
Team LOB: 10.

BASERUNNING -
CS: Dugan (1,2nd base by Haines/O'Farrell); Ruth (1,2nd base by Alexander/O'Farrell).

PITCHING

St. Louis Cardinals	IP	H	R	ER	BB	SO	HR
Haines W(2-0)	6.2	8	2	2	5	2	1
Alexander SV(1)	2.1	0	0	0	1	1	0
Totals	9	8	2	2	6	3	1

IBB: Haines (1,Ruth).

New York Yankees	IP	H	R	ER	BB	SO	HR
Hoyt L(1-1)	6	5	3	0	0	2	0
Pennock	3	3	0	0	0	0	0
Totals	9	8	3	0	0	2	0

Umpires: George Hildebrand, Bill Klem, Bill Dinneen, Hank O'Day

Time of Game: 2:15   **Attendance:** 38093

	1	2	3		4	5	6		7	8	9		R	H	E
STL N	0	0	0		3	0	0		0	0	0		3	8	0
NY A	0	0	1		0	0	1		0	0	0		2	8	3

1927 _____ Pittsburgh Pirates vs. New York Yankees

The myth behind the 1927 World Series is that the Pittsburgh Pirates folded after watching the New York Yankees' Murderers Row take batting practice before Game 1. In fact, the opener was a one-run game; the Pirates kept Games 2 and 3 close before Yankee outbursts decided things in the eighth and seventh innings, respectively; and Game 4 was another one-run loss.

The embarrassment came only at the end. With Game 4 tied at 3-3 and the Yankees batting in the bottom of the ninth, Pirate reliever Johnny Miljus walked Earle Combs on four pitches and allowed a bunt single to Mark Koenig. Both runners advanced on a wild pitch. Miljus intentionally walked Babe Ruth and then stiffened, getting Lou Gehrig and Bob Meusel on strikes. But with a one-strike count on Tony Lazzeri, Miljus threw another wild pitch, and Combs scored to end the Series. The Pirates watched, helpless and embarrassed.

World Series—Game 4
Sunday, October 8, 1927
Yankee Stadium

	1	2	3	4	5	6	7	8	9	R	H	E
PIT N	1	0	0	0	0	0	2	0	0	3	10	1
NY A	1	0	0	0	2	0	0	0	1	4	12	2

1931 _____ Philadelphia Athletics vs. St. Louis Cardinals

The Cardinals led Game 7 of the 1931 World Series 4-2, but the Philadelphia Athletics edged off all three bases with two out in the ninth inning. America held its collective breath when Max Bishop lashed a sinking liner off reliever Wild Bill Hallahan that had "two-run single" written all over it. It looked like extra innings—or better—for the A's. But center fielder Pepper Martin, who had stolen five bases in the Fall Classic, had another theft in mind. He raced in and caught the ball to become the World Series' Most Valuable Player…and a national darling.

World Series—Game 7
Saturday, October 10, 1931
Sportsman's Park III

	1	2	3	4	5	6	7	8	9	R	H	E
PHI A	0	0	0	0	0	0	0	0	2	2	7	1
STL N	2	0	2	0	0	0	0	0	x	4	5	0

Pepper Martin, OF, 1928-1944

G	PO	A	ERR	DP	FPCT.	LF-G	CF-G	RF-G
613	1299	59	37	14	.973	31	314	273

Born in Havana, Cuba, Adolfo Domingo de Guzman Luque became the major leagues' first great Latino after debuting briefly with the 1914 Boston Braves and sticking in the Show with the 1918 Cincinnati Reds. He went 10-3 for the 1919 World Champion Reds. Primarily a reliever up to that point, he became a starter with shockingly mixed results: Luque was 13-9 in 1920, then 17-19 and 13-23 the next two seasons before rebounding in 1923 to lead the league in wins (27), percentage (.771) and ERA (1.93) while finishing 27-8.

In the 1930s, he returned to relief for the New York Giants and at age forty-two pitched effectively for the Carl Hubbell-led team that reached the 1933 World Series. The Giants faced a strong Washington Senators lineup led by outfielder Heinie Manush and first baseman Joe Kuhel. Washington shortstop Joe Cronin and New York first baseman Bill Terry shouldered the dual role of player-manager, having just replaced Walter Johnson and John McGraw, respectively.

Leading three games to one, the Giants took a 3-0 lead in Game 5. The Senators tied the score on Fred Schulte's three-run homer in the bottom of the sixth before Luque put out the fire with two on and two out, and he kept the Senators scoreless into extra innings.

With two outs in the top of the 10th, Mel Ott drove a pitch into the bleachers to give the Giants a 4-3 lead. In the bottom of the inning, Luque recorded two quick outs before allowing a single to Joe Cronin and a walk to Fred Schulte. The next batter, Joe Kuhel, was the Senators' leading home run hitter with 11 (Jimmie Foxx led the AL with 48). Three pitches later, Kuhel went down on strikes to end the Series. Over 4⅔ innings, Luque allowed no runs on two hits and two walks while fanning five.

Retiring after the 1935 season with a 194-179 record, Luque remains the oldest pitcher to win a World Series game. Had Roger Clemens won Game 1 of the 2005 Series, he would have been older. Both men were born on October 4—Luque in 1890, Clemens in 1962. Luque won on October 7. Clemens pitched Game 1 on October 22 (he lasted two innings in a no-decision) and would have been the oldest by fifteen days.

World Series—Game 5
Saturday, October 7, 1933
Griffith Stadium

BATTING

New York Giants	AB	R	H	RBI	BB	SO	PO	A
Moore lf	5	0	1	0	0	1	3	0
Critz 2b	5	0	0	0	0	0	2	4
Terry 1b	5	0	2	0	0	0	13	1
Ott rf	5	1	1	1	0	2	1	0
Davis cf	5	1	2	0	0	0	1	0
Jackson 3b	3	1	1	0	0	1	2	4
Mancuso c	3	1	1	0	0	0	7	1
Ryan ss	2	0	1	0	1	1	0	5
Schumacher p	3	0	1	2	0	2	0	0
Luque p	1	0	1	0	0	0	1	0
Totals	**37**	**4**	**11**	**4**	**2**	**7**	**30**	**15**

FIELDING -
DP: 1. Jackson-Terry.
E: Jackson (1).

BATTING -
2B: Davis (1,off Crowder); Mancuso (1,off Crowder).
HR: Ott (2,10th inning off Russell 0 on 2 out).
SH: Ryan (1,off Crowder); Jackson (2,off Crowder).
Team LOB: 7.

Washington Senators	AB	R	H	RBI	BB	SO	PO	A
Myer 2b	5	0	0	0	0	1	3	1
Goslin rf	4	0	1	0	1	1	4	1
Manush lf	5	0	1	0	0	0	3	0
Cronin ss	5	1	3	0	0	0	3	3
Schulte cf	4	1	2	3	1	0	1	0
Kerr pr	0	0	0	0	0	0	0	0
Kuhel 1b	5	0	2	0	0	1	8	0
Bluege 3b	4	1	0	0	2	1	1	1
Sewell c	4	0	0	0	0	0	7	0
Crowder p	2	0	0	0	0	0	0	2
Russell p	1	0	0	0	1	1	0	2
Totals	**39**	**3**	**10**	**3**	**3**	**6**	**30**	**10**

FIELDING -
DP: 1. Cronin-Kuhel.

BATTING -
HR: Schulte (1,6th inning off Schumacher 2 on 2 out).
Team LOB: 9.

PITCHING

New York Giants	IP	H	R	ER	BB	SO	HR
Schumacher	5.2	8	3	3	1	1	1
Luque W(1-0)	4.1	2	0	0	2	5	0
Totals	**10**	**10**	**3**	**3**	**3**	**6**	**1**

WP: Schumacher (2).

Washington Senators	IP	H	R	ER	BB	SO	HR
Crowder	5.1	7	3	3	2	4	0
Russell L(0-1)	4.2	4	1	1	0	3	1
Totals	**10**	**11**	**4**	**4**	**2**	**7**	**1**

WP: Crowder (1).

Umpires: Charlie Moran, George Moriarty, Cy Pfirman, Red Ormsby

Time of Game: 2:38 **Attendance:** 28454

	1	2	3		4	5	6		7	8	9	10		R	H	E
NY N	0	2	0		0	0	1		0	0	0	1		4	11	1
WAS A	0	0	0		0	0	3		0	0	0	0		3	10	0

St. Louis Cardinals vs. Detroit Tigers

With Dizzy Dean pitching Game 7 on one day's rest, the St. Louis Cardinals scored seven times in the fourth inning and embarrassed the Detroit Tigers, 11-0. What's more, the Detroit fans embarrassed the Tigers. When the Cardinals' Joe Medwick took left field after sliding hard into third baseman Marv Owen, Tiger fans pelted him with "pop bottle, oranges, apples and anything else that came ready to hand," in the words of New York *Times* writer John Drebinger. Four times Medwick left the field; four times, he returned to a torrent of trash. Finally, Commissioner Kennesaw Mountain Landis ordered him removed from the game for safety reasons.

This was the stinker of all World Series games.

World Series—Game 7
Tuesday, October 9, 1934
Navin Field

	1	2	3	4	5	6	7	8	9	R	H	E
STL N	0	0	7	0	0	2	2	0	0	11	17	1
DET A	0	0	0	0	0	0	0	0	0	0	6	3

Cincinnati Reds vs. New York Yankees

Concluding another four-game sweep by the Bronx Bombers, the New York Yankees and Cincinnati Reds were tied 4-4 after nine innings. Frank Crosetti walked to open the Yankee 10th, and Red Rolfe sacrificed him to second. When Reds shortstop Billy Myers fumbled Charlie Keller's grounder, Keller was safe at first and Crosetti went to third. Then came the uncomfortable denouement before the Queen City faithful: Joe DiMaggio singled to right to score Crosetti, and after Ival Goodman bobbled the ball, Keller raced for home. Goodman's throw arrived simultaneously with Keller's slide, and Keller was safe when he accidentally kicked catcher Ernie Lombardi in the groin; Lombardi dropped the throw. With the catcher writhing on the ground and the ball resting a few feet away, DiMaggio stretched his single into a run. Goodman and Lombardi were both charged with errors on the play. With the score now 7-4, the Yankees held on for a hard-earned win.

World Series—Game 4
Sunday, October 8, 1939
Crosley Field

	1	2	3	4	5	6	7	8	9	10	R	H	E
NY A	0	0	0	0	0	0	2	0	2	3	7	7	1
CIN N	0	0	0	0	0	0	3	1	0	0	4	11	4

Detroit Tigers vs. Cincinnati Reds

The Detroit Tigers' Bob Newsom and the Cincinnati Reds' Paul Derringer each threw seven-hitters in the shortest (1:47) Game 7 ever. Newsome pitched his second complete game in three days, Derringer his second in four. Almost anything could have tipped the balance, but who'd have expected that a sacrifice fly by .202-hitting Billy Myers would give the Reds a 2-1 victory?

World Series—Game 7
Tuesday, October 8, 1940
Crosley Field

	1	2	3	4	5	6	7	8	9	R	H	E
DET A	0	0	1	0	0	0	0	0	0	1	7	0
CIN N	0	0	0	0	0	0	2	0	x	2	7	1

Last Lick

1944 showcased the only all-St. Louis World Series, with every game played in Sportsman's Park and the Cardinals winning four games to two. George McQuinn hit the Browns' only home run of the Series in Game 1.

1945   Detroit Tigers vs. Chicago Cubs

The Detroit Tigers scored five times in the top of the first and never looked back as they beat the Chicago Cubs 9-3 in Game 7. Winning pitcher Hal Newhouser struck out 10 batters even though he was just trying to pace himself by throwing strikes without painting the corners. The Cubs out-hit the Tigers 10-9, but once again there was no joy in Cubville; the Cubs would not reach the World Series again in the twentieth century.

World Series—Game 7
Wednesday, October 10, 1945
Wrigley Field

	1	2	3	4	5	6	7	8	9	R	H	E
DET A	5	1	0	0	0	0	1	2	0	9	9	1
CHI N	1	0	0	1	0	0	0	1	0	3	10	0

1946   St. Louis Cardinals vs. Boston Red Sox

First, some foreshadowing: In the fourth inning of the 1946 World Series opener, St. Louis Cardinals outfielder Enos Slaughter was kept at third by coach Mike Gonzalez, who held the runner rather than let him try for an inside-the-park home run. Furious, Slaughter complained to manager Eddie Dyer. "All right, all right," Dyer said. "If it happens again, and you think you can make it, go ahead."

With the score tied 3-3 in Game 7, Slaughter singled leading off the eighth. The next two batters failed to advance the baserunner. Always aggressive, Slaughter took off on a pitch that Harry Walker swatted into left-center. Centerfielder Dom DiMaggio had injured his ankle earlier and been replaced by Leon Culbertson, but the blurry film clip doesn't show Culbertson fielding the ball and throwing it in to the cut-off man, shortstop Johnny Pesky. What we do know is that Pesky hesitated momentarily before throwing home and fired to the catcher's right while Slaughter slid safely to the left for the go-ahead run. The Cardinals hung on to win, 4-3.

We'll never know if Culbertson fielded and threw less expertly than the sure-gloved, sure-armed DiMaggio would have; in *Red Sox Century*, Pesky told authors Glenn Stout and Richard A. Johnson that Culbertson "kind of lofted the ball." What anyone viewing the clip should conclude is that even if he had caught the relay, turned and threw perfectly in one motion—without bothering to gauge distance and direction—Pesky wouldn't have nailed Slaughter, who slid needlessly. The fault was not Pesky's hesitation; instead, credit Slaughter's haste.

World Series—Game 7
Tuesday, October 15, 1946
Sportsman's Park III

	1	2	3	4	5	6	7	8	9	R	H	E
BOS A	1	0	0	0	0	0	0	2	0	3	8	0
STL N	0	1	0	0	2	0	0	1	x	4	9	1

Johnny Pesky, SS, 1942-1954

G	PO	A	ERR	DP	FPCT.
591	1175	1810	111	387	.964

It was a familiar matchup and a familiar conclusion—the New York Yankees beat the Brooklyn Dodgers in seven—but the events of Game 4 were anything but familiar. With the Yanks leading the Series two games to one, both teams had tough choices to make in selecting their starters. The Yankees turned to Bill Bevens, a right-hander with a 7-13 record during the regular season. The Dodgers countered with 10-5 Harry Taylor.

Taylor didn't last very long; in fact, he didn't retire a batter. He gave up singles to Snuffy Stirnweiss and Tommy Henrich before Yogi Berra reached on an error by Pee Wee Reese to load the bases. When Taylor walked Joe DiMaggio to force in a run, manager Burt Shotton brought in Hal Gregg to prevent further damage. Gregg got out of the inning unscathed.

Armed with a 1-0 lead, Bevens walked leadoff hitter Eddie Stanky before eventually stranding him on first. Bevens walked Spider Jorgenson in the second but left him on base as well. In the third, Bevens again walked Stanky, who advanced to second on a wild pitch, but advanced no further before the inning was through.

The Yanks finally scored another run in the fourth on a Johnny Lindell RBI double to take a 2-0 lead. They needed the second run, because Bevens allowed a fifth-inning run on two walks, a sacrifice and a fielder's choice. But by the time the Dodgers came to bat in the last of the ninth, Bevens still hadn't allowed a hit.

Dodger catcher Bruce Edwards led off with a flyball to center. Carl Furillo then worked Bevens for the Dodgers' ninth walk of the game. When Jorgensen fouled out to first, Bevens was one out away from immortality. Al Gionfriddo ran for Furillo, and Pistol Pete Reiser pinch hit for reliever Hugh Casey. With a 3-1 count on Reiser, Gionfriddo stole second base, and the Yankees took the risky step of putting the winning run on first by intentionally walking Reiser. Eddie Miksis pinch ran for him.

Every delay, every substitution ratcheted up the tension. Shotton sent up Harry (Cookie) Lavagetto to pinch hit for Stanky. This move infuriated Dodger fans as well as Stanky, who slammed his bat to the ground as he walked back to the dugout. But on the second pitch from Bevens, Lavagetto lined a drive to deep right field.

Tommy Henrich raced back but quickly realized he would have to play it off the Gem Razorblade sign on the right field wall. Gionfriddo had already scored the tying run when Henrich grabbed the ball and threw to the plate—too late to catch Miksis sliding in with the winning run.

Bevens lost his no-hitter *and* the game, although he still does hold the record for most walks in a World Series game: 10. Bevens appeared in relief in Game 7 (he did not face Lavagetto); Lavagetto pinch hit in Games 5, 6 and 7; and in Game 6, Al Gionfriddo robbed Joe DiMaggio of a hit by making one of baseball history's greatest postseason catches. But Bevens, Lavagetto and Gionfriddo never appeared in another regular season major league game.

World Series—Game 4
Friday, October 3, 1947
Ebbets Field

	1	2	3	4	5	6	7	8	9	R	H	E
NY A	1	0	0	1	0	0	0	0	0	2	8	1
BRO N	0	0	0	0	1	0	0	0	2	3	1	3

Bill Bevens, P, 1944-1947

G	GS	CG	SHO	GF	SV	IP	H	BFP	HR	R	ER	BB	SO	SH	WP	HBP	BK	W	L	ERA	PW
96	84	46	6	8	0	642.1	598	2692	40	253	220	236	289	57	4	4	1	40	36	3.08	1.6

Cookie Lavagetto, 3B, 1934-1947

G	AB	R	H	2B	3B	HR	RBI	BB	SO	HBP	SH	GDP	SB	AVG	OBP	SLG	BFW
1043	3509	487	945	183	37	40	486	485	244	12	33	86	63	.269	.360	.377	-3.5

Al Gionfriddo, OF, 1944-1947

G	PO	A	ERR	DP	FPCT.	LF-G	CF-G	RF-G
157	316	9	14	2	.959	32	96	29

Last Lick

In Game 7, the New York Yankees beat the Brooklyn Dodgers 5-2 behind Bobby Brown's double, Tommy Henrich's single, and five shutout innings of one-hit relief by Joe Page. No Game 7 reliever has ever been that effective.

In the seventh inning of Game 7, the New York Yankees led the Brooklyn Dodgers, 4-2. But the Dodgers' Carl Furillo drew a walk, Rocky Nelson popped out to short, Billy Cox singled, and Pee Wee Reese walked to load the bases. Surprising almost everyone, Yankee manager Casey Stengel summoned left-hander Bob Kuzava from the bullpen. The moved seemed to pay off when Duke Snider popped out to third. Kuzava threw another great pitch, and Jackie Robinson lofted a pop fly eight feet to the right of the mound. The ball arced high over Ebbets Field, directly into the sun, and Joe Collins—a defensive replacement at first base—lost it. Kuzava froze; two Dodgers had crossed the plate and another was rounding third.

"There were four Dodgers tearing around the bases, and nobody was close enough to the ball to wave hello to it," right fielder Hank Bauer said. It looked for all the world like a three-run infield hit and a one-run Dodger lead—until into the void raced second baseman Billy Martin, who made a knee-high catch. The inning was over, and the Yankees hung on to win, 4-2.

1954   New York Giants vs. Cleveland Indians

Pinch hitting for Monte Irvin in the series opener with one out in the 10th inning, Dusty Rhodes hit a three-run home run off the Cleveland Indians' Bob Lemon to give the New York Giants a 5-2 walk-off victory. This feat is often forgotten, because two innings earlier Willie Mays made one of the most memorable catches in baseball history to rob Vic Wertz of extra bases.

World Series—Game 1
Wednesday, September 29, 1954
Polo Grounds V

	1	2	3		4	5	6		7	8	9		10	R		H	E
CLE A	2	0	0		0	0	0		0	0	0		0	2		8	0
NY N	0	0	2		0	0	0		0	0	0		3	5		9	3

World Series—Game 7
Tuesday, October 7, 1952
Ebbets Field

BATTING

New York Yankees	AB	R	H	RBI	BB	SO	PO	A
McDougald 3b	5	1	2	0	0	0	2	3
Rizzuto ss	4	1	1	0	0	0	1	1
Mantle cf	5	1	2	2	0	1	1	0
Mize 1b	3	0	2	1	1	0	6	0
Collins 1b	0	0	0	0	0	0	1	0
Berra c	4	0	0	0	0	1	7	0
Woodling lf	4	1	2	1	0	0	5	0
Noren rf	2	0	0	0	0	0	1	0
Bauer ph,rf	1	0	0	0	1	0	0	0
Martin 2b	4	0	1	0	0	0	2	4
Lopat p	1	0	0	0	0	0	0	1
Reynolds p	1	0	0	0	0	0	1	0
Houk ph	1	0	0	0	0	0	0	0
Raschi p	0	0	0	0	0	0	0	0
Kuzava p	1	0	0	0	0	0	0	0
Totals	36	4	10	4	2	2	27	9

FIELDING -
DP: 1. Rizzuto-Martin-Mize.
E: McDougald 2 (4), Woodling (1), Reynolds (2).
BATTING -
2B: Rizzuto (1,off Black).
HR: Woodling (1,5th inning off Black 0 on 0 out); Mantle (2,6th inning off Black 0 on 1 out).
SH: Rizzuto (1,off Roe).
Team LOB: 8.

Brooklyn Dodgers	AB	R	H	RBI	BB	SO	PO	A
Cox 3b	5	1	2	0	0	1	2	3
Reese ss	4	0	1	1	1	0	2	2
Snider cf	4	1	1	0	1	0	4	0
Robinson 2b	4	0	1	0	0	0	0	4
Campanella c	4	0	2	0	0	1	2	0
Hodges 1b	4	0	0	1	0	0	13	0
Shuba lf	3	0	1	0	0	1	1	0
Pafko ph	1	0	0	0	0	1	0	0
Holmes lf	0	0	0	0	0	0	0	0
Furillo rf	3	0	0	0	1	0	3	0
Black p	2	0	0	0	0	2	0	0
Roe p	0	0	0	0	0	0	0	0
Nelson ph	1	0	0	0	0	0	0	0
Erskine p	0	0	0	0	0	0	0	0
Morgan ph	1	0	0	0	0	0	0	0
Totals	36	2	8	2	2	7	27	9

FIELDING -
DP: 1. Robinson-Reese-Hodges.
E: Cox (1).
BATTING -
2B: Cox (2,off Reynolds).
Team LOB: 9.

PITCHING

New York Yankees	IP	H	R	ER	BB	SO	HR
Lopat	3	4	1	1	0	3	0
Reynolds W(2-1)	3	3	1	1	0	2	0
Raschi	0.1	1	0	0	2	0	0
Kuzava SV(1)	2.2	0	0	0	0	2	0
Totals	9	8	2	2	2	7	0

Lopat faced 3 batters in the 4th inning

Brooklyn Dodgers	IP	H	R	ER	BB	SO	HR
Black L(1-2)	5.1	6	3	3	1	1	2
Roe	1.2	3	1	1	0	1	0
Erskine	2	1	0	0	1	0	0
Totals	9	10	4	4	2	2	2

Umpires: Larry Goetz, Bill McKinley, Babe Pinelli, Art Passarella, Dusty Boggess, Jim Honochick

Time of Game: 2:54   **Attendance:** 33195

	1	2	3		4	5	6		7	8	9		R	H	E
NY A	0	0	0		1	1	1		1	0	0		4	10	4
BRO N	0	0	0		1	1	0		0	0	0		2	8	1

Brooklyn Dodgers vs. New York Yankees

The Brooklyn Dodgers' Sandy Amoros made perhaps the best play in any Game 7. How he appeared in left field is a story in itself. Manager Walter Alston's starting pitcher, left-hander Johnny Podres, led 2-0 heading into the bottom of the sixth inning. Because he had pinch hit for second baseman Don Zimmer in the top of the inning, Alston moved Junior Gilliam from left field to second base and inserted Amoros, a little-used reserve, in left. It seemed of little significance that the left fielder was now left-handed.

Billy Martin led off the Yankee half of the sixth with a walk, and Gil McDougald beat out a bunt. With the tying runs on base and no outs, Yogi Berra sliced a ball just fair down the left field line. Quickly the mood shifted in New York City: Gloom descended on Brooklyn, while spirits rose in the Bronx.

There were only two conceivable options. If the ball dropped into the stands, the Yankees would lead, 3-2; if it dropped onto the field, it would clear the bases for a double or triple, depending on how Amoros played it. McDougald was so sure the ball wouldn't be caught that he raced around second at full tilt.

But the inconceivable happened. Running at full speed for more than thirty yards, Amoros appeared to be on a collision course with the fence. But as he approached, he somehow slowed, stuck out his right, gloved hand and snared the ball.

"What made Amoros' catch great," Vin Scully said, "was that he caught it on the dead run, one-handed, with his arm extended. If he hadn't been left-handed, he wouldn't have caught it. And if he hadn't caught it, the Dodgers might never have won a World Series in Brooklyn."

And that wasn't all. Righting himself, Amoros threw to shortstop Pee Wee Reese, who relayed to first baseman Gil Hodges to double up McDougald.

Before 62,465 depressed partisans at Yankee Stadium, but also before a televised nation full of supporters, the "people's team" hung on to win, 2-0. After seven fruitless trips to the postseason, the Brooklyn Dodgers won their only World Championship.

World Series—Game 7
Tuesday, October 4, 1955
Yankee Stadium

BATTING

Brooklyn Dodgers	AB	R	H	RBI	BB	SO	PO	A
Gilliam lf,2b	4	0	1	0	1	0	2	0
Reese ss	4	1	1	0	0	1	2	6
Snider cf	3	0	0	0	0	2	2	0
Campanella c	3	1	1	0	0	0	5	0
Furillo rf	3	0	0	0	1	0	3	0
Hodges 1b	2	0	1	2	1	0	10	0
Hoak 3b	3	0	1	0	1	0	1	1
Zimmer 2b	2	0	0	0	0	1	0	2
Shuba ph	1	0	0	0	0	0	0	0
Amoros lf	0	0	0	0	1	0	2	1
Podres p	4	0	0	0	0	0	0	1
Totals	29	2	5	2	5	4	27	11

FIELDING -
DP: 1. Amoros-Reese-Hodges.

BATTING -
2B: Campanella (3,off Byrne).
SH: Snider (1,off Byrne); Campanella (1,off Byrne).
SF: Hodges (1,off Grim).
IBB: Furillo (1,by Byrne).
Team LOB: 8.

BASERUNNING -
CS: Gilliam (1,2nd base by Grim/Berra).

New York Yankees	AB	R	H	RBI	BB	SO	PO	A
Rizzuto ss	3	0	1	0	1	0	1	3
Martin 2b	3	0	1	0	1	0	1	6
McDougald 3b	4	0	3	0	0	1	1	1
Berra c	4	0	1	0	0	0	4	1
Bauer rf	4	0	0	0	0	1	1	0
Skowron 1b	4	0	1	0	0	0	11	1
Cerv cf	4	0	0	0	0	5	0	0
Howard lf	4	0	1	0	0	0	2	0
Byrne p	2	0	0	0	0	2	0	2
Grim p	0	0	0	0	0	0	1	0
Mantle ph	1	0	0	0	0	1	0	0
Turley p	0	0	0	0	0	0	0	0
Totals	33	0	8	0	2	4	27	14

FIELDING -
E: Skowron (1).

BATTING -
2B: Skowron (2,off Podres); Berra (1,off Podres).
Team LOB: 8.

PITCHING

Brooklyn Dodgers	IP	H	R	ER	BB	SO	HR
Podres W(2-0)	9	8	0	0	2	4	0

New York Yankees	IP	H	R	ER	BB	SO	HR
Byrne L(1-1)	5.1	3	2	1	3	2	0
Grim	1.2	1	0	0	1	1	0
Turley	2	1	0	0	1	1	0
Totals	9	5	2	1	5	4	0

WP: Grim (1).
IBB: Byrne (1,Furillo).

Umpires: Jim Honochick, Frank Dascoli, Bill Summers, Lee Ballanfant, Red Flaherty, Augie Donatelli

Time of Game: 2:44 **Attendance:** 62465

	1	2	3	4	5	6	7	8	9	R	H	E
BRO N	0	0	0	1	0	1	0	0	0	2	5	0
NY A	0	0	0	0	0	0	0	0	0	0	8	1

Don Larsen pitched the only perfect game in the post-season for arguably the greatest feat ever accomplished by an American athlete in a single event.

"This one can only be tied," Larsen says.

In baseball, the term "perfect" is an absolute that can't be modified. One pitcher can't be "more perfect" than another, nor can a pitcher throw a "relatively perfect game." The game is either perfect, or it is not. There have been only 16 other perfect games in baseball's history, and while none is more perfect than the other, Larsen threw his perfect game at the most prominent time and against the highest level of competition.

The date was October 8, 1956; the place was Yankee Stadium. Tied at two games apiece, the New York Yankees and defending-champion Brooklyn Dodgers were both supremely talented teams. The Yankees were led by center fielder Mickey Mantle, the 1956 winner of the Triple Crown. Yogi Berra was behind the plate, Joe Collins at first, Billy Martin at second, Andy Carey at third, and Gil McDougald at shortstop. Joining Mantle in the outfield were right fielder Hank Bauer and left fielder Enos Slaughter. The Dodgers were comprised of the players we have all read about: Jackie Robinson, Duke Snider, Pee Wee Reese, Gil Hodges, Roy Campanella, Carl Furillo, Sandy Amoros, Junior Gilliam…the Boys of Summer.

At first, Yankee pitching coach Jim Turner and manager Casey Stengel were mum (a rare occurrence in itself) about who would pitch Game 5. The stories about how Don Larsen spent the night prior have become a cottage industry. Long known as a partier, Larsen didn't deny that the reputation was well-deserved when we spent the day with him in his beautiful Idaho home. Indeed, he enjoyed his favorite potable throughout the day. On October 2, 1956, *TIME* magazine described Larsen as "a lighthearted playboy noted most for spectacular achievements such as wrapping his car around a Florida telephone pole during spring training."

As Mantle wrote in *My Favorite Summer, 1956,* "It makes a better story to say Larsen was out all night the night before he pitched, partying, and drinking, and falling down drunk." It simply wasn't true. Larsen had a couple of drinks and a pizza with his friend, the newspaperman Artie Richman, and went to bed before midnight. Richman and Larsen were friends from back in the days when Larsen pitched for the St. Louis Browns. The last active Brownie to play in the majors, Larsen went 3-21 in 1954, the year the Browns moved to Baltimore and became the Orioles.

Richman reportedly had been told by Stengel that Larsen would pitch the next day and told Larsen, "We can't have too much to drink because you're pitching tomorrow." Larsen responded that if he did pitch, he might throw a no-hitter, according to Richman.

When Larsen entered the clubhouse the next day, he found that Frank Crosetti, the Yankees' third base coach, had placed the warm-up ball for that day's game in Larsen's spikes inside his locker, signifying he was the starting pitcher. So Game 5 pitted Larsen (11-5, 3.26) against the Brooklyn Dodgers' Sal Maglie (13-5, 2.89).

Jim Gilliam led off by striking out, and Pee Wee Reese did the same on a 3-2 slider. No one among the 64,519 fans in attendance could have ever imagined that Reese's first at-bat would be the only time that day Larsen

World Series—Game 5
Monday, October 8, 1956
Yankee Stadium

BATTING

Brooklyn Dodgers	AB	R	H	RBI	BB	SO	PO	A
Gilliam 2b	3	0	0	0	0	1	2	0
Reese ss	3	0	0	0	0	1	4	2
Snider cf	3	0	0	0	0	1	1	0
Robinson 3b	3	0	0	0	0	0	2	4
Hodges 1b	3	0	0	0	0	1	5	1
Amoros lf	3	0	0	0	0	0	3	0
Furillo rf	3	0	0	0	0	0	3	0
Campanella c	3	0	0	0	0	1	7	2
Maglie p	2	0	0	0	0	1	0	1
Mitchell ph	1	0	0	0	0	1	0	0
Totals	**27**	**0**	**0**	**0**	**0**	**7**	**24**	**10**

FIELDING -
DP: 2. Reese-Hodges, Hodges-Campanella-Robinson-Campanella-Robinson.

New York Yankees	AB	R	H	RBI	BB	SO	PO	A
Bauer rf	4	0	1	1	0	1	4	0
Collins 1b	4	0	1	0	0	2	7	0
Mantle cf	3	1	1	1	0	0	4	0
Berra c	3	0	0	0	0	0	7	0
Slaughter lf	2	0	0	0	1	0	1	0
Martin 2b	3	0	1	0	0	1	3	4
McDougald ss	2	0	0	0	1	0	0	2
Carey 3b	3	1	1	0	0	0	1	1
Larsen p	2	0	0	0	0	1	0	1
Totals	**26**	**2**	**5**	**2**	**2**	**5**	**27**	**8**

BATTING -
HR: Mantle (3,4th inning off Maglie 0 on 2 out).
SH: Larsen (1,off Maglie).
Team LOB: 3.

PITCHING

Brooklyn Dodgers	IP	H	R	ER	BB	SO	HR
Maglie L(1-1)	8	5	2	2	2	5	1

New York Yankees	IP	H	R	ER	BB	SO	HR
Larsen W(1-0)	9	0	0	0	0	7	0

Umpires: Babe Pinelli, Hank Soar, Dusty Boggess, Larry Napp, Tom Gorman, Ed Runge

Time of Game: 2:06 **Attendance:** 64519

	1	2	3	4	5	6	7	8	9	R	H	E
BRO N	0	0	0	0	0	0	0	0	0	0	0	0
NY A	0	0	0	1	0	1	0	0	x	2	5	0

would run the count to three balls. Duke Snider then lined out to Hank Bauer, retiring the side.

Maglie quickly disposed of the Yanks 1-2-3. Leading off the second inning was the immortal Jackie Robinson, who would retire after the Series. When he announced his retirement in an article for *Look* magazine, the thirty-seven-year-old star explained that "my legs are gone and I know it." Those words were telling in this most crucial of at-bats. Robinson fouled off a fastball, then hit the second pitch on a line toward third baseman Andy Carey. The ball caromed off his glove to shortstop Gil McDougald, who nipped the struggling Robinson by a step.

Through 3½ innings, neither team had recorded a run or a hit. When Mickey Mantle stepped to the plate, Larsen had retired 12 in a row, Maglie had retired 11 straight, and the combined 23 in a row retired is a World Series record that still stands. Mantle led the league in hitting (.353), home runs (52) and RBI (130) in 1956, on the strength of borrowed bats. Using a loaner from Jerry Lumpe, a Yankee reserve who wasn't on the postseason roster (Mantle usually swung Hank Bauer's bats), Mantle hit his third homer of the series to give Larsen a 1-0 lead. Later Mantle said, "This will be the first time a home run by me will not make the headlines."

A critical inning for any pitcher is the one immediately following the inning in which he gets the lead. Larsen started the fifth inning by inducing Robinson to flyout to Bauer. Up stepped Gil Hodges. In every game there are "mistake" pitches; the winning pitcher is the one who gets away with them. On a 2-2 pitch to Gil Hodges, Larsen made what Yogi Berra referred to as his only mistake all day. Larsen threw Hodges a slider that hung, and Hodges hit a tremendous shot to left-center. It would have been a home run in any other ballpark—certainly in Ebbets Field, Larsen says. But this was Yankee Stadium with its huge center field alleys.

Because Hodges was so strong, Mantle had backed up and moved over a bit to his left. He took off with the crack of the bat and ran full speed. Just when it appeared the ball would hit the ground, Mantle stretched and made a backhanded stab. "It was the greatest catch I ever made," Mantle said later.

With a 1-1 count on Sandy Amoros, the fielding star of the 1955 Series, Larsen was still shaken. Amoros hit a long drive down the right field line,

deep enough to tie the game…but was it fair or foul? World Series games have six umpires instead of the usual four so that outfield calls can be made with greater accuracy. Ed Runge, the ump down the right field line, quickly signaled "foul." The speed of the call did not reflect how close the ball was to being fair. When asked after the game how foul the ball had been, Runge held his fingers four inches apart. Two pitches later, Amoros grounded out to Billy Martin.

In the sixth, Larsen easily retired Carl Furillo, Roy Campanella and Sal Maglie, although Maglie stretched him to seven pitches, the most Larsen would throw to any batter that day. Eventually, Maglie struck out. Larsen had faced 18 Dodgers and retired them all.

In the bottom of the sixth, Andy Carey led off with a single. It was only the second hit of the game for the Yankees. Larsen was next. Often used as a pinch hitter, Larsen ended his fourteen-year career with a .242 batting average, 14 homers, and 72 RBI, yet only 11 sacrifice bunts. After failing twice to sacrifice, Larsen laid down a successful two-strike bunt to move Carey to second. Carey scored on a Hank Bauer single, making it a 2-0 game.

Larsen retired the Dodgers in the seventh on just eight pitches: 21 up and 21 down. As the Yankees came to bat in the bottom of the inning, Larsen looked at the scoreboard. He has said in all sincerity that he had no idea he was pitching a no-hitter. "All I cared about was winning the game. That's all I was focused on."

If Larsen didn't know, he was the last one to notice. Vin Scully was announcing the game for the Dodgers, Mel Allen was calling the game for the Yankees, and Bob Wolff was doing radio play-by-play for the independent Mutual Network. Wolff recalls that he didn't want to jinx Larsen by using the term "no-hitter," instead saying things like "21 up and 21 down."

Larsen has also said that he didn't know it was a perfect game until someone told him in the shower. Larsen remembers that the Yankee dugout was as quiet as a morgue. Everybody sat in the same place inning after inning, hoping not to whammy their pitcher. They would occasionally talk to one another, but never to Larsen. At the end of the seventh, he was having a smoke in the runway when he looked up and saw nothing but goose eggs following "BKLYN" on the scoreboard. Larsen turned to Mantle and said, "Look at the scoreboard! Wouldn't it be something? Two more innings to go!" Mantle shook his head, said nothing, and walked back to his seat.

Maglie held the Yankees in the seventh, and Larsen retired the Dodgers in order in the eighth. By the time Larsen came to the plate in the bottom of the inning, the announcers were running out of words to describe the tension.

Wolff recalls, "I was pitching the game with Larsen."

Scully thought, "Don't make a mistake. Don't say it's a no-hitter."

In the bottom of the eighth, Maglie struck out Bauer, Collins and, greeted by a tremendous roar when he came to the plate, Larsen himself. We asked him if he just wanted to strike out and get to the mound, and he responded with disdain, "I was trying for a hit, I wanted to win the damn game."

As Larsen prepared to pitch in the ninth, he felt genuinely nervous for the first time. "My legs were like rubber when I headed out there," he recalls, "but I had a game to win."

Furillo fouled off four pitches before he flied out to right for the first out. Campy grounded meekly to Billy Martin. Excited during the late innings, Martin was running to the outfield on flies to make sure they wouldn't drop.

Now it was time for "Number 27," as Larsen refers to the batter with two outs in the ninth. With Maglie due up, Larsen knew the Dodgers had a number of choices on the bench, including Charlie Neal, Gino Cimoli, Rube Walker and Don Zimmer. The logical one to expect was Dale Mitchell. A lifetime .312 hitter, he had joined the Dodgers in July after a successful ten-year career with the Cleveland Indians. Perhaps even more impressive than Mitchell's lifetime average was the fact that in 3,984 at-bats he had struck out only 119 times.

Waiting for Mitchell to be announced had a chilling effect on Larsen. "I remember my knees shaking. He really scared me," Larsen said. "I knew how much pressure he was under. He must have been paralyzed. That made two of us." But when asked who was more nervous, Larson answered with an unequivocal, "Me!"

"I walked to the back of the mound and looked out to center field and said a little prayer, 'Old man,

get me through one more.' I was very nervous."

The first pitch was a fastball low and outside, the next a slider that Mitchell took for a strike. The umpire behind the plate was Babe Pinelli. A major league player for eight seasons and a National League umpire for twenty-two more, he called Jackie Robinson's first game. This would be Pinelli's last game behind the plate, because he had already announced his retirement. According to Larsen, Pinelli did not miss a call the entire game.

A swing and a miss on a slider made it 1-2. Larsen looked in for the sign, and Berra signaled for a fastball. Larsen hadn't shaken off a sign all day. "Why should I? Yogi was perfect!"

Berra has said, "Everything I put down he got over. His breaking ball was good and usually his breaking ball wasn't that good. Hitters probably figured he had a good fastball and slider, but his breaking ball was good that day. Anything he threw went over the plate."

Larsen used the no-windup delivery that he adopted late in the season. As the pitch was about to cross the plate, Mitchell swung and fouled it back.

The 97th pitch: With the count 1-2, Yogi called for a fastball. Two hours and six minutes into the game, Don Larsen threw a pitch that looked to many to be a little high and a little outside, but that he insists was in the strike zone. Mitchell checked his swing, but Pinelli agreed with Larsen and raised his hand to call strike three. Mitchell turned to complain to Pinelli but as Larsen recalls, "There was no one there."

"I knew Yogi would do something if I got the no-hitter, I just didn't know what," Larsen remembers. Yogi came running out to Larsen, waving the ball in the air, and leaped into Larsen's arms to create a picture as vivid as any from that era. Acclaimed author Jerry Crasnick said, "Fifty years after the fact, Don Larsen's World Series perfect game remains one of the most powerful and enduring achievements in baseball history. And the images—Larsen's called third strike on Dale Mitchell and his celebratory embrace with catcher Yogi Berra—are as vivid as ever. We might never see anything like it again."

Vin Scully in his broadcast that day said, "Ladies and gentlemen, it's the greatest pitched game ever pitched in baseball history." The next day in the Washington *Post*, the great baseball writer Shirley Povich led off his column, "The million-to-one shot came in. Hell froze over. A month of Sundays hit the calendar. Don Larsen today pitched a no-hit, no-run, no-man-reach-first game in a World Series."

Recalling the event, Yankees public-address announcer Bob Sheppard said, "If Nolan Ryan had done it, if Sandy Koufax had done it, if Don Drysdale had done it, I would have nodded and said, 'Well, it could happen.' But Don Larsen?"

Recently, the great Cleveland *Plain-Dealer* reporter Paul Hoynes recalled the magnitude of covering this event: "I read a story somewhere about the writers who were covering that game. One writer was overwhelmed by the event. He couldn't get going on his story. Hall of Famer Dick Young was sitting next to him, saw he was in trouble, leaned over and typed one of the deathless leads of our business on the writer's typewriter: 'The imperfect man pitched the perfect game.' It captures the unlikelihood and greatness of the event perfectly."

It took Larsen 97 pitches to retire 27 Brooklyn Dodgers in front of 64,519 Yankee Stadium fans. Does he worry that someone else will pitch a perfect game? "Records are made to be broken," Larsen says, "but they can only tie me, they can never beat me."

Sports reporter Dan LeBatard told us, "[It's] not humanly possible to be better than perfect...add the stakes to it, and you have the best game ever pitched... Jim Edmonds has made 10 catches as good as the one Willie Mays did...but Mays did it in a World Series...pressure bursts pipes, so it is pretty hard on the human psyche...and Larsen, otherwise mediocre, was perfect when pressurized..."

Pulitzer-Prize-winning retired New York *Times* writer Ira Berkow puts the achievement in perspective: "Larsen's perfect game in a World Series is perhaps the most unbeatable record in all of sports. The feat can be tied, though profoundly improbable, but to be topped someone has to pitch a pair of perfect games in a World Series. I think a million monkeys at typewriters over a million years would produce *Hamlet* quicker."

ESPN's Jayson Stark said, "Is there any player—especially any pitcher, and mega-especially any *Yankees* pitcher—who is more associated with one game than Don Larsen? He's one of the most magical names in baseball history. Yet I doubt most people, even most baseball fans, can tell you *anything* else about his career. But they can see Yogi Berra jumping into his arms in the grainy black-and-white replay machine in their heads. They know that no one else in the history of the sport—not a single Hall of Famer, Cy Young, or 20-game winner—has ever pitched a no-hitter in a postseason game. And they know that says something about the beauty of the sport, even when it comes down to the games that matter most. Anyone can have that game, that moment, which cements his place in the lore of baseball forever. So Don Larsen is more than just a human trivia answer. He embodies what makes baseball great."

According to baseball analyst Bill James, Larsen's feat holds even greater meaning. "Pitching a perfect game in the World Series is sort of like having the President of the United States call you on your cell phone when you're on a first date with your dream girl. It's a combination of eerily random good fortune and the exact right moment for random good fortune to find you. It's like winning the lottery ten minutes after you find that perfect house you've spent the last four years looking for, although you know you could never afford it. Larsen wasn't that *good*, really, and anyway, nobody is good enough to throw a perfect game in the World Series. It's random. It's a kiss from God. Don Larsen carries God's lipstick on his collar for the rest of his life."

Anyone who loves baseball should share in the joy of Larsen's achievement. Larsen represents every baseball fan. His lifetime record of 81-91 over fourteen seasons with eight teams proved that any person can have that one moment, that one touch with immortality. There are those who have had fifteen minutes of fame, but this fun-loving man and his wonderful wife, Corrine, have been celebrating this achievement for fifty-two years.

Don Larsen, P, 1953-1967

G	GS	CG	SHO	GF	SV	IP	H	BFP	HR	R	ER	BB	IB	SO	SH	SF	WP	HBP	BK	2B	3B	GDP	ROE	W	L	ERA	PW
412	171	44	11	132	23	1548	1442	6708	130	728	650	725	35i	849	80	28i	39	26	0	123i	24i	58i	56i	81	91	3.78	4.5

New York Yankees manager Casey Stengel sent everyone but the starter, Don Larsen, to the bullpen for Game 7 of the 1958 World Series. When it became apparent that Larsen was far from perfect that day, Bullet Bob Turley was told to warm up.

It didn't matter that Turley had started in 31 of his 33 appearances during the regular season; he was the natural choice. At 6'2" and 215 pounds, he was built to throw hard and throw long. After leading the league in wins (21), winning percentage (.750), complete games (19), and opponents' batting average (.206) in a Cy Young Award season, he had won Game 5 with a shutout and then registered the save in Game 6.

Moreover, warming up in a hurry was no problem for him. "Before my starts, I would warm up for only 13 minutes—a little more if it was cold, a little less if it was hot," he says. "I'd throw my fastball, curve and slider, at the end throwing with the same motion and speed as in a game."

After a few minutes' warm-up, pitching coach Jim Turner called bullpen catcher Darrell Johnson. "How does he look?" asked Turner.

"As good as he was yesterday and the day before," Johnson said.

It was only the third inning when Turley began the slow walk to the mound. When he passed Mickey Mantle in center field, Mantle said, "If you get them out and do the job, you deserve the car." He meant the Corvette given to the World Series Most Valuable Player.

Turley had to do the job right away. With the Yankees holding a precarious 2-1 lead, the Milwaukee Braves had runners on first and second and one out. Turley got the dangerous Wes Covington on a weak grounder in front of the plate—catcher Yogi Berra throwing to first while the runners advanced. Then Turley deflected Del Crandall's grounder to second baseman Gil McDougald, who threw to first to end the inning.

Yielding only one run on Crandall's game-tying home run in the sixth, Turley pitched 6⅔ innings of two-hit ball and got the 6-2 win on Elston Howard's run-scoring single and Moose Skowron's three-run homer in the eighth. His no-windup delivery worked almost as well as Larsen's had two autumns before.

Thanks to Turley's two wins and one save, the Yankees became the first club since the 1925 Pirates to win a Series after trailing three games to one. When Mantle squeezed Red Schoendienst's line drive for the last out, Turley's legs started, as he puts it, to "cave." But he wouldn't need to walk. He had won the car.

In a span of six days, Turley had thrown 20 innings in four games. "If you protect your arm, you get hurt," he says. "We didn't know anything about rotator cuffs and Tommy John surgeries." Johnny Sain—a teammate of Turley's who later became a successful pitching coach—"believed you should pitch every day, just as hitters hit every day."

Two days later, in fact, Turley threw four innings for a Hawaiian team warming up the St. Louis Cardinals before their trip to Japan. Two of his teammates were Lew Burdette and Eddie Mathews of the vanquished Braves.

"The scouting report said you had no curve," said Mathews, victimized twice in Game 7 by Turley hooks. "That's crazy."

Turley didn't win 10 games in any of his remaining five seasons. In his last appearance, pitching for the Red Sox on September 21, 1963, he got his final batter, George Bank of the Minnesota Twins, on a foul popout to first. His career was shortened by two years in the military and a bone-chips operation. Turley retired with a 101-85 record and a 3.64 ERA before spending one year as the Boston Red Sox pitching coach.

Bob Turley, P, 1958 World Series

G	GS	CG	SHO	GF	SV	IP	H	BFP	HR	R	ER	BB	IB	SO	SH	SF	WP	HBP	BK	2B	3B	GDP	ROE	W	L	ERA
4	2	1	1	2	1	16.1	10	64	2	5	5	7	1	13	1	0	0	0	0	1	0	1	0	2	1	2.76

For spills, thrills, unexpected heroes and dramatic reversals, only 1960 rates with the 1924 Fall Classic. Game 7 began with an upstart manager having already outmaneuvered an Olympian. It wasn't so much that the Pirates' Danny Murtaugh out-managed the Yankees' Casey Stengel, but how Stengel foiled himself by mismanaging his ace, Whitey Ford. Unaccountably, he failed to start Ford in the opener. Ford beat the Pirates 10-0 in Game 3 and 12-0 in Game 6, but Casey never considered saving his ace for emergency relief in Game 7 by removing him early in the second blowout. Perhaps Stengel was over-confident. After all, in the first six games, the Yankees had outscored the Pirates 46-17 and out-hit them, 78-42.

In the Forbes Field finale, the Pirates took a 3-0 lead over Bob Turley, and Pirates pitcher Vernon Law still had a 4-1 margin after five innings. When Bobby Richardson singled and Tony Kubek walked to begin the sixth, Murtaugh turned to his closer Elroy Face, who had saved 24 games and all three Pirate wins in the series. Roger Maris fouled out before Mickey Mantle rapped a run-scoring single to make it 4-2. The Forbes faithful stirred uneasily before Yogi Berra caught a hanging forkball and pulled it just fair down the right field line and into the upper deck. The Yankees led, 5-4.

The Pirates failed in the sixth and seventh and looked as good as gone, when Johnny Blanchard's two-run homer in the eighth made it 7-4. After Pirate pinch hitter Gino Cimoli singled, Bobby Shantz got Bill Virdon to hit a grounder to the sure-handed Yankee shortstop, Tony Kubek. In 1960, fields weren't groomed during the game, and the ball hit a spike mark and struck Kubek in the Adam's apple, leaving runners on first and second and forcing Kubek out of the game. Dick Groat singled home a run to make it 7-5. In a Stengel decision that was endlessly second-guessed, the slick-fielding Shantz was out and Jim Coates was in. Bob Skinner sacrificed the runners to second and third. Nelson flied to short right field for the second out. Coates fooled the immortal Roberto Clemente, jamming him with a pitch he could only lash toward first base. But the ball was chopping, Clemente was running, and Coates was slow covering first. Clemente beat it out for a single, with Bill Virdon scoring. Groat advanced to third and the lead was just one. Turley says Coates' failure to cover first was the key play of the game.

Hal Smith, who had replaced catcher Smokey Burgess when Burgess was replaced by a pinch runner one inning earlier, strode to the plate and clocked a three-run homer. After reliever Ralph Terry secured the final out, the Pirates led 9-7 going into the ninth.

World Series—Game 7
Thursday, October 13, 1960
Forbes Field

BATTING

New York Yankees	AB	R	H	RBI	BB	SO	PO	A
Richardson 2b	5	2	2	0	0	0	2	5
Kubek ss	3	1	0	0	1	0	3	2
DeMaestri ss	0	0	0	0	0	0	0	0
Long ph	1	0	1	0	0	0	0	0
McDougald pr,3b	0	1	0	0	0	0	0	0
Maris rf	5	0	0	0	0	0	2	0
Mantle cf	5	1	3	2	0	0	0	0
Berra lf	4	2	1	4	1	0	3	0
Skowron 1b	5	2	2	1	0	0	10	2
Blanchard c	4	0	1	1	0	0	1	1
Boyer 3b,ss	4	0	1	1	0	0	0	3
Turley p	0	0	0	0	0	0	0	0
Stafford p	0	0	0	0	0	0	0	1
Lopez ph	1	0	1	0	0	0	0	0
Shantz p	3	0	1	0	0	0	3	1
Coates p	0	0	0	0	0	0	0	0
Terry p	0	0	0	0	0	0	0	0
Totals	40	9	13	9	2	0	24	15

FIELDING -
DP: 3. Stafford-Blanchard-Skowron, Richardson-Kubek-Skowron, Kubek-Richardson-Skowron.
E: Maris (1).

BATTING
2B: Boyer (2,off Face).
HR: Skowron (2,5th inning off Law 0 on 0 out); Berra (1,6th inning off Face 2 on 1 out).
Team LOB: 6.

Pittsburgh Pirates	AB	R	H	RBI	BB	SO	PO	A
Virdon cf	4	1	2	2	0	0	3	0
Groat ss	4	1	1	1	0	0	3	2
Skinner lf	2	1	0	0	1	0	1	0
Nelson 1b	3	1	1	2	1	0	7	0
Clemente rf	4	1	1	1	0	0	4	0
Burgess c	3	0	2	0	0	0	0	0
Christopher pr	0	0	0	0	0	0	0	0
Smith c	1	1	1	3	0	0	1	0
Hoak 3b	3	1	0	0	1	0	3	2
Mazeroski 2b	4	2	2	1	0	0	5	0
Law p	2	0	0	0	0	0	0	1
Face p	0	0	0	0	0	0	0	1
Cimoli ph	1	1	1	0	0	0	0	0
Friend p	0	0	0	0	0	0	0	0
Haddix p	0	0	0	0	0	0	0	0
Totals	31	10	11	10	3	0	27	6

BATTING -
HR: Nelson (1,1st inning off Turley 1 on 2 out); Smith (1,8th inning off Coates 2 on 2 out); Mazeroski (2,9th inning off Terry 0 on 0 out).
SH: Skinner (1,off Coates).
Team LOB: 1.

PITCHING

New York Yankees	IP	H	R	ER	BB	SO	HR
Turley	1	2	3	3	1	0	1
Stafford	1	2	1	1	1	0	0
Shantz	5	4	3	3	1	0	0
Coates	0.2	2	2	2	0	0	1
Terry L(0-2)	0.1	1	1	1	0	0	1
Totals	8	11	10	10	3	0	3

Turley faced 1 batter in the 2nd inning
Shantz faced 3 batters in the 8th inning
Terry faced 1 batter in the 9th inning

Pittsburgh Pirates	IP	H	R	ER	BB	SO	HR
Law	5	4	3	3	1	0	1
Face	3	6	4	4	1	0	1
Friend	0	2	2	2	0	0	0
Haddix W(2-0)	1	1	0	0	0	0	0
Totals	9	13	9	9	2	0	2

Law faced 2 batters in the 6th inning
Friend faced 2 batters in the 9th inning

Umpires: Bill Jackowski, Nestor Chylak, Dusty Boggess, Johnny Stevens, Stan Landes, Jim Honochick

Time of Game: 2:36 **Attendance:** 36683

	1	2	3		4	5	6		7	8	9		R	H	E
NY A	0	0	0		0	1	4		0	2	2		9	13	1
PIT N	2	2	0		0	0	0		0	5	1		10	11	0

But the Yankees could never be counted out. Not at Guadalcanal, not at Iwo Jima, not at Pittsburgh. Bobby Richardson and pinch hitter Dale Long singled to open the ninth off the latest, but not the last, Pirate pitcher: Bob Friend. Murtaugh replaced him with Harvey Haddix, who got Roger Maris to foul out, but Mantle scored Richardson with a single and sent Long to third as the would-be tying run.

First baseman Nelson held Mantle close to the bag. When Berra scorched a hard grounder down the line, Nelson speared it and instinctively stepped on the bag, removing the force on Mantle. Just a few feet down the line—and a dead duck if he tried for second—Mantle dove back to first, barely eluding Nelson's tag with a contortionist's twist. One could almost forget that Long scored the tying run on the play, forever scratching Hal Smith's earlier home run from being remembered as the most famous in World Series history.

The Pirates got out of the top of ninth. Up first to face the Yankees' Ralph Terry was second baseman Bill Mazeroski, known for his extraordinary glove and good-but-not-great-bat. Mazeroski was a noted high-ball hitter, and when Terry got his first pitch up, catcher John Blanchard headed out to the mound and warned him. Terry nodded. He knew what was needed. And he threw the next pitch low, except that it never dropped.

At 3:36 P.M., Mazeroski launched a tremendous drive, and all that left fielder Berra could do was watch it disappear over the vine-covered wall. Mazeroski waved his cap and dodged fans to get around the bases and make history official: He had just become the only player to achieve every boy's dream and end a seven-game World Series with a home run.

It took a while for the magnitude of the event to sink in. The Pirates won, 10-9. No one struck out. The mighty Casey Stengel had managed his last game with the Yankees.

Though he arguably hit a more meaningful homer, Mazeroski doesn't mind playing second lick to Bobby Thomson and his 1951 Shot Heard 'Round the World.

Any baseball fan over the age of sixty is bound to be asked, "What were you doing when Thomson came to bat?" Mazeroski, the Hall of Fame second baseman, remembers. "I was a freshman at Tiltonsville [Ohio]

High School that year," he says. "I was walking down the street, and there were so many radios playing on porches that it was like one gigantic loudspeaker. As I recall, I was walking into the ice cream parlor when he hit it.

"What did I think? Wow! What a fantastic comeback! I was as excited as everyone else."

Mazeroski doesn't remember if he was happy about the New York Giants' victory. "I was an Indians fan, but I don't know who I was rooting for," he says.

He has a much clearer memory of a homer many baseball fans consider the equal—or better of—Thomson's blast. His dramatic ninth-inning shot off the Yankees' Ralph Terry to win Game 7 of the World Series concluded perhaps the most exciting game in Series history, not to mention what some call the most skilled era baseball has ever known.

Consider baseball at the moment of his historic home run. With only sixteen major league teams and the addition of a fabulous new player pool in black athletes, almost any game was an All-Star Game. Now consider baseball, post-Mazeroski's blast. In 1961, the American League added two teams; the National League followed suit a year later and baseball never really was the same again.

Epic moments can produce atypical behavior. Just as the quiet, unassuming Thomson leaped high before landing on home plate at the Polo Grounds, the quiet, unassuming Mazeroski waved his hands in the air as he rounded the bases at Forbes Field. But something even stranger happened to Maz. Even as he was reeling with joy, even as the city of Pittsburgh was staging its most boisterous celebration—with confetti streaming out of the office buildings, paper clogging trolley tracks, bridges and tunnels closed, and commuters sleeping in hotel lobbies—a small, nagging doubt interrupted his elation.

Many baseball historians already considered Mazeroski, then a twenty-four-year-old in his fifth big league season, the greatest defensive second baseman of all-time. And what might he now be remembered for? Maz wondered. When later that day, he and his wife retired to a hill in order to take stock of the day's events he thought—a home run! That's what he would be remembered for.

Although it's possible his home run pulled attention from his fielding prowess and delayed his induction into Cooperstown, he did eventually make it to the

Hall of Fame. These days, he revels in his momentous at-bat, indeed considers it an unmitigated thrill.

"I can imagine that from the time [Thomson] hit it, he felt like I did," says Mazeroski. "You think you just hit a homer to win a game or a pennant or a World Series. People won't let you forget about it. It gets bigger and bigger, bigger than when you hit it.

"It made me more well known than my fielding ever would. People still approach me and say, 'Oh, you're the guy who hit the homer.' I've gone to golf tournaments and banquets I probably wouldn't have been invited to, and I went to the BAT [Baseball Assistance Team] banquet for walk-off homers. That certainly wouldn't have happened."

Is there ever a time when he wishes the homer would go away? "In October I get so many calls there's no time to do anything else," he says. "But I wouldn't change anything."

He chuckles. "People in New York are still getting over it."

Bill Mazeroski, 2B, 1956-1972

G	AB	R	H	2B	3B	HR	RBI	BB	IBB	SO	HBP	SH	SF	XI	ROE	GDP	SB	CS	AVG	OBP	SLG	BFW
2163	7755	769	2016	294	62	138	853	447	110	706	20	87	70	0	135i	194	27	23	.260	.299	.367	35.2

San Francisco Giants vs. New York Yankees

The pitch left Ralph Terry's hand, and Willie McCovey rocketed it back toward right-center. If the ball was caught, the New York Yankees would repeat as World Champions. If it dropped, the New York Giants would win their first World Series ever in San Francisco. Last licks don't get any tenser than that.

Game 7, Candlestick Park. The Giants were used to going the distance in 1962. The Giants and the Los Angeles Dodgers had ended the 162-game regular season tied for the National League pennant, and it wasn't until game 165 that the Giants won the best-of-three playoff and moved on to the World Series.

The day after the playoff ended, the World Series began. The Yankees behind Whitey Ford took Game 1, 6-2. Game 2 pitted Giants ace Jack Sanford against Ralph Terry. Sanford limited the Yankees to three hits. The Giants only mustered six hits against Terry, but one was a home run by Willie McCovey that gave the Giants the victory and evened the series at one game apiece. Terry and McCovey would meet again.

Bill Stafford won Game 3 for the Yanks 3-2, with Roger Maris driving home two runs and scoring the third. Game 4 went to the Giants 7-3, when second baseman Chuck Hiller hit a grand slam, the first in Series history by a National Leaguer. The winning pitcher was Don Larsen, who later mentioned he had won "on my day," recognizing the sixth anniversary of his perfect game.

When asked if the 1956 Yankee team was the best he ever played on, Larsen hedged. "That '62 Giants with Mays, McCovey, Cepeda, Alou and Bailey were an awfully good team."

Larsen remembers wanting to win the series for Giants owner Horace Stonham, whom he liked very much. Game 5 was a rematch of Terry and Stanford, and this time the Yankees won, 5-3. As they headed to San Francisco, they held a three-games-to-two lead. They held that lead for the next three days while it rained and rained, and in Game 6 Giant left-hander Billy Pierce reigned, 5-2.

For the third time in the series, Ralph Terry faced Jack Sanford. In the fifth, the Yankees loaded the bases on singles by Moose Skowron and Clete Boyer and a walk to Terry. Tony Kubek hit into a double play and a run scored, but that's all the Yankees could push across.

The Giants entered the last of the ninth still trailing, 1-0. Pinch hitter extraordinaire Matty Alou beat out a drag bunt single. Felipe Alou and Chuck Hiller struck out. Down to the last out, Willie Mays hit a line drive down the right field line. As good a fielder as he was a hitter, right fielder Roger Maris cut the ball off and fired quickly to second baseman Bobby Richardson,

World Series—Game 7
Tuesday, October 16, 1962
Candlestick Park

BATTING

New York Yankees	AB	R	H	RBI	BB	SO	PO	A
Kubek ss	4	0	1	0	0	0	1	0
Richardson 2b	2	0	0	0	2	0	3	0
Tresh lf	4	0	1	0	0	0	6	0
Mantle cf	3	0	1	0	1	1	3	0
Maris rf	4	0	0	0	0	0	0	0
Howard c	4	0	0	0	0	1	5	0
Skowron 1b	4	1	1	0	0	0	6	0
Boyer 3b	4	0	2	0	0	0	2	2
Terry p	3	0	1	0	1	2	1	1
Totals	32	1	7	0	4	4	27	3

San Francisco Giants	AB	R	H	RBI	BB	SO	PO	A
F. Alou rf	4	0	0	0	0	1	1	0
Hiller 2b	4	0	0	0	0	1	1	3
Mays cf	4	0	1	0	0	0	1	0
McCovey lf	4	0	1	0	0	0	3	0
Cepeda 1b	3	0	0	0	0	2	12	0
Haller c	3	0	0	0	0	0	5	0
Davenport 3b	3	0	0	0	0	0	3	4
Pagan ss	2	0	0	0	0	0	1	2
Bailey ph	1	0	0	0	0	0	0	0
Bowman ss	0	0	0	0	0	0	0	1
Sanford p	2	0	1	0	0	0	0	1
O'Dell p	0	0	0	0	0	0	0	0
M. Alou ph	1	0	1	0	0	0	0	0
Totals	31	0	4	0	0	4	27	11

FIELDING -
DP: 2. Pagan-Hiller-Cepeda, Davenport-Cepeda.
E: Pagan (1).

BATTING -
2B: Mays (2,off Terry).
3B: McCovey (1,off Terry).
Team LOB: 4.

PITCHING

New York Yankees	IP	H	R	ER	BB	SO	HR
Terry W(2-1)	9	4	0	0	0	4	0

San Francisco Giants	IP	H	R	ER	BB	SO	HR
Sanford L(1-2)	7	7	1	1	4	3	0
O'Dell	2	0	0	0	0	1	0
Totals	9	7	1	1	4	4	0

Sanford faced 3 batters in the 8th inning

Umpires: Stan Landes, Jim Honochick, Al Barlick, Charlie Berry, Ken Burkhart, Hank Soar

Time of Game: 2:29 **Attendance:** 43948

	1	2	3	4	5	6	7	8	9	R	H	E
NY A	0	0	0	0	1	0	0	0	0	1	7	0
SF N	0	0	0	0	0	0	0	0	0	0	4	1

holding Mays at second and Alou at third.

Who better to bat, the Candlestick faithful must have thought, than Willie (Stretch) McCovey, a fine clutch hitter and for good measure one of the most popular players in San Francisco history?

Before Stretch came to the plate, Yankee manager Ralph Houk visited Terry on the mound. There was no discussion of removing Terry; the only question was whether the right-hander wanted to face McCovey, the left-handed slugger who amassed 20 home runs and 54 RBI in only 91 games, or intentionally walk him and take his chances with the right-handed Orlando Cepeda (35 homers, 114 RBI). Terry was confident he could get McCovey out, and that was good enough for Houk.

Before the pitch, Richardson looked to the dugout for advice on where to play Stretch. Houk looked down at his feet, meaning, "You decide." More than forty years later, Larsen remembers looking and watching Richardson move. Reasoning that the tiring Terry wouldn't be throwing with much speed and that McCovey was a dead pull hitter with tremendous topspin, Richardson moved a few steps to his left.

"I sure hope they don't hit the ball to you," shortstop Tony Kubek called over.

"Why?"

"Well, I'd hate to see you blow it this time." Nonetheless, money-ball Richardson wanted the ball hit his way.

Just a few seconds before Terry wound up, the second base umpire said, "Hey, Rich, I'd like your cap after the game for my little cousin."

Terry threw. McCovey swung. Richardson stayed on the balls of his feet, and when McCovey hit one of the hardest line drives in World Series history, he moved a step or two to his left, reached up and snagged the ball—an easy play.

Except that it wasn't. "I thought for a second that it would be a hit because of the height of the ball," Richardson explained to author David Falkner, "but I picked up that topspin right away…I was ready. I was on my way off the field."

"A man hits the ball as hard as he can," McCovey said, smiling ruefully. "He can't feel bad about what he does."

After the game, the classy McCovey headed downtown to hear some jazz. As Art Rosenbaum and Bob Stevens wrote in *The Giants of San Francisco*, Duke Ellington himself noticed Stretch in the crowd and played an Ellington classic with the title slightly changed: "You hit it good, and that ain't bad."

Thirteen days after the World Series began, the Yankees were champions once again.

Forty-five years later the Yankees returned to San Francisco to play an interleague game. The night before the opener the Giants hosted a party to salute the 1962 Fall Classic. Bobby Richardson told us that he saw his now good friend, Willie McCovey. McCovey, with a smile, asked Richardson if his hand still hurt from catching that liner.

1965 — Los Angeles Dodgers vs. Minnesota Twins

The inimitable Mickey Rivers once said, "Pitching is 80 percent of the game, and the other half is hitting and fielding." He must have been referring to the fact that, in World Series Game 7s, pitchers have held hitters to a .235 batting average.

Perhaps the greatest performance of the nine shutouts and numerous tight seventh games was Sandy Koufax' 2-0 victory over Minnesota in 1965. Koufax was in the news from the start of that Fall Classic. First, he sat out his expected start in the opener because it was played on Yom Kippur, one of the most sacred Jewish holidays. Then he unexpectedly lost when Jim Kaat beat him 5-1 in Game 2 (Koufax was charged with just one earned run). Koufax rebounded to win Game 5, 7-0, striking out 10 and yielding only four hits and one walk. When the Twins tied the Series at three games apiece, Koufax was pressed into service on just two days' rest. That's hardly unusual in the postseason, but what Koufax accomplished at Minnesota's Metropolitan Stadium on October 16 was mind-bending.

It's axiomatic in baseball that no one can win consistently with a single pitch, other than possibly the knuckler. If a guy throws a blazing fastball and nothing else, batters will anticipate and eventually catch up to it. In Game 7, Koufax lost his curveball and was reduced to throwing one fastball after another. Although he walked two batters in the first, he only gave up one more free pass and three hits in nine innings. Meanwhile, the Dodgers did just enough damage against Kaat in the fourth, when Lou Johnson hit the foul pole for a home run, Ron Fairly doubled, and Wes Parker singled him home. Strong throughout the game, Koufax struck out Earl Battey and Bob Allison for his ninth and tenth of the day—ending the game. Final score: 2-0 Dodgers in a neat, concise two hours and twenty-seven minutes.

World Series—Game 7
Thursday, October 14, 1965
Metropolitan Stadium

	1	2	3	4	5	6	7	8	9	R	H	E
LA N	0	0	0	2	0	0	0	0	0	2	7	0
MIN A	0	0	0	0	0	0	0	0	0	0	3	1

Sandy Koufax, P, 1965 World Series

G	GS	CG	SHO	GF	SV	IP	H	BFP	HR	R	ER	BB	IB	SO	SH	SF	WP	HBP	BK	2B	3B	GDP	ROE	W	L	ERA
3	3	2	2	0	0	24	13	87	0	2	1	5	0	29	1	0	0	0	0	2	0	2	1	2	1	0.38

1968 — Detroit Tigers vs. St. Louis Cardinals

Bob Gibson looked unstoppable. After compiling a 22-9 regular-season record, with a jaw-dropping 1.12 ERA, he won the 1968 World Series opener by beating 31-game winner Denny McLain, shutting out the Detroit Tigers 4-0 and fanning a postseason-record 17 men. Three games later Gibson beat them, 10-1. By Game 7, what could go wrong? After retiring 20 of his first 21 batters, Gibson allowed eighth-inning singles to Norm Cash and Willie Horton. Then Jim Northrup hit a long fly that center fielder Curt Flood misplayed into a two-run triple. When Bill Freehan doubled home Northrup, the Tigers had a 3-0 lead, and Mickey Lolich hung on to win, 4-1.

There was no getting around it: Flood's misjudgment cost the St. Louis Cardinals dearly. It's disingenuous, perhaps, to pin the "G-word" on a great defensive center fielder and a regular .300 hitter. Fortunately, Flood's obituaries accented his brave challenge to the reserve clause—not his World Series miscue.

World Series—Game 7
Thursday, October 10, 1968
Busch Stadium II

	1	2	3	4	5	6	7	8	9	R	H	E
DET A	0	0	0	0	0	0	3	0	1	4	8	1
STL N	0	0	0	0	0	0	0	0	1	1	5	0

Pittsburgh Pirates vs. Baltimore Orioles

While the Pittsburgh Pirates' Steve Blass tossed a memorable Game 7 and beat the Baltimore Orioles 2-1, Willie Stargell scored the winning run on Jose Pagan's double (see p. 87, 1979).

World Series—Game 7
Sunday, October 17, 1971
Memorial Stadium

	1	2	3	4	5	6	7	8	9	R	H	E
PIT N	0	0	0	1	0	0	0	1	0	2	6	1
BAL A	0	0	0	0	0	0	0	1	0	1	4	0

The Oakland Athletics led the Cincinnati Reds two games to one, but trailed Game 4 of the World Series 2-1 going into the bottom of the ninth inning.

With one down, Oakland's Gonzalo Marquez pinch hit for George Hendrick and singled off Cincinnati reliever Pedro Borbon. Allan Lewis ran for Marquez, and Clay Carroll replaced Borbon. Gene Tenace singled, bringing up Don Mincher to pinch hit for Dick Green. Mincher singled in the tying run, sending Tenace to third.

And then the unlikeliest of heroes, Angel Mangual, singled to right, driving home the winning run for his only RBI in 17 career postseason at-bats. The A's eventually won the series behind Rollie Fingers' two innings of relief work in Game 7.

World Series—Game 4
Thursday, October 19, 1972
Oakland-Alameda
County Coliseum

BATTING

Cincinnati Reds	AB	R	H	RBI	BB	SO	PO	A
Rose lf	4	0	0	0	0	0	3	0
Morgan 2b	3	1	0	0	1	0	2	1
Tolan cf	4	0	1	2	0	0	0	0
Bench c	4	0	2	0	0	0	4	0
Perez 1b	4	0	2	0	0	1	11	0
McRae rf	4	0	1	0	0	1	2	0
Geronimo rf	0	0	0	0	0	0	0	0
Menke 3b	4	0	0	0	0	0	1	4
Concepcion ss	3	1	1	0	0	0	2	5
Gullett p	2	0	0	0	0	0	0	1
Javier ph	0	0	0	0	0	0	0	0
Borbon p	0	0	0	0	0	0	0	0
Carroll p	0	0	0	0	0	0	0	0
Totals	32	2	7	2	1	2	25	11

FIELDING -
DP: 1. Concepcion-Perez.
E: Perez (1).

BATTING -
2B: Tolan (1,off Blue).
SH: Javier (1,off Holtzman).
Team LOB: 5.

BASERUNNING -
SB: Bench (1,2nd base off Holtzman/Tenace).

Oakland Athletics	AB	R	H	RBI	BB	SO	PO	A
Campaneris ss	4	0	0	0	0	0	3	3
Alou rf	3	0	0	0	1	0	2	0
Rudi lf	4	0	2	0	0	1	2	0
Bando 3b	3	0	2	0	1	0	1	4
Epstein 1b	3	0	0	0	0	0	7	0
Hegan 1b	1	0	0	0	0	0	3	1
Hendrick cf	3	0	0	0	0	1	3	0
Marquez ph	1	0	1	0	0	0	0	0
Lewis pr	0	1	0	0	0	0	0	0
Tenace c	4	2	2	1	0	1	2	1
Green 2b	3	0	1	0	0	1	4	6
Mincher ph	1	0	1	1	0	0	0	0
Odom pr	0	0	0	0	0	0	0	0
Holtzman p	3	0	0	0	0	0	0	2
Blue p	0	0	0	0	0	0	0	0
Fingers p	0	0	0	0	0	0	0	1
Mangual ph	1	0	1	1	0	0	0	0
Totals	34	3	10	3	2	4	27	18

FIELDING -
DP: 1. Holtzman-Green-Hegan.
E: Holtzman (1).

BATTING -
2B: Green (1,off Gullett).
HR: Tenace (3,5th inning off Gullett 0 on 1 out).
IBB: Bando (1,by Gullett).
Team LOB: 8.

PITCHING

Cincinnati Reds	IP	H	R	ER	BB	SO	HR
Gullett	7	5	1	1	2	4	1
Borbon	1.1	2	1	1	0	0	0
Carroll L(0-1)	0	3	1	1	0	0	0
Totals	8.1	10	3	3	2	4	1

IBB: Gullett (1,Bando).

Oakland Athletics	IP	H	R	ER	BB	SO	HR
Holtzman	7.2	5	1	1	0	1	0
Blue	0.1	2	1	1	1	0	0
Fingers W(1-0)	1	0	0	0	0	1	0
Totals	9	7	2	2	1	2	0

Blue faced 1 batter in the 9th inning

Umpires: Frank Umont, Bob Engel, Bill Haller, Chris Pelekoudas, Jim Honochick, Mel Steiner

Time of Game: 2:06   **Attendance:** 49410

	1	2	3		4	5	6		7	8	9		R	H	E
CIN N	0	0	0		0	0	0		0	2	0		2	7	1
OAK A	0	0	0		0	1	0		0	0	2		3	10	1

Oakland Athletics vs. New York Mets

Oakland Athletics reliever Darold Knowles did unprecedented work in the World Series. Not only was he the only pitcher to appear in all seven games, he threw 6⅓ scoreless innings against the New York Mets, allowing four hits and five walks while striking out five and earning two saves.

Darold Knowles, P, 1973 World Series

G	GS	CG	SHO	GF	SV	IP	H	BFP	HR	R	ER	BB	IB	SO	SH	SF	WP	HBP	BK	2B	3B	GDP	ROE	W	L	ERA
7	0	0	0	2	2	6.1	4	30	0	1	0	5	2	5	0	0	0	1	0	0	0	1	2	0	0	0.00

Many historians recount the exploits of pitchers, hitters and fielders, but in Game 3 of the 1975 World Series, the story was home plate umpire Larry Barnett. The series was tied at one game apiece, and Game 3 was tied 5-5 when the Cincinnati Reds came up in the bottom of the 10th inning.

Cesar Geronimo led off with a single against Jim Willoughby. Reds manager Sparky Anderson then called upon Ed Armbrister to pinch hit for Rawly Eastwick and sacrifice Geronimo into scoring position. Armbrister bunted a chopper right in front of the plate. Boston catcher Carlton Fisk went after the ball, Armbrister was slow heading to first, and they got tangled up. Fisk eventually freed himself, and in attempting to force Geronimo at second base

threw the ball into center field.

Fisk immediately turned to Barnett looking for the interference call. Fisk is still looking. Barnett ruled that the play was clean because Armbrister did not intentionally impede Fisk.

Armbrister admitted to the Cincinnati *Enquirer* after the game, "The ball bounced high and I just stood there for a moment watching it. Then he [Fisk] came up from behind me and bumped me as he took the ball."

The play stood, and the Reds had runners on second and third and no one out. The Sox walked Pete Rose intentionally to load the bases and set up a force play, but Joe Morgan hit a flyball over drawn-in center fielder Fred Lynn's head. In a game that featured six home runs in regulation, the Reds were

World Series—Game 6
Thursday, October 19, 1972
Fenway Park

BATTING

Cincinnati Reds	AB	R	H	RBI	BB	SO	PO	A
Rose 3b	5	1	2	0	0	0	0	2
Griffey rf	5	2	2	2	1	0	0	0
Morgan 2b	6	1	1	0	0	0	4	4
Bench c	6	0	1	1	0	2	8	0
Perez 1b	6	0	2	0	0	2	11	2
Foster lf	6	0	2	2	0	0	4	1
Concepcion ss	6	0	1	0	0	0	3	4
Geronimo cf	6	1	2	1	0	3	2	0
Nolan p	0	0	0	0	0	0	1	0
Chaney ph	1	0	0	0	0	0	0	0
Norman p	0	0	0	0	0	0	0	0
Billingham p	0	0	0	0	0	0	0	0
Armbrister ph	0	1	0	0	1	0	0	0
Carroll p	0	0	0	0	0	0	0	0
Crowley ph	1	0	1	0	0	0	0	0
Borbon p	1	0	0	0	0	0	0	0
Eastwick p	0	0	0	0	0	0	0	0
McEnaney p	0	0	0	0	0	0	0	0
Driessen ph	1	0	0	0	0	0	0	0
Darcy p	0	0	0	0	0	0	0	1
Totals	50	6	14	6	2	7	33	14

FIELDING -
DP: 1. Foster-Bench.

BATTING -
2B: Foster (1,off Tiant).
3B: Griffey (1,off Tiant).
HR: Geronimo (2,8th inning off Tiant 0 on 0 out).
HBP: Rose (1,by Drago).
Team LOB: 11.

BASERUNNING -
SB: Concepcion (3,2nd base off Drago/Fisk).

Boston Red Sox	AB	R	H	RBI	BB	SO	PO	A
Cooper 1b	5	0	0	0	0	1	8	0
Drago p	0	0	0	0	0	0	0	0
Miller ph	1	0	0	0	0	0	0	0
Wise p	0	0	0	0	0	0	0	0
Doyle 2b	5	0	1	0	1	0	0	2
Yastrzemski lf,1b	6	1	3	0	0	0	7	1
Fisk c	4	2	2	1	2	0	9	1
Lynn cf	4	2	2	3	1	0	2	0
Petrocelli 3b	4	1	0	1	1	1	1	1
Evans rf	5	1	1	0	0	2	5	1
Burleson ss	3	0	0	0	2	0	3	2
Tiant p	2	0	0	0	0	2	0	2
Moret p	0	0	0	0	0	0	0	1
Carbo ph,lf	2	1	1	3	0	1	1	0
Totals	41	7	10	7	7	7	36	11

FIELDING -
DP: 1. Evans-Yastrzemski-Burleson.
E: Burleson (1).

BATTING -
2B: Doyle (1,off Norman); Evans (1,off Billingham).
HR: Lynn (1,1st inning off Nolan 2 on 2 out); Carbo (2,8th inning off Eastwick 2 on 2 out); Fisk (2,12th inning off Darcy 0 on 0 out).
SH: Tiant (1,off Billingham).
IBB: Fisk 2 (2,by Norman,by McEnaney).
Team LOB: 9.

PITCHING

Cincinnati Reds	IP	H	R	ER	BB	SO	HR
Nolan	2	3	3	3	0	2	1
Norman	0.2	1	0	0	2	0	0
Billingham	1.1	1	0	0	1	1	0
Carroll	1	0	0	0	0	0	0
Borbon	2	1	2	2	2	1	0
Eastwick	1	2	1	1	1	2	1
McEnaney	1	0	0	0	1	0	0
Darcy L(0-1)	2	2	1	1	0	1	1
Totals	11	10	7	7	7	7	3

Borbon faced 2 batters in the 8th inning
Eastwick faced 2 batters in the 9th inning
Darcy faced 1 batter in the 12th inning.
IBB: Norman (1,Fisk); McEnaney (1,Fisk).

Boston Red Sox	IP	H	R	ER	BB	SO	HR
Tiant	7	11	6	6	2	5	1
Moret	1	0	0	0	0	0	0
Drago	3	1	0	0	0	1	0
Wise W(1-0)	1	2	0	0	0	1	0
Totals	12	14	6	6	2	7	1

Tiant faced 1 batter in the 8th inning.
HBP: Drago (1,Rose).

Umpires: Satch Davidson, Art Frantz, Nick Colosi, Larry Barnett, Dick Stello, George Maloney.

Time of Game: 4:01   **Attendance:** 35205

	1	2	3	4	5	6	7	8	9	10	11	12	R	H	E
CIN N	0	0	0	0	3	0	2	1	0	0	0	0	6	14	0
BOS A	3	0	0	0	0	0	0	3	0	0	0	1	7	10	1

victorious 6-5 on a sketchy bunt and what Red Sox fans will forever say was an even sketchier non-call.

But Fisk would be featured again, this time in Game 6, in what may have been the greatest baseball game ever played.

On October 21, 1975, Fisk led off the 12th inning with a homer that hit the mesh net on the left field foul pole at Fenway Park, giving the Red Sox a 7-6 win over the Reds. But this game had much more than a dramatic walkoff.

Back in the ninth inning, the Reds were about to win the World Series and Rawley Eastwick was about to be crowned World Series Most Valuable Player when Boston's Bernie Carbo hit a three-run homer off Eastwick that sent the game into extra innings. In the 11th, Sox right fielder Dwight Evans robbed Joe Morgan of a probable two-run homer with a circus catch that he then turned into a double play. Finally, Fisk willed his 12th-inning shot to stay fair, waving his arms as he bounded toward first, and Fenway organist John Kiley broke into Handel's *Hallelujah Chorus* when it did.

Said Jim Kaplan, who was covering the game, "It was the only time I ever saw press row spontaneously roar to its feet three times in one game."

A good series morphed into a classic, even though the Reds disappointed all New England fans by winning Game 7. But perhaps had sports telecasting not been forever changed (as the camera focused on Fisk "willing the ball fair") we would be writing about Game 7 instead.

The Sox jumped out to a quick 3-0 lead off Don Gullett, and after four innings the Reds were forced to go to the bullpen. But as the triumvirate of Jack Billingham, Clay Carroll and Will McEnaney held the Sox to one mere hit, the Reds picked and picked, scoring two in the sixth, tying it in the seventh, and scoring what proved to be the winner in the ninth. Had Fisk's walkoff never happened, this book might have showcased a 4-3 Reds victory in Game 7. But we cannot escape the impact, power and drama of Game 6.

Indeed, Game 6 has often been referred to as "the game that saved baseball." Some felt it resurrected the national pastime as popular entertainment. Others retrospectively said it deflected the anger and envy that arose over the free-agency salaries that followed.

But baseball most likely would have survived without Game 6. It always survives the sins of the people who play it, the men in blue who umpire it, those of us who cover it, those of you who watch it, and especially those who run it.

1976 _____ New York Yankees vs. Cincinnati Reds

It would be fair to say that shortstop Jim Mason was not a good hitter. His lifetime batting average was .203, and in nine seasons he hit only 12 home runs. But while playing for the New York Yankees in 1976, Mason entered Game 3 for defensive purposes in the fifth inning and homered off winning pitcher Pat Zachary in the seventh. The Cincinnati Reds swept the series 4-0, and Mason hit the only homer for the Yankees. It also was the only Series at-bat of Mason's career, making him the only man to hit a home run in his lone World Series appearance.

Jim Mason, SS, 1976 World Series

G	AB	R	H	2B	3B	HR	RBI	BB	IBB	SO	HBP	SH	SF	XI	ROE	GDP	SB	CS	AVG	OBP	SLG
3	1	1	1	0	0	1	1	0	0	0	0	0	0	0	0	0	0	0	1.000	1.000	4.0000

New York Yankees vs. Los Angeles

New York Yankee star Reggie Jackson revealed his alter ego, "Mr. October," in Game 6—the finale of the 1977 World Series against the Los Angeles Dodgers. Jackson was relatively quiet the first three games, but he homered in Games 4 and 5. The Yankees led the Dodgers three games to one before falling 10-4 in Game 5. In his last time up, Jackson hit a meaningless home run off Don Sutton.

In Game 6, L.A.'s Burt Hooton walked Jackson on four pitches in his first at-bat. In his next, with New York trailing 3-2 in the fourth and Thurman Munson on first, Jackson hit Hooton's first pitch over the right field wall for a 4-3 Yankee lead. Facing Elias Sosa in the fifth, with the crowd chanting "Reg-gie, Reg-gie!" he hit another home run on his first swing. Finally in the eighth, with the Yankees leading 7-4, he came to the plate against knuckleball pitcher Charlie Hough. Once again, Reggie hit the first pitch, this time into the center field bleachers. Two games, four pitches, four swings, four consecutive home runs.

Reggie also set numerous records, including home runs in a Series (5), runs scored (10) and total bases (25). All this was good enough to win his second World Series Most Valuable Player Award (also a record) and the name Mr. October.

Reggie Jackson, OF, 1977 World Series

G	AB	R	H	2B	3B	HR	RBI	BB	IBB	SO	HBP	SH	SF	XI	ROE	GDP	SB	CS	AVG	OBP	SLG
6	20	10	9	1	0	5	8	3	0	4	1	0	0	0	0	1	0	0	.450	.542	1.250

Pittsburgh Pirates vs. Baltimore Orioles

In Game 7 of the 1979 World Series, Willie Stargell went 4-for-5 and scored the decisive run while the Pittsburgh Pirates beat the star-crossed Baltimore Orioles, 4-1. Pops is the only player to score the winning run in two Game 7s (see p. 82, 1971).

World Series—Game 7
Wednesday, October 17, 1979
Memorial Stadium

	1	2	3		4	5	6		7	8	9		R	H	E
PIT N	0	0	0		0	0	2		0	0	2		4	10	0
BAL A	0	0	1		0	0	0		0	0	0		1	4	2

St. Louis Cardinals vs. Kansas City Royals

The Series was tied at three games apiece, but it was over before Game 7 began. Leading the Kansas City Royals 1-0 in the ninth inning of Game 6 and preparing to sip champagne for the second time in four years, the St. Louis Cardinals appeared to get an easy first out when pinch hitter Jorge Orta bounced to first baseman Jack Clark. Clark flipped to pitcher Todd Worrell; Orta was out on a close play—but first base umpire Don Denkinger blew the call. The Cards protested heatedly to no avail. Although the game was far from lost, the Cardinals imploded. Clark then failed to catch a foul pop, catcher Darrell Porter gave up a passed ball, and the Royals loaded the bases before Dane Iorg won the game with a two-run single.

Any reporter visiting either clubhouse was tempted to bet the house on K.C. in Game 7. Cardinal manager Whitey Herzog and his players had lost control of themselves and were still venting over Denkinger's call. By contrast, the Royals, who had remained calm after going down three games to one (credit Manager Dick Howser) were coolly contemplating Game 7. No one should have been surprised when K.C.'s sophomore right-hander Bret Saberhagen throttled the Cards and veteran pitcher John Tudor, 11-0.

World Series—Game 6
Saturday, October 26, 1985
Royals Stadium

	1	2	3		4	5	6		7	8	9		R	H	E
STL N	0	0	0		0	0	0		0	1	0		1	5	0
KC A	0	0	0		0	0	0		0	0	2		2	10	0

New York Mets vs. Boston Red Sox

Champagne was on ice in the Boston Red Sox clubhouse and the lockers were covered with plastic. That's how close they were to winning the 1986 World Series. For the briefest moment someone who ran the scoreboard at Shea Stadium flicked on a congratulatory message to the Bostonians—that's how close they were to winning it all. On October 25, the Sox led the New York Mets three games to two, and were leading Game 6, 5-3, with two outs and none on in the bottom of the 10th inning. All that stood between the Mets and oblivion was Gary Carter.

Watching the game in his Manhattan apartment, author Jim Kaplan was ready to head to the nearest bar and risk his neck ordering drinks on the house. In his Brookline, Massachusetts, apartment, author Bill Chuck sat in the throes of depression fearing his Mets would be soon be finished. Even Kevin Mitchell, the Mets backup outfielder, was in the clubhouse having a smoke.

Hanging tough with two strikes, Carter singled to left. Calvin Schiraldi still only needed to get Mitchell, who came running from the locker room to pinch hit for pitcher Rick Aguilera. With two strikes, Mitchell singled to center. When Ray Knight singled to drive in Carter, sending Mitchell to third and cutting the Red Sox lead to 5-4, John McNamara called for veteran Bob (Steamer) Stanley to nail down the victory.

McNamara had a lot of faith in his veterans and was happy to reward them. His first baseman, Bill Buckner (and his rickety legs), despite having been removed from every winning game of the series for defensive purposes, was still on the field so that he could be part of the inevitable celebration.

Stanley's first two pitches to Mookie Wilson were balls. Then Wilson fouled off three pitches. The Shea Stadium crowd was deafening as Stanley threw what was officially scored a wild pitch, sending Mitchell in with the tying run. Some blamed catcher Rich Gedman for missing the ball, some blamed Stanley for throwing it, and some claimed he threw a spitball and got what he deserved. In any case, the score was now 5-5.

Meanwhile, Wilson was still at the plate, the count 3-2, and potential-winning-run Ray Knight was on second. Wilson hit a foul pop into the stands, and then a liner foul and out of play. On the 10th pitch of this momentous at-bat he hit a roller—not a spinner, not a bouncer, not a tricky hopper—but a *roller* down the first base line and Buckner, who in 1,555 regular season games had made just 128 errors, let it go through his legs. Knight hopped, skipped and danced his way home to give the Mets a 6-5 victory.

Never has a team been closer to winning it all only to blow

World Series—Game 6
Saturday, October 25, 1986
Shea Stadium

BATTING

Boston Red Sox	AB	R	H	RBI	BB	SO	PO	A
Boggs 3b	5	2	3	0	1	0	1	0
Barrett 2b	4	1	3	2	2	0	1	4
Buckner 1b	5	0	0	0	0	0	5	0
Rice lf	5	0	0	0	1	2	5	0
Evans rf	4	0	1	2	1	0	1	0
Gedman c	5	0	1	0	0	1	9	0
Henderson cf	5	1	2	1	0	0	5	0
Owen ss	4	1	3	0	0	1	2	2
Clemens p	3	0	0	0	0	1	0	1
Greenwell ph	1	0	0	0	0	1	0	0
Schiraldi p	1	0	0	0	0	1	0	1
Stanley p	0	0	0	0	0	0	0	0
Totals	42	5	13	5	5	7	29	8

FIELDING -
DP: 1. Barrett-Owen-Buckner.
E: Buckner (1), Evans (1), Gedman (2).

BATTING -
2B: Evans (1,off Ojeda); Boggs (3,off Aguilera).
HR: Henderson (2,10th inning off Aguilera 0 on 0 out).
SH: Owen (1,off McDowell).
HBP: Buckner (1,by Aguilera).
IBB: Boggs (1,by McDowell).
Team LOB: 14.

New York Mets	AB	R	H	RBI	BB	SO	PO	A
Dykstra cf	4	0	0	0	0	2	4	0
Backman 2b	4	0	1	0	0	1	0	4
Hernandez 1b	4	0	1	0	1	0	6	1
Carter c	4	1	1	1	0	1	9	0
Strawberry rf	2	1	0	0	2	0	5	0
Aguilera p	0	0	0	0	0	0	0	0
Mitchell ph	1	0	1	0	0	0	0	0
Knight 3b	4	2	2	1	1	1	0	0
Wilson lf	5	0	1	0	0	1	2	1
Santana ss	1	0	0	0	0	1	0	1
Heep ph	1	0	0	0	0	0	0	0
Elster ss	1	0	0	0	0	0	3	3
Johnson ph,ss	1	0	0	0	0	1	0	0
Ojeda p	2	0	0	0	0	1	0	0
McDowell p	0	0	0	0	0	0	0	1
Orosco p	0	0	0	0	0	0	0	0
Mazzilli ph,rf	2	1	1	0	0	0	1	0
Totals	36	6	8	3	4	9	30	11

FIELDING -
DP: 1. Backman-Elster-Hernandez.
E: Knight (1), Elster (1).

BATTING -
SH: Dykstra (2,off Schiraldi); Backman (1,off Schiraldi).
SF: Carter (1,off Schiraldi).
IBB: Hernandez (1,by Schiraldi).
Team LOB: 8.

BASERUNNING -
SB: Strawberry 2 (3,2nd base off Clemens/Gedman 2).

PITCHING

Boston Red Sox	IP	H	R	ER	BB	SO	HR
Clemens	7	4	2	1	2	8	0
Schiraldi L(0-1)	2.2	4	4	3	2	1	0
Stanley	0	0	0	0	0	0	0
Totals	9.2	8	6	4	4	9	0

WP: Stanley (1).
IBB: Schiraldi (1,Hernandez).

New York Mets	IP	H	R	ER	BB	SO	HR
Ojeda	6	8	2	2	2	3	0
McDowell	1.2	2	1	0	3	1	0
Orosco	0.1	0	0	0	0	0	0
Aguilera W(1-0)	2	3	2	2	0	3	1
Totals	10	13	5	4	5	7	1

HBP: Aguilera (1,Buckner).
IBB: McDowell (2,Boggs).

Umpires: Dale Ford, John Kibler, Jim Evans, Harry Wendelstedt, Joe Brinkman, Ed Montague

Attendance: 55078

	1	2	3		4	5	6		7	8	9		10		R	H	E
BOS A	1	1	0		0	0	0		1	0	0		2		5	13	3
NY N	0	0	0		0	2	0		0	1	0		3		6	8	2

it. And things only got worse when they lost Game 7. In the aftermath, Boston *Globe* columnist Dan Shaughnessy coined the term "Curse of the Bambino" to describe Red Sox fortunes since selling Babe Ruth to the New York Yankees in 1918. Bostonians hadn't celebrated a World Series since, and they would have to wait eighty-six years in all before uncorking the champagne...and finally forgiving Bill Buckner.

Last Lick

Perhaps no reliever has ever finished a World Series more jubilantly than the New York Mets' Jesse Orosco. Brought in to hold a 6-5 lead over the Boston Red Sox in Game 7, with runners on second and third and no outs in the eighth, he got Rich Gedman on a liner to second, Dave Henderson on a strikeout, and Don Baylor on a grounder. When the Mets scored twice more in the ninth, Orosco himself knocked in the last run. And when he struck out Marty Barrett to end the series, Orosco threw his glove high in the air. It still hasn't come down.

No one gave the Los Angeles Dodgers much chance against the Oakland Athletics in the 1988 World Series. Dodgers manager Tommy Lasorda finished the regular season with a 94-57 record and needed the maximum seven games to beat the New York Mets in the National League Championship Series. By contrast, A's manager Tony La Russa had gone 104-58 and beat the Boston Red Sox in four games in the American League Championship Series.

As expected, Oakland took a 4-3 lead into the ninth inning of Game 1, with baseball's best reliever, Dennis Eckersley, on the mound. A gloomy crowd at Dodger Stadium looked on, anticipating the first Dodger loss of a four-game sweep. L.A. didn't even have its sparkplug, because convalescing outfielder Kirk Gibson had sprained a ligament in his right knee and was nursing a strained left hamstring.

Earlier that evening, broadcaster Vin Scully told a national television audience, "The man who is the spearhead of the Dodger offense…will not see any action." Gibson, who was sitting in the trainer's room at the time, reacted vehemently.

"*Bleep* it," he said. "I'll be there."

With an ice bag on his knee, Gibson grabbed a bat and told batboy Mitch Poole to start placing balls on a tee so he wouldn't have to bend. "Clang!" went ball after ball against the metal-frame batting cage. "This could be our script," Gibson told Poole.

After half a bucket of balls, Gibson sent Poole to his manager to announce he was available. Lasorda ran down the runway to hear for himself. "As soon as he heard that I was ready to hit, he took off," Gibson said. "I never got the chance to say, 'I think…'"

Lasorda didn't want to use Gibson until a man was on base. Pinch hitter Mike Davis had a 3-1 count, but Lasorda knew that Eckersley had unintentionally walked only nine batters all season. Therefore, he had Davis step out. That wasn't all. Lasorda placed right-handed-hitting Dave Anderson as a decoy on the on-deck circle. Eckersley, a righty, would have pitched more carefully with Gibson, a noted left-handed clutch hitter, waiting to bat.

"If Davis gets on, wait 'til you see the crowd's reaction," Tracy Woodson told Mickey Hatcher on the Dodger bench. Plainly bothered by Davis' delay ("The guy's hitting a buck-ninety—what the hell's he calling time out for?" Eck complained later), Eckersley walked Davis on the next pitch.

As Davis headed to first, Gibson limped to the plate and 55,983 fans rose to their feet cheering. The drama built. Gibson fouled off the first two pitches. He hit a weak grounder down the first base line and limped toward the bag. But the ball curved foul. On the fourth pitch, Eckersley tried to lay a backdoor slider over the outside corner. "That was the key pitch," Gibson said, "because I was able to stay back, lay off it. And it just missed the strike zone."

Gibson fouled one off again, and when Eckersley missed outside for ball two, Davis stole second. "All I had to think about was shortening my swing and trying to get a hit to score him," Gibson said. So Gibson took a short swing and hit a slider out over the plate to a spot five rows deep in the right field bleachers.

Amid shock and astonishment around the country, amid disbelieving joy in Dodger Stadium, Gibson hobbled around the bases pumping his fist. "It was the one pitch he could pull for power," Eckersley said. "He hit the dog meat out of it."

Though he was never used again, Gibson set the tone for the series. The Dodgers, not the A's, won in five games. And now strangers approach Gibson and tell him what they were doing when he teed off against Eckersley.

"Arguably the most dramatic at-bat in baseball history," said Arizona Diamondbacks manager Bob Melvin, who hired Gibson as his bench coach for the 2007 season.

The derivation of "walk-off homer" is credited to Dennis Eckersley in *The New Dickson Baseball Dictionary*. Eck reportedly coined the term after yielding a game-losing homer and walking dejectedly off the mound in 1993, but the seed was surely planted by Kirk Gibson in 1988.

World Series—Game 1
Saturday, October 15, 1988
Dodger Stadium

	1	2	3		4	5	6		7	8	9		R	H	E
OAK A	0	4	0		0	0	0		0	0	0		4	7	0
LA N	2	0	0		0	0	1		0	0	2		5	7	0

The Minnesota Twins' Kirby Puckett led off the 11th inning with a home run to beat the Atlanta Braves 4-3 in Game 6 of the 1991 World Series—a series that boasted three extra-inning games and five games decided by one run, including a memorable Game 7.

"I'm just glad it's over. I feel like I went 15 rounds with Evander Holyfield," Puckett told the postgame reporters. "This game, I'll never forget right here. It's pretty awesome. Our backs were against the wall. If we didn't win, we would have had to go home. I've never felt so drained in my life. But we've got to do it one more time."

Something memorable was bound to happen in the postseason: This was the year Montreal's Dennis Martinez threw a perfect game, Puckett got six hits in a game for a record second time, and Toronto became the first franchise to draw four million fans.

Starters John Smoltz (Atlanta) and Jack Morris (Minnesota) took a tense pitching duel into the eighth inning at the Hubert H. Humphrey Metrodome in downtown Minneapolis. The Braves seemed about to break it open when Lonnie Smith led off with a walk and Terry Pendleton lined a shot into left-center, a certain double that would likely score the sure-footed Smith. As he was heading into second, however, Smith saw second baseman Chuck Knoblauch pantomime fielding the ball. Fooled by the decoy play and possibly overwhelmed by the crowd noise, Smith hesitated and had to stop at third.

Still, there were runners on second and third with none out. The Twins moved their infield in, anticipating a play at the plate, and when Ron Gant grounded to first, Kent Hrbek stepped on the bag while the runners held. Morris deliberately walked David Justice to set up a force at any base, then induced Sid Bream to hit a grounder for an inning-ending double play.

Could the Braves do any less in the field? The Twins also loaded the bases, with one out in their half of the eighth. But Kent Hrbek hit a liner off Mike Stanton that second baseman Mark Lemke caught and turned into a double play.

The Braves turned another double play in the ninth, and the game went into extra innings. Morris refused to leave the field. The only starter other than Christy Mathewson to pitch into the 10th inning of any World Series Game 7, Morris set down the Braves in order. Leading off for the Twins, Dan Gladden dropped a broken-bat blooper into short left-center. As heads-up as Lonnie Smith had been heads-down, Gladden knew the ball would bounce high off the artificial turf, and he raced into second. Chuck Knoblauch sacrificed him to third, and the Braves elected to walk the next two batters to load the bases.

World Series—Game 6
Sunday, October 27, 1991
Hubert H. Humphrey Metrodome

BATTING

Atlanta Braves	AB	R	H	RBI	BB	SO	PO	A
Smith dh	4	0	2	0	1	1	0	0
Pendleton 3b	5	0	1	0	0	0	0	5
Gant cf	4	0	0	0	0	2	4	0
Justice rf	3	0	1	0	1	1	4	0
Bream 1b	4	0	0	0	0	0	7	2
Hunter lf	4	0	1	0	0	1	1	0
Olson c	4	0	0	0	0	1	5	0
Lemke 2b	4	0	1	0	0	1	4	1
Belliard ss	2	0	1	0	0	1	2	2
Blauser ph,ss	1	0	0	0	0	0	0	0
Smoltz p	0	0	0	0	0	0	1	1
Stanton p	0	0	0	0	0	0	0	0
Pena p	0	0	0	0	0	0	0	0
Totals	35	0	7	0	2	8	28	11

FIELDING -
DP: 3. Bream-Belliard-Bream, Lemke, Lemke-Belliard-Bream.

BATTING -
2B: Hunter (1,off Morris); Pendleton (3,off Morris).
SH: Belliard (2,off Morris).
IBB: Justice (1,by Morris).
Team LOB: 8.

Minnesota Twins	AB	R	H	RBI	BB	SO	PO	A
Gladden lf	5	1	3	0	0	1	2	0
Knoblauch 2b	4	0	1	0	0	0	2	2
Puckett cf	2	1	0	1	3	1	2	0
Hrbek 1b	3	0	0	0	1	0	10	2
Davis dh	4	0	1	0	0	1	0	0
Brown pr,dh	0	0	0	0	0	0	0	0
Larkin ph,dh	1	0	1	1	0	0	0	0
Harper c	4	0	2	0	0	0	10	2
Mack rf	4	0	1	0	0	0	2	0
Pagliarulo 3b	3	0	0	0	1	0	0	1
Gagne ss	2	0	0	0	0	1	1	1
Bush ph	1	0	1	0	0	0	0	0
Newman pr,ss	0	0	0	0	0	0	0	1
Sorrento ph	1	0	0	0	0	1	0	0
Leius ss	0	0	0	0	0	0	0	1
Morris p	0	0	0	0	0	0	1	0
Totals	34	1	10	1	5	5	30	10

FIELDING -
DP: 1. Hrbek-Harper-Hrbek.
PB: Harper (1).

BATTING -
2B: Gladden 2 (2,off Smoltz,off Pena).
SH: Knoblauch (1,off Pena).
HBP: Hrbek (1,by Smoltz).
IBB: Puckett 2 (4,by Stanton,by Pena); Pagliarulo (1,by Pena); Hrbek (1,by Pena).
Team LOB: 12.

PITCHING

Atlanta Braves	IP	H	R	ER	BB	SO	HR
Smoltz	7.1	6	0	0	1	4	0
Stanton	0.2	0	0	0	1	0	0
Pena L(0-1)	1.1	2	1	1	3	1	0
Totals	9.1	10	1	1	5	5	0

Stanton faced 2 batters in the 9th inning
HBP: Smoltz (1,Hrbek).
IBB: Stanton (2,Puckett); Pena 3 (3,Pagliarulo,Puckett,Hrbek).

Minnesota Twins	IP	H	R	ER	BB	SO	HR
Morris W(2-0)	10	7	0	0	2	8	0

IBB: Morris (1,Justice).

Umpires: Don Denkinger, Harry Wendelstedt, Drew Coble, Terry Tata, Rick Reed, Ed Montague

Time of Game: 3:23 **Attendance:** 55118

	1	2	3		4	5	6		7	8	9	10		R	H	E
ATL N	0	0	0		0	0	0		0	0	0	0		0	7	0
MIN A	0	0	0		0	0	0		0	0	0	1		1	10	0

The outfield drew in to cut off any more bloopers. Pinch hitter Gene Larkin's fly to left would have been an out on any other day, but it sailed over drawn-in Brian Hunter's head for a Series-winning single.

Asked how long he could have stayed in the game, the red-mustachioed Morris said, "A hundred and twelve innings." Tight pitching, clutch double plays, telling baserunning, and a walk-off hit—some call it the greatest Series game ever.

1993

Toronto Blue Jays vs. Philadelphia Phillies

All Joe Carter's career lacked, people said, as his Toronto Blue Jays defended their World Series title in 1993, was a defining moment.

In Game 6—the Blue Jays led the Philadelphia Phillies three games to two—Carter came to bat in the ninth inning with the Phillies ahead 6-5 and one out. Rickey Henderson stood on second base, Paul Molitor on first. The pitcher was Mitch (Wild Thing) Williams, who had induced as much terror in the eyes of his fans as he did in his opponents, even as he saved 43 games during the regular season. In the words of Phillies owner Bill Giles, "Every time [Williams] pitches, it takes me an extra hour and a vodka martini to get to sleep."

With the count 2-2, Williams tried to throw a fastball up and away. Trouble was, it behaved like a slider down and in, where Carter loved his pitches. He smacked it down the left field line and it headed into the stands, just fair. While the crowd at Toronto's SkyDome erupted and his teammates poured from the dugout, Carter literally danced around the bases, leaving his feet as he rounded second and again as he passed the vacated shortstop position.

"I actually dreamed of that moment many times," Carter told ESPN.com's Rick Weinberg. "I dreamed of that moment when I was a little kid. I'd be sitting at my father's garage and daydreaming about that moment. I even wrote it down a few times: 'My dream is to hit a home run to win the World Series.'"

Carter grinned and crossed his arms over his chest in a gesture Weinberg described as "satisfying and heartwarming." Then he added: "It was the ultimate sports fantasy."

Now the Carter and Mazeroski homers will be spoken of in the same breath. True, Maz ended a seven-game Series with the quintessential walk-off homer. But Maz broke a tie, and Carter capped a come-from-behind thriller. Moreover, it produced the first World Series repeat since the 1977-78 Yankees. And it ended another era in baseball history: the pre-wild card era.

Carter's blow helped nail down Paul Molitor's bid for Cooperstown well before his 3,000th hit. Batting .500, Molitor was selected World Series Most Valuable Player—an award that might not have been his if the Blue Jays hadn't won. And the homer virtually nailed shut the career of Mitch Williams, who received death threats during the series. After saving 102 games over three seasons with the Phillies, he was traded to Houston, where he saved just six in 1994. A year later he was out of baseball.

World Series—Game 6
Saturday, October 23, 1993
SkyDome

	1	2	3	4	5	6	7	8	9	R	H	E
PHI N	0	0	0	1	0	0	5	0	0	6	7	0
TOR A	3	0	0	1	1	0	0	0	3	8	10	2

Playing second base for the Cleveland Indians in the World Series, an aging Tony Fernandez (who made his reputation as a good defensive shortstop) unfortunately left the wrong lasting impression against the Florida Marlins. With the score tied, a runner on first and one out in the 11th, Fernandez booted Craig Counsell's double-play ball and a runner advanced. Jim Eisenreich was deliberately walked to load the bases. When Devon White grounded to Fernandez, he fielded it cleanly and threw home for the second out. Then Edgar Renteria grounded one up the middle to give the Marlins a 3-2 win. To be fair, there were three batters after Tony's blunder. But all would have stayed on the bench if he'd done the job on Counsell.

World Series—Game 7
Sunday, October 26, 1997
Pro Player Stadium

	1	2	3	4	5	6	7	8	9	10	11	R	H	E
CLE A	0	0	2	0	0	0	0	0	0	0	0	2	6	2
FLA N	0	0	0	0	0	0	1	0	1	0	1	3	8	0

LAST LICK

How does such a collapse affect the people who suffer it? The game occurred on the forty-eighth birthday of Cleveland Indians manager Mike Hargrove. "I haven't celebrated that birthday yet," Hargrove told the Seattle *Times* in 2007. "I had a guy ask me once how long it took me to get over it. I told him as soon as I did, I'd let him know. I have the same answer now." Maybe the lingering disappointment contributed to Hargrove's surprise announcement that he was quitting as Seattle Mariners manager during the 2007 season.

W ith the New York Yankees leading the Arizona Diamondbacks 2-1 in Game 7, Arizona's Mark Grace
led off the ninth with a single. When Damian Miller
laid down a poor sacrifice bunt, Yankee closer Mariano Rivera
threw wildly to second for only the second error of his career.
Now there were runners on first and second with no outs. Jay
Bell also bunted, an atrocious bunt that Rivera fielded and
threw to third baseman Scott Brosius in plenty of time. Trouble
was, Brosius should have doubled up Bell at first but forgot to
throw there. Maybe Rivera was shaken, maybe he'd just lost it,
but he promptly gave up run-scoring singles to Tony Womack
and Luis Gonzalez, and the Diamondbacks were champs.

Pitching for the Diamondbacks at age thirty-eight, Randy
Johnson became the only pitcher to win Game 6 as a starter and
Game 7 as a reliever.

World Series—Game 7
Sunday, November 4, 2001
Bank One Ballpark

BATTING

New York Yankees	AB	R	H	RBI	BB	SO	PO	A
Jeter ss	4	1	1	0	0	1	1	4
O'Neill rf	3	0	2	0	0	1	0	0
Knoblauch ph,lf	1	0	0	0	0	0	0	0
Williams cf	4	0	0	0	0	1	2	1
Martinez 1b	4	0	1	1	0	1	6	1
Posada c	4	0	0	0	0	2	13	1
Spencer lf,rf	3	0	0	0	0	0	0	0
Soriano 2b	3	1	1	1	0	1	1	2
Brosius 3b	3	0	0	0	0	2	2	0
Clemens p	2	0	0	0	0	1	0	0
Stanton p	0	0	0	0	0	0	0	0
Justice ph	1	0	1	0	0	0	0	0
Rivera p	0	0	0	0	0	0	0	0
Totals	32	2	6	2	0	10	25	10

FIELDING -
E: Soriano (3), Clemens (1), Rivera (1).

BATTING -
2B: O'Neill (1,off Schilling).
HR: Soriano (1,8th inning off Schilling 0 on 0 out).
Team LOB: 3.

Arizona Diamondbacks	AB	R	H	RBI	BB	SO	PO	A
Womack ss	5	0	2	1	0	1	1	1
Counsell 2b	4	0	1	0	0	0	2	1
Gonzalez lf	5	0	1	1	0	2	2	0
Williams 3b	4	0	1	0	0	2	1	1
Finley cf	4	1	2	0	0	1	5	0
Bautista rf	3	0	1	1	1	1	4	1
Grace 1b	4	0	3	0	0	0	2	1
Dellucci pr	0	0	0	0	0	0	0	0
Miller c	4	0	0	0	0	3	10	0
Cummings pr	0	1	0	0	0	0	0	0
Schilling p	3	0	0	0	0	3	0	0
Batista p	0	0	0	0	0	0	0	0
Johnson p	0	0	0	0	0	0	0	0
Bell ph	1	1	0	0	0	0	0	0
Totals	37	3	11	3	1	13	27	5

BATTING -
2B: Bautista (2,off Clemens); Womack (3,off Rivera).
HBP: Counsell (1,by Rivera).
Team LOB: 11.

BASERUNNING -
CS: Womack (1,2nd base by Stanton/Posada).

PITCHING

New York Yankees	IP	H	R	ER	BB	SO	HR
Clemens	6.1	7	1	1	1	10	0
Stanton	0.2	0	0	0	0	0	0
Rivera L(1-1)	1.1	4	2	1	0	3	0
Totals	8.1	11	3	2	1	13	0

HBP: Rivera (1,Counsell).

Arizona Diamondbacks	IP	H	R	ER	BB	SO	HR
Schilling	7.1	6	2	2	0	9	1
Batista	0.1	0	0	0	0	0	0
Johnson W(3-0)	1.1	0	0	0	0	1	0
Totals	9	6	2	2	0	10	1

Umpires: Steve Rippley, Mark Hirschbeck, Dale Scott, Ed
Rapuano, Jim Joyce, Dana DeMuth

Time of Game: 3:20 **Attendance:** 49589

	1	2	3		4	5	6		7	8	9		R	H	E
NY A	0	0	0		0	0	0		1	1	0		2	6	3
ARI N	0	0	0		0	0	1		0	0	2		3	11	0

2002 — Anaheim Angels vs. San Francisco Giants

In the first World Series between two wild-card teams, Angels manager Mike Scoscia examined his exhausted pitching staff and chose rookie John Lackey to start Game 7 against the Giants. Lackey had gone 9-4 with a 3.66 ERA in 18 appearances after a mid-season call-up, but he had pitched spottily in two Series games. What Scoscia saw in him was resolve.

Giants pitcher Livan Hernandez screamed at the home-plate umpire after a tense first inning; Lackey remained focused. He gave up just one run in five innings and left with a 4-1 lead. With spotless relief from Brendan Donnelly, Francisco Rodriguez and Troy Percival, the Angels held their lead and Lackey became the second and last rookie to start and win Game 7.

World Series—Game 7
Sunday, October 27, 2002
Edison International Field
of Anaheim

	1	2	3	4	5	6	7	8	9	R	H	E
SF N	0	1	0	0	0	0	0	0	0	1	6	0
ANA A	0	1	3	0	0	0	0	0	x	4	5	0

2004 — Boston Red Sox vs. St. Louis Cardinals

Edgar Renteria won the World Series with a hit for the Florida Marlins in 1997 and made the final out for the St. Louis Cardinals in 2004. Renteria was also the last out in the 2005 American League Division Series, this time playing for the Boston Red Sox against the Chicago White Sox. Renteria is the only player to win a World Series and lose both a playoff and World Series in the last at-bat.

In fairness, it should also be noted that on September 29, 1997, in Game 1 of the NLDS, Renteria's two-out, bases-loaded single in the bottom of the ninth gave Florida a 2-1 victory over the San Francisco Giants.

Edgar Renteria, SS, 1996-Present

G	AB	R	H	2B	3B	HR	RBI	BB	IBB	SO	HBP	SH	SF	XI	ROE	GDP	SB	CS	AVG	OBP	SLG	BFW
1722	6637	1021	1934	370	24	117	762	597	33	941	29	84	62	0	97	190	274	101	.291	.349	.407	3.2

Perfect Games

Catcher Yogi Berra and pitcher Don Larsen celebrate perfection in 1956.

American League

Pitcher (age) Lifetime Record	Date, Venue Attendance Time of Game	Pitches Thrown Catcher Umpire	Result Losing Team Record Final Out	Ks
David Cone (36) 194-126	07-18-1999 Yankee Stadium day game, 41,930 2:16 (not including a 33-minute rain delay)	88 Joe Girardi U: Ted Barrett	New York 6, Montreal 0 68-94—fourth in NL East Pinch hitter Ryan McGuire flied out to left.	10
David Wells (34) 229-146 (still active)	05-17-1998 Yankee Stadium day game, 49,820 2:40	120 Jorge Posada U: Tim McClelland	New York 4, Minnesota 0 70-92—fourth in AL Central Pat Meares flied to right.	11
Mike Witt (24) 117-116	09-30-1984 Arlington Stadium day game, 8,375 1:49	94 Bob Boone U: Greg Kosc	California 1, Texas 0 69-92—seventh in AL West Pinch hitter Marv Foley grounded to second.	10
Kenny Rogers (29) 205-137 (still active)	07-28-1994 The Ballpark in Arlington, night game, 46,581, 2:08	98 Ivan Rodriguez U: Ed Bean	Texas 4, California 0 47-68—fourth in AL West Gary DiSarcina flied to center.	8
Len Barker (25) 74-76	05-15-1981 Cleveland Stadium night game, 7,290 2:09	103 Ron Hassey U: Rich Garcia	Cleveland 3, Toronto 0 37-69—seventh in AL East Pinch hitter Ernie Whitt flied to center.	11
Catfish Hunter (22) 224-166 HOF	05-08-1968 Oakland-Alameda County Coliseum night game, 6,298 2:28	107 Jim Pagliaroni U: Jerry Neudecker	Oakland 4, Minnesota 0 79-83—seventh in AL Pinch hitter Rich Reese took a called third strike.	11
Don Larsen (27) 81-91	10-08-1956 Yankee Stadium day game (Game 5 of the World Series) 64,519, 2:06	97 Yogi Berra U: Babe Pinelli	New York 2, Brooklyn 0 Game 5, 1956 World Series 93-61—first in NL Pinch hitter Dale Mitchell took a called third strike.	7
Charlie Robon (26) 49-80	04-30-1922 Navin Field day game, 25,000 1:55	90 Ray Schalk U: Dick Nallin	Chicago 2, Detroit 0 79-75—third in AL	6
Addie Joss (28) 160-97 HOF	10-02-1908 League Park day game, 10,598 1:29	74 Nig Clarke U: Tommy Connolly	Cleveland 1, Chicago 0 88-64—third in AL	3

Pitcher (age) Lifetime Record	Date, Venue Attendance Time of Game	Pitches Thrown Catcher Umpire	Result Losing Team Record Final Out	Ks
Cy Young (37) 511-316 HOF	05-05-1904 Huntington Avenue Grounds, day game, 10,267, 1:23	Lou Criger U: Frank Dwyer	Boston 3, Philadelphia 0 81-70—fifth in AL Opposing pitcher Rube Waddell flied out.	3

National League

Pitcher (age) Lifetime Record	Date, Venue Attendance Time of Game	Pitches Thrown Catcher Umpire	Result Losing Team Record Final Out	Ks
Randy Johnson (40) 280-146 (still active)	05-18-2004 Turner Field night game, 23,381 2:13	117 Robby Hammock U: Greg Gibson	Arizona 2, Atlanta 0 96-66—first in NL East Pinch hitter Eddie Perez struck out.	13
Dennis Martinez (36) 245-193	07-28-1991 Dodger Stadium day game, 45,560 2:14	95 Ron Hassey U: Larry Poncino	Montreal 2, Los Angeles 0 93-69—second in NL West Pinch hitter Chris Gwynn, brother of Tony Gwynn, flied to center field.	5
Tom Browning (28) 123-90	09-16-1988 Riverfront Stadium night game, 16,591 1:51	102 Rick Dempsey U: Jim Quick	Cincinnati 1, Los Angeles 0 94-67—first in NL West Pinch hitter Tracy Woodson struck out.	7
Sandy Koufax (29) 165-87 HOF	09-09-1965 Dodger Stadium night game, 29,139 1:43	113 Jeff Torborg U: Ed Vargo	Los Angeles 1, Chicago 0 72-90—eighth in NL Pinch hitter Harvey Kuenn struck out.	14
Jim Bunning (32) 224-184 HOF	06-21-1964 Shea Stadium day game, 32,026 2:19	90 Gus Triandos U: Ed Sudol	Philadelphia 6, New York 0 53-109—10th in NL Pinch hitter John Stephenson struck out.	10
John Montgomery Ward (20) 164-102 HOF	06-17-1880 day game	Emil Gross U: Daniels	Providence 5, Buffalo 0 24-58 - seventh in NL Future Hall of Famer Pud Galvin.	i
John Lee Richmond (23) 75-100	06-12-1880 Worcester Agricultural Fairgrounds, day game	Charlie Bennett U: Bradley	Worcester 1, Cleveland 0 47-37—third in NL.	i

Perfect Points

- Ten perfect games have been thrown by American League pitchers.
- Seven perfect games have been thrown by National League pitchers.
- Five perfect games have been thrown by National League pitchers since 1900.
- Two perfect games have been interleague: Don Larsen's in the World Series and David Cone's during the regular season (for the New York Yankees against the Montreal Expos).
- The Dodgers have been on the losing side of three perfect games and on the winning side once.
- The Yankees have been involved in three perfect games, winning them all.
- Two Cleveland Indians pitchers have hurled perfect games.
- The Texas Rangers and California Angels were involved in two perfect games, against each other, with each team winning once.
- The Minnesota Twins have been victims of two perfect games.
- The Chicago White Sox are 1-1 in perfect games.
- Yankee Stadium has been the site of three perfect games.
- Dodger Stadium has been the site of two perfect games.
- The Ballpark in Arlington has been the site of two perfect games.
- There have been 10 daytime perfect games and seven nighttime perfect games.
- Jim Bunning's was thrown on Father's Day in the first game of a Sunday doubleheader.
- The final out of Sandy Koufax' perfect game was Harvey Kuenn, who had earlier made the last out in Koufax' no-hitter on May 11, 1963.
- Don Larsen and David Wells attended Point Loma High School in San Diego.
- Don Larsen attended David Cone's perfect game to celebrate Yogi Berra Day.
- Between innings of David Wells' perfect game, Wells sat next to David Cone.
- Randy Johnson, Cy Young and Jim Bunning are the only pitchers to throw a perfect game in one league and a no-hitter in the other.
- At forty years and 251 days, Johnson is the oldest pitcher to throw a perfect game.
- At just over twenty years old, John Montgomery Ward was the youngest man to throw a perfect game.
- Mike Witt's perfect game happened on the final day of the season.
- Future basketball star Danny Ainge played third base for the Toronto Blue Jays when they were perfected by Len Barker.
- Sandy Koufax' perfect game was his fourth no-hitter.
- The losing pitcher in Koufax' perfect game was Bob Hendley, who allowed just one hit. One hit between two teams in a nine-inning game is a major league record.
- Hall of Famer Addie Joss defeated Hall of Famer Ed Walsh in his perfect game.
- Hall of Famer Cy Young defeated Hall of Famer Rube Waddell in his perfect game.
- John Montgomery Ward and John Lee Richmond's perfect games were five days apart.
- Tom Browning's perfect game started late because of a two-hour, 27-minute rain delay.
- David Cone's game was delayed by rain for thirty-three minutes in the bottom of the third inning.
- Jim Bunning had two hits and two RBI in his perfect game.
- Ron Hassey was the catcher for Len Barker's and Dennis Martinez' perfect games.
- Paul O'Neill was the right fielder in the perfect games of Tom Browning, David Wells and David Cone.

The Streaks

The ultimate Iron Man, Cal Ripken, Jr.

Nothing intrigues baseball fans like a record-threatening streak. It builds upon itself and attracts more attention each day. In the end, it overshadows everything else—including races for postseason berths. Sometimes it even eclipses baseball.

Robert W. Creamer wrote in *Baseball in '41*:

...[Joe] DiMaggio's 56-game hitting streak transcended the Yankees and Yankees fans. It transcended New York; it even transcended baseball. Everyone was caught up in it. No athlete before or since—not Babe Ruth or Jack Dempsey or Bobby Jones; not Jackie Robinson or Mary Lou Retton; not Muhammad Ali; not even Bo Jackson—has held the country's fascinated attention day after day, week after week, the way DiMaggio did in 1941. [Colleague] Andy Crichton told me that he and his brother Bob and two high school friends drove across the country that summer in an old jalopy. In Montana they stopped for coffee at a dusty cafe in a dusty town. Farm hands and ranch hands came into the cafe for breakfast. This was before television, remember, and radio news was sketchy before we got into the war, particularly in smaller towns. You found out what was happening from newspapers. Almost every man who came into the café, Crichton said, would glance toward a newspaper lying on the counter and ask the proprietor, "He get one yesterday?" He didn't have to explain who "he" was, even though this was two thousand miles from New York and a thousand miles west of the westernmost major league city, which in those days was St. Louis. Every day, all over the country, people asked, "Did he get one yesterday?"

Volumes have been written about Joe DiMaggio's 56-game hitting streak, but a book about grand finales can't ignore baseball's greatest exhibition of persistent mastery. The 1941 streak ran from May 15 through July 16. Interestingly, Joltin' Joe was in one of the worst slumps of his career, a 20-game stretch in which he hit .184, before he took off.

Over the next 56 games, DiMaggio went 91-for-223 to bat .408. He had 56 singles and 56 runs, 16 doubles and four triples, 15 home runs and 55 RBI, 21 walks and—perhaps the most remarkable statistic of all—only seven strikeouts.

By Game 56, DiMaggio was charting new territory with each outing. He had long since broken the Yankee record of 29 held by Roger Peckinpaugh and Earle Combs (after game 30, DiMaggio hit .457), and he was well past George Sisler's 41-game American League record set in 1922. DiMaggio tied and broke that mark in a June 29 doubleheader in Washington, despite the fact that a fan stole his favorite bat between games. On July 2, DiMaggio homered off Boston's Dick Newsome to break Wee Willie Keeler's major league record of 44 that had been set in 1897. In Game 56, played at Cleveland's League Park before 15,000 fans (the Indians averaged only 9,625 for the season), DiMaggio hit the first pitch he saw from Al Milnar up the middle for a single. He ended the game 3-for-4, with Milnar giving up two hits and reliever Joe Krakauskas the third. Yankee starter Atley Donald went the distance to win 10-3, giving the Yankees a six-game lead over the Indians in the American League standings.

Afterward, DiMaggio admitted that the pressure had lessened for him, as reflected by his .510 batting average over his last twelve games. The Yankee Clipper had two goals: to equal the 61-game streak he compiled with the Pacific Coast League's San Francisco Seals in 1933 (Joe Wilhoit hit in 69 straight in 1919 for Wichita of the Western Association); and to catch Ted Williams in the batting race. DiMaggio trailed Williams .375 to .395 and wasn't gaining on him. During DiMaggio's streak, Williams hit .412 in 55 games.

There was nothing to indicate that Game 57 would be the end of DiMaggio's streak. Cleveland played in two ballparks at the time, and the game was held at Municipal Stadium. On the hot evening of July 17, 67,468 fans—before that time the largest crowd ever to see a night game—were on hand. Facing Al Smith in the first inning, DiMaggio slammed a grounder down the third base line. Playing him almost on the outfield grass, third baseman Ken Keltner backhanded the ball in foul territory and threw him out. DiMaggio walked in the fourth and hit another grounder headed for the left field corner in the seventh. Again, Keltner made a magnificent backhand stop and threw him out as DiMaggio strained to reach first ahead of the throw.

DiMaggio had one last opportunity in the eighth. With the bases filled and the Yankees ahead 4-1, the Cleveland crowd screamed their support. Reliever Jim Bagby, Jr. threw a 1-1 pitch that DiMaggio hit on the ground toward shortstop Lou Boudreau. The crowd held its collective breath when the ball took a tricky hop, but Boudreau fielded it at shoulder level and threw to second baseman Ray Mack for the force before Mack relayed to first for an inning-ending double play.

There might have been one last at-bat for DiMaggio, but the Indians' two-run rally in the ninth fell short after they put the tying run on third with nobody out. The Yankees won, 4-3. Had the Indians tied the score, DiMaggio could have been the fourth Yankee batter in the 10th inning.

"I can't say that I'm glad it's over," DiMaggio told John Drebinger of the New York *Times*. "Of course, I wanted it to go on as long as it could. Now that the streak is over, I just want to get out there and keep helping to win ballgames."

DiMaggio was incredibly successful at that as well. At the beginning of his streak, the Yankees were 5½ games out of first place. After going 41-13-2, they were in first place. The Yankees eventually won the pennant by 17 games over the Red Sox and the World Series in 5 games over the Brooklyn Dodgers. Perhaps it was DiMaggio's value to his team, perhaps it was personality, but most likely it was the Streak. Whatever the case, the Yankee Clipper was voted Most Valuable Player over Williams, who finished with a .406 batting average and a league-leading 37 home runs.

Even Williams admitted, "I believe there isn't

a record in the books that will be harder to break than Joe's 56 games. It may be the greatest batting achievement of all."

There was another reason that the parsimonious DiMaggio was disappointed when his streak ended. "Did you know if I got a hit tonight I would have made $10,000?" he said. "The Heinz 57 people wanted to make some kind of deal."

In one of the great last licks of movie history, the mighty King Kong lay dead on the ground after being shot down from the top of the Empire State Building.

A New York City policeman turned to Kong's captor and said, "Well, Denham, the airplanes got him." To which Carl Denham replied, "Oh, no. It wasn't the airplanes. It was beauty killed the beast."

DiMaggio's streak was stopped by the son of former big league pitcher Jim Bagby, just as his 61-game minor league streak had been stopped by Ed Walsh Jr., son of the Hall of Fame right-hander. But it wasn't pitching that did DiMaggio in: It was Cleveland third baseman Keltner stopped the Streak.

Joe DiMaggio, CF, New York Yankees, 1941

G	AB	R	H	2B	B	HR	RBI	BB	SO	HBP	SH	GDP	SB	CS	AVG	OBP	SLG	BFW
139	541	122	193	43	11	30	125	76	13	4	0	6	4	2	.357	.440	.643	6.6

269

An outstanding reliever for the San Francisco Giants in the late 1970s and early 1980s, Greg Minton had a nasty sinkerball that produced many grounders and few flyballs. On September 6, 1978, Minton relieved Jim Barr in the fourth inning.

Lacking his usual stuff, he surrendered a home run to Joe Ferguson. On May 2, 1982, 179 games and 269 innings later, Minton gave up a homer to the New York Mets' John Stearns. The Giants still won 4-3, and Minton picked up the save.

Greg Minton, P, 1975-1990

G	GS	CG	SHO	GF	SV	IP	H	BFP	HR	R	ER	BB	IB	SO	SH	SF	WP	HBP	BK	2B	3B	GDP	ROE	W	L	ERA	RS	PW
710	7	0	0	415	150	1130.2	1082	4810	43	452	389	483	131	479	74	35	56	16	9	141	21	153	90	59	65	3.10	3.86	10.4

369

Darren Lewis debuted in center field for the Oakland Athletics on August 21, 1990. In December of that year, he was traded across the Bay to the San Francisco Giants. On June 30, 1994, Lewis overran a ground single to center by Cliff Floyd, enabling Floyd to reach second. It was Lewis' first error after 369 flawless games.

Darren Lewis, OF, 1990-2002

G	GS	CG	INN	PO	A	ERR	DP	TP	FPCT.	RFg	LF	CF	RF
1273	1024	881	9483	2778	42	16	14	0	.994	2.14	98	1032	187

59

On August 30, 1988, Orel (Bulldog) Hershiser started for the Los Angeles Dodgers against the Montreal Expos. Leading 4-0 with two outs in the fifth inning, Hershiser yielded a Rex Hudler single, a Tim Raines double that scored Hudler, and a Dave Martinez single that scored Raines, but Hershiser hung on to win, 4-2. The next time out, he pitched a four-hit shutout over the Braves. Then he won his 20th game of the season by shutting out the Reds on seven hits. On September 14, Hershiser and Rick Mahler engaged in a pitcher's duel that remained scoreless until the bottom of

the ninth, when Mike Marshall singled home Kirk Gibson to give Hershiser his 21st victory, 1-0. All of a sudden, everyone was aware that Bulldog had three straight shutouts and 31 consecutive scoreless innings.

His next time out, the Houston Astros mustered just four hits against him, but the Dodgers managed only three. Fortunately for Hershiser, one was a John Shelby homer, and the Dodgers won, 1-0. On September 23, the San Francisco Giants' Atlee Hammaker matched Hershiser through seven innings. Once again, the Dodgers got a big hit: Mickey

Hatcher's three-run homer gave them a 3-0 victory. Hershiser's shutout streak was now up to 49 innings, and he took dead aim at the 58-inning record held by Dodger broadcaster Don Drysdale. Unfortunately, Hershiser had only one more start remaining, which meant even if he threw another shutout, he wouldn't break the record until the following season.

Unless…

On September 28, Hershiser faced Andy Hawkins and the San Diego Padres. This time, the weak Dodger bats worked in Hershiser's favor. No score through three innings of play; no score through seven; no score through nine. Both starters were still in the game and Hershiser had tied the record of 58 scoreless innings. Leading off the bottom of the 10th for San Diego, Marvell Wynne swung and missed on strike three but reached first on a wild pitch. Benito Santiago sacrificed and moved the streak-breaking run to second. Randy Ready grounded to short, but the winning run was now on third. Garry Templeton

was intentionally walked and went to second on defensive indifference. Keith Moreland batted with the Streak and the game on the line. When he flied out to right, the Dodgers mobbed their star pitcher and celebrated his record 59-inning shutout streak. Hershiser was through for the night in a game that the Padres eventually won in 16 innings.

Unless you count the eight shutout innings in the opener of the National League Championship Series against the Mets, the streak ended there. The next season, on April 5, 1989, Hershiser was tabbed the Opening Day starter. Cincinnati's Barry Larkin led off the Reds' half of the first with a single and advanced to second on an errant pickoff attempt. Chris Sabo and Eric Davis both struck out before Kal Daniels walked and Todd Benzinger singled to right, scoring Larkin with an unearned run to end the Streak at 59 scoreless innings.

Don Drysdale still holds the record for consecutive shutouts, throwing six from May 14 through June 4, 1968.

Orel Hershiser, SP, Los Angeles Dodgers. 1988

G	GS	CG	SHO	GF	SV	IP	H	BFP	HR	R	ER	BB	IB	SO	SH	SF	WP	HBP	BK	2B	3B	GDP	ROE	W	L	ERA	RS	P
35	34	15	8	1	1	267	208	1068	18	73	67	73	10	178	9	6	6	4	5	28	6	18	15	23	8	2.26	4.03	4.5

George Stallings, manager of the 1914 Miracle Braves, hated bases on balls. According to an apocryphal story, as he lay on his deathbed in 1929, Stallings was asked what had caused his bad heart. Supposedly he groaned, "Oh, those bases on balls!" Then he turned to the wall and died.

Stallings would have loved Bill Fischer.

In July, 1913, the great Christy Mathewson set a record of 68 consecutive innings without issuing a free pass. The record held up until 1962.

On August 3, 1962, Fischer—pitching for the Kansas City Athletics—faced the Cleveland Indians. Leading off the bottom of the first, Bubba Phillips drew a walk. Fischer allowed no more free passes but lost, 1-0.

On August 7, Fischer again went the distance, issuing no walks and beating the Senators, 10-3. Two days later he pitched an inning in relief, gave up a hit, and blew the save, but didn't walk anyone. Fischer started again on August 12 and pitched eight innings, yielding a Jim Landis home run and losing to the Chicago White Sox, 1-0. But he walked no one. Fischer threw a six-hitter against the New York

Yankees, winning 7-2 on August 17—still no walks.

On August 21, Fischer lasted four innings, gave up seven runs (six earned), and lost to the Boston Red Sox—walkless. In his next start he had his stuff again, but he lost for the third time 1-0, this time to the Minnesota Twins, without walking a batter.

By September 1, it had been almost a month since Fischer's last walk. Facing the Yankees, he walked no one in six innings of work, but the Yankees sent the A's to a 3-1 loss. In his next start, Fischer lasted 2⅓ innings in which the Red Sox hammered him for five runs without a walk. Fischer was more effective his next start while losing to the White Sox, and he was walk-free.

The pattern continued until Fischer's last start of the season on September 30, when in the fifth inning he walked Bubba Morton. The streak of 84 consecutive innings without a walk began with a Bubba and ended with a Bubba. During the streak, Fischer went 2-10, with one blown save and one no-decision. For the season, he walked only eight batters in 127⅔ innings.

As an aside, one must wonder whether it is sometimes better not to throw the ball over the plate. On May 24, 1964, Fischer, now pitching for the Twins, came on in relief with the score tied in the bottom of the ninth, two out, and a 3-0 count on Baltimore Orioles catcher Johnny Orsino. Fischer didn't walk him; instead, he threw a strike and then another good pitch that Orsino hit for a game-winning home run. Fischer went into the clubhouse, packed his bags, and never played again.

Bill Fischer, P, Kansas City Athletics, 1962

G	GS	CG	SHO	GF	SV	IP	H	BFP	HR	R	ER	BB	IB	SO	SH	SF	WP	HBP	BK	2B	3B	GDP	ROE	W	L	ERA	RS	P
34	16	5	0	6	2	127.2	150	533	16	61	56	8	2	38	7	5	2	1	0	23i	7	7i	6i	4	12	3.95	3.19	0.2

115

Hall of Famer Joe Sewell went from May 17 through September 19, 1929, without striking out: a span of 115 games. That season, Sewell struck out four times, an average of once every 144.5 at-bats.

Joe Sewell, SS, Cleveland Indians, 1929

G	AB	R	H	2B	3B	HR	RBI	BB	SO	HBP	SH	SB	CS	AVG	OBP	SLG	BFW
152	578	90	182	38	3	7	73	48	4	5	41	6	6	.315	.372	.427	2.4

50

On September 15, 1988, Vince Coleman of the St. Louis Cardinals singled leading off the game against Shane Rawley of the Philadelphia Phillies. With one down, Rawley picked him off, which goes down in the books as a caught-stealing. Three games later, Coleman drag-bunted for a hit, then stole second off Greg Maddux and catcher Jody Davis. It was Coleman's 76th stolen base of the season. He was successful on his final five attempts that year, finishing with 81 steals and 27 caught-stealings (a 75% success rate).

The following season, Coleman succeeded in his first 42 attempts. On July 26, 1989, Coleman stole second against the Chicago Cubs' Rick Sutcliffe in the third and the eighth innings, then immediately stole third against Sutcliffe's replacement, Steve Wilson. That gave Coleman 44 steals in 44 attempts and 50 in a row.

In his next game against the Montreal Expos on July 28, Coleman was thrown out trying to steal second by catcher Nelson Santovenia. Coleman's streak of 50 steals in a row had come to an end, but later in the game he stole third and scored the final run in the Cardinals' 2-0 victory. Coleman finished the season 65-for-75 (87%) in steal attempts.

Vince Coleman, OF, St. Louis Cardinals, 1989

G	AB	R	H	2B	3B	HR	RBI	BB	IBB	SO	HBP	SH	SF	XI	ROE	GDP	SB	CS	AVG	OBP	SLG	BFW
145	563	94	143	21	9	2	28	50	0	90	2	7	2	0	6	4	65	10	.254	.316	.334	-1.7

1,096

Cecil Fielder, nicknamed Big Daddy because he was 6'3" (at least), 240 pounds (at least), holds a dubious record for a streak that he was more than happy to see end.

On April 2, 1996, Fielder's Detroit Tigers were leading the Minnesota Twins 9-6, with Fielder on first after drawing a walk from Dan Naulty. With Melvin Nieves at the plate, manager Buddy Bell ordered a hit-and-run. Now, one of the bad things that can happen on such a play is that the batter swings and misses—which is exactly what Nieves did for strike three. What often happens under these circumstances is that the runner is thrown out attempting to steal, which is what had happened to Fielder five previous times in his career.

But this time, something odd occurred. Fielder lumbered toward second base. (To time Fielder in the 100-yard dash, you would use a calendar, not a stopwatch.) Twins catcher Greg Myers had more than enough time to nab him, and Myers' throw was on the mark. Too much on the mark; it nicked Fielder's helmet and bounded off the glove of shortstop Pat Meares.

Fielder was safe. His streak of 1,096 major

league games without a steal was over. After the game, he was presented with the base, a reminder that sometimes—rarely—crime does pay.

Cecil Fielder, 1B, 1985-1998

G	AB	R	H	2B	3B	HR	RBI	BB	IBB	SO	HBP	SH	SF	XI	ROE	GDP	SB	CS	AVG	OBP	SLG	BFW
1470	5157	744	1313	200	7	319	1008	693	76	1316	43	0	46	0	72	169	2	6	.255	.345	.482	6.6

As much as baseball is a team game, the closer's role is more like a goalie in soccer: Everybody knows when he stops a score and everybody knows when he allows one.

In baseball's current age of specialization, the closer is no longer a "short man" in the pen but one who closes the door on the opponents—tight. That's what Tom Gordon did for the Boston Red Sox, 54 times in a row, from April 19, 1998 to June 5, 1999.

Eric Gagné broke Gordon's record with something to spare. Pitching out of the Los Angeles Dodgers' bullpen, Gagné blew a save on Aug. 26, 2002, when David Dellucci of the Arizona Diamondbacks hit a game-tying double. The next save chance Gagné blew was when he came in to hold a 5-3 Dodgers lead, again against the Diamondbacks, on July 5, 2004. That's 84 consecutive save opportunities converted over a twenty-three-month period. In those 84 games, Gagné allowed 71 hits while striking out 207 batters for 55% of the outs he recorded. On top of that, 48% of the time he retired the minimum number of batters necessary to record the save. His ERA was 0.82, and he allowed no inherited runners to score. No wonder the Dodger scoreboard flashed "Game Over" when Gagné entered a game.

Pinch hitter Luis Gonzalez drove home the first run with a double and Chad Tracy drove home the game-tying, streak-busting run on an 0-2 single that eluded diving first baseman Olmedo Saenz.

As Jayson Stark of ESPN.com pointed out, during Gagné's streak, other relievers combined to blow 969 saves, and 28 of the blown saves were against the Dodgers. "I never really thought about the streak at all," Gagné told reporters. "I'm not really relieved about it, but it was fun to be a part of it."

Eric Gagne, P, 1999-Present

G	GS	CG	SHO	GF	SV	IP	H	BFP	HR	R	ER	BB	IB	SO	WP	HBP	BK	W	L	ERA
352	48	0	0	253	177	597.1	472	2461	65	240	220	204	11	680	23	15	17	29	23	3.31

On August 23, 1972, Jim Barr of the fifth-place San Francisco Giants faced the first-place Pittsburgh Pirates. Barr was a second-year pitcher with decent numbers and no indication that he would do something extraordinary. The way he started that day, there was nothing to indicate anything might be different at all.

In the second inning, he gave up singles to Willie Stargell and Milt May but left them stranded. In the top of the third, Barr walked the opposing pitcher, Bob Moose, but retired the next three batters. To be exact, he retired the next 21 batters, pitching seven perfect innings against the likes of Willie Stargell, Roberto Clemente, Richie Hebner and Bill Mazeroski. It was an outstanding 8-0 victory for the twenty-four-year old.

The next time out, Barr dueled with Reggie Cleveland of the Cardinals. St. Louis had hitters like Lou Brock, Joe Torre and Ted Simmons. The game was scoreless through six innings, and Barr was pitching a perfect game. By retiring Ted Sizemore for the second out in the seventh, he set a record for most consecutive batters retired with 41. Barr's streak ended when Bernie Carbo doubled with two down in the seventh.

In 2007, the Chicago White Sox' Bobby Jenks tied Barr's record by retiring 41 straight batters between July 19 and Aug. 20. Alas, in his next appearance, Jenks lost a six-pitch duel to his first batter, the Kansas City Royals' Joey Gathright, who singled.

Jim Barr, P, San Francisco Giants, 1972

G	GS	CG	SHO	GF	SV	IP	H	BFP	HR	R	ER	BB	IB	SO	SH	SF	WP	HBP	BK	2B	3B	GDP	ROE	W	L	ERA	RS	PW
44	18	8	2	13	2	179	166	732	16	66	57	41	8	86	9	5	1	3	1	21	7	11	12	8	10	2.87	3.50	1.3

Bobby Jenks, P, 2007

G	GS	CG	SHO	GF	SV	IP	H	BFP	HR	R	ER	BB	IB	SO	WP	HBP	BK	W	L	ERA
66	0	0	0	62	40	65	45	249	2	20	20	13	4	56	5	3	4	3	5	2.77

The National League and major league record for consecutive team wins is 26, set by the New York Giants in 1916. But the streak comes with an asterisk, because the Giants won 12 straight, then tied a game, then won another 14 in a row. If the asterisk disqualifies the Giants' claim, the Chicago Cubs hold the all-time record of 21 straight wins in 1935.

The American League record is another matter. In 2002, Art Howe's Oakland Athletics went on a streak that managers dream about—they won 19 straight games to tie the AL record shared by the 1906 Chicago White Sox and the 1947 New York Yankees.

On September 4, the A's hosted the Kansas City Royals before 55,528 deliriously excited fans, the largest regular-season crowd in Oakland history. All the fans wanted to do was celebrate their first-place team's defeat of the Royals, who were 29 games under .500. The streak up to then had been nerve-wracking. The A's won number 18 when Miguel Tejada hit a three-run walk-off homer against the Minnesota Twins to win, 7-5. Victory number 19 came when Tejada singled through a drawn-in infield in the ninth to beat Kansas City, 7-6.

The celebration started early as the A's beat up starter Paul Byrd by scoring six times in the first. By the end of the third they led, 11-0.

Nobody felt discouraged when the Royals bounced back with five in the fourth inning. In fact, 11-5 was the score entering the eighth inning. Then the Royals did a funny thing—not funny ha-ha, but funny scary. They scored five more times in the eighth to make it 11-10. In the ninth, Royal Luis Alicea singled off A's closer Billy Koch and the game was tied.

Much as it felt like Mudville after the A's Jermaine Dye flew out to right to start the home half of the ninth, it did not turn out to be. Pinch hitting for Eric Byrnes, Scott Hatteberg sent Jason Grimsley's second pitch deep into the right-center field stands. For the third straight game, the A's had a walk-off victory, this one for a record 20-straight wins.

There were no histrionics, no gatherings at home plate, no dancing around the base paths on Friday, September 6, 2002, in Minnesota. Brad Radke and the Twins, quickly and efficiently, dispatched the A's, 6-0. The winning streak was over.

Wednesday, September 4, 2002
Network Associates Coliseum

BATTING

Kansas City Royals	AB	R	H	RBI	BB	SO	PO	A
Tucker rf	5	0	2	2	0	3	1	0
Beltran cf	4	0	0	1	0	2	3	0
Sweeney 1b	5	1	3	3	0	0	5	2
Ibanez lf	5	1	2	0	0	1	2	0
Randa 3b	5	1	3	0	0	0	0	0
Pellow pr,3b	0	1	0	0	0	0	0	0
Mayne c	3	2	1	0	1	0	10	0
Brown dh	4	2	1	2	1	2	0	0
Perez ss	4	2	2	1	0	0	1	1
Alicea ph,ss	1	0	1	1	0	0	0	0
Ordaz 2b	4	1	0	1	0	0	1	2
Byrd p	0	0	0	0	0	0	0	0
May p	0	0	0	0	0	0	2	1
Stein p	0	0	0	0	0	0	0	0
Affeldt p	0	0	0	0	0	0	0	0
Grimsley p	0	0	0	0	0	0	0	0
Totals	40	11	15	11	2	8	25	6

FIELDING -
E: Ibanez (3).
BATTING -
2B: Tucker 2 (23,off Hudson 2).
HR: Sweeney (20,8th inning off Tam 2 on 2 out).
SH: Mayne (4,off Koch).
SF: Beltran (5,off Rincon).
Team LOB: 6.
BASERUNNING -
CS: Alicea (3,3rd base by Koch/Hernandez).

Oakland Athletics	AB	R	H	RBI	BB	SO	PO	A
Durham dh	5	2	2	0	0	1	0	0
Mabry 1b	5	2	2	0	0	0	10	1
Tejada ss	4	1	1	0	0	1	2	6
Chavez 3b	5	2	3	0	3	0	3	3
Dye rf	5	1	1	1	0	2	1	0
Justice lf	4	1	0	0	1	0	0	0
Byrnes lf	0	0	0	0	0	0	0	0
Hatteberg ph	1	1	1	1	0	0	0	0
Ellis 2b	3	1	1	2	0	1	5	4
Long cf	3	1	2	0	1	0	1	0
Hernandez c	4	1	2	2	0	0	8	0
Hudson p	0	0	0	0	0	0	0	1
Bradford p	0	0	0	0	0	0	0	0
Rincon p	0	0	0	0	0	0	0	0
Tam p	0	0	0	0	0	0	0	0
Bowie p	0	0	0	0	0	0	0	0
Koch p	0	0	0	0	0	0	0	1
Totals	39	12	15	11	1	9	27	16

FIELDING -
DP: 1. Ellis-Tejada-Mabry.
E: Tejada (19).
BATTING -
2B: Long 2 (30,off Byrd,off Stein); Hernandez 2 (18,off Byrd,off May); Justice (18,off May).
3B: Durham (6,off Byrd); Dye (1,off Byrd).
HR: Mabry (10,2nd inning off May 0 on 0 out); Hatteberg (13,9th inning off Grimsley 0 on 1 out).
SF: Ellis (3,off Byrd).
HBP: Tejada (11,by Byrd).
Team LOB: 5.

PITCHING

Kansas City Royals	IP	H	R	ER	BB	SO	HR
Byrd	1	6	6	6	0	1	0
May	5	6	5	5	1	6	1
Stein	1	1	0	0	0	1	0
Affeldt	0.2	0	0	0	0	0	0
Grimsley L(3-6)	0.2	2	1	1	0	1	1
Totals	8.1	15	12	12	1	9	2

HBP: Byrd (6,Tejada).

Oakland Athletics	IP	H	R	ER	BB	SO	HR
Hudson	6.2	11	5	2	0	6	0
Bradford	0.1	1	4	4	2	0	0
Rincon	0.2	0	0	0	0	1	0
Tam	1	1	1	1	0	0	1
Bowie	0.1	0	0	0	0	0	0
Koch W(9-2)	1	2	1	1	0	1	0
Totals	9	15	11	8	2	8	1

Bradford faced 4 batters in the 8th inning
WP: Koch (4).

Umpires: Chuck Meriwether, Ted Barrett, Brian Runge, Tim McClelland

Time of Game: 3:38 **Attendance:** 55528

	1	2	3	4	5	6	7	8	9	R	H	E
KC A	0	0	0	5	0	0	0	5	1	11	15	1
OAK A	6	1	4	0	0	0	0	0	1	12	15	1

On Sunday, September 20, 1998, Cal Ripken, Jr. took the day off. For most, one day off is no big deal; but for Ripken, it was his first day off in 16 years—2,632 games to be exact.

The folks who attended the game that evening at Camden Yards expected to see Ripken at third, just as they had seen him for many years, earlier in his career, at shortstop. But with one week left in the season, Ripken felt the time was right. Over three years had gone by since he had broken Lou Gehrig's "unbreakable" streak of 2,130 straight games on September 6, 1995.

"I was going to take the last day of the season off in Boston, but I thought about it a long time and decided if this is going to end, let it end where it started, in Baltimore," the thirty-eight-year-old Ripken said after the game (a 5-4 victory by the New York Yankees). Ripken had gone hitless in his last 12 at-bats. For the year he was hitting .273 with 14 home runs and 61 RBIs when the streak ended.

Fortunately, Ripken was healthy and uninjured, but with the Orioles only playing out the season, he decided to end the streak that began a generation before on May 30, 1982. Rookie Ryan Minor, who started in Ripken's place on the day the streak ended, had been eight years old when Ripken began his incredible run.

Ripken had been a rookie, batting eighth and playing third base in a game against Toronto. On June 5, Ripken played the first of 8,243 consecutive innings, spanning 904 games. When the season ended, Ripken had played in 118 games and was named the American League Rookie of the Year. On September 14, 1987, Ripken's record-setting, consecutive innings streak ended in Toronto when manager Cal Ripken, Sr. replaced him with Ron Washington in the bottom of the eighth inning. The Blue Jays won, 18-3.

On September 5, 1995, Ripken tied Lou Gehrig's record of 2,130 consecutive games played. In the bottom of the fifth, when the game became official, Ripken received a standing ovation of more than five minutes from a sellout crowd at Camden Yards. In the sixth inning, he homered.

On September 6, 1995, Ripken homered in the fourth inning. When the game became official, he was the record holder. There was a twenty-two-minute ovation for Ripken at Camden Yards. During that ovation, he took a lap around the ballpark, shaking hands and receiving the warm wishes of his adoring fans.

On the night the streak ended, it was the opposing team, the New York Yankees, who stood on the dugout steps and applauded the future Hall of Famer. Ripken emerged from the Orioles dugout, tipped his hat toward the Yankees, and stepped back down to the bench. He then re-emerged and bowed to the cheering fans.

Ripken played 86 games in 1999 and 83 games in 2000. His final game was played on October 1, 2001, and ended with him waiting in the on-deck circle.

Cal Ripken, Jr., SS, 1981-2001

G	AB	R	H	2B	3B	HR	RBI	BB	IBB	SO	HBP	SH	SF	XI	ROE	GDP	SB	CS	AVG	OBP	SLG	BFW
3001	11551	1647	3184	603	44	431	1695	1129	107	1305	66	10	127	0	176	350	36	39	.276	.340	.447	43.0

Stadiums

Crosley Field, Cincinnati, OH.

When a team leaves a cherished stadium, regret and nostalgia languish in its wake. Plenty of great parks have been deemed outmoded and torn down: Shibe Park, Old Comiskey and Ebbets Field, for openers. A cause for sadness? Sure. On the other hand, the cookie-cutter, artificial-turf fields that opened in Philadelphia, Cincinnati, Pittsburgh and St. Louis in the 1960s and '70s were so reviled from the start that their eventual abandonment was cause for celebration. When the New York Mets' uncreative and noisy Shea Stadium is buried under rubble in a few years, Mets fans will dance on its grave.

Atlanta   Atlanta-Fulton County Stadium

In Game 5 of the 1996 World Series, the New York Yankees beat the Atlanta Braves, 1-0. The only run scored when Cecil Fielder doubled home Charlie Hayes. John Wetteland recorded Atlanta-Fulton County Stadium's final out and final save by getting Luis Polonia on a fly to right fielder Paul O'Neill. Andy Pettitte got the win and John Smoltz took the loss. The day before, Jim Leyritz hit a three-run, game-tying home run in the eighth inning for the ballpark's last home run.

The Braves played their last regular-season home game there on September 23, when the Braves' Greg Maddux beat the Montreal Expos' Al Leiter, 3-1. David Segui got the last hit, Moises Alou made the last out, and Mike Bielecki picked up the save. The day before, John Smoltz and Marquis Grissom went back-to-back for the last regular-season home runs at the stadium.

The ballpark was imploded on August 2, 1997.

Atlanta-Fulton County Stadium (1966-1997)

Opened for MLB...... 1966
Team.......................... Atlanta Braves
Turf............................ Natural
Fences....................... 325-L. 402-C, 325-R (original)
                                 330-L, 402-C, 330-R (final)
Capacity .... 50,893 (original)
                                 52,900 (final)

Baltimore   Memorial Stadium

Since he played more regularly than anyone, it was somehow fitting that Cal Ripken, Jr. was the last batter at Baltimore's Memorial Stadium. He hit into a round-the-horn double play against the Detroit Tigers' Frank Tanana on October 6, 1991. With this disappointing at-bat, Ripken finished what was perhaps the best season of his career, hitting .323 with 210 hits, 34 home runs, 144 RBI, 368 total bases and just 46 strikeouts. He was both the American League's Most Valuable Player and the All-Star MVP, and he won the All-Star Game Home Run Derby.

The first-place Tigers won the final game 7-1, with Frank Tanana throwing a complete game. Mike Flanagan pitched the last inning for the Orioles and retired the final batters 1-2-3. It was also Ernie Harwell's "last" Tigers broadcast...before he returned two years later. A total of 51,268,097 fans saw five World Series, six no-hitters, 4,743 home runs and 23,471 runs in 27,727 innings. The Orioles' record at Memorial was 1,706 wins, 1,321 losses, and nine ties. After the final game, more than 100 Orioles legends bid adieu to "the Grand Old Lady of 33rd Street," and transplanted home plate to its new location at Camden Yards—the ballpark that set the stage for the great ballpark Renaissance.

Out with the beloved old, in with the even more beloved new.

Memorial Stadium (1950-1991)

Opened for MLB...... 1954
Team.......................... Baltimore Orioles
Turf............................ Natural
Fences....................... 309-L, 410-C, 309-R (original)
                                 309-L, 405-C, 309-R (final)
Capacity .... 20,000 (original)
                                 54,000 (final)

Boston _____ Braves Field

In 1953, the Boston Braves moved to Milwaukee—understandably, given that on September 21, 1952, the Braves played their last home game ever before a crowd of 8,822 for their second-largest draw of the season. Granted, the team didn't officially announce its move to Milwaukee until the following spring, but during that last Boston season, the Braves failed to attract 500,000 fans.

In the final game, they fell to Joe Black and the Brooklyn Dodgers, 8-2. Jackie Robinson recorded the last hit and Roy Campanella the last home run.

Jim Wilson took the loss for the Braves; the Dodgers' Andy Pafko recorded the final out on a Walker Cooper fly ball.

Braves Field (1915 -1952)
Opened for MLB...... 1915
Team........................ Boston Braves
Turf.......................... Natural
Fences...................... 402-L, 550-C, 402-R (original)
Capacity 42,000

Brooklyn _____ Washington Park

On October 5, 1912, the Brooklyn Superbas (soon to become the Trolley Dodgers, or simply, the Dodgers) lost 1-0 to the New York Giants. Pat Ragan took the loss. After the Dodgers moved to Ebbets Field the following season, the Brooklyn Federals (or Tip-Tops) of the Federal League used the park.

Washington Park (1898 -1912)
Opened for MLB...... 1898
Team........................ Brooklyn Superbas
Turf.......................... Natural
Fences...................... 335-L, 445-C, 215-R (original)
　　　　　　　　　　　 300-L, 400-C, 275-R (final)
Capacity 18,000

The last batter at Ebbets Field was Dee Fondy of the Pirates, who grounded out to shortstop Don Zimmer. The last putout was recorded by first baseman Gil Hodges, who was also the last Brooklyn Dodger to record a RBI and at-bat. Hodges struck out swinging.

On February 23, 1960, about 200 people gathered to watch the demolition of Ebbets Field. Lucy Monroe, who often sang the National Anthem during the season, did so on this day as well. Bricks were later sold for a dollar; flowerpots were sold with infield soil for a quarter. The cornerstone was sold to Warren Giles, the National League president, who donated it to the Hall of Fame. Roy Campanella was given an urn of dirt from behind home plate.

The same wrecking ball was used again four years later to demolish the Polo Grounds, in Manhattan. Now there are apartments on the former site of Ebbets Field, and a school that was once known as Crown Heights Intermediate School. Its assistant principal at the time, Marty Adler, successfully campaigned to have it renamed the Jackie Robinson School after Robinson's death in 1972.

Brooklyn-born Bob Aspromonte can claim his distinguished place in history as the last active member of the Brooklyn Dodgers. He finished his career with the New York Mets on September 28, 1971. At age eighteen, Aspro had one at-bat with the 1956 Dodgers and struck out; he returned to the Dodgers in Los Angeles in 1960 after spending time in the minor leagues. A third baseman, Aspromonte was one of the original expansion-draft picks made by the Houston Colt .45s after the 1961 season.

In his last game, Aspromonte went 0-for-3 with a sacrifice fly against the St. Louis Cardinals' Steve Carlton, who won his 20th game of the season. Nolan Ryan lost his 14th game that day; he started and faced five batters in the first inning, giving up three runs on one hit and four walks. It was Carlton's last appearance as a member of the Cardinals and Ryan's last appearance as a Met.

Ebbets Field (1913–1957)

Opened for MLB...... 1913
Team........................ Brooklyn Dodgers
Turf........................... Natural
Fences...................... 419-L, 450-C, 301-R (original)
348-L, 393-C, 297-R (final)
Capacity .... 23,000 (original)
32,000 (final)

Last Lick

Born in Van Nuys, California, Don Drysdale was the last active Brooklyn Dodger still playing with the Dodgers when he bowed out on August 5, 1969, pitching six innings and allowing eight hits and three runs, two earned. The last batter Drysdale hit was Al Oliver.

The Chicago White Sox beat the Seattle Mariners 2-1 on September 30, 1990. All the Sox' scoring occurred in the sixth inning, the winning run coming when Lance Johnson tripled, Frank Thomas singled him home, and Thomas scored on a triple by Dan Pasqua.

Designed primarily by architect Zachary Taylor Davis, White Sox Park, also known as Old Comiskey Park, opened in 1910. Offering input were owner Charles Comiskey and pitcher Ed Walsh, which explained the odd dimensions: 362 feet down each line and 420 feet to straight-away center field. During the life of the park, 72,801,381 fans saw some very exciting (and some not-so-exciting) baseball.

The Mariners' Harold Reynolds grounded out to end the game against Bobby Thigpen, who notched the save. Jack McDowell was the winning pitcher, and Rich DeLucia went the distance to take the loss for the Mariners.

The last home run was hit by the Mariners' Alvin Davis on Sept. 29, and the last grand slam was hit by Davis the day before.

Comiskey Park (1910-1990)

Opened for MLB...... 1910
Team......................... Chicago White Sox
Turf.......................... Natural (1910-1968)
　　　　　　　　　　　Artificial (1969)
　　　　　　　　　　　Natural (1970-1990)
Fences...................... 363-L, 420-C, 363-R (original)
　　　　　　　　　　　347-L, 409-C, 347-R (final)
Capacity .... 28,800 (original)
　　　　　　　　　　　43,951 (final)

On Sunday, September 28, 1969, 28,018 fans showed up at Crosley Field to watch the Cincinnati Reds' "final" game at this unique old ballpark. The Reds beat the Houston Astros 4-1, and Wayne Granger recorded the last out by getting Norm Miller to fly out to Pete Rose in right field. The only problem was that it wasn't the last game. Delays in construction of the new Riverfront Stadium forced the Reds to remain in Crosley until their actual last game there on June 24, 1970.

They say that everything works out for the best, and this was certainly true for Reds fans who saw a classic in the final, *final* game at Crosley Field. Jon McGlothlin started against San Francisco Giants great Juan Marichal. The Giants took an early 4-2 lead, and they were still on top 4-3 heading into the bottom of the eighth. Johnny Bench led off the inning, and tied the game with a home run. Next up, first baseman Lee May. With the call are Reds radio announcers Jim McIntyre and Joe Nuxhall.

McIntyre: *Johnny Bench's home run has just tied it at 4-4, and Mr. Marichal has now allowed the Reds nine hits, and we've got a brand-new ball game here in the eighth inning. Two and two to May. On deck, Bernie Carbo...Now the pitch. Swung on, a high drive, deep center field!*

Nuxhall shouted: *Get outta here, outta here, babe get outta here! I tell ya, out, out, outta here!*

McIntyre finished: *...it's over the center-field fence!*

A home run for Lee May! And the Reds have taken the lead, 5-4.

That was the score when the Giants batted in the ninth. Hal Lanier and Bob Taylor both grounded out, Darrel Cheney to Lee May. The next batter Bobby Bonds bounced back to pitcher Wayne Granger, who threw to May, and the Reds had a memorable 5-4 win. The winning pitcher, with two perfect innings to end the game, was Granger.

In the last game, the final single was recorded by the Giants' Tito Fuentes, the last double by the Reds' Bernie Carbo, the last triple by Pete Rose, and of course, the last home run by Lee May.

During the closing ceremonies, Cincinnati Mayor Gene Ruehlmann lifted home plate out of the Crosley Field ground and transported it by helicopter to the artificial turf of Riverfront Stadium. The last fan to leave Crosley Field was one Frank O'Toole, an everyman and lifelong fan of the Reds.

Crosley Field (1912-1970)

Opened for MLB...... 1912
Team......................... Cincinnati Reds
Turf............................ Natural
Fences....................... 360-L, 420-C, 360-R (original)
                                        328-L, 387-C, 366-R (final)
Capacity .... 20,000 (original)
                                        29,400 (final)

Some farewells are restrained and pay proper homage to the ballpark's history. The last game at Riverfront Stadium was played on September 22, 2002, when the Cincinnati Reds lost to the Philadelphia Phillies 4-3 before 40,964 fans. Loyal to a fault, the fans applauded the banned but cherished Pete Rose in pregame ceremonies. A total of 64,650,553 attended 2,572 games over 32 seasons. The Reds' record was 1,412 wins, 1,159 losses, and four ties. Johnny Bench's 154 home runs at Riverfront were the most by any player.

Todd Walker hit into a routine 4-3 groundout for the last out. Aaron Boone hit the last home run (Hank Aaron hit the first), Jason Michaels got the last hit, and Brandon Duckworth picked up the final win, with Jose Rijo taking the loss. Following the game, the Reds grounds crew, dressed in tuxedos, dug up home plate while fifty-two former Reds greats watched. The plate was then transported by "The Big Red Machine," a Zamboni used to dry the artificial turf field at Riverfront. With Cincinnati police escort, the plate arrived at the Reds' new stadium—the Great American Ball Park, right next door.

"They can tear it down but they can't take it away from me," Sparky Anderson, who managed the Big Red Machine teams of the 1970s, told the Cincinnati *Enquirer.* "I'll never forget."

Riverfront Stadium was demolished on December 29, 2002, and the site is now part of the Great American Ball Park.

Riverfront Stadium (1970-2002)

Opened for MLB...... 1970
Team......................... Cincinnati Reds
Turf........................... Astroturf (original)
Natural (final)
Fences...................... 330-L, 404-C, 330-R (original)
325-L, 393-C, 325-R (final)
Capacity .... 52,952 (original)
40,008 (final)

Cleveland _____ League Park II

The Cleveland Indians lost to the Detroit Tigers 5-3 in 11 innings on September 21, 1946. A gathering of 2,772 saw Jack Conway line into a double play to end the game. Gene Woodling hit the last single, Dizzy Trout picked up the final win, and Joe Berry took the loss. Dick Wakefield hit the last home run at League Park II on Sept. 20, and Ted Williams got the last inside-the-park home run on Sept. 13.

The Indians often played games at both Municipal Stadium and League Park, because League Park was the only ballpark in major league baseball to never install lights before it was torn down.

League Park II (1910-1946)

Opened for MLB...... 1910
Team......................... Cleveland Indians
Turf........................... Natural
Fences...................... 375-L, 420-C, 290 (240)-R
Capacity 21,414

Municipal Stadium

On October 3, 1993, the Cleveland Indians lost to the Chicago White Sox, 4-0. Winning pitcher Jason Bere went seven innings, and Charles Nagy started and lost for the Tribe. Drew Denson's single in the top of the eighth was the last hit in "The Mistake by the Lake"—otherwise known as Municipal Stadium.

Jose DeLeon pitched the final inning for the White Sox and hit leadoff batter Sam Horn. Manny Ramirez came in to run for Horn, but Ramirez was wiped out when Jeff Treadway hit into a double play.

Mark Lewis struck out to close the ballpark forever.

Cleveland Municipal Stadium (1931-1993)

Opened for MLB...... 1931
Team......................... Cleveland Indians
Turf........................... Natural
Fences...................... 322-L, 470-C, 322-R (original)
320-L, 404-C, 320-R (final)
Capacity .... 78,000 (original)
74,483 (final)

Denver _____ Mile High Stadium

On August 11, 1994, the Atlanta Braves defeated the Colorado Rockies 11-0 in front of 65,043 fans. Not only did Greg Maddux go all the way, pitching a three-hit shutout, but he also drove home the final run with a single in the ninth inning. Lance Painter was the starter and losing pitcher for the Rockies; Atlanta's David Justice hit the last home run.

The book was closed on Mile High Stadium when Maddux got Dante Bichette to ground out, third to first. Bichette had stolen the last base on Aug. 9, and he hit the last grand slam on July 17.

Mile High Stadium (1948-1994)
Opened for MLB...... 1993
Team......................... Colorado Rockies
Turf........................... Natural
Fences...................... 335-L, 420-C, 370-R
Capacity 76,098

Detroit _____ Bennett Park

The Detroit Tigers beat the Cleveland Indians 2-1 in 13 innings before 8,756 fans on September 10, 1911. Bill Donovan started and went the distance for the winners, while Fred Blanding went all the way and took the loss.

Jim Delahanty, who reached on an error, was the last batter, and Ty Cobb got the last hit (he also hit the last grand slam on May 13). Nap Lajoie registered the last RBI, and Jack Coombs hit the last home run on August 29.

Bennett Park (1896-1911)
Opened for MLB...... 1901
Team......................... Detroit Tigers
Turf........................... Natural
Fences...................... 308-L, 390-C, 324-R (original)
                              285-L, 390-C, 324-R (final)
Capacity .... 5,000 (original)
                              11,000 (final)

_____ Tiger Stadium

Prior to the 6,873rd and final game at Detroit's Tiger Stadium, on September 27, 1999, Hall of Famers Al Kaline of the Tigers and George Brett of the Kansas City Royals brought out the lineup cards. Introduced to the crowd by Ernie Harwell, Kaline bit his lip and swallowed before speaking:

While common materials may have been used to build this place—concrete, steel and bricks—the memories are the cement that held it together for 86 wonderful seasons…Is it a specific game that you will remember most about Tiger Stadium? Maybe Ty Cobb sliding hard into third. George Kell diving to his left. Norm Cash or Kirk Gibson blasting one into the lights in right field. Or will it be a memory of your family and friends, sharing a story with your best buddy or listening closely as your dad tells you of the first time he came to the park years ago?

Author Tom Stanton, who attended all 81 home games in 1999, in his book *The Final Season* said:

This ballpark challenges the notion that you can never go home again. For no matter how my life has evolved and how many years have passed and how far my hairline has shifted, I feel like a kid when I come here. This place awakens those spirits and allows me to reclaim parts of myself that otherwise might be lost.

In the spirit of the occasion, the 1999 Tigers took the field wearing the numbers of old greats. Brian Moehler pitched in Jack Morris' 47. Tony Clark patrolled first in Hank Greenberg's 5, and Damion Easley carried Charlie Gehringer's number 2. Rookie Gabe Kapler, wearing Cobb's numberless uniform, stole a base. Karim Garcia, in Kaline's 6, hit a home run.

The signs in the stands read, "So long old girl," "This will always be home," "Baseball cries today." Most of the 43,356 fans were standing (the attendance for the final season was 2,026,441), many with tears flowing down their cheeks. Here's Harwell's call of the last out at 7:07 P.M.:

Tigers lead it 8-2. Two down in the ninth inning. Jones is ready. He delivers. Here's a swing and a miss. The game is over, and Tiger Stadium is no more.

Detroit's Todd Jones threw the last pitch, striking out Carlos Beltran. Moehler was the winning pitcher, while Jeff Suppan took the loss. The Tigers' Rob Fick hit the last grand slam. But the best part of the show was just beginning. Unannounced, familiar Tigers of old emerged onto the center field bluegrass and took their former positions: pitcher Mickey Lolich (stirring memories of his heroics in the 1968 World Series), center fielder Ron LeFlore (much heavier now), left fielder Willie Horton (weeping), shortstop Alan Trammel and second baseman Lou Whitaker (the brilliant double-play combination who stayed together a record 19 seasons), Mark Fidrych (falling to his knees to take a sample from the pitcher's mound), as well as old-timers few had seen actually play, like Elden Auker and Billy Rogell, all with the Old English "D" on their ballcaps.

"What got me is that some of the former players walked and ran exactly the way they did when they played," Joe Falls recalled in the Detroit *News*. "Like pitcher Billy Hoeft when he approached the pitching mound and Steve Kemp when he ran from center field to left field. That was incredible."

They handed the Tiger flag, one to another, all the way to home, where Auker told current catcher Brad Ausmus, "Each of us has touched this flag today as Tiger Stadium has touched each of us. Take this flag to Comerica Park, your new home."

Tiger Stadium (1912-1999)

Opened for MLB	1912
Team	Detroit Tigers
Turf	Natural
Fences	345-L, 467-C, 370-R (original)
	340-L, 440-C, 325-R (final)
Capacity	23,000 (original)
	52,400 (final)

Houston _____ Colt Stadium

On September 27, 1964, the old ballpark did not die easily. It took 12 innings before the Houston Colts .45s defeated the Los Angeles Dodgers 1-0 before 6,246 fans. Bob Bruce pitched all 12 innings for Houston, limiting the Dodgers to five hits. Don Drysdale went the first 10 for the Dodgers, and Ron Perranoski took the loss.

In the 12th, Houston's Joe Morgan led off with an infield single. Attempting to bunt him over, Rusty Staub forced him at second. The next batter Walt Bond bounced back to the mound and Staub advanced to second. After Bob Aspromonte, who hit the stadium's last grand slam on June 29, 1964, walked intentionally, Jimmy Wynn singled home Staub for the victory.

The Dodgers' Tommy Davis hit the last double in this game and the day before hit the last home run and the last sacrifice fly.

Colt Stadium (1962-1964)

Opened for MLB	1962
Team	Houston Colt .45's
Turf	Natural
Fences	400-L, 450-C, 400-R
Capacity	33,000

On October 3, 1999, the Houston Astros beat the Los Angeles Dodgers 9-4 and clinched Houston's third straight National League Central crown. Mike Hampton (22-4) was the winning pitcher, and rookie Robinson Checo took the loss after allowing four runs on five walks and Darryl Ward's bases-loaded, bases-clearing double in the first inning. The game was played before 52,033 fans who saw Ken Caminiti hit the last home run in the Astrodome.

The Dodgers scored three runs in the ninth, just to drag out the excitement, but Raul Mondesi struck out to kick off the Astros' celebration, the Astrodome's celebration, and a Willie Nelson concert.

The last time the Astros played at the Dome was Game 4 of the National League Division Series on Saturday, Oct. 9, 1999, when the Atlanta Braves defeated Houston, 7-5. John Smoltz was the winning pitcher, Shane Reynolds the loser.

The Astros had the tying run at the plate in the ninth after Stan Javier worked a walk off John Rocker. Rocker threw a wild pitch and Javier advanced to second. But both Jeff Bagwell and Carl Everett struck out before Ken Caminiti, who had hit the last home run earlier in the game, closed the "Eighth Wonder of the World" with a flyout to center.

The Astrodome (1965-1999)

Opened for MLB...... 1965
Team......................... Houston Astros
Turf........................... Tifway Bermuda Grass (1965)
Artificial (1966-1999)
Fences....................... 340-L, 406-C, 340-R (original)
325-L, 375-C, 325-R (final)
Capacity .... 42,217 (original)
54,816 (final)

Jersey City — Roosevelt Stadium

While the Brooklyn Dodgers let the mayor of New York know that Ebbets Field was not a suitable environ, they played a total of 14 home games in 1956 and '57 at Roosevelt Stadium in Jersey City, New Jersey. Though the capacity of the art-deco Roosevelt was smaller than Ebbets Field, the parking was significantly better. Primarily a minor league ballpark, it was the site where Jackie Robinson made his first appearance in 1946 as a member of the Montreal Royals.

In the Dodgers' last game at Roosevelt, on September 3, 1957, the Philadelphia Phillies defeated them in 12 innings, 3-2. When Elmer Valo struck out to end the game, Dick Farrell picked up the win and Don Drysdale took the loss. Chico Fernandez scored the winning run on a triple and a sacrifice fly by Willie Jones. Harry Anderson hit the last single and home run.

Roosevelt Stadium (1937-1985)

Opened for MLB...... 1956
Team......................... Brooklyn Dodgers
Turf........................... Natural
Fences....................... 330-L, 411-C, 330-R
Capacity 24,000

Kansas City ———————————————————————————— Municipal Stadium

The Kansas City Monarchs of the Negro leagues played at Municipal Stadium until 1955; the Kansas City Athletics played there until September 27, 1967, when they swept a doubleheader from the Chicago White Sox. Despite that sweep, the A's finished in last place with a record of 62-99 and lost 30 of their last 40 games. Catfish Hunter pitched a 4-0 shutout in the nightcap before 5,325 fans.

The ballpark's last game was on October 4, 1972, when the innagural Royals franchise defeated the Texas Rangers, 4-0. Roger Nelson pitched the complete-game shutout, and Don Stanhouse took the loss. Ted Ford lined out to center fielder Joe Keough for the final out, while Ed Kirkpatrick's single was the last hit. Gene Tenace had hit the last home run on Sept. 30.

Municipal Stadium was demolished in 1976, and the site is now a community garden.

Municipal Stadium (1923-1972)
Opened for MLB...... 1955
Team......................... Kansas City Athletics, Kansas City Royals
Turf........................... Natural
Fences....................... 312-L, 430-C, 347-R (original) 369-L, 421-C, 338-R (final)
Capacity .... 17,500 (original) 30,611 (final)

Last Lick

It may be difficult to picture Hall of Fame outfielder Reggie Jackson in Kansas City, but Mr. October started his career with owner Charlie Finley and the Kansas City Athletics in June of 1967. He spent his rookie season there.

Los Angeles ———————————————————————————— Los Angeles Coliseum

On September 20, 1961, the Los Angeles Dodgers beat the Chicago Cubs 3-2 in 13 innings, with Ron Fairly hitting a walk-off single to drive home Wally Moon. Winning pitcher Sandy Koufax threw a complete game and struck out 15 Cubs. Barney Schultz took the loss.

Los Angeles Coliseum (1932-Present)
Opened for MLB...... 1958
Team......................... Los Angeles Dodgers
Turf........................... Natural
Fences....................... 250-L, 425-C, 301-R (original) 252-L, 420-C, 300-R (final)
Capacity 92,572

———————————————————————————— Wrigley Field (LA)

In the California Angels' first season, they played at Wrigley Field in Los Angeles. In their final game there on October 1, 1961, before 9,868 fans, the Cleveland Indians beat the Angels, 8-5. Both starters were involved in the decision when Jim (Mudcat) Grant defeated Ryne Duren. Grant went the distance for the win, retiring George Thomas on a grounder to short, Jack Kubiszyn to Hal Jones, for the final out. With two outs in the ninth, local legend Steve Bilko pinch hit for Tom Satriano and hit the last home run at Wrigley. The Indians' Walt Bond fell one double short of the cycle, going 4-for-5, including a grand slam.

Wrigley Field (LA) (1961)
Opened for MLB...... 1961
Team......................... Los Angeles Angels
Turf........................... Natural
Fences....................... 340-L, 412-C, 339-R
Capacity 20,457

Chavez Ravine (Dodger Stadium of the American League)

The Los Angeles Dodgers were very possessive of their territory and particularly their new ballpark, Dodger Stadium. So when the Dodgers were at home, they played at Dodger Stadium, but when the American League California Angels played there, in the same park, it was known by its location: Chavez Ravine.

On September 22, 1965, the Angels ended their rental by playing a doubleheader against the Boston Red Sox before 3,353 fans. The Angels won the first game 10-1. In the second game, George Brunet of the Angels shut out the Red Sox 2-0 with Jerry Stephenson taking the loss. Angels bonus baby Rick Reichardt recorded the last hit (he also hit the last home run on September 15), while the Sox' Tony Conigliaro made the final out, grounding out, third baseman Paul Schall to Vic Power at first.

Chavez Ravine (1962-Present)
Opened for MLB...... 1962
Team......................... Los Angeles Angels
Turf............................ Natural
Fences........................ 330-L, 400-C, 330-R
Capacity 56,000

Milwaukee

Once known as the Boston Braves, the Milwaukee Braves moved to Atlanta following the 1965 season. Fans knew throughout the season that this was to be the final year for the Braves in Milwaukee, and they stayed away from County Stadium in droves, racking up only 555,584 in season attendance—including 12,577 for the final home game on September 12. Frank Clines of the Milwaukee *Journal Sentinel* wrote that while there were plenty of candidates for "Best Night at County Stadium," there was no contest as to which was the worst: the night the Milwaukee Braves played their final home game.

Their opponent was Sandy Koufax and the soon-to-be-World-Champion Los Angeles Dodgers. Koufax had little stuff that night, and by the time he left in the third inning, having given up five runs on a grand slam by Frank Bolling and a solo homer by Mack Jones, he bore little resemblance to a man on the way to his first Cy Young Award. This game had a little bit of everything, including a Gene Oliver inside-the-park home run that gave the Braves a 6-1 lead.

A Dodgers comeback tied it up in the fifth. The

County Stadium (Milwaukee Braves)

score remained tied in the eighth, when the fans gave Eddie Mathews, the last remaining Brave from Opening Day, 1953, a standing ovation.

"I'm not ordinarily a sentimental guy, but this really shook me up," Mathews said.

Like the first game at County Stadium, the last one went into extra innings. The Dodgers went ahead 7-6 in the top of the 11th, and in the bottom of the inning the Braves got the tying run on base when Mack Jones' one-out infield single became the last hit at the stadium. The next batter, Hank Aaron, lined out to center fielder Willie Davis, and Jones was then doubled off first to give the Dodgers and Ron Perranoski the win and Chi-Chi Olivo the loss.

County Stadium (1953-2000)
Opened for MLB...... 1953
Team......................... Milwaukee Braves, Milwaukee Brewers
Turf............................ Natural
Fences........................ 320-L, 404-C, 320-R (original)
                      315-L, 402-C, 315-R (final)
Capacity .... 28,111 (original)
                      53,192 (final)

County Stadium (Milwaukee Brewers)

The Milwaukee Brewers' last game at County Stadium was on September 28, 2000. While the Brew Crew did not desert the city, after playing in the American League from their 1970 inception to their final game in 1997, they had moved to the National League in 1998.

So it was a National League game that closed the park before 56,354 fans. The Brewers faced the

Cincinnati Reds, and Hall of Fame pitcher Warren Spahn, who threw the first pitch (for the Braves) when the stadium opened, came back to toss the ceremonial first pitch.

The Reds won the finale 8-1, with winning pitcher Elmer Dessens retiring the Brewers' Mark Loretta on a groundout to shortstop Juan Castro. The Reds' Michael Tucker got an infield single in the eighth for the last hit, and the Reds' Sean Casey hit the last home run in the fifth (the last of 5,807 dingers at the ballpark). Jeff D'Amico took the loss.

A total of 64,865,253 watched baseball at County Stadium for 1,023 Braves games and 2,433 Brewers games.

The last Sausage Race winner was the Bratwurst.

Last Lick

Phil Niekro played his last game on September 27, 1987, as a member of the Atlanta Braves. He played his first game on April 15, 1964, pitching for the Milwaukee Braves. When he and his 318 wins retired, so did the last active member of the Milwaukee Braves.

Minnesota _____ Metropolitan Stadium

The Kansas City Royals defeated the Minnesota Twins 5-2 on September 30, 1981. Larry Gura went the distance for the win, while Fernando Arroyo took the loss. Roy Smalley popped to short for the final out. By winning, Kansas City clinched at least a tie for the American League second-half title (in that strange strike season there were actually two seasons, the pre-strike one and the post-strike one), becoming the only team to make the postseason with a sub-.500 record.

In the ninth inning, Gary Ward got the last hit, a single. Clint Hurdle hit the last home run. There were 2,866 homers hit at the ballpark, led by Harmon Killebrew's 246.

Metropolitan Stadium (1956-1981)
Opened for MLB...... 1956
Team......................... Minnesota Twins
Turf........................... Natural
Fences...................... 329-L, 412-C, 329-R (original)
329-L, 412-C, 329-R (original)
343-L, 402-C, 330-R (final)
Capacity .... 18,200 (original)
45,919 (final)

Montréal _____ Parc Jarry

The Montréal Expos played their final game at their first home, Parc Jarry (Jarry Park), before 14,166 fans on September 26, 1976. Competing with the Summer Olympics in Montreal, the Expos did not fare well at the gate and drew only 646,704 fans. In the final game, the Philadelphia Phillies led 2-1 after seven innings in the second game of a doubleheader, when the game was halted by rain. Ron Schueler was the winner and Dennis Blair took the loss. Pat Scanlon struck out to end the bottom of the seventh, the game, and the ballpark.

Pepe Frias singled for the last hit of the game, Ellis Valentine got the last double, and in the first game of the doubleheader, Larry Bowa slugged the last triple, Greg Luzinski the last home run. The Phils won Game 1 as well, 4-1.

Parc Jarry (1969-1976)
Opened for MLB...... 1969
Team......................... Montreal Expos
Turf........................... Natural
Fences...................... 340-L, 415-C, 340-R
Capacity 29,125

The Montréal Expos lost to the Florida Marlins 9-1 on September 29, 2004, before 31,395 fans—the largest crowd of the season at Stade Olympique (Olympic Stadium). The lone and last run scored when Juan Rivera's two-out double in the fourth inning scored Tony Batista, who had doubled. Carl Pavano picked up the win for Florida, while Sun-Woo Kim took the loss for the Expos. Marlin Miguel Cabrera hit the last home run.

Following the game, Montreal players and coaches came onto the field, spoke to the fans and threw souvenirs into the bleachers. The Expos played 2,786 games in Montréal: 2,145 at Stade Olympique, and 641 at Parc Jarry.

Stade Olympique (1976-2004)

Opened for MLB...... 1977
Team.......................... Montreal Expos
Turf............................ Artificial
Fences........................ 325-L, 404-C, 370-R
Capacity.................... 46,500

New York — The Polo Grounds III

On April 13, 1911, the Philadelphia Phillies beat the New York Giants 6-1 in 18 innings. Christy Mathewson went the distance and took the loss. Later that night, an enormous fire engulfed the park and burned for two solid days. President Frank Farrell of the New York Highlanders invited the Giants to use Hilltop Park, setting the stage for a return-favor ten years later.

Polo Grounds III (1891-1911)

Opened for MLB...... 1911
Team.......................... New York Giants
Turf............................ Natural
Fences........................ Unknown
Capacity.................... Unknown

Hilltop Park (New York Giants)

On May 30, 1911, the New York Giants shut out the Brooklyn Dodgers 3-0 in the second game of a doubleheader. Bugs Raymond, the starter and winner, got Bob Coulson to ground out for the final out. Nap Rucker started and took the loss; Zack Wheat got the last hit.

Hilltop Park (1903-1912)

Opened for MLB...... 1903
Team.......................... New York Highlanders,
                                      New York Giants
Turf............................ Natural
Fences........................ 365-L, 542-C, 400-R
Capacity.................... 16,000

Hilltop Park (New York Yankees)

The New York Yankees beat the Washington Senators 8-6 on October 5, 1912. A crowd of approximately 5,000 saw a raucous game of baseball and comedy because the Senators learned they had clinched second place and the Yanks were just playing out the schedule. Nick Altrock and Germany Schaefer were the leading comics. The forty-two-year-old manager of the Senators, Clark Griffith, made his only appearance of the season on the mound (as did Nick Altrock) and gave up a home run to Hal Chase.

Hilltop Park was demolished in 1914, and Columbia Presbyterian Hospital was built on the site in the 1920s. In 1993, the Yankees presented a home plate-shaped plaque to the hospital to commemorate Hilltop Park. According to The New York Times, the plaque was placed at the original location of Hilltop's home plate which happened to be in a garden at the hospital off West 165th Street.

The Polo Grounds IV (New York Giants/New York Mets)

New York's Polo Grounds had two lives: first as host to the New York Giants and then as home to the nascent New York Mets.

The Giants played in what was actually the Polo Grounds IV starting June 28, 1911. They played their last game there—and their last game as the New York Giants—on September 29, 1957, losing 9-1 to the Pittsburgh Pirates. Bob Friend picked up the win, while Johnny Antonelli took the loss. The Bucs' John Powers got the last hit, a home run. Hall of Famer Bill Mazeroski hit the last double. The last sacrifice fly was hit by the Giants' Dusty Rhodes, who also became the last batter when he grounded out, shortstop Dick Groat to first baseman Frank Thomas.

Polo Grounds IV (1911-1963)
Opened for MLB...... 1911
Team .... New York Giants
Turf .... Natural
Fences .... 277-L, 433-C, 256-R (original)
279-L, 483-C, 258-R (final)
Capacity .... 34,000 (original)
55,000 (final)

Last Lick

Willie Mays is one of four players who began their careers and ended their careers playing in the same city...but for different teams. Mays debuted on May 25, 1951, for Leo Durocher's New York Giants. His struggling start is legendary: After going 0-for-12, the Say Hey Kid homered off Hall of Fame pitcher Warren Spahn. But Mays struggled at the end of his career as well. Now with the New York Mets, Mays hit only .211 in 209 at-bats and played his last regular season game on September 9, 1973.

The Polo Grounds (New York Yankees)

From 1912 to 1922, the New York Highlanders sublet the Polo Grounds from the Giants after their lease ran out on Hilltop Park. In the move, the Highlanders became the Yankees.

In the Yankees' last game at the Polo Grounds, on September 10, 1922, they defeated the Philadelphia Athletics 2-1 in the second game of a doubleheader. Joe Hauser struck out to end the game. The last home run was hit in the first game of the twinbill by Wally Pipp. Babe Ruth got the last triple, and Waite Hoyt was the last winning pitcher. The Yankees played their final 18 games on the road before Yankee Stadium opened the following spring.

Polo Grounds (1891-1922)
Opened for MLB...... 1891
Team .... New York Yankees
Turf .... Natural
Fences 277-L, 455-C, 258-R
Capacity 16,000

On April 13, 1962, the Mets returned National League baseball to New York. On September 18, 1963, the Mets played and lost their final game at the Polo Grounds to the Philadelphia Phillies, 5-1. Chris Short picked up the win, and Craig Anderson took the loss. Attendance was a meager 1,752 when the Mets' Jim Hickman hit the last home run and Chico Fernandez got the last hit. Ted Schreiber, the last batter, hit into a 4-6-3 double play, Cookie Rojas to Bobby Wine to Roy Sievers, to close the Polo Grounds at 4:21 P.M.

Last Lick

On June 18, 1962, Hank Aaron hit a 470-foot shot into the center field bleachers of the Polo Grounds for probably the longest home run of his career. The first homer to the stadium's center field stands was by Joe Adcock in 1953 and the second by the Chicago Cubs' Lou Brock the day before Aaron's.

Philadelphia _____ Shibe Park

Shibe Park was originally named for Ben Shibe, a Philadelphia Athletics stockholder and baseball manufacturer. The ballpark was then renamed Connie Mack Stadium in 1953 after Mack—longtime manager of the A's—retired. All told, the stadium was the home of the American League Philadelphia Athletics from 1909 through September 19, 1954.

In the final game, the New York Yankees beat the A's 4-2 before 1,715 lonely fans (it was not announced that the A's were moving to Kansas City until after the season). Johnny Sain picked up the win, Jim Konstanty recorded the save, and Moe Burtschy took the loss. Gil McDougald hit the final home run, scored the final run, and collected the last RBI.

The A's attracted only 305,362 fans that final season.

Shibe Park (1909-1971)

Opened for MLB...... 1909
Team......................... Philadelphia Athletics,
                         Philadelphia Phillies
Turf........................... Natural
Fences....................... 360-L, 515-C, 360-R (original)
                         334-L, 410-C, 329-R (final)
Capacity .... 20,000 (original)
                         33,000 (final)

_____ Connie Mack Stadium

Shibe Park was the temporary home for the National League's Philadelphia Phillies for about two weeks in May 1927, and their permanent home from July 4, 1938, to October 1, 1970. In the last game there, the Phillies edged the Montreal Expos 2-1 in 10 innings, with Dick Selma winning and Howie Reed recording the loss. The Phillies' Tim McCarver singled, stole second, and scored the final run on Oscar Gamble's single. During the game, McCarver hit the last triple and Bobby Wine the last double. The final home run was hit by John Bateman of the Expos on September 29. A's star Jimmie Foxx hit the most the homers at the ballpark with 181; Babe Ruth led visitors with 68.

After the final game, the crowd of 31,822 ran onto the field and began destroying the stadium. As a result, the postgame ceremony—there were even prizes to be awarded—was canceled. The ballpark was torn down in June, 1976. The site now houses the Deliverance Evangelistic Church.

Connie Mack Stadium (1953-1971)

Opened for MLB...... 1909
Team......................... Philadelphia Athletics,
                         Philadelphia Phillies
Turf........................... Natural
Fences....................... 360-L, 515-C, 360-R (original)
                         334-L, 410-C, 329-R (final)
Capacity .... 20,000 (original)
                         33,000 (final)

The Vet hosted 2,617 regular season games and 25 postseason games. On September 27, 2003, Jim Thome became the last player to hit two home runs in a game at the Vet; his second homer, off Will Cunnane, was also the last home run ever hit there. In the same game, Jesse Garcia of the Atlanta Braves hit the ballpark's last triple and Rheal Cormier picked up the last Phillies win 8-7 in 10 innings.

On Sept. 28, 2003, Pat Burrell of the Phillies singled in the ninth inning off Jason Marquis of the Braves. Then Chase Utley, the last batter at Veterans Stadium, grounded into a double play. The Braves won the finale, 5-2. Greg Maddux recorded the last win, Kevin Millwood the last loss, and Jason Marquis the last save.

After the final game ended at 3:55 P.M., Hall of Fame announcer Harry Kalas took the microphone and said, "Like a 3-1 fastball to Jim Thome or Mike Schmidt, it's a long drive and Veterans Stadium is outta here!"

On March 21, 2004, Veterans Stadium was demolished. The site is now a parking lot for the sports complexes that replaced it.

Veterans Stadium (1971-2003)

Opened for MLB...... 1971
Team.......................... Philadelphia Phillies
Turf............................ Artificial
Fences........................ 330-L, 408-C, 330-R
Capacity 62,623

Last Lick

Vic Power spent most of his 1953 rookie season playing center field for the Philadelphia Athletics, and ended his career on October 3, 1965, as a member of the California Angels. In his last game he went 1-for-5 with an RBI against the Minnesota Twins. Facing Johnny Klippstein, he struck out to end the game, the season and his career—the last active member of the Philadelphia A's.

Pittsburgh — Forbes Field

Some farewells are almost too good to be true. On June 28, 1970, the Pittsburgh Pirates' Bill Mazeroski, who hit the most famous home run in Forbes Field history (see page 77), fielded a grounder by the Chicago Cubs' Don Kessinger and stepped on second base to record the final out.

Forbes Field (1909-1970)

Opened for MLB...... 1909
Team.......................... Pittsburgh Pirates
Turf............................ Natural
Fences........................ 360-L, 422-C, 376-R (original)
　　　　　　　　　　　　 365-L, 400-C, 329-R (final)
Capacity .... 25,000 (original)
　　　　　　　　　　　　 35,000 (final)

On October 1, 2000, Pittsburgh Pirates third baseman and local boy John Wehner went 3-for-5 in the Bucs' 10-9 loss to the Chicago Cubs. In the fifth inning, he hit the last home run in Three Rivers Stadium history off Jon Lieber. And in the bottom of the ninth, after John Vander Wal singled to right (driving in a run), Wehner grounded out, third to first, laying the ballpark to rest.

Kyle Farnsworth notched the last win and Scott Sauerbeck the last loss. It was also the final game for Pirates skipper Gene Lamont, who had been fired earlier but was allowed to manage his last game. When he was introduced before the game, he feared the worst from the fans. To the contrary, Lamont told Bob Smizik of the Pittsburgh *Post-Gazette*, "You walk out there hoping you don't get booed, then you get a standing ovation."

Following the game, former Pirates saluted their ballpark and the fans who loved them. Kent Tekulve was preparing to throw one final pitch to Jason Kendall when the recorded voice of the late public address announcer, Art McKennan, introduced Willie Stargell. The Hall of Fame slugger was immediately embraced by his old Pirates teammates. Stargell was in ill health and died the following April.

Three Rivers Stadium (1970-2000)
Opened for MLB...... 1970
Team.......................... Pittsburgh Pirates
Turf............................ Artificial
Fences....................... 340-L, 410-C, 340-R (original)
335-L, 400-C, 335-R (final)
Capacity 47,952

St. Louis

Sportsman's Park / Busch Stadium I

Sportsman's Park was renamed and retro-fitted after Anheuser-Busch purchased the club in 1953. On May 8, 1966, the St. Louis Cardinals lost to the San Francisco Giants, 10-5. Lindy McDaniel pitched five innings of one-hit relief to pick up the win, while Tracy Stallard took the loss. Final batter Alex Johnson hit into a 6-4-3 double play. Jim Ray Hart hit the last single and Willie Mays the last home run. A helicopter transferred home plate to the new Busch Stadium.

Sportsman's Park/Busch Stadium I (1902-1966)
Opened for MLB...... 1902
Team.......................... St. Louis Browns,
St. Louis Cardinals
Turf............................ Natural
Fences....................... 368-L, 430-C, 335-R (original)
351-L, 422-C, 310-R (final)
Capacity .... 8,000 (original)
30,500 (final)

The last regular-season game was played at the new Busch Stadium on October 2, 2005. The St. Louis Cardinals beat the Cincinnati Reds, 7-5. One of nine pitchers used in the game, Brad Thompson notched the win and Reds starter Brandon Claussen earned the loss. Jason Isringhausen nailed down the save when he struck out Chris Denorfia to end the game. Chris Duncan, son of Cardinal coach Dave Duncan, hit the final home run.

But there were more games to play at Busch Stadium in the postseason. When the Cardinals lost 5-1 to the Houston Astros in Game 6 of the National League Championship Series, the Astros headed to the World Series against the Chicago White Sox and Busch Stadium closed after 3,227 games. Last batter Yadier Molina, facing Dan Wheeler, flied out to right fielder Jason Lane. Mark Grudzielanek got the last hit—a single—and Jason Lane hit the last home run. Roy Oswalt notched the win, and Mark Mulder took the loss.

Following the game, there was a ten-minute video tribute featuring former Cardinals players like Ozzie Smith, Bob Gibson and legendary broadcaster Jack Buck. In November 2005, an auction was held for various parts of the old ballpark. The foul pole brought in $4,347, while a Cardinals clubhouse urinal was purchased by a urologist for $2,174.

Busch Stadium II (1966-2005)

Opened for MLB	1966
Team	St. Louis Cardinals
Turf	Natural (1966-1969)
	Artificial (1970-1995)
	Natural (final)
Fences	330-L, 414-C, 330-R (original)
	372-L, 402-C, 372-R (final)
Capacity	49,676

San Diego

On September 28, 2003, the Colorado Rockies defeated the San Diego Padres, 10-8. Javier Lopez was the winning pitcher, Jay Witasick the loser. Justin Speier struck out the side in the ninth inning, fanning Gary Bennett to pick up the save. The Padres' Mark Loretta hit the last Qualcomm home run. The attendance for the game was 60,988.

Qualcomm Stadium (1966-2003)

Opened for MLB	1966
Team	San Diego Padres
Turf	Natural
Fences	327-L, 405-C, 330-R
Capacity	49,676

San Francisco

On September 20, 1959, the soon-to-be-world-champion Los Angeles Dodgers defeated the San Francisco Giants, 8-2, with Johnny Podres beating Sam Jones. Eddie Bressoud ended the game by hitting into a 4-6-3 double play, Charlie Neal to Maury Wills to Gil Hodges, off Clem Labine. Dodger greats Duke Snider got the last homer and Maury Wills the last hit. The attendance was 22,923.

Seals Stadium (1958-1959)

Opened for MLB	1958
Team	San Francisco Giants
Turf	Natural
Fences	365-L, 410-C, 355-R (original)
	361-L, 400-C, 350-R (final)
Capacity	18,600 (original)
	22,900 (final)

Perpetual tormenters, the Los Angeles Dodgers beat the San Francisco Giants 9-4 before 61,389 fans on September 30, 1999. Jeff Williams won over Shawn Estes, and Marvin Benard hit a weak grounder to Eric Karros, who stepped on first for the final out. The Dodgers' Raul Mondesi hit the last home run, in the sixth inning off Mark Gardner, and the Giants' Ramon Martinez tallied the last hit. The game ended at 4:35 P.M. exactly the same time as the Giants' last out had been recorded at the Polo Grounds in 1957. Following the game, the closing ceremony ended with Giants great Willie Mays throwing the last pitch to his godson, Barry Bonds. A helicopter then appeared and carried home plate to the Giants' new home at Pacific Bell Park, now called AT&T Park.

Candlestick Park (1960-1999)

Opened for MLB...... 1960
Team.......................... San Francisco Giants
Turf........................... Natural
Fences....................... 330-L, 420-C, 330-R (original)
                            335-L, 400-C, 330-R (final)
Capacity 45,744-57,546

The Toronto Blue Jays played their last game at Exhibition Stadium on May 28, 1989, against the Chicago White Sox, eleven years after opening the park against the same team (but in the snow) on April 7, 1977.

If they weren't quite sure how to open a stadium, they certainly knew how to close it. With the score 5-5 in the bottom of the 10th, Toronto's Kelly Gruber led off with a double off Bobby Thigpen. Then George Bell hit a walk-off, shutdown homer to win the game for Tom Henke.

Exhibition Stadium (1977-1999)

Opened for MLB...... 1977
Team.......................... Toronto Blue Jays
Turf........................... Artificial
Fences....................... 330-L, 410-C, 330-R
Capacity 44,649

The original Washington Senators played their last game on October 2, 1960, losing to the Baltimore Orioles 2-1 before 4,768 fans at Griffith Stadium. Milt Pappas went all the way for the victory. Catcher Hal Naragon singled and scored on Billy Consolo's fifth-inning triple for Washington's last run.

Less than one month later, on Oct. 27, the American League—seeking to get first dibs on new expansion territory—granted franchises to Los Angeles (the Angels) and Washington. (The Senators' current owner had been given permission to move his team to Minnesota.) The old Senators were renamed the Twins, but carried the franchise's oft-humiliating history.

The new Washington franchise was named the Senators. On April 10, 1961, the new Senators made their debut before 26,724 at Griffith Stadium. President John F. Kennedy threw out the first pitch. These Senators picked up where the old Senators left off by losing to the White Sox, 4-3. On Apr. 11, 1961, the Twins debuted at Yankee Stadium and won, 6-0. The winning pitcher was Pedro Ramos—the last losing pitcher for the old Senators.

On September 21, 1961, with DC Stadium well under construction, doubts lingered about whether the new stadium would be ready to open the following season. Consequently, there was no farewell planned for the old ballpark. That game in September saw the new Washington Senators face the "old" Washington Senators: now known as the Minnesota Twins. The Twins would finish the season 70-90, while the expansion team finished 61-100, 47½ games behind the first-place New York Yankees of Maris and Mantle.

In that last game, the Senators threw Bennie Daniels against the Twins' Jack Kralick. With the Twins leading 5-1 in the bottom of the sixth, Gene Green led off with a single, and Don Lee replaced Kralick. Lee walked Willie Tasby, and Ken Retzer singled to right to score Green. When the ball eluded right fielder Bob Allison for an error, Tasby became the last Senator to score at Griffith. The Twins won, 6-3.

In the bottom of the ninth, Bud Zipfel grounded out to first, Gene Woodling flew out to center, and Danny O'Connell grounded out, shortstop Zoilo Versalles to first baseman Harmon Killebrew. The attendance for the game was 1,498.

Former Senators player, coach and clown Nick Altrock, who claimed to have been present for the first game played at the stadium, was there for the last. According to The Washington Post's Shirley Povich, the eighty-five-year-old Altrock watched the game from "his customary corner of the Washington dugout."

Kansas City Athletics catcher Billy Bryan hit his first major league home run in the sixth inning off Senators pitcher Hector Maestri on Sept. 17, 1961. This was the last home run hit at Griffith Stadium. (Bryan ended his career striking out as a pinch hitter for the Washington Senators on July 23, 1968.)

Griffith Stadium was demolished in 1965, and is now the site of Howard University Hospital.

Griffith Stadium (1911-1965)

Opened for MLB...... 1911
Team......................... Washington Senators
Turf........................... Natural
Fences...................... 407-L, 421-C, 320-R (original)
                                      388-L, 421-C, 320-R (final)
Capacity 27,410

Last Lick

Jim (Kitty) Kaat had cups of coffee in 1959 and 1960 with the Senators, and retired following the game of July 1, 1983, with the St. Louis Cardinals. Katt was the last active member of the Washington Senators/Minnesota Twins franchise. He won 16 consecutive Gold Gloves starting in 1962—and made no errors as a member of the Senators.

RFK Stadium

RFK Stadium hosted the former Expos franchise when it moved from Montreal to Washington, DC, and became the Nationals in 2005. The final game was on September 23, 2007. The Nationals hosted the Philadelphia Phillies, who were in the midst of a pennant race that had long since left the Nationals behind. Before a crowd of 40,519, the Nationals' largest of the season, Washington defeated Philadelphia, 5-3. It was the Nats' 122nd win over three years at RFK, against 121 losses. In postgame ceremonies, hosted by broadcaster Don Sutton, fans were given game-worn jerseys. Nationals manager Manny Acta and team owner Ted Lerner helped dig out home plate, which was moved to their new ballpark.

Luis Ayala picked up the final win in relief. Chad Cordero earned the save. Antonio Alfonseca was the loser in relief. Jayson Werth ended the game by striking out—swinging. Chase Utley tallied the final hit with a ground-rule double in the ninth. Wily Mo Peña had the final hit for the Nationals when he poked a pinch hit single in the eighth.

RFK Stadium (1962-Present)

Opened for MLB...... 1962
Team......................... Washington Senators,
                                      Washington Nationals
Turf........................... Natural
Fences...................... 335-L, 410-C, 335-R
Capacity 46,382

The Final Goodbye

Roberto Clemente (1934-1972).

Ballplayers say, "He died" when referring to a teammate demoted to the minor leagues. A. E. Housman (1859-1936) wrote the poem "To an Athlete Dying Young" in lament to the physical lad who peaks long before his maturity, only to live the rest of his life in decline. It reads, in part:

> Smart lad, to slip betimes away
> From fields where glory does not stay
> And early though the laurel grows
> It withers quicker than the rose.

But these are mere metaphors. When a ballplayer actually dies in what should be his prime, we are all affected. The loss of a young man reminds us of our own vulnerability; the unexpected message of mortality socks us in the gut.

New York Yankees infielder Alex Burr played his only game on April 21, 1914. He was killed on October 12, 1918, in Cazaux, France, at the age of twenty-five.

Larry Chappell died of influenza in a San Francisco hospital on November 8, 1918. The outfielder made his final appearance on April 25, 1917, while playing for the Boston Braves. He was twenty-eight.

After playing ten National League seasons, Captain Eddie Grant of the 307th Infantry, 77th Division, Company H was hit by two shells and died in the Argonne Forest in France on Oct. 5, 1918. Grant, thirty-five, played his last game on Oct. 6, 1915, as an outfielder for the New York Giants.

Ralph Sharman played in 13 games as an outfielder for the Philadelphia Athletics in 1917. His last appearance was Oct. 3, 1917. Sharman drowned on May 24, 1918, at Camp Sheridan in Alabama. He was twenty-three.

Bun Troy pitched his only game on September 15, 1912, for the Detroit Tigers. He was the starting and losing pitcher, giving up four runs on nine hits in 6⅓ innings. Born in Bad Wurzach, Germany, on August 27, 1888, Troy, thirty, was killed in action on Oct. 7, 1918, in Petit Maujouym, France.

Alex Burr, OF, 1914

G	AB	R	H	2B	3B	HR	RBI	BB	SO	HBP	SH	SB	CS	AVG	OBP	SLG	BFW	PO	A	ERR	DP	FPCT.
1	0	0	0	0	0	0	0	0	0	0	0	0	0	-	-	-	0.0	0	0	0	0	0

Larry Chappell, OF, 1913-1917

G	AB	R	H	2B	3B	HR	RBI	BB	SO	HBP	SH	SB	CS	AVG	OBP	SLG	BFW	PO	A	ERR	DP	FPCT.
109	305	27	69	9	2	0	26	25	42	2	5	9	0i	.226	.289	.269	-2.6	149	5	8	1	.951

Eddie Grant, 3b, 1905-1916

G	AB	R	H	2B	3B	HR	RBI	BB	SO	HBP	SH	SB	CS	AVG	OBP	SLG	BFW	PO	A	ERR	DP	FPCT.
990	3385	399	844	79	30	5	277	233	0i	181i	11	129	0i	.249	.300	.295	-10.2	962	1423	148	105	.942

Ralph Sharman, OF, 1917

G	AB	R	H	2B	3B	HR	RBI	BB	SO	HBP	SH	SB	AVG	OBP	SLG	BFW
13	37	2	11	2	1	0	2	3	2	1	2	1	.297	.366	.405	-0.1

Bun Troy, P, 1912

G	GS	CG	SHO	GF	SV	IP	H	BFP	HR	R	ER	BB	SO	SH	WP	HBP	BK	W	L	ERA
1	1	0	0	0	0	6.2	9	30	0	4	4	3	1	0	0	1	0	0	1	5.40

1920   Ray Chapman

Cleveland Indians shortstop Ray Chapman was twenty-nine years old when the Tribe faced the New York Yankees on August 16, 1920, at the Polo Grounds in New York. Submarine pitcher Carl Mays faced Chapman, who was hitting .303 with 97 runs and a .380 on-base percentage when he led off the fifth inning. Mays had a reputation for throwing high and tight, and Chapman liked to crowd the plate. It proved to be a fatal combination.

On the first pitch, Mays threw an almost underhand pitch that quickly rose and hit Chapman on the temple. The sound of Chapman's skull fracturing could be heard all over the park. In fact, Mays thought the ball had hit Chapman's bat—he fielded the carom and tossed the ball to first base.

Chapman immediately collapsed. Blood ran from his ears, nose and eyes. A doctor rushed onto the field and temporarily revived Chapman, but as he was being helped off the field he lapsed back into unconsciousness. He was driven by ambulance to St. Lawrence Hospital, where at 10:00 P.M. doctors, with the assent of the Cleveland Indians management, decided that surgery was necessary to relieve the condition caused by the depressed fracture on the left side of Chapman's skull. The surgery, which included the removal of a piece of his skull, was unsuccessful. Chapman died at 4:30 the next morning. He remains the only on-field fatality in major league history.

Ray Chapman, SS, 1912-1920

G	AB	R	H	2B	3B	HR	RBI	BB	SO	HBP	SH	SB	CS	AVG	OBP	SLG	BFW	PO	A	ERR	DP	FPCT.
1051	3785	671	1053	162	81	17	364	452	414i	19	334	233	47i	.278	.358	.377	16.6	2204	2950	336	350	.939

1928 — Urban Shocker

One of the last legal spitballers, Urban Shocker went 18-6 for the great New York Yankees team of 1927. Following the season, he announced plans to retire and spend his time in the radio business and aviation. But once the 1928 season began, Shocker un-retired and returned to the Yankees. He pitched only two scoreless innings on May 30, 1928.

Shocker then retired to the Denver area and pitched once more, on August 6, in a semi-pro game. He was beaten by a Cheyenne, Wyoming team. The following week, Shocker was hospitalized with pneumonia. He seemed to recover, but on September 8 he suffered a relapse and died one day later from congenital congestive heart disease. He was thirty-eight years old.

Urban Shocker, P, 1916-1928

G	GS	CG	SHO	GF	SV	IP	H	BFP	HR	R	ER	BB	SO	SH	WP	HBP	BK	W	L	ERA	RS	PW
412	317	200	28	68	25	2681.2	2709	11140	126	1127	945	657	983	203	20	37	3	187	117	3.17	4.93	27.0

1935 — Len Koenecke

A back-up outfielder for the Brooklyn Dodgers, Len Koenecke played his last game on September 15, 1935, grounding out in a pinch hit at-bat. On Sept. 16, following the Dodgers' 1-0 loss to the St. Louis Cardinals, he was told he was finished for the season. Sometime after midnight, he chartered a three-seat plane to fly from Detroit, Michigan, to Buffalo, New York, where he had much success as a minor leaguer.

According to the pilot, William Joseph Mulqueeney, Koenecke appeared to be under stress when boarding the plane and for the first part of the flight sat quietly drinking. Then Koenecke moved into the seat next to the pilot. After repeatedly asking Koenecke to stop nudging him with his shoulder, Mulqueeney insisted that Koenecke sit in the back with his assistant, Irwin Davis. Moments later, Koenecke resumed poking Mulqueeney, and Davis grabbed his hand to make him stop.

When Koenecke bit Davis on the shoulder, the two grappled for fifteen minutes while the plane dangerously rocked. The pilot did everything he could to keep the craft on an even keel, but it was lurching out of control. Mulqueeney then made a decision that he felt would save the lives of all of them—he walloped Koenecke over the head with a fire extinguisher and quickly landed the plane in an open field.

Koenecke, thirty-one, was dead on landing.

Len Koenecke, OF, 1932, 1934-1935

G	AB	R	H	2B	3B	HR	RBI	BB	SO	HBP	SH	GDP	SB	AVG	OBP	SLG	BFW	PO	A	ERR	DP	AVG
265	922	155	274	49	9	22	114	124	96	4	14	10i	11	.297	.383	.441	2.1	593	9	15	0	.976

1940 — Willard Hershberger

A catcher with the Cincinnati Reds from 1938 through August 2, 1940, Hershberger primarily served as a backup to Hall of Fame catcher Ernie Lombardi. On Aug. 3, 1940, Hershberger, thirty, cut his jugular vein in the shower. He is the only player ever to commit suicide during the season.

Hershberger went to Fullerton Union High School in California with future Hall of Fame shortstop Arky Vaughn and President Richard Nixon.

Willard Hershberger, C, 1938-1940

G	AB	R	H	2B	3B	HR	RBI	BB	SO	HBP	SH	GDP	SB	AVG	OBP	SLG	BFW	PO	A	ERR	DP	PB	.FPCT
160	402	41	127	16	5	0	70	20	16	5	13	12	2	.316	.356	.381	0.3	433	45	10	4	6	.980

Elmer Gedeon starred for the University of Michigan in football, track and baseball. Gedeon played five games in the outfield for the Washington Senators, his last on September 24, 1939. On August 9, 1942, now-Lieutenant Gedeon was injured in a plane crash after a failed takeoff in Raleigh, North Carolina. In terrible pain, he managed to crawl from the burning wreckage but hero-ically returned to rescue his crewmate. He survived the crash, but was later killed at age twenty-seven when he was shot out of the sky over St. Pol, France on April 20, 1944.

Harry O'Neill caught his only game for the Philadelphia Athletics on July 23, 1939. He was killed in action on March 6, 1945, in the Battle of Iwo Jima. He was twenty-six.

Elmer Gedeon, OF, 1939

G	AB	R	H	2B	3B	HR	RBI	BB	SO	HBP	SH	GDP	SB	AVG	OBP	SLG	BFW	PO	A	ERR	DP	.FPCT
5	15	1	3	0	0	0	1	2	5	0	0	0	0	.200	.294	.200	-0.1	17	0	0	0	1.000

Harry O'Neill, C, 1939

G	AB	R	H	2B	3B	HR	RBI	BB	SO	HBP	SH	GDP	SB	AVG	OBP	SLG	BFW	PO	A	ERR	DP	.FPCT
1	0	0	0	0	0	0	0	0	0	0	0	0	0	-	-		0.0	0	0	0	0	-

Harry Agganis graduated from Boston University holding fifteen Terrier records. Red Grange said Agganis, a quarterback, was the best player he had seen all year. Despite his success in football (as a junior, he was the No. 1 draft pick of the National Football League's Cleveland Browns), Agganis signed with his hometown Boston Red Sox in 1953.

A first baseman in his second year on the roster, Agganis was stricken by viral pneumonia early in the 1955 season and hospitalized ten days before rushing back to the Red Sox. He was stricken again a week later, and his condition was complicated by phlebitis. Agganis appeared to be recovering, but on June 27, he died suddenly of a massive pulmonary embolism at Sancta Maria Hospital in Cambridge.

In his final game, on June 2, 1955, he went 2-for-4 against the Chicago White Sox at Comiskey Park. Agganis hit the last triple in Philadelphia's Shibe Park history on September 5, 1954, in the second game of a doubleheader. He was twenty-six and batting .313 at the time of his death.

Harry Agganis, 1B, 1954-1955

G	AB	R	H	2B	3B	HR	RBI	BB	SO	HBP	SH	GDP	SB	AVG	OBP	SLG	BFW	PO	A	ERR	DP	.FPCT
157	517	65	135	23	9	11	67	57	67	0	7	9	8	.261	.331	.404	-0.9	1272	103	15	116	.989

As a freshman at star-crossed Boston University, Tom Gastall played end to make room for Harry Agganis at quarterback. As a senior quarterback, Gastall was the school's Athlete of the Year and captain of both the basketball and baseball teams. He was drafted by the Detroit Lions of the National Football League, but instead he signed a bonus contract with the Baltimore Orioles as a catcher.

On September 20, 1956, Gastall was killed piloting a small plane that crashed into Chesapeake Bay, just one day after he played his last game against the Detroit Tigers. He was twenty-four years old.

Tom Gastall, C, 1955-1956

G	AB	R	H	2B	3B	HR	RBI	BB	SO	HBP	SH	GDP	SB	AVG	OBP	SLG	BFW	PO	A	ERR	DP	PB	.FPCT
52	83	7	15	3	0	0	4	6	13	1	1	3	0	.181	.242	.217	-0.8	95	7	1	2	1	.990

1964 _____ Ken Hubbs

The 1962 National League Rookie of the Year for the Chicago Cubs and the first rookie to win a Gold Glove, Hubbs, twenty-two, died on February 15, 1964, when his private plane crashed.

His last appearance was September 29, 1963, against Warren Spahn and the Milwaukee Braves. On his last at-bat, Hubbs grounded into a force play.

Ken Hubbs, 2B, 1961-1963

G	AB	R	H	2B	3B	HR	RBI	BB	SO	HBP	SH	GDP	SB	CS	AVG	OBP	SLG	BFW	PO	A	ERR	DP	.FPCT
324	1255	148	310	44	13	14	98	74	230	5	16	37	11	16	.247	.290	.336	-0.6	714	997	37	201	.979

1972 _____ Roberto Clemente

On September 30, 1972, Hall of Fame right fielder Roberto Clemente doubled off the New York Mets' Jon Matlack in the fourth inning for his 3,000th and last regular-season hit. Manny Sanguillen singled him home for the 1,416th run of his eighteen-year career. In the fifth inning, Bill Mazeroski pinch hit for Clemente.

Clemente's last appearance was in Game 5 of the National League Championship Series on October 11, 1972, at Riverfront Stadium. The Cincinnati Reds' Tom Hall intentionally walked Clemente in his last plate appearance after Pedro Borbon had struck him out in his last official at-bat.

Clemente, thirty-eight, was killed when his plane crashed into the sea off the coast of Puerto Rico on December 31, 1972. He was flying relief supplies to Nicaraguan earthquake victims.

Roberto Clemente, OF, 1955-1972

G	AB	R	H	2B	3B	HR	RBI	BB	IBB	SO	HBP	SH	GDP	SB	CS	AVG	OBP	SLG	BFW	PO	A	ERR	DP	FPCT.
2433	9454	1416	3000	440	166	240	1305	621	167	1230	35	36	275	83	46	.317	.359	.475	35.4	4696	266	140	42	.973

1976 _____ Bob Moose

Pittsburgh Pirates pitcher Bob Moose faced the St. Louis Cardinals on September 25, 1976, and threw two innings in relief, giving up two hits, two walks and no runs. The final batter he faced,

Mike Anderson, popped out to second base.

On his way to his twenty-ninth birthday party, on October 9, 1976, Moose was killed in a car accident.

Bob Moose, P, 1967-1976

G	GS	CG	SHO	GF	SV	IP	H	BFP	HR	R	ER	BB	IB	SO	SH	SF	WP	HBP	BK	2B	3B	GDP	ROE	W	L	ERA	RS	PW
289	160	35	13	59	19	1304.1	1308	5501	75	566	507	387	59	827	63	35	25	30	6	192i	30i	132i	86i	76	71	3.50	4.34	-0.3

1978 _____ Lyman Bostock

An up-and-coming outfielder, Lyman Bostock hit .323 and .336 for the 1976-77 Minnesota Twins and batted .296 for the 1978 California Angels.

On September 23, 1978, Bostock, twenty-seven, went 2-for-4 against the Chicago White Sox. In his last at-bat, he grounded out against Paul Hartzell to end the game. The Angels lost, 5-4. Later that night,

Bostock was riding in the backseat of his uncle's car in Gary, Indiana, with his uncle's goddaughter, Barbara Smith. Leonard Smith, her estranged husband, pulled up beside the vehicle at a stop sign and killed Bostock with a shot to the temple. Smith was found not guilty of murder by reason of insanity and twenty-one months later was released after being judged no longer a danger.

Lyman Bostock, OF, 1975-1978

G	AB	R	H	2B	3B	HR	RBI	BB	SO	HBP	SH	SF	GDP	SB	CS	AVG	OBP	SLG	BFW	PO	A	ERR	DP	TP	FPCT.
526	2004	305	624	102	30	23	250	171	174	9	10	20	64	45	28	.311	.365	.427	4.6	1223	30	15	4	0	.988

1979 —————————————————————————————— Thurman Munson

The first New York Yankees captain since Lou Gehrig, catcher Thurman Munson led the Yankees to three straight American League titles (1976-1978) and two World Series championships (1977-1978). The 1970 AL Rookie of Year, he was the AL Most Valuable Player in 1976, a seven-time All-Star, winner of three Gold Gloves, and a .292 career hitter in eleven seasons with the Yankees.

On August 2, 1979, Munson was killed while piloting his private plane in Canton, Ohio. In his last appearance (playing first base) on August 1, 1979, Munson struck out against the Chicago White Sox' Ken Kravec. Munson was thirty-two. His locker in the Yankee clubhouse remains vacant to this day.

Thurman Munson, C, 1969-1979

G	AB	R	H	2B	3B	HR	RBI	BB	SO	HBP	SH	GDP	SB	AVG	OBP	SLG	BFW	PO	A	ERR	DP	PB	SB	CS	FPCT.
1423	5344	696	1558	229	32	113	701	438	571	42	21	160	48	292	.346	.410	25.0	6253	742	127	82	93	533	427	.982

1993 —————————————————————————— Steve Olin and Tim Crews

Spring training is a time of hopeful beginnings, but on March 22, 1993, in Winter Haven, Florida, it was a time of tragic endings. At 7:30 P.M., three Cleveland Indians pitchers—Bobby Ojeda, Steve Olin and Tim Crews—were involved in a one-boat accident on Little Lake Nellie in central Florida. Spending an off-day with their families at a barbecue, the three went for one last spin around the lake and crashed into and under a neighbor's dock.

Olin, who last pitched for the Indians on October 4, 1992, throwing three shutout innings against Baltimore in a game eventually won by the Orioles in the 13th inning, was killed instantly. He was twenty-seven. Crews, who last pitched on Oct. 3, 1992, for the Los Angeles Dodgers, throwing 2⅔ innings before giving up the winning run to the Houston Astros in the 13th, was airlifted to Orlando Medical Center, where he later died. He was thirty-one. Post-mortem tests indicated that Crews had a blood alcohol content of .14 percent, operating the boat while legally drunk.

Ojeda, bleeding badly and in shock from head lacerations, was taken to the hospital. He recovered and eventually returned to pitch in the major leagues.

Steve Olin, P, 1989-1992

G	GS	CG	SHO	GF	SV	IP	H	BFP	HR	R	ER	BB	IB	SO	SH	SF	WP	HBP	BK	2B	3B	GDP	ROE	W	L	ERA	RS	PW
195	1	0	0	118	48	273	272	1155	14	108	94	90	17	173	13	4	3	11	1	37	4	41	16	16	19	3.10	4.00	4.6

Tim Crews, P, 1987-1992

G	GS	CG	SHO	GF	SV	IP	H	BFP	HR	R	ER	BB	IB	SO	SH	SF	WP	HBP	BK	2B	3B	GDP	ROE	W	L	ERA	RS	PW
281	4	0	0	83	15	423.2	444	1797	34	181	162	110	43	293	22	16	10	7	1	75	13	17	19	11	13	3.44	3.25	0.7

1996 ———————————————————————————————— John McSherry

On April 1, 1996, the Cincinnati Reds hosted the Montreal Expos on Opening Day at Riverfront Stadium. Pete Schourek threw the first pitch of the season to Mark Grudzielanek at 2:09 P.M. and later told Tim Sullivan of the Cincinnati *Enquirer* that he was stunned when home plate umpire John McSherry did not call it a strike.

"It was right down the middle, and he called it a ball, and it was like he didn't react to it," Schourek said. "But he seemed fine after that."

Grudzielanek flied out to right field, and Mike Lansing struck out swinging. Seven pitches into the season, with the count 1-1 on Rondell White, McSherry stepped away from the plate and signaled that something was wrong. Then his knees buckled. As he shakily walked toward the dugout, McSherry collapsed.

"Once we rolled John over, John never was conscious," fellow umpire Jerry Crawford said. "I don't think he ever heard me, when I was talking to him."

Third base umpire Tom Hallion went with McSherry, his friend, to University Hospital, but within the hour McSherry was pronounced dead.

The umpires were prepared to officiate the game with just two umpires, but the players knew better.

"I want you to know that right now, you do not have to worry about not playing this game," Reds manager Ray Knight told Crawford. "And I'll support you one hundred percent."

"I've had a lot of deaths in my family," Knight continued. "In good conscience, out of respect for life, I can't go out there."

The only ugliness occurred when Reds owner Marge Schott publicly complained about the game being cancelled—there had been a sellout crowd at the ballpark. In addition, the Dayton *Daily News* reported a basket of flowers that she sent to the umpires in "sympathy" had actually been re-gifted. Reportedly, she scribbled a sympathy note, attached it to flowers that had been given to her on Opening Day by the team's television affiliate, and had the flowers sent to the umpires' dressing room.

An autopsy later revealed McSherry died of coronary disease caused by arterial blockage, an irregular heartbeat, and an enlarged heart. He was fifty-one.

John McSherry, Umpire, 1971-1995

G	HP	1B	2B	3B	EJ
3396	846	847	841	862	23

❧❦

2002   Darryl Kile

On June 22, 2002, Kile was scheduled to pitch a nationally televised game at Wrigley Field. When he was late arriving at the ballpark, his St. Louis Cardinals teammates became concerned. Authorities checked his room and found that he had died in his sleep. The cause of death was listed as "coronary atherosclerosis, narrowing of the arter-ies supplying the heart muscle."

In Kile's final appearance on June 18, he pitched 7⅓ innings against the Los Angeles Angels, giving up one run on six hits and one walk while striking out five. The last batter he faced was Garrett Anderson, who singled. Kile was the winning pitcher and ended his career 133-119. He was thirty-three.

Darryl Kile, P, 1991-2002

G	GS	CG	SHO	GF	SV	IP	H	BFP	HR	R	ER	BB	IB	SO	SH	SF	WP	HBP	BK	2B	3B	GDP	ROE	W	L	ERA	RS	PW
359	331	28	9	8	0	2165.1	2135	9429	214	1099	992	918	41	1668	121	75	97	117	19	390	60	191	112	133	119	4.12	4.69	4.2

❧❦

2006   Cory Lidle

The New York Yankees had been eliminated from the American League Division Series by the Detroit Tigers. Pitcher Cory Lidle, acquired from the Philadelphia Phillies at the end of July, spoke to the media about his disappointment. He had played in the major leagues for nine seasons with seven different clubs and had been looking forward to appearing in his first World Series.

On October 11, 2006, Lidle, an inexperienced pilot with less than eighty-eight hours of total flying experience—forty-eight as "'pilot in command'"—crashed his new private plane into a building on the Upper East Side of Manhattan. Lidle, thirty-four, and his flying instructor, Tyler Stanger, twenty-six, were both killed.

In his last regular-season appearance, on Oct. 1, Lidle pitched one inning in relief, giving up one run on one hit with one strikeout against the Toronto Blue Jays. His last batter, John McDonald, struck out.

In his last postseason appearance on Oct. 7, Lidle pitched 1⅓ innings and gave up four hits and three runs. His last batter, Carlos Guillen, doubled.

Cory Lidle, P, 1997-2006

G	GS	CG	SHO	GF	SV	IP	H	BFP	HR	R	ER	BB	IB	SO	SH	SF	WP	HBP	BK	2B	3B	GDP	ROE	W	L	ERA	RS	PW
277	199	11	5	26	2	1322.2	1400	5639	159	738	671	356	34	838	49	35	47	54	1	289	37	121	67	82	72	4.57	5.00	-1.3

❧❦

S t. Louis Cardinals pitcher Josh Hancock was killed early in the morning of April 29, 2007, when he plowed his car into the back of a tow truck parked on Highway 40 in St. Louis, Missouri. Hancock was legally drunk, talking on a cell phone, and traveling at 68 mph in a 55 mph zone. The police chief said 8.55 grams of marijuana were found in his car.

The Cardinals canceled their Sunday night game against the Chicago Cubs and wore commemorative number "32" patches—Hancock's jersey number—for the remainder of the season. The team also planned a memorial for the bullpen.

Hancock joined the Cardinals before the 2006 season after pitching for Boston, Philadelphia and Cincinnati. In his last appearance on April 28, Hancock pitched three innings of relief in the Cards' 8-1 loss to the Chicago Cubs, yielding one run on two hits. The last batter he faced, Ryan Theriot, grounded out to third. Hancock was twenty-nine.

Josh Hancock, P, 2002-2006

G	GS	CG	SHO	GF	SV	IP	H	BFP	HR	R	ER	BB	IB	SO	SH	SF	WP	HBP	BK	2B	3B	GDP	ROE	W	L	ERA	RS	PW
277	199	11	5	26	2	1322.2	1400	5639	159	738	671	356	34	838	49	35	47	54	1	289	37	121	67	82	72	4.57	5.00	-1.3

Hall of Famers

Umpire Bill Klem calls it "safe."

What was the last at-bat by any Hall of Fame player? The last pitch? A comfortable image forms in the mind: The old fellow, who has, however improbably, spent his entire career with one team, takes his final bow in front of the homefolk. In a pregame ceremony, he accepts warm, glowing praise—everyone from the mayor to team officials—and thanks the fans with a memorable speech that tries to equal the magnitude of Lou Gehrig's, "Today I consider myself the luckiest man on the face of the earth." Then he starts the game and is replaced at some moment when he's still on the field, preferably after a career-ending grand slam (if he's an everyday player) or a strikeout (if he's a pitcher). He exits the field to a standing ovation, and trots a victory lap around the perimeter, high-fiving the front-row fans. The following day, newspapers are filled with his touching remembrances.

It's a happy thought, but one that hardly jibes with reality. Most Hall of Famers had sad farewells. Let's face it: Their skills have declined, and they're about to stop doing what they most love in the world. It's hard to end a career of highs on anything but a low note.

Of course, there are some touching and even heroic last licks, but not everyone can orchestrate his exit. Sometimes a Hall of Famer doesn't even know that he's taken his last lick. As a result, the subject ranges from the heroic to the tragic, the happy to the morose, the purposeful to the unintended.

Hank Aaron and Babe Ruth are inextricably tied in baseball history because of their home run prowess, but they are literally tied in another category that Aaron was none too pleased about.

On September 29, 1976, the Milwaukee Brewers faced the Baltimore Orioles at Memorial Stadium. The Brewers were well on their way to a last-place finish, while the Orioles would finish in second place, 10½ games behind the New York Yankees. In his second-to-last major league game, Hank Aaron led off the sixth with a double to left field off Scott McGregor. He advanced to third when Sixto Lezcano reached on an error, and Aaron scored on Dan Thomas' single to right.

The 8,119 fans had just witnessed Aaron's 2,174th run scored, which tied him with the Babe for second place on the all-time list, behind only Ty Cobb (they were all eventually passed by Rickey Henderson). Aaron had three games left in his career.

But you can't score if you don't get on base, and you can't get on base if you don't play. More interested in watching younger players than veterans so late in the season, Brewers manager Alex Grammas sat Aaron for the next two games.

On October 3, the Brewers played the Detroit Tigers at Milwaukee's County Stadium in the final game of Aaron's career. With only 6,808 in attendance, Aaron was penciled in as the designated hitter, in the clean-up slot. First, he grounded out to short. Then he grounded out to third. In his final at-bat against Dave Roberts, Aaron hit a two-out, sixth-inning single to deep short, scoring Charlie Moore and sending George Scott to third. Then, to Aaron's dismay, Grammas sent Jim Gantner in to pinch run for him. Grammas wanted to give the fans one final opportunity to cheer for their hero, but their hero wanted one more opportunity to beat the Babe. Lezcano struck out, leaving Scott and Gantner stranded, and Hank and the Babe tied. Gantner stayed in the game as the DH and had one unsuccessful at-bat in the eighth inning.

Aaron, second on the all-time home run list with 755, hit his last home run off California Angels pitcher Dick Drago on July 20, 1976. A fastball pitcher, Drago hung a slider in the seventh inning and Aaron hit it over the left field fence.

"I remember being upset because I had gotten him out [earlier in the game] with fastballs," recalled Drago, who surrendered only seven homers in 79 innings that season. "I was a fastball pitcher and I out-thought myself."

According to the Milwaukee *Journal Sentinel*, there were only 10,134 fans in County Stadium, and groundskeeper Richard Arndt had no trouble beating them to the ball. Arndt offered to return it to Aaron in exchange for the opportunity to hand it to him in person. The Brewers refused and fired Arndt for refusing to deliver the baseball with no strings attached. Reportedly, $5.00 was docked from his final paycheck for the cost of the ball.

But living well is always the best revenge. Years later, Arndt had Aaron autograph the ball at a card show (he wasn't aware that it was *the* ball), and in 1999 Arndt sold it to Andrew J. Knuth, a Connecticut portfolio manager, for $650,000.

As for Aaron, he just wishes the ball was in the Hall of Fame. As reported by the Milwaukee *Journal Sentinel* of Aug. 28, 1999, Arndt donated $155,800 (25%) from the sale to Aaron's charitable Chasing the Dream Foundation, established to help underprivileged children develop their artistic talents. But Aaron believes the ball belongs in the Baseball Hall of Fame in Cooperstown, N.Y.

"If I had the ball, that's what I would have done with it," said Aaron. "I tried getting it from that kid."

Hank Aaron, OF, 1954-1976

G	AB	R	H	2B	3B	HR	RBI	BB	IBB	SO	HBP	SH	SF	XI	ROE	GDP	SB	CS	AVG	OBP	SLG	BFW
3298	12364	2174	3771	624	98	755	2297	1402	293	1383	32	21	121	0i	182i	328	240	73	.305	.374	.555	83.0

Walter Alston

As manager of the Brooklyn Dodgers, Walter Alston certainly boasted Hall of Fame credentials. It's a good thing, because he never would have made it as a player. Smokey's only at-bat came on September 27, 1936, as a member of the St. Louis Cardinals. Alston entered the game and took over at first base after Johnny Mize was ejected in the eighth inning.

Making one putout and one error while striking out in his only at-bat, Alston became the only member of the Hall of Fame to play in just one game.

Walter Alston, Manager, 1954-1976

G	W	L	PCT	RS	RA	EJ
3658	2040	1613	.558	15472	13791	36

Luis Aparicio

Playing shortstop (where else?) for the Boston Red Sox at Fenway Park, Luis Aparicio went 1-for-3 against the Milwaukee Brewers on September 28, 1973. In his last at-bat, facing Ed Sprague, Luis popped out to second baseman Pedro Garcia.

Of the 227 players elected to the Hall of Fame, Little Louie holds a unique spot. Beyond the fact that he was the first South American native to be inducted at Cooperstown, in his eighteen-year career spanning 2,601 games, Aparicio was the only Hall of Fame position player to have played every game at one position.

When the Chicago White Sox clinched the pennant on Sept. 22, 1959, the final outs were recorded when Vic Power of the Indians hit a grounder to Aparicio, who stepped on second and threw to first baseman Ted Kluszewski for a 6-3 double play.

Luis Aparicio, SS, 1956-1973

G	AB	R	H	2B	3B	HR	RBI	BB	IBB	SO	HBP	SH	SF	XI	ROE	GDP	SB	CS	AVG	OBP	SLG	BFW
2599	10230	1335	2677	394	92	83	791	736	22	742	27	161	76	0i	195i	184	506	136	.262	.311	.343	15.6

Ernie Banks

On September 26, 1971, Ernie Banks came to the plate in the first inning at the friendly confines of Wrigley Field and received a standing ovation from the Cubs' faithful. Facing the Philadelphia Phillies' Ken Reynolds, he responded by slamming an infield single behind third for the 2,583rd and last base hit of his career. Still facing Reynolds in the eighth, Mr. Cub popped out to third baseman Deron Johnson and finished his career with 2,528 games played and not one first-place finish. As the old player and manager Jimmy Dykes said, "Without him, the Cubs would finish in Albuquerque."

Ernie Banks, SS, 1953-1971

G	AB	R	H	2B	3B	HR	RBI	BB	IBB	SO	HBP	SH	SF	XI	ROE	GDP	SB	CS	AVG	OBP	SLG	BFW
2528	9421	1305	2583	407	90	512	1636	763	201i	1236	70	45	96i	0i	138i	229	50	53	.274	.330	.500	27.8

Roger Bresnahan / Martin DiHigo

Roger Bresnahan and Martin DiHigo were the only members of the Hall of Fame to play all nine positions.

In seventeen seasons, Bresnahan caught 974 times, played outfield for 281 games, third for 42, first for 33, second for 28, pitcher for nine, and shortstop for eight.

DiHigo did the same while playing in the Negro leagues. The exact number at each position is unknown.

Roger Bresnahan, C, 1897-1915

G	AB	R	H	2B	3B	HR	RBI	BB	IBB	SO	HBP	SH	XI	ROE	GDP	SB	CS	AVG	OBP	SLG	BFW
1446	4481	682	1252	218	71	26	530	714	1i	99i	67	112	0i	3i	4i	212	10i	.279	.386	.377	22.5

Martin DiHigo, 2B etc., 1923-1935 (Negro Leagues)

G	AB	R	H	2B	3B	HR	RBI	BB	IBB	SO	HBP	SH	SF	XI	ROE	GDP	SB	CS	AVG	OBP	SLG	BFW
i	1404	292	431	61	17	64	227	143	i	i	i	i	i	i	i	i	41	i	.307	i	i	i

George Brett

George Brett's career ended on October 3, 1993, against the Texas Rangers at Arlington Stadium. It was also Nolan Ryan's final game, and the two future Hall of Famers carried the lineup cards to home plate. As Brett stepped into the batter's box for his last at-bat, players from both dugouts stood on the top steps. Ryan tipped his cap to Brett, while catcher Ivan Rodriguez put his arm on Brett's shoulder and told him that pitcher Tom Henke would be throwing nothing but fastballs. Brett bounced a 1-2 pitch up the middle for a single, and he subse-quently scored on Gary Gaetti's home run.

Brett said:

It found a hole up the middle. Good way to end a career. I really felt good [about] the first three at-bats. The results weren't good, but the last at-bat was really emotional. The most emotional at-bat I've ever had. I knew it was my last one. I could have played one more year but, if I'd played one more year, I'd have played for the money, and the game didn't deserve that.

George Brett, 3B, 1973-1993

G	AB	R	H	2B	3B	HR	RBI	BB	IBB	SO	HBP	SH	SF	XI	ROE	GDP	SB	CS	AVG	OBP	SLG	BFW
2707	10349	1583	3154	665	137	317	1595	1096	229	908	33	26	120	1	130	235	201	97	.305	.369	.487	42.8

Mordecai (Three Finger) Brown / Christy Mathewson

On September 4, 1916, Mordecai (Three Finger) Brown pitched a 19-hit complete game for the Chicago Cubs and lost, 10-8. On the mound for Cincinnati that day, Reds manager Chris-ty Mathewson pitched his only game of the season. He threw a complete-game 15-hitter. It was the last major league appearance for both future members of the Hall of Fame.

Mordecai (Three Finger) Brown, P, 1903-1916

G	GS	CG	SHO	GF	SV	IP	H	BFP	HR	R	ER	BB	IB	SO	SH	WP	HBP	BK	2B	3B	GDP	ROE	W	L	ERA	RS	PW
481	332	271	55	138	49	3172.1	2708	12642	43	1044	725	673	0i	1375	277	59	63	4	41i	14i	13i	27i	239	130	2.06	4.47	32.7

Christy Mathewson, P, 1900-1916

G	GS	CG	SHO	GF	SV	IP	H	BFP	HR	R	ER	BB	IB	SO	SH	WP	HBP	BK	2B	3B	GDP	ROE	W	L	ERA
635	551	434	79	74	28	4780.2	4218	19136	91	1616	1133	844	0i	2502	397	114	59	6	47i	11i	12i	38i	373	188	2.13

Steve Carlton

By the time Steve Carlton finished his career, he had pitched for too many teams. When he worked his last game for the Philadelphia Phillies, going five innings and yielding six runs to the St. Louis Cardinals on June 21, 1986, Lefty had played seven years with St. Louis and fourteen-plus with the Phils. He had also earned 318 wins and the respect of thousands of fans and players.

But following his June 24 release, Carlton began the odyssey of a player who doesn't know when his time is up. He joined the San Francisco Giants (last game: August 5, 1986, pitching 3⅔ innings and giving up seven runs to the Cincinnati Reds) then the Chicago White Sox (last game: September 30, 1986, pitching seven innings and giving up three runs, two earned, to the Seattle Mariners).

Alas, he didn't quit. Carlton started 1987 with the Cleveland Indians. He ended that tour on July 30 (6⅓ innings, four runs to the Baltimore Orioles) and ended the season in Minnesota with a combined 6-14 record and a 5.74 ERA. He pitched again for the Twins in 1988 and finally, *finally*, on April 23 in the Metrodome against the Indians, Carlton pitched his last game. Facing his last three batters, Carlton surrendered an infield single to Mel Hall, a walk to Ron Washington, and a two-run double to Andy Allanson. After his five-plus-inning performance in which he gave up nine hits and nine runs (eight earned), the Twins ran out of patience and Carlton ran out of teams willing to give him a chance.

Steve Carlton, P, 1965-1988

G	GS	CG	SHO	GF	SV	IP	H	BFP	HR	R	ER	BB	IB	SO	SH	SF	WP	HBP	BK	2B	3B	GDP	ROE	W	L	ERA	RS	PW
741	709	254	55	13	2	5217.1	4672	21683	414	2130	1864	1833	150	4136	235	122	183	53	90	807	137	405	298	329	244	3.22	4.37	34.0

The one-time games, at-bats, singles, hits, runs and steals king, Ty Cobb batted .262 for losing Detroit Tigers teams in the 1907-1909 World Series. Exonerated of gambling charges by Commissioner Kennesaw Mountain Landis and hoping for one last shot at the postseason, Cobb decided not to retire and signed with the Philadelphia Athletics in 1927. His contract, reportedly between $70,000 and $75,000 a year, made him the highest paid player in baseball.

The 1927 A's finished second, 19 games behind the Yankees, with Cobb batting .357—the league's fifth-best average—in 134 games. Well, nobody was going to catch the '27 New York Yankees, so Cobb stayed on for another season.

The 1928 A's were much more competitive. In fact, they led the Yankees by half a game on September 8. The following day they opened a critical series in Yankee Stadium. Because visiting teams had to pass through the Yankee dugout to reach their own at the time, the A's ran the gauntlet before a Sunday doubleheader.

"You bums!" a young Yankees shortstop, Leo Durocher, shouted at them. "So you're in first. By the end of the day you'll be in second." And, after losing both games, they were.

Now 1½ games out, the A's handed the ball to Lefty Grove for an unforgettable game on Monday, Sept. 12. Grove had won 14 straight, and he led the Yankees 3-1 through the seventh. In the eighth, Grove walked Earle Combs on a 3-2 pitch. When Mark Koenig hit a smash to the left side, third baseman Jimmy Dykes threw wildly to first, leaving runners on first and third. Unraveling now, Grove threw a wild pitch to Lou Gehrig, Combs scored, Koenig scooted to second, and the Yanks cut the lead to one run. When Grove threw unintentionally close to Gehrig, the Iron Horse leaned back and his bat somehow hit the ball into left, scoring Koenig and tying the game 3-3, with Gehrig going to second on the throw home.

Up stepped Babe Ruth. Always the showman, he surprised everyone by bunting the first pitch…foul by inches. After taking a ball, Ruth unloaded on a fastball and drove it deep into the right field stands, giving the Yankees a 5-3 lead.

On the bench and seething, Cobb was finally called on to pinch hit for Dykes leading off the ninth. He came to the plate in just his 95th game of the year and drew boos from the crowd of 50,000. Facing journeyman right-hander Henry Johnson, Cobb swung at a high pitch and hit a pop foul to shortstop Koenig behind third base. Johnson quickly retired the A's and preserved the 5-3 victory, leaving the A's 2½ out with two weeks remaining.

As far as Cobb was concerned, the season was over. He and his .323 batting average left the team immediately. The Yankees won the pennant by the same 2½ games: The Georgia Peach was done.

Ty Cobb, OF, 1905-1928																	
G	AB	R	H	2B	3B	HR	RBI	BB	SO	HBP	SH	SB	CS	AVG	OBP	SLG	BFW
3035	11434	2246	4189	724	295	117	1937	1249	357i	94	295	891	212i	.366	.433	.512	85.7

Last Lick

On September 3, 1928, Ty Cobb pinch hit for Joe Boley and doubled off the Washington Senators' Bump Hadley for the last of his 4,189 hits and 724 two-baggers. His record for career hits would stand until 1985. He remains the leader with the highest all-time career batting average of .366.

Other than Ted Williams, Mickey Cochrane is the only Hall of Fame player to end his career with a home run in his last official at-bat. The key word is "official." After homering off the New York Yankees' Bump Hadley (the same pitcher who surrendered Ty Cobb's last hit in 1928) on May 25, 1937, the Detroit Tigers' catcher-manager was hit on the temple by a fastball on an errant 3-1 pitch. Black Mike was unconscious and critical for forty-eight hours and hospitalized for ten days. While in the hospital, Cochrane indicated that getting hit was his own fault: "I lost the ball." He never played another inning.

Cochrane resumed managing the team from the bench on July 26 and stayed on until he was fired on August 6, 1938. He never managed again in the major leagues.

Mickey Cochrane, C, 1925-1937

G	AB	R	H	2B	3B	HR	RBI	BB	SO	HBP	SH	SB	CS	AVG	OBP	SLG	BFW
1482	5169	1041	1652	333	64	119	832	857	217	29	151	64	46	.320	.419	.478	34.7

Talk about a guy who did it all. Joe Cronin was a player, player-manager, manager, general manager—even the American League president. His playing career ended at the age of thirty-nine with the Boston Red Sox. On April 19, 1945, he caught his spikes at second base and fractured his right leg in a 4–3 loss to the New York Yankees (who else!). Cronin continued to manage the Sox after his retirement as a player, then became the general manager, and in 1959 emerged as the first former player to assume the role of league president. Cronin was a great ballplayer—lucky, because he never would have made the Hall of Fame on his post-ballplaying skills.

Joe Cronin, SS, 1926-1945

G	AB	R	H	2B	3B	HR	RBI	BB	SO	HBP	SH	GDP	SB	CS	AVG	OBP	SLG	BFW
2124	7579	1233	2285	515	118	170	1424	1059	700	34	166	57i	87	71i	.301	.390	.468	39.6

In 1951, Joe DiMaggio's baseball skills finally began to erode. He slumped to a .263 batting average with 12 home runs and 71 RBI in 116 games. On September 30, the New York Yankees played the Boston Red Sox, but while Frank Shea and Johnny Sain shut them out 3-0, New York fans were more interested in the cross-town Giants and cheered when the Giants beat the Braves in Boston while the Dodger-Phillie game was still in progress. (The Giants were heading home while the Dodgers struggled in Philadelphia.) You might recall that Bobby Thomson and Ralph Branca still had some excitement ahead of them before the winner could face the Yanks in the World Series. Upon hearing that the Giants and Dodgers would be facing one another in a playoff, Yankee manager Casey Stengel joked, "Somebody ought to be pretty tired about the time they get ready to play us."

There was a ceremony before the Yankee Clipper's final regular-season game. Pitching star Allie Reynolds was called to home plate and presented with the pitching rubber he used when throwing his second no-hitter of the season, the day the Yankees clinched the pennant. The rubber was signed by all the Yankees, as well as his Sox opponents.

In his first at-bat, DiMaggio singled off Boston's Harley Hisner, the day's losing pitcher. DiMaggio came around to score the 1,390th run of his career and was then replaced by Archie Wilson. Wilson went to right field and rookie Mickey Mantle moved over to center.

The torch had been passed, but there was no mention in the New York *Times* the next day—exactly nineteen years after DiMaggio made his professional, minor league debut at shortstop for the San Francisco Seals—that the Yankee Clipper may have had his last regular-season at-bat.

In 13 seasons with the Yankees (he lost three seasons to military service), DiMaggio appeared in ten World Series: nine on the winning side. The 1951 Series against the Giants would be his grand finale.

In Game 1, facing Dave Koslo, DiMaggio went 0-for-4. He was 0-for-3 in Game 2, the day Mickey Mantle suffered a career-altering knee injury. Because of bone spurs in DiMaggio's heel, Yankee manager

Casey Stengel told Mantle, his fleet, young right fielder, to go after anything he could reach. In the top of the fifth, both outfielders converged on a fly ball hit by Giants rookie Willie Mays. A rookie himself, Mantle always pulled up short whenever DiMaggio called for the ball. Unfortunately, Mantle caught his cleats in an outfield storm drain and injured his knee. This injury would plague him for the rest of his career. DiMaggio biographer Richard Ben Cramer recounts:

In 1951, when Mantle arrived, he was so shy he couldn't say a word to DiMaggio unless the big guy spoke to him first. In fact, the first words that Joe addressed to Mantle occurred at the end of that season, the World Series, when Joe bent over the injured Mantle in right-center field and said, "Don't move, they're bringing a stretcher."

In Game 3, Joltin' Joe continued to struggle, going 0-for-4. He was now 0-for-11 for the Series. The Yanks trailed two games to one. In Game 4, DiMaggio struck out in the first but singled in the third. Then he came alive. In the fifth, he hit a long homer off Sal Maglie, the key blow in a 6-2 Yankees victory.

In Game 5, DiMaggio went 3-for-5 with a double and drove home three men in a Yankee rout. On October 10, the Yankees led the Giants three games to two, and DiMaggio headed to center field for the last time. The New York *Times* wrote the next day:

DiMaggio played a rather quiet role in this final battle. It marked his fifty-first game in world series [sic] play, putting him one over Frankie Frisch. Apart from two intentional passes, Joe figured in none of the scoring but in the eighth he blasted a double into right center and after being tagged out at third on a fielder's choice got a rousing cheer from the crowd as he jogged into the dugout.

Larry Jansen was the pitcher who gave up the last hit, fielding Gil McDougal's sacrifice bunt attempt and throwing DiMaggio out at third. But the Yankees won the game, 4-3, and they won the World Series, four games to two.

Following the game, Stengel congratulated the team. "Without you, we couldn't have done it," he said, slapping DiMaggio on the back.

Someone asked the Yankee Clipper if he were quitting. "With this victory…I don't know how I feel," he said. "Right now I haven't a thing to say on the subject. Maybe in a couple of days I'll have an answer to that."

On December 11, DiMaggio officially retired, saying, "When baseball is no longer fun, it's no longer a game. And so, I've played my last game."

Joe DiMaggio, OF, 1936-1951																		
G	AB	R	H	2B	B	HR	RBI	BB	SO	HBP	SH	GDP	SB	CS	AVG	OBP	SLG	BFW
1736	6821	1390	2214	389	131	361	1537	790	369	46	14	130i	30	9	.325	.398	.579	45.8

Last Lick

Harley Hisner was the losing pitcher for the Boston Red Sox in Joe DiMaggio's last regular-season game. It was the only game Hisner pitched in the major leagues.

Carlton Fisk

On June 22, 1983, Carlton Fisk caught game 2,226, passing Bob Boone for the most games played by a catcher in baseball history. Fisk was forty-five, and the Chicago White Sox had wanted him to retire for years. In twenty-five seasons he'd built up enough memories for two careers, including the most memorable walk-off home run ever hit: "the Fisk stay fair wave" that ended Game 6 of the 1975 World Series (see p. 85-86). But now he was hitting under .200, and the last 20 baserunners who had attempted to steal on Fisk had succeeded. But a record is a record, and there he was on a June day at Comiskey Park.

Before the game, played against the Texas Rangers, Fisk was given a motorcycle by his teammates and a shadow box of home plate by the team. Signs like "Fisk Forever" and "The Commander" festooned the stands. He lasted until the seventh inning, when he flied out deep to center fielder Tom Hulse, off Kenny Rogers. When Sox manager Gene Lamont sent in Mike LaValliere to catch for him in the ninth, Fisk took a seat on the bench. It was just as well. Now that the ceremony was over, he could comfortably prepare to catch some more games that season.

Fisk rode the bench five more days. On the sixth, with the White Sox in Cleveland, Sox general manager Ron Scheuler summoned Fisk to his hotel room. Fisk thought he would be asked to discuss his role on the team. Scheuler said the team had to look to the future and, after all the ceremony of breaking the record, unceremoniously gave him his release. He was hitting .189 with one homer and four RBI in 53 at-bats.

Overall, Fisk caught more games for Chicago than for Boston, but he entered the Hall of Fame wearing a Red Sox cap. Fisk also requested that White Sox owner Jerry Reinsdorf and Schueler not be there for the induction ceremony.

Carlton Fisk, C, 1969-1993

G	AB	R	H	2B	3B	HR	RBI	BB	IBB	SO	HBP	SH	SF	XI	ROE	GDP	SB	CS	AVG	OBP	SLG	BFW
2499	8756	1276	2356	421	47	376	1330	849	105	1386	143	26	79	0	116	204	128	58	.269	.341	.457	38.8

Last Lick

Carlton Fisk wore jersey number 72, and is the only player to have that high a number retired. Fisk chose 72 when he joined the Chicago White Sox because it was the reverse of his 27 with the Boston Red Sox. The Red Sox retired 27 in Fisk's honor in 2000. The last person to wear number 27 for the Red Sox was Kip Gross in 1999; Fisk is the only member of the White Sox to wear 72.

Lou Gehrig

The Iron Horse went 0-for-4 in a 3-2 loss to the Washington Senators at Yankee Stadium on Sunday, April 30, 1939. In Lou Gehrig's last plate appearance, facing Senators reliever Pete Appleton, he grounded out. Gehrig had left runners on in each of his plate appearances.

The team took the train to Detroit for a Tuesday game, but Gehrig made a decision Sunday night. Arthur E. Patterson wrote in the New York Herald Tribune that when manager Joe McCarthy arrived at the Book Cadillac Hotel, Gehrig asked to speak with him.

"Sure thing, Lou. C'mon around the corner here and sit down," McCarthy said.

"I know I look terrible out there," Gehrig said. "This string of mine doesn't mean a thing to me. It isn't fair to the boys."

As reluctant as McCarthy was in making the move, that's how insistent Gehrig was. The Iron Horse brought the lineup card to the umpires before the start of the next game. At first for the Yankees was Babe Dahlgren. Gehrig had played 2,164 games in his career, the last 2,130 in a row.

He never played again.

On September 27, 1923, Gehrig hit his first homer in the majors off Bill Piercy of the Boston Red Sox. On Sept. 27, 1938, exactly 15 years later, Gehrig hit his 493rd and last homer off Dutch Leonard of the Senators.

On August 20, 1938, Gehrig hit his 23rd and last grand slam off Lee Ross of the Philadelphia A's.

Gehrig was the only Yankee to ever wear uniform number 4, with the Yankees retiring the number on Lou Gehrig Day, July 4, 1939. It was the first number retired by any team. In 1929, the Yankees and Cleveland Indians became the first teams to display numbers as a permanent part of their uniforms. The Yankee numbers were assigned by position in the batting order, with Earle Combs the lead-off batter getting number 1, Mark Koenig 2, Babe Ruth 3, and Gehrig 4. Gehrig's number was retired just two months after the Iron Horse played his final game.

Ruth's number 3 was finally retired more than 13 years after he left the Yankees and was worn in the interim by George Selkirk, Bud Metheny, Roy Weatherly, Eddie Bockman, Frank Colman, Allie Clark and Cliff Mapes.

Lou Gehrig, 1B, 1923-1939

G	AB	R	H	2B	3B	HR	RBI	BB	SO	HBP	SH	GDP	SB	CS	AVG	OBP	SLG	BFW
2164	8001	1888	2721	534	163	493	1995	1508	790	45	106	2i	102	101	.340	.447	.632	70.9

It would be fair to say that whether you are rich or poor, black or white, life consists of three stages: birth, life, death. The same is true for a baseball player's major league career. He breaks in, he plays his career, and then he retires or he is released. It doesn't matter whether he's a scrub or a future member of the Hall of Fame: That's the way it goes. Sooner or later, every game ends, every streak halts, every career bows out.

Here's a story about a player in his first major league game, Buddy Schultz of the Chicago Cubs. It's also about Pete LaCock, a third-year guy, although officially still a rookie. But this story is really about Bob Gibson, the great Hall of Fame pitcher in the last game of his storied career.

LaCock came up for cups of coffee with the Chicago Cubs in 1972 and 1973, but September 22, 1974, was the first time he had ever faced Bob Gibson. LaCock pinch hit for Rob Sperring in the sixth inning and singled to right. Next time up in the seventh, Gibson brushed back LaCock before coaxing him to fly out to left.

Five days later the two teams met again, this time with LaCock in the starting lineup. In the third, he doubled to right. When LaCock told this to the authors, he jokingly mentioned that he "owned" Gibson. LaCock laughed and then in all seriousness added, "No one owned Bob Gibson, I just got my licks at the right time." In his next at-bat, Gibson hit LaCock with a fastball.

Fast-forward to June 21, 1975, Gibson's last season. LaCock went 0-for-4 against him, but the rest of the Cubs fared better and won the game, 6-1. Gibson's record dropped to 1-6. On August 4, Gibson pitched in relief and threw 3⅓ scoreless innings. LaCock struck out to end the bottom of the eighth in his only at-bat facing Gibson.

Gibson's last appearance in the majors was on Sept. 3, when he came in to face the Cubs with the score tied, 6-6. The St. Louis Cardinals had tied the game by scoring five times in the bottom of the sixth, including Lou Brock's two-out, bases-loaded double that drove in three. In came Cubs pitcher Buddy Schultz, making his major league debut in relief. As he walked to the mound, he looked over at second base and saw Lou Brock. Schultz has said that was the moment he thought, "Wow! I'm really in the big leagues!"

Nonetheless, Schultz threw two pitches and got Bake McBride on a grounder to second.

Bill Madlock led off the top of seventh against Gibson by flying out, but Jose Cardenal drew a walk. Champ Summers reached on an infield single and Cardinal moved to third when Mike Tyson committed an error.

The hot-hitting Andre Thornton, who had taken LaCock's starting job, drew a walk to load the bases. Manny Trillo bounced a ball back to Gibson, who threw to Ted Simmons for a force at the plate. Then Gibson gave an indication that the end was near by throwing a wild pitch, allowing the go-ahead run to score. He intentionally walked Jerry Morales to reload the bases.

It was Buddy Schultz's turn at the plate, but up stepped LaCock, who was generally frustrated at being a bench player. Cubs manager Jim Marshall spent forty-five minutes before the game listening to LaCock's request to be traded. Marshall told reporters, "Pete is a very ambitious young man. He needs a lot of time for someone to explain to him what it's all about."

Pete had taken extra batting practice prior to the start of the game and also had a good run around the ballpark with his Siberian Husky puppy. The combination must have worked: LaCock blasted the only grand slam of his career, deep to right field.

After Don Kessinger bounced to Reggie Smith at first, who tossed it to Gibson for the final out, Gibson was done as a player and eventually on his way to Cooperstown. Before he left the clubhouse that day, Gibson said, "When I gave up a grand slam to Pete LaCock, I knew it was time to quit."

But the story isn't over. In 1986, former stars like Warren Spahn, Whitey Ford, Brooks Robinson and Gibson played a series of old-timers' games, three-to-five innings each, at major league ball parks to raise money for former ballplayers not covered by the current pension system. The games were sponsored by the Equitable Life Assurance Company.

According to LaCock, one day Bob Feller was on the mound and having trouble getting pitches to the plate. "I come up to the plate and all of a sudden

Gibson comes running out to the mound and starts warming up, LaCock told us. "First pitch, he gets me right in the back."

At the banquet that night, Gibson was serving as the Master of Ceremony and introduced all the players…except for LaCock. "The other players are going, 'What about your friend LaCock?'" Pete recalls. Gibson laughed and went on with the evening.

Bob Gibson, P, 1959-1975

G	GS	CG	SHO	GF	SV	IP	H	BFP	HR	R	ER	BB	IB	SO	SH	SF	WP	HBP	BK	2B	3B	GDP	ROE	W	L	ERA	RS	PW
528	482	255	56	21	6	3884.1	3279	16068	257	1420	1258	1336	118	3117	171	94	108	102	13	457	83	292	208	251	174	2.91	4.08	45.0

Goose Goslin

Facing the Boston Red Sox' Lefty Grove in his last at-bat, on September 25, 1938, the Washington Senators' Goose Goslin strained a back muscle while swinging and missing a pitch. He was immediately replaced by a pinch hitter. In other words, his last at-bat wasn't an at-bat; it was the only time Goslin was pinch hit for in his career.

Goslin also has the distinction of being the final batter in both the 1925 and 1935 World Series. Unsuccessful in 1925, Goslin made the final out for the Senators when he took a called third strike against the Pittsburgh Pirates' Red Oldham in Game 7. Successful in 1935 for the Detroit Tigers, Goslin singled home the winning run in Game 6 against the Chicago Cubs.

Goose Goslin, OF, 1921-1938

G	AB	R	H	2B	3B	HR	RBI	BB	SO	HBP	SH	SB	CS	AVG	OBP	SLG	BFW
2287	8656	1483	2735	500	173	248	1609	949	585	55	162	175	89	.316	.387	.500	23.3

Last Lick

Goose Goslin, elected to the Hall of Fame in 1968, is the only man to have played in all 19 Washington Senators World Series games. Goslin hit .308 in 78 at-bats.

Hank Greenberg

Hank Greenberg had a Hall of Fame career, but he had an even more important impact on American society.

As recounted in the award-winning documentary, *The Life and Times of Hank Greenberg*, he landed in the capital of American anti-Semitism when he joined the Detroit Tigers in 1933. Father Coughlin spewed his venom on the radio; Henry Ford sold his fiction about "the international Jew."

Greenberg combated his detractors with his intelligence and his actions. In addition to winning or sharing four RBI and four home run titles as a slugger on par with the likes of Lou Gehrig and Joe DiMaggio, he won respect for sitting out a game on Yom Kippur and maintaining his composure when bigots hurled abuses at him during his challenge to Babe Ruth's single-season home run record. Widely considered the country's most important—and certainly most beloved—Jew, by the time he became the first major leaguer to enlist after Pearl Harbor, Greenberg was an American hero to more than just followers of his religion.

He returned to baseball on July 1, 1945, before a welcoming crowd of 55,000 at Briggs Stadium, and he hit a home run to help win the game. "I was playing from memory," he told Lawrence Ritter in *The Glory of Their Times*. "I'd hardly had a bat in my hands since I'd left in 1941, and after I hit that home run, they gave me an unbelievable standing ovation."

Greenberg was just getting warmed up. Needing a win on the final day of the season to clinch the American League pennant, the Tigers trailed the St. Louis Browns 3-2 in the top of the ninth inning. The bases were loaded with two outs when Greenberg came to the plate in a too-good-to-be-true opportunity. He hit a grand slam on his first swing. The Tigers held on to win, 6-3.

Finally, Greenberg clouted a three-run homer to

win Game 2 of the World Series. The Tigers beat the Chicago Cubs, four games to three. Granted, none of these dingers was technically a walk-off homer, but Greenberg had already walked off with America's heart.

After a salary dispute with the Detroit Tigers following the 1946 season, Greenberg was waived and later claimed by the Pittsburgh Pirates. In his final season, Greenberg openly supported Jackie Robinson, who cited Greenberg's "class." Greenberg played his final game for the Bucs on September 18, 1947, at Forbes Field against the Brooklyn Dodgers.

Hank Greenberg, 1B, 1930-1947

G	AB	R	H	2B	3B	HR	RBI	BB	SO	HBP	SH	GDP	SB	CS	AVG	OBP	SLG	BFW
1394	5193	1051	1628	379	71	331	1276	852	844	16	35	66i	58	26i	.313	.412	.605	32.6

Burleigh Grimes

Major League Baseball banned the spitball in 1920 but grandfathered in seventeen pitchers who relied upon the pitch for their success. The last to set a spittoon alongside his resin bag was Burleigh Grimes, who ended his career against the Brooklyn Dodgers on September 20, 1934, having returned to the Pittsburgh Pirates, his original team, at the age of forty. Ol' Stubblebeard was inducted into the Hall of Fame in 1964.

Grimes won 270 games over his nineteen-year career in large part because of his spitball. However, that didn't mean he was infallible, as Arthur Daley described in the New York *Times*:

> The one team that constantly maltreated the hard-to-hit spitballer was the Philadelphia Phils. This puzzled Uncle Wilbert Robinson, the manager of the Dodgers. He called over the catcher, Zack Taylor. Daley recreated the conversation.

"They're stealing your signs," Robinson said.

"They can't," Taylor protested. "I'm covering them up too well."

That afternoon Taylor covered up the signs so well that even Grimes had trouble seeing them. Yet the Phillies slugged away. Grimes and Taylor changed the sign pattern from inning to inning. Still, the Phillies waited for the spitter and let blast.

Eagle-eyed Art Fletcher, the Phillies' manager, had noticed something. On every pitch Grimes held the ball in front of his mouth, shielding it with his glove and either spitting on the ball or faking. But when he worked his jaws to generate saliva for a genuine spitter, the muscles in his head made his cap bobble. On the fake spitter, no muscles moved. Grimes solved this dead give-away easily enough: He wore a larger cap to protect his secret.

Burleigh Grimes, P, 1916-1934

G	GS	CG	SHO	GF	SV	IP	H	BFP	HR	R	ER	BB	IB	SO	SH	WP	HBP	BK	2B	3B	GDP	ROE	W	L	ERA	RS	PW
616	497	314	35	94	18	4179.2	4412	17959	148	2048	1638	1295	2i	1512	443	92	97	12	39i	13i	17i	34i	270	212	3.53	5.00	18.3

Last Lick

The last legal spitballers and their final games:

Doc Ayers, Detroit Tigers, May 21, 1921
Ray Caldwell, Cleveland Indians, Sept. 29, 1921
Stan Coveleski, Cleveland Indians, Aug. 3, 1928
Bill Doak, St. Louis Cardinals, May 13, 1929
Phil Douglas, New York Giants, July 30, 1922
Red Faber, Chicago White Sox, Sept. 20, 1933
Dana Fillingim, Boston Braves, May 12, 1925
Ray Fisher, Cincinnati Reds, Oct. 2, 1920

Marv Goodwin, St. Louis Cardinals, Oct. 4, 1925
Dutch Leonard, Detroit Tigers, July 19, 1925
Clarence Mitchell, Brooklyn Dodgers, June 21, 1932
Jack Quinn, New York Yankees, July 7, 1933
Dick Rudolph, Boston Braves, Sept. 11, 1927
Allan Russell, Boston Red Sox, Sept. 19, 1925
Urban Shocker, St. Louis Browns, May 30, 1928
Allen Sothoron, St. Louis Browns, Sept. 6, 1926

All eyes would ordinarily be focused on a pitcher seeking his 300th win, but that wasn't the case for the great Lefty Grove in 1941. That year, the baseball world focused on Ted Williams, who would bat .406, and Joe DiMaggio, who would run off a 56-game hitting streak. Meanwhile, the rest of the world worried about impending war.

Though he'd slipped to a 7-6 record and a 3.99 ERA in 1940, everyone assumed Grove would get the last seven of his 300 victories in 1941. Sure enough, pitching for the Boston Red Sox, Grove started the season with a two-hitter, but left after seven innings trailing, 2-1. Having become a "Sunday pitcher" who rarely worked more than once a week, he didn't pitch for another eleven days and was shelled by the Detroit Tigers in a three-inning outing. His 11-4 win over the St. Louis Browns on May 4 was overshadowed by President Franklin Delano Roosevelt's declaration that "We are ready to fight again."

Eight days later, Grove out-pitched someone he was often confused with: the New York Yankees' Lefty Gomez, 8-4. Next, Grove threw seven innings for a no-decision against the Tigers. Returning to the mound at Yankee Stadium on May 25, Grove silenced the Bombers 10-3 for win 296. On June 8, he out-pitched old rival and trivia-twin Ted Lyons (they were the only two pitchers involved in DiMaggio's streak and Babe Ruth's 60-homer season in 1927) and beat the Chicago White Sox for victory 297.

Grove was whacked by the White Sox and Browns in his next two starts, but on June 25, he beat Jim Bagby, Jr. and the Cleveland Indians, 7-2. Alas, number 298 occurred the same day DiMaggio homered to run his hitting streak to 37, four short of George Sisler's twentieth century mark and seven behind Wee Willie Keeler's nineteenth century standard. Baseball wasn't watching Grove closely anymore.

On July 2, Grove beat the Philadelphia Athletics, 5-2 for win 299. "Just as long as any club will give me the chance, I'll keep on pitching," he told Boston sportswriter Joe Cashman.

On July 11, Grove lost to the Tigers 2-0, despite his 59-18 record against them. Grove also lost a 10-inning, 4-3 decision to the White Sox when right fielder Lou Finney dropped a fly.

Before the July 25 game against the Indians at Fenway Park, Red Sox manager Joe Cronin told Grove, "Pop, this is a nine-inning game. I'm not coming out to get you." Cronin was true to his word. Amid "Take him out!" calls from the Fenway unfaithful, Grove remained in a game that would never be confused with a pitcher's duel. A Lou Boudreau homer gave Cleveland a 6-4 lead in the seventh, but in the bottom of the inning, Red Sox third baseman Jim Tabor tied it up with a home run. After Johnny Peacock singled, on-deck hitter Grove took a seat while the Indians changed pitchers, prompting some to think his day was over.

It wasn't. Years later, Boston *Globe* columnist Ray Fitzgerald wrote, "That shiny 300 apple was still on the tree, and Grove was reaching for it." Grove almost won the game himself when his single skipped past the center fielder and then was bobbled by the left fielder, but Peacock was thrown out at home. With the score still 6-6 in the eighth, Grove's best friend in baseball and his teammate for 15 seasons, Jimmie Foxx, won it with a three-run homer. When he headed into the dugout, Grove hugged and kissed him. Tabor put the icing on the cake with another homer, and Grove hung on to win his 12-hitter, 10-6 for his 300th and, despite six more appearances, last win.

On Sunday, September 21, his last day at Fenway, Grove snuck in early during the morning, packed his belongings, and hustled home to Lonaconing, Maryland, without telling his teammates. Grove reappeared in Philadelphia for the season-ending series and the tail end of Williams' pursuit of .400.

On Sept. 28, after receiving a silver chest from Philadelphia Athletics scout Ira Thomas in a ceremony between games of a Sunday doubleheader, Grove pitched in the second game and lasted one inning, surrendering four hits and three runs and taking the loss.

"It was bitingly sad," Harold Kaese wrote in the Boston *Globe*, "because while the greatest pitcher of his generation stumbled toward oblivion, cheers were ringing for the new idol, for a new Ted Williams who was making six hits in eight times at-bat to be the first American Leaguer in eighteen years to hit over .400. The contrast was painfully perfect."

Walking through Red Sox owner Tom Yawkey's hunting preserve in South Carolina that December, Grove told his boss he was quitting. When his retirement was announced Dec. 9, it was little-noticed amid developments at baseball's winter meetings and, of course, the aftermath of Pearl Harbor.

Lefty Grove, P, 1925-1941

G	GS	CG	SHO	GF	SV	IP	H	BFP	HR	R	ER	BB	SO	SH	WP	HBP	BK	W	L	ERA	RS	PW
616	457	298	35	123	55	3940.2	3849	16633	162	1594	1339	1187	2266	277	51	42	1	300	141	3.06	5.48	59.1

Rogers Hornsby

Too frequently, Rogers Hornsby's name is overlooked when recounting the game's greatest hitters. He was the only right-handed hitter to hit .400 in three seasons as well as lead the league in batting average six straight years. He also won two Triple Crowns. His career .358 batting average is the highest ever by a right-handed hitter.

But just being a great hitter doesn't make you a great guy. Charlie (Jolly Cholly) Grimm, the old player and manager, described Hornsby:

Hornsby never chewed tobacco or smoked or drank anything at all, and he expected all his ballplayers to live that way. He didn't know how to handle men. We were not allowed to smoke in the clubhouse, not allowed to eat in the clubhouse.

The owners whom Hornsby reported to were even less complimentary. While Hornsby eschewed reading and going to the movies for fear it would affect his eyesight, he found an outlet at the racetrack. Not only that, the cranky Hornsby often lived with the reputation of reneging on gambling debts.

In 1937, Hornsby was near the end of career both as player and manager of the lowly St. Louis Browns. At one point, he didn't endear himself to anyone by calling his club "a bunch of banjo hitters." That should have been warning enough that the Rajah was in trouble, even after he claimed he hadn't seen the writer who quoted him in a year. (The old "misquoted" bit goes back quite a ways, apparently.)

Browns president Donald Barnes gave Hornsby the kiss of death: a vote of confidence. By July 20, 1937, the Browns had lost 11 of 14 but scored three runs in the eighth for a pitcher named Oral Hildebrand to send the game into extra innings tied, 4-4. Alas, in the top of the 10th, Tim (Scoops) Carey, who had the fewest errors (eight) among league shortstops at game time, booted two grounders, and the Yankees went ahead, 5-4.

The king was in a rage—even when Beau Bell led off the bottom of the inning with a single, Bill Knickerbocker advanced him to third with a double, and the Yankees intentionally walked Sunny Jim Bottomley. The bases were loaded with none out, but Scoops Carey was up.

"Carey, sit down!" Hornsby barked, grabbing a bat himself and heading to the plate for his 8,173rd at-bat. The crowd at the home field, Sportsman's Park, hadn't had much to cheer all season. Now they were on their feet.

With no sense of drama, Hornsby went after the first pitch and topped it a few feet in front of the plate. Yankees catcher Bill Dickey grabbed it and stepped on the plate for the first out of the inning. Whereupon pinch hitter Ethan Allen lashed a hard liner to right fielder Tommy Henrich, and Old Reliable gunned down Knickerbocker at the plate.

Just like that it was all over: the game, Hornsby's playing career, and his managerial stint with St. Louis. Possibly looking for an excuse to fire him (other than the team's 25-52 record), the club's business manager, Bill DeWitt, called in the Rajah and said he was shocked, *shocked*, to find that Hornsby had been spending time at the racetrack. Hornsby was through.

It was true that Hornsby at times had a gambling problem, but he stoutly denied this was one of those times. Barnes would only tell the St. Louis newspapers, "Just say he was released for cause. Draw your own conclusions."

Rogers Hornsby, 2B, 1915-1937

G	AB	R	H	2B	3B	HR	RBI	BB	IBB	SO	HBP	SH	XI	ROE	GDP	SB	CS	AVG	OBP	SLG	BFW
2259	8173	1579	2930	541	169	301	1584	1038	7i	679	48	216	0i	5i	4i	135	64i	.358	.434	.577	86.0

Last Lick

Rogers Hornsby was the only player-manager to win the Triple Crown when he batted .403, with 39 home runs and 143 RBI in 1925.

Cal Hubbard was an American League baseball umpire for 16 years and then a league supervisor for 18 years. He worked four World Series and three All-Star games. Umpire Cal Hubbard is the only member of both the baseball and the football Hall of Fame.

Carl Hubbard, Umpire, 1936-1951

G	HP	1B	2B	3B	LF	RF	EJ
2470	862	813	76	719	0	0	55

Carl Hubbard, Offensive Tackle, 1927-1936

G	Rec.	TD	Int.
105	1	2	1

Jim (Catfish) Hunter

Jim Hunter was from North Carolina, and that was the only true part of owner Charles O. Finley's story about his nickname. Catfish, said Finley, was so named because Hunter enjoyed catching the fish in the backwoods creeks of his home. But back home everyone called him Jimmy.

Hunter's career ended on September 17, 1979, while he was pitching for the New York Yankees at Cleveland Stadium. Hunter threw 6⅓ innings, giving up eight hits and five runs, four earned. In the seventh, he gave up a leadoff single to Duane Kuiper. On the last pitch of his career, Hunter took care of business himself when Tom Veryzer bunted and the pitcher tagged him out. Don Hood replaced Hunter and gave up a single to Mike Hargrove that drove home Kuiper and closed the books on Hunter's Hall of Fame career.

The Athletics retired his number 27 jersey in 1993.

Jim (Catfish) Hunter, P, 1965-1979

G	GS	CG	SHO	GF	SV	IP	H	BFP	HR	R	ER	BB	IB	SO	SH	SF	WP	HBP	BK	2B	3B	GDP	ROE	W	L	ERA	RS	PW
500	476	181	42	6	1	3449.1	2958	14032	374	1380	1248	954	57	2012	132	93	49	49	7	525	70	183	157	224	166	3.26	4.30	9.8

Walter Johnson

On September 30, 1927, the great Walter Johnson made his last major league appearance. Baseball aficionados will also remember that same game as the one in which Babe Ruth slugged his then-record 60th home run of the season. How well did the Big Train pitch against the Sultan of Swat? He never faced him that day. Johnson actually made his last appearance as a pinch hitter in the ninth inning. Coming to the plate for Tom Zachary (the pitcher who surrendered Ruth's 60th the inning before), Johnson flew out to Ruth in right field.

In Johnson's first appearance of the season, on May 30, 1927 (he had broken his foot in spring training when hit by a Joe Judge liner), he threw the 110th and last shutout of his career, topping Boston 3-0 on a three-hitter.

One of the nicest men ever to play baseball, Johnson didn't throw at batters, criticize teammates, or argue with umpires. So let's be gentle when considering his last start on September 12, 1927, at home-field Griffith Stadium against the St. Louis Browns, and say the following: At least he didn't lose the game.

At thirty-nine, Barney, as he was often called, was struggling, and his final game pushed his ERA over 5.00. This from a guy who ended his twenty-one-year career with an ERA of 2.17. And the reason he didn't lose on Sept. 12 was that teammates bailed him out. Johnson homered off the Browns' Sam Jones in the top of the fourth, but in the bottom of the inning he gave up a single to Spencer Adams, doubles to Wally Gerber and Jones and a single to Harry Rice. Johnson was replaced after 3⅓ innings trailing 6-1, but the Senators got him off the hook when they rallied to win.

Walter Johnson, P, 1907-1927

G	GS	CG	SHO	GF	SV	IP	H	BFP	HR	R	ER	BB	SO	SH	WP	HBP	BK	W	L	ERA	RS	PW
802	666	531	110	129	34	5914.2	4913	23749	97	1902	1424	1363	3509	534	155	203	4	417	279	2.17	3.98	89.9

"It ain't nothin' till I call it." These were the closing words of a "discussion," as proclaimed by the Old Arbitrator, arguably baseball's most famous and greatest umpire. Bill Klem, who umpired from 1905 to 1941, called 18 World Series, was the first umpire to use the inside chest protector, and was an early adoptee of arm signals to reinforce calls. But being an umpire doesn't exclude Klem from having his own last lick.

His skills as an arbiter were so superior that for the first sixteen years of his career he served almost exclusively at home plate. It was a salute to his stature that he umpired the first All-Star Game in 1933, working behind the plate for the second half of the game. In 1953, Klem and Tommy Connolly were the first two umpires inducted into the Baseball Hall of Fame.

Many changes took place during Klem's career. In 1912, two umpires were required to cover each game, and by 1933, three-man crews were used during the regular season. The 1940 season was Klem's last full year as an umpire because at sixty-six, he felt he was slowing down. On December 10, Klem retired and was appointed chief of the National League umpires.

In 1941, the NL started experimenting with four-man umpiring crews, and Klem umpired a few games to fill the role of fourth umpire. In his last game, the St. Louis Cardinals were visiting the Dodgers in Brooklyn. St. Louis had a runner on first who took off on a stolen base attempt. Klem called the runner out when Billy Herman put the tag on him. The runner protested vehemently, but Klem—in typical fashion—walked away.

Shortly before he died, Klem talked about that play and said that as he walked away he said to himself, "I'm almost certain Herman tagged him." Recalling that moment, he said he was almost brought to tears because, "For the first time in all my career, I only 'thought' a man was out."

Klem immediately retired and never umpired another game.

Bill Klem, Umpire, 1905-1941

G	HP	1B	2B	3B	LF	RF	EJ
5368	3543	1198	25	602	0	0	241

The Chicago Cubs' Ken Holtzman faced his hero at Wrigley Field on September 25, 1966—all because Sandy Koufax had refused to play the day before on the Jewish holiday of Yom Kippur. Koufax gave up a pair of runs (one earned) in the first inning and only four hits that day; Holtzman carried a no-hitter into the seventh and only allowed two Dodger hits in a 2-0 victory. It was Koufax' ninth defeat of the season and the 87th and last regular-season loss of his career.

But when Koufax took the mound on October 2, 1966, in the second game of a doubleheader, there was no reason to suspect that this would be the great lefty's last game. Baseball fans knew that Koufax was pitching in pain, but he was simply too magnificent to do anything but continue to play.

When he beat Jim Bunning of the Philadelphia Phillies that day, Koufax won his 27th game of the season against only nine losses. Even when he surrendered three runs in the ninth (two earned), his ERA was still 1.73. And when he struck out Jackie Brandt to end the game, it was Koufax' 27th complete game of the season, his 10th strikeout of the game and his 317th for the season. He would go on to win his third Cy Young Award.

So it was shocking when this remarkable pitcher announced his retirement at age thirty, on November 18, citing a severely-arthritic elbow. On the editorial page of the New York *Times*, recounting his on-field experiences and balancing those with Koufax's off-field dignity, an editorial concluded, "Sandy's private life was kept private and his public appearances were exemplary. He has retired from the diamond; but he will be long remembered as a great player and a great human being."

Sandy Koufax, P, 1955-1966

G	GS	CG	SHO	GF	SV	IP	H	BFP	HR	R	ER	BB	IB	SO	SH	SF	WP	HBP	BK	2B	3B	GDP	ROE	W	L	ERA	RS	PW
500	476	181	42	6	1	3449.1	2958	14032	374	1380	1248	954	57	2012	132	93	49	49	7	525	70	183	157	224	166	3.26	4.30	9.8

Last Lick

Not only was 1966 the last Cy Young Award for Sandy Koufax—he was elected unanimously for the second straight year to become the first three-time winner—it was the last year in which only one Cy Young Award was presented. Starting in 1967, each league awarded their own.

One of the first stars of the American League, Napoleon Lajoie owns the highest AL batting average ever for a single season: an incredible .422 while playing for the Philadelphia Athletics in 1901. In the last game of his career, against the Cleveland Indians' Stan Coveleski on August 26, 1916, Lajoie went 1-for-3 with a triple, flying out to right field in his final at-bat. Joe Bush, who had been knocked out by Cleveland in three innings just the day before, sought revenge. It would be fair to assume he took it: He threw a no-hitter and won, 5-0.

Nap Lajoie, 2B, 1896-1916

G	AB	R	H	2B	3B	HR	RBI	BB	SO	HBP	SH	SB	CS	AVG	OBP	SLG	BFW
2480	9589	1504	3242	657	163	83	1599	516	85i	134	221	380	21i	.338	.380	.467	95.2

Tommy Lasorda

How does a guy with an 0-4 lifetime pitching record and a lifetime .071 batting average make the Hall of Fame? With a record of 1,599-1,439 as a manager.

In his final managerial game on June 23, 1996, Tommy Lasorda's Los Angeles Dodgers beat the Houston Astros 4-3 at Dodger Stadium. Lasorda repeatedly stated, "My heart bleeds Dodger blue,"

and the following day that Dodger heart attacked him. Lasorda recovered, and although he never managed in the major leagues again, he became a great ambassador for baseball around the world.

Tommy Lasorda, Manager, 1976-1996

G	W	L	PCT	RS	RA	EJ
3040	1599	1439	.526	12498	11600	44

Mickey Mantle

On May 22, 1963, Mickey Mantle broke a 7-7 tie in the 13th inning with a home run off the façade of the right field roof behind the third deck in Yankee Stadium. Mantle stopped on his way to first base to see if the ball would become the first ever to leave the stadium. He called the prodigious blast, off the Kansas City Athletics' Bill Fischer, the hardest-hit ball he ever walloped. When Mantle pronounced façade "fuh-card," the New York *Post*'s Maury Allen wrote, "When you hit them as far as Mickey Mantle does, it hardly matters how you pronounce them."

Five years later on September 20, 1968, Mantle doubled off the Boston Red Sox' Jim Lonborg in the first inning for his 14th two-bagger of the season and the 344th—and last—of his career. In the Yankee third, he hit his farewell home run, a bases-empty shot off Lonborg, for his 18th of the season and 536th of his career. He grounded out and struck out his last two times at the plate.

Mantle last appeared at Yankee Stadium on Sept.

25. Facing the Cleveland Indians' Luis Tiant, Mantle hit a two-out, first-inning single to center. This was the only Yankee hit, as Tiant threw his ninth shutout of the year to win, 3–0. In his last at-bat at Yankee Stadium, Mantle walked in the ninth—only one of two free passes allowed by Tiant.

He played his 2,401st and last game, the most ever for a Yankee, on Saturday, September 28, at Fenway Park. Facing Lonborg in the Yankees first, Mantle popped out to shortstop Rico Petrocelli. In the bottom of the inning Andy Kosco replaced Mantle at first base. Rico said, "If I had known it was his last at-bat, I would have kept the ball. I just tossed it on the mound as I left the field."

Mantle, a switch-hitter, homered from each side of the plate in the same game 10 times—the last on August 12, 1964. The Yankees beat the White Sox, 7-3 at Yankee Stadium.

An ill and dying Mickey Mantle made his final public appearance on July 11, 1995, in an effort to increase awareness of organ-donation programs.

Mickey Mantle, OF, 1951-1968

G	AB	R	H	2B	3B	HR	RBI	BB	IBB	SO	HBP	SH	SF	XI	ROE	GDP	SB	CS	AVG	OBP	SLG	BFW
2401	8102	1677	2415	344	72	536	1509	1733	126i	1710	13	14	47i	0i	73i	113	153	38	.298	.421	.557	71.8

Eddie Mathews

Eddie Mathews ended his playing career with the Detroit Tigers. But most baseball fans picture him wearing the uniform of the Braves, because he was the only person who played for the Boston, Milwaukee and Atlanta Braves. Not only that, but he played for Milwaukee and Atlanta in the minor leagues before they were major league cities.

Mathews debuted on April 15, 1952, the last year the Braves were in Boston. After thirteen years in

Milwaukee, the thirty-four-year-old Mathews played for the Atlanta Braves when they made their debut in 1966.

But he ended his career with the Tigers. In Mathews' last at-bat, on September 27, 1968, he pinch-hit for pitcher Pat Dobson and forced Don Wert on a grounder off Joe Coleman of the Washington Senators. Mathews advanced to second on an error by first baseman Frank Howard. Dick Tracewski pinch ran for Mathews, who left the field as a player for the last time. Four days earlier, he pinch hit for Denny McLain and singled off Roger Nelson of the Orioles for his last hit. (Tracewski pinch ran for Mathews then as well.)

The only time Mathews had a multi-home run game in his last season was on May 27 against the California Angels, when he homered off Sammy Ellis in the fifth and the seventh innings for the last two dingers of his career (511 and 512).

Mathews went on to manage the Braves in 1974. Despite a 50-49 record, the Braves had lost six of seven games, and on July 21 they fired Mathews. The 6-2 loss to the Pittsburgh Pirates that day was the last game of Mathews' managerial career. He oversaw former teammate Hank Aaron's breaking the all-time home run record and was the only player, coach and manager of the same team. Mathews' managerial record was 149-161.

Eddie Mathews, 3B, 1952-1968

G	AB	R	H	2B	3B	HR	RBI	BB	IBB	SO	HBP	SH	SF	XI	ROE	GDP	SB	CS	AVG	OBP	SLG	BFW
2391	8537	1509	2315	354	72	512	1453	1444	122i	1487	26	36	58i	0i	78i	123	68	39	.271	.376	.509	53.0

Last Lick

The last active member of the Boston Braves was Eddie Mathews.

Willie Mays

Sometimes the end is embarrassing. The San Francisco Giants traded Willie Mays to the New York Mets in May of 1972 so he could end his career where he'd started in 1951. Mays hit home run number 660, the last of his career, off Cincinnati Reds pitcher Don Gullett at Shea Stadium on August 17, 1973. The Mets lost, 2-1.

Later in 1973, Mays was carrying three cracked ribs and forty-two years—in short, playing on reflexes alone. He had grown querulous and selfish. Late one game, observers looked for him on the Mets bench, where he might be available as a pinch hitter. He was gone. When asked why afterward, manager Yogi Berra shrugged and said, "Maybe somebody told him something."

Appearing in only 66 games, Mays batted .211 with six homers and 25 RBI, and announced his retirement. Playing first base on September 9, 1973, in his last regular-season game, he went 0-for-2 with two walks. In his last at-bat, against Chuck Taylor of the Montreal Expos, Mays went down swinging. That should have been it, but the Mets went on to a World Series where Mays had one last chance to distinguish—or disgrace—himself.

In Game 2, the most exciting baserunner of his time fell down rounding second base. That should

have been warning enough, but there was more. With the Mets leading 6-4 in the ninth, the center fielder who made the most endlessly replayed catch in Series history back in 1954, took off slowly after a Deron Johnson liner, dived awkwardly, and missed the ball by two feet. It fell in for a double, and the game went into extra innings. In the 12th, Mays actually drove in the game-winning run when he met a Rollie Fingers pitch on the end of the barrel and sent it bouncing into center field. With the Mets protecting a 10-6 lead in the bottom of the inning, however, Oakland's Reggie Jackson hit a liner right at him that he apparently never saw. Mays retreated to the wall and brushed along it, raised his glove and watched the ball bounce in front of him.

The Mets hung on to win, but Berra took no more chances with Mays in the field. Mays only pinch hit in Game 4 and grounded out to the shortstop against Paul Lindblad. For Games 5, 6 and 7, Mays sat on the bench.

A member of the Hall of Fame, Mays is still the only player in baseball history to hit four home runs in one game and three triples in another. On Sept. 15, 1960, Mays hit three triples in a game against the Philadelphia Phillies, and on April 30, 1961, he hit four homers against the Milwaukee Braves.

Willie Mays, OF, 1951-1973

G	AB	R	H	2B	3B	HR	RBI	BB	IBB	SO	HBP	SH	SF	XI	ROE	GDP	SB	CS	AVG	OBP	SLG	BFW
2992	10881	2062	3283	523	140	660	1903	1464	206i	1526	44	13	91i	0i	143i	251	338	103	.302	.384	.557	84.4

Willie McCovey

In his fourth major league decade, Willie McCovey played his final game on July 6, 1980. Pinch hitting for Rennie Stennett, Stretch hit a sacrifice fly off Rick Sutcliffe in the final at-bat of his career.

McCovey's final homer, on May 3, 1980, against the Montreal Expos' Scott Sanderson, was the 521st of his career, tying him with his idol Ted Williams.

Willie McCovey, 1B, 1959-1980

G	AB	R	H	2B	3B	HR	RBI	BB	IBB	SO	HBP	SH	SF	XI	ROE	GDP	SB	CS	AVG	OBP	SLG	BFW
2588	8197	1229	2211	353	46	521	1555	1345	260	1550	69	5	70	5	112	176	26	22	.270	.374	.515	39.3

Bill McKechnie

Bill McKechnie was elected to the Hall of Fame by the Veterans Committee in 1962, primarily for his work as a manager (1922-26, 1928-46). He remains the only skipper to win pennants with three different National League clubs: the Pittsburgh Pirates (1925), the St. Louis Cardinals (1928), and the Cincinnati Reds (1939-40). In his final year as manager he was 67-87 with the 1946 Reds, finishing sixth in the National League. At least he finished in style, sweeping the Pirates in a doubleheader (1-0, 3-2).

An infielder, McKechnie played his final game as a member of the Pirates on September 28, 1920, against the Reds. Never a great hitter (.251 lifetime), McKechnie ended the season batting .218.

Bill McKechnie, Manager, 1915-1946

G	W	L	PCT	RS	RA	EJ
3647	1896	1723	.524	15638	15094	20

Paul Molitor

Denny Hocking, a reserve on the 1998 Minnesota Twins, clearly remembers Paul Molitor's farewell. As a Metrodome crowd of 12,049 stood to cheer on September 27, Molitor, the designated hitter, came to the plate somewhat unsteadily.

"When he got his 3,000th hit, it was like 'O.K., let's play the game,'" Hocking says. "But this last at-bat, it was the one time I saw him take a step back and kind of refresh himself of all the things he accomplished, and how important this last at-bat was. He literally had tears in his eyes."

By day's end, Molitor would have a lot of accomplishments to consider, including his 3,319 hits, 1,782 runs scored, 504 stolen bases, seven All-Star selections, and the Most Valuable Player Award in the 1993 World Series. He played every position during his career but pitcher and catcher.

In the bottom of the eighth inning, with the Twins leading, 3-2, Matt Lawton led off by getting hit by a pitch. In came Cleveland Indians closer Doug Jones, who was best known for his changeup. Molitor anticipated the pitch, but Jones threw a fastball.

"I swung anyway, and somehow I was able to fight it off and get a base hit," Molitor said. His single to center ignited a three-run inning, and the Twins won, 6-2.

Molitor finished the day 2-for-4 with a run scored. "I forgot to kiss the plate," he said, "but other than that it was perfect."

Paul Molitor, DH, 1978-1998

G	AB	R	H	2B	3B	HR	RBI	BB	IBB	SO	HBP	SH	SF	XI	ROE	GDP	SB	CS	AVG	OBP	SLG	BFW
2683	10835	1782	3319	605	114	234	1307	1094	100	1244	47	75	109	7	170	209	504	131	.306	.369	.448	36.6

Last Lick

Paul Molitor and Dennis Eckersley were inducted into the Hall of Fame together in 2004. They last met competitively on August 22, 1998, at the Metrodome when Molitor was playing for the Twins, Eck was back with the Boston Red Sox, and both teams were out of the race. With two down in the bottom of the ninth and the bases loaded, Molitor placed a perfect bunt down the third base line for the game-winning hit.

"Eck was swearing at me as we went off the field," recalled Molitor.

"I'd like to think that at-bat would be forgotten," Eckersley told USA *Today*. "But he didn't forget it and neither did I. I hoped that one day we'd both be going to the Hall of Fame, which we are and that's a miracle. He didn't have to bunt to get on—I was forty-three years old, they were 25 games out of first place, and he drops a bunt. Guess what? It worked. He's a little weasel, that's what he is."

Joe Morgan

Late in the 1983 season, Philadelphia Phillies second baseman Joe Morgan stood in a Pittsburgh bar drinking beer and talking baseball with two *Sports Illustrated* writers. If he could just get his bat going, Morgan said, the Phillies might reach the World Series.

The writers looked at each other in amazement. Morgan was thirty-nine years old. For a man 5'7", he had the ego of a giant. Morgan finished the season batting .230, but he did hit 16 homers, drove in 59 runs—and the Phillies did reach the Series. It was a good way to end his Hall of Fame career.

Between seasons, however, Morgan formed a friendship with Oakland Athletics executive Roy Eisenhardt, who suggested that Morgan might want to finish in Oakland, where he went to high school. He might also help the A's rebuild the team by mentoring younger players. And there was history to consider; Morgan needed only three more home runs to pass Rogers Hornsby's career total of 264—the most ever hit by a second basemen. Morgan signed with the A's.

By September 29, 1984, Morgan already had six homers (he broke Hornsby's record on June 24) and was penciled in one last time at his familiar number two spot in the order. It was officially Fan Appreciation Day, but really it was Joe Morgan Appreciation Day. Before a crowd of 23,036 in the Oakland Coliseum, his father Leonard threw the ceremonial first pitch to him. Then Morgan stuck around just long enough to get an at-bat. In the first inning, facing Mark Gubicza of the Kansas City Royals, Morgan took his stance, twitched his left elbow as he always did, slapped a line drive to left-center, and coasted into second base with his 449th double and 2,517th hit. How perfectly wonderful: a second baseman ending his career at second base.

Tony Phillips came in to run for Morgan, who waved to the crowd and disappeared into the dugout. He was voted the Most Valuable Player of the National League two times; he was a five-time Gold Glove winner and an All-Star nine times (MVP once)…but as a player, Joe Morgan never did like to have a fuss made over him.

He became the last Cincinnati Red to wear number 8 when it was officially retired in a pregame ceremony on June 6, 1998.

Joe Morgan, 2B, 1963-1984

G	AB	R	H	2B	3B	HR	RBI	BB	IBB	SO	HBP	SH	SF	XI	ROE	GDP	SB	CS	AVG	OBP	SLG	BFW
2649	9277	1650	2517	449	96	268	1133	1865	76	1015	40	51	96	0	130i	105	689	162	.271	.392	.427	68.5

Stan Musial

Broadcaster Vin Scully answered his own question when he queried, "How good was Stan Musial? He was good enough to take your breath away." But at forty-two, the St. Louis Cardinals' Musial was slipping, and on August 12, 1963, he announced he would retire at the end of the season. The .331 lifetime batter was merely ordinary, hitting in the .250s. But on September 29, Stan Musial Day in St. Louis, Stan showed he was still the Man. When he delivered his second hit of the game, a single off the Cincinnati Reds' Jim Maloney to score Curt Flood in the sixth inning at Busch Stadium, he had 3,630 hits in his career, 1,815 hits at home, and 1,815 on the road. Musial batted .336 at home and .326 on the road, .340 in day games and .320 at night. The crowd of 27,576 roared when he left the field for the last time, replaced by a pinch runner. The Donora Greyhound had two hits in his debut on September 17, 1941, and two hits in his finale, prompting one

sportswriter to write, "He hasn't improved at all."

Sportscaster Bob Costas elegantly described Musial on ESPN's *SportsCentury*:

> He didn't hit a homer in his last at-bat; he hit a single. He didn't hit in 56 straight games. He married his high school sweetheart and stayed married to her, never married a Marilyn Monroe. He didn't play with the sheer joy and style that goes alongside Willie Mays' name. None of those easy things are there to associate with Stan Musial. All Musial represents is more than two decades of sustained excellence and complete decency as a human being.

Commenting upon Musial's retirement, baseball Commissioner Ford Frick said, "Here stands baseball's perfect warrior. Here stands baseball's perfect knight." Those words reside on the pedestal of the ten-foot bronze statue honoring him that sat outside the old Busch Stadium and sits in front of the new Busch Stadium.

Like Jimmie Foxx, Mickey Mantle, Frank Robinson and Babe Ruth, Musial blasted 12 walk-off homers. One that stands out occurred in the 12th inning of the 1955 All-Star Game, when he hit Frank Sullivan's pitch into the stands of Milwaukee's County Stadium to win the game, 6-5.

Musial even pitched once. As a child, he had dreamed of being a major league pitcher, and on September 29, 1952, his dream came true. Musial made his only appearance.

Cardinal management devised a gimmick. With his sixth batting title wrapped up. Musial took the mound against the Chicago Cubs' Frank Baumholtz, runner-up to him in the batting race (Musial finished with a .336 average to Baumholtz' .325). A lefty, Baumholtz hit right-handed and reached base on an error by the third baseman. "Outfielder" Harvey Haddix relieved Musial after facing his only batter, swapping positions. This was also Haddix' only appearance as an outfielder.

Stan Musial, OF, 1941-1963

G	AB	R	H	2B	3B	HR	RBI	BB	IBB	SO	HBP	SH	SF	XI	ROE	GDP	SB	CS	AVG	OBP	SLG	BFW
3026	10972	1949	3630	725	177	475	1951	1599	142i	696	53	35	35	53i	0i	44i	243	78	31i	.331	.417	.559	76.0

Leroy (Satchel) Paige

Leroy (Satchel) Paige became the oldest player to make his major league debut when his contract was sold to the Cleveland Indians on his 42nd birthday, July 7, 1948. He pitched two days later.

Paige at times showed through his "retirement" in 1953 how his stuff could be judged as some of the greatest in the Negro leagues or the major leagues. He was old when he debuted and even older when he called it a career (although Paige returned to pitch in the Negro leagues after he was released by the St. Louis Browns). That's why it was even more remarkable when, on September 25, 1965, Paige pitched his first major league game in twelve seasons. He was showcased on a rocking chair in the dugout being rubbed with liniment by a nurse. Then Paige,

fifty-nine, delighted everyone but the visiting Boston Red Sox by pitching three scoreless innings of one-hit ball. After throwing genuine fastballs on his first two pitches, he needed just 26 more to face 10 men, one more than the minimum. He threw overhand, underhand and three-quarters. The last man he faced, Jim Gosger, grounded out to short.

"The old gentleman can still pitch," Roger Birtwell wrote in the Boston Globe. And the old gentleman still knew how to perform. When he was relieved at the start of the fourth inning, he removed his hat and bowed to his right and to his left. The few lucky fans, 9,289 of them in Kansas City, roared their approval.

Paige was the last St. Louis Brown to play in the All-Star Game, pitching the eighth inning of the 1953 contest in Cincinnati.

Satchel Paige, P, 1948-1965

G	GS	CG	SHO	GF	SV	IP	H	BFP	HR	R	ER	BB	IB	SO	SH	SF	WP	HBP	BK	2B	3B	GDP	ROE	W	L	ERA	RS	PW
179	26	7	4	109	32	476	429	2005	29	191	174	183	0i	290	34	0i	6	7	5	1i	0i	0i	1i	28	31	3.29	3.69	4.3

Jim Palmer

On May 12, 1984, facing the Oakland Athletics, Jim Palmer gave up four runs in two innings, pitching, as always, for the Baltimore Orioles. In the last two outs of his storied career, Bill Almon, hitting for Rickey Henderson, flied out and Mark Wagner grounded out as a pinch hitter for Joe Morgan.

After refusing to pitch mopup relief or go on the Voluntarily Retired list, Palmer was released by the Orioles eleven days later. With a 9.17 ERA for the

season but a lifetime 2.86 ERA, he looked for another pitching job, thought better of it, and went home.

Palmer was the only pitcher to win World Series games in three decades. He shut out Sandy Koufax and the Dodgers on October 6, 1966. He subsequently beat Gary Nolan and the Cincinnati Reds on October 10, 1970; Bob Johnson and the Pittsburgh Pirates on October 11, 1971; and Steve Carlton and the Philadelphia Phillies (in relief) on October 14, 1983. Palmer was 4-2 in the World Series and 8-3 in postseason appearances.

Jim Palmer, P, 1965-1984

G	GS	CG	SHO	GF	SV	IP	H	BFP	HR	R	ER	BB	IB	SO	SH	SF	WP	HBP	BK	2B	3B	GDP	ROE	W	L	ERA	RS	PW
558	521	211	53	15	4	3948	3349	16112	303	1395	1253	1311	37	2212	133	84	85	38	11	512	88	272	161	268	152	2.86	4.38	35.0

After 22 moist big league seasons, Gaylord Perry pitched his final game as a spitballer as a member of the Kansas City Royals. On September 21, 1983, he was the starting and losing pitcher against the California Angels, going five innings, giving up three runs on 10 hits, striking out four, and walking none.

His last batter was Ellis Valentine, whom Perry coaxed into a force out. No doubt, the ball was muddy by the time it arrived in second baseman U.L. Washington's hands.

In six of his last seven seasons, Perry hit one home run for a grand total of six home runs for his career. We could have written about his only homer for each of those seasons, but none of the others has as good a story as this: The date was July 20, 1969—not a minor day in world history. Perry was a lifetime .131 hitter, certainly not good, but not the worst. On this day in baseball history, Perry, pitching for the San Francisco Giants, got his first hit of the year and the first homer of his career by going deep on the Los Angeles Dodgers' Claude Osteen. Sportswriters around the country scrambled to find the quote his manager Alvin Dark had given San Francisco *Examiner* sportswriter Harry Jupiter about Perry's hitting, years prior in a game against the Pittsburgh Pirates. Watching Perry, Jupiter told Dark, "Hey Alvin, this prairie lad might hit some home runs for you." Dark responded, "They'll put a man on the moon before he hits a home run." Perry's homer on July 20, 1969, came about 20 minutes after Apollo 11 touched down on the moon with Buzz Aldrin and Neil Armstrong aboard.

On Sept. 15, 1974, Perry won his 20th game of the season by beating the Baltimore Orioles, 1-0. He went 21–13, the last Indian pitcher in the twentieth century to win 20 games.

Gaylord Perry, P, 1962-1983

G	GS	CG	SHO	GF	SV	IP	H	BFP	HR	R	ER	BB	IB	SO	SH	SF	WP	HBP	BK	2B	3B	GDP	ROE	W	L	ERA	RS	PW
777	690	303	53	33	11	5350.1	4938	21953	399	2128	1846	1379	164	3534	217	111	160	108	6	708	142	451	344	314	265	3.11	3.92	32.9

At forty-four, Sam Rice played his last game with the Cleveland Indians on September 18, 1934, and retired 13 hits shy of 3,000. Rice is the only member of the Hall of Fame to hit a home run off Babe Ruth.

Sam Rice, OF, 1915-1934

G	AB	R	H	2B	3B	HR	RBI	BB	SO	HBP	SH	SB	CS	AVG	OBP	SLG	BFW
2404	9269	1514	2987	498	184	34	1078	708	275	56	213	351	143i	.322	.374	.427	8.4

Brooks Robinson was announced as a pinch hitter for Al Bumbry on August 13, 1977, at Baltimore's Memorial Stadium. But before Robinson could bat, Doug Bair replaced Oakland Athletics pitcher Bob Lacey, and Tony Muser was announced as the pinch hitter for Robinson. In other words, Robinson's last at-bat wasn't even an at-bat. Robinson watched Muser strike out to end the game. Eight days later, the Human Vacuum Cleaner went on the Voluntarily Retired list.

On Aug. 5, 1977, Robinson had been sent in to pinch hit for Mark Belanger and actually had the opportunity to swing the bat. Facing Frank Tanana of the California Angels, he lined out to Rance Mulliniks at shortstop.

Robinson ended his career 0-for-14, most of which came as a pinch hitter. He got his last hit, an infield single to third (where else?), on June 3, 1977, off the Royals' Steve Mingori in Kansas City.

On April 19, 1977, Robinson pinch hit for Larry Harlow in the bottom of the 10th and hit a three-run, walk-off homer off Dave LaRoche to beat the Cleveland Indians, 6-5.

Brooks Robinson, 3B, 1955-1977

G	AB	R	H	2B	3B	HR	RBI	BB	IBB	SO	HBP	SH	SF	XI	ROE	GDP	SB	CS	AVG	OBP	SLG	BFW
2896	10654	1232	2848	482	68	268	1357	860	120	990	53	101	114	0i	158i	297	28	22	.267	.322	.401	14.5

LAST LICK

On August 6, 1967, Brooks Robinson became the only batter to hit into four triple plays in his career. In the fifth inning of the second game of a doubleheader, the Chicago White Sox' John Buzhardt walked Boog Powell to lead off the inning, hit Frank Robinson, then induced a Robinson grounder that went around the horn, Ken Boyer to Don Buford to Tom McCraw: 5-4-3 for those fans scoring at home.

Frank Robinson

On September 18, 1976, Cleveland Indians manager Frank Robinson sent future Hall of Fame outfielder Frank Robinson to the plate in the eighth inning as a pinch hitter. In his last appearance as a player, Robby singled off Baltimore Orioles hurler Rudy May.

Frank Robinson, OF, 1956-1976

G	AB	R	H	2B	3B	HR	RBI	BB	IBB	SO	HBP	SH	SF	XI	ROE	GDP	SB	CS	AVG	OBP	SLG	BFW
2808	10006	1829	2943	528	72	586	1812	1420	218	1532	198	17	102	1i	165i	269	204	77	.294	.389	.537	65.0

Babe Ruth

On May 25, 1935, Babe Ruth hit the last three home runs of his career. Finishing his playing days with the Boston Braves, he hit three homers at Pittsburgh's Forbes Field, including home run 714, the first fair ball hit over the right field roof of that estimable park. He should have retired then. His wife Claire and the club's traveling secretary, Duffy Lewis, urged him to quit. In the end, though, Ruth ceded to the wishes of club President Emil Fuchs, who pointed out that National League cities had scheduled Babe Ruth Days in his honor. Fuchs was also thinking about Braves attendance, sure to dip once his terrible team lost its greatest draw. Finally, Fuchs had a large carrot on the end of the stick: He gave Ruth the idea that he might manage the club one day.

So Ruth, his knee aching, his condition disgraceful, his average below the Mendoza Line, limped off to Cincinnati and Philadelphia. And on May 30, facing Jim Bivin at the Phillies' Baker Bowl, he grounded out in the first inning to first baseman Dolph Camilli, unassisted. When Ruth hobbled out to left and fell diving for a triple by Lou Chiozza, he'd had enough. He walked into the clubhouse…and out of baseball.

Hal Lee replaced Ruth in left field.

The Braves headed to New York to play the Giants. Invited to a party aboard the ocean liner *Normandie*, Ruth asked Fuchs' permission to take the series off and was refused. Fuchs told The New York *Times* that manager Bill McKechnie and he thought the Babe belonged with the team. When Ruth wouldn't budge, Fuchs released him. Ruth left baseball with a .181 average in his final season, and he never did manage.

Ruth is the only pitcher to hit somewhere other than the ninth slot in the batting order during a World Series. He batted sixth for the Boston Red Sox in Game 4 against the Chicago Cubs on September 9, 1918. He went 1-for-2 with a triple and a sac fly to drive home two runs and win his own game, 3-2. When Guy Bush relieved him in the ninth, after Ruth had given up a single and a walk, the Babe moved to left field.

September 20, 1919, was Babe Ruth Day at Boston's Fenway Park. Unbeknownst to all, Ruth was playing his last home games for the Red Sox. An indication of the "curse" to come was that Ruth scored the winning run in both ends of the doubleheader.

According to the Sanford *Tribune* of Friday, October 3, 1919, the Boston Red Sox and the Sanford Professionals met at Goodall Park the prior Wednesday in an exhibition game that marked the Babe's last appearance in a Sox uniform. The Sox won 4-3, with Ruth homering in the eighth. It was described in this fashion:

It wasn't a case of just letting the big swat artist bat the ball for four sacks to please the crowd of fans, who had been reading of his tremendous wallops during the big league season. When Ruth caught the old pill and sailed it over the right field fence, thirty feet or more inside the foul line and with a clearance of full forty feet, Sanford had his team in the hole 3-1, and it was the eighth inning. There were two out, and Gilholey was on third, with Roth on first, the result of a base on balls and a fielder's choice. Ruth had swung hard at the first ball pitched, and missed. Then came a called strike. There were few present who expected the blow that followed. Sanford's pitcher tried to pass the batter, but Babe reached out for a ball eight or ten inches wide of the plate, picked out the

seam he wanted to hit it on, and slammed the sphere out of the park, whereafter taking his time in jogging around the bases in the wake of the two men who preceded him across the plate, putting the score at 4 to 3 against the locals, which count remained without change until the finish.

Ruth won his only batting title in 1924, hitting .378. In 1923, he hit .393 but Harry Heilmann was the leader with .403 batting average.

The last man to pinch hit for Ruth was Ben Paschal, on Opening Day, April 12, 1927. After the Babe went 0-for-3 and struck out twice, Yankee manager Miller Huggins sent Paschal to the plate in the sixth inning. Pascal singled.

Only once was Ruth ever pinch hit for after he became a fulltime outfielder, when Bobby Veach singled for the Babe in the eighth inning of a 12-inning game against the Chicago White Sox on August 9, 1925. Veach subsequently moved to center field, with Earle Combs moving from center to right.

After Chicago's 4-3 win at Yankee Stadium, a Chicago *Tribune* reporter wrote, "The fans were treated to the unusual spectacle of His Royal Highness being yanked for a pinch hitter."

Ruth's last pitching performance occurred on Oct. 1, 1933. He beat Boston's Bob Kline, 6-5.

In 1934, Ruth hit .288 with 22 home runs (including career home run 700) and 84 RBI. On Sept. 24, Ruth made his final appearance at Yankee Stadium, appropriately against the Red Sox, who won, 5-0. Hobbled by a bad knee, Ruth caught a ball in right field during the top of the first inning that he barely had to move for; he then drew a walk in the bottom of the inning, limped to first, and called for a pinch runner. The 2,000 fans in attendance cheered as loud as they could.

On Sept. 29, Ruth hit his 22nd homer of the season and his 659th for the Yankees while they split a doubleheader with the Senators in Washington.

On Sept. 30, Ruth played his last game in a Yankee uniform, on the road in Washington. He went 0-for-3 and drew a walk off Orville Armbrust. Before the game, Ruth received a scroll signed by President Roosevelt, members of his cabinet, local officials and thousands of fans. Afterward, Ruth told reporters that he hoped to remain in baseball as a manager and play two or three times a week.

Babe Ruth Day was celebrated at every ballpark in the major leagues and in Japan on June 13, 1948. The main ceremony was held at Yankee Stadium on the stadium's 25th anniversary. Weakened by throat cancer, wearing a uniform (number 3) that would be retired, Ruth leaned on Bob Feller's bat in order to stand. He spoke to the fans, who sat in rapt silence:

Thank you very much ladies and gentlemen. You know how bad my voice sounds. Well, it feels just as bad. You know this baseball game of ours comes up from the youth. That means the boys. And after you've been a boy, and grow up to know how to play ball, then you come to the boys you see representing themselves today in our national pastime. The only real game—I think—in the world is baseball.

The Babe died of cancer at 8:01 P.M. August 16, 1948.

Babe Ruth, OF/P, 1914-1935

G	AB	R	H	2B	3B	HR	RBI	BB	SO	HBP	SH	GDP	SB	CS	AVG	OBP	SLG	BFW
2503	8399	2174	2873	506	136	714	2213	2062	1330	43	113	2i	123	118i	.342	.474	.690	112.0

Babe Ruth, P, 1914-1933

G	GS	CG	SHO	GF	SV	IP	H	BFP	HR	R	ER	BB	SO	SH	WP	HBP	BK	W	L	ERA	RS	PW
163	148	107	17	11	4	1221.1	974	5006	10	398	309	441	488	132	25	29	4	94	46	2.28	4.32	17.0

Last Lick

During the 1915 season, Ruth became the only pitcher in history to hit more home runs (four) than he allowed (three).

Nolan Ryan

Pitching until the age of forty-six, Nolan Ryan was 5-5, with (for him) a low total of 46 strikeouts in 66 innings, for the 1993 Texas Rangers. In his last outing, nursing a sore right elbow with ligament damage at Seattle's Kingdome on September 22, he got no one out, surrendering two hits, four walks and five runs. Dann Howitt's grand slam finished him off. The Mariners won 7-4, and Ryan took the loss. But by then, more fans were celebrating his career rather than bemoaning its end. An uncompromising fastballer who started 773 games in 807 appearances—he refused to finish his career as a closer—Ryan won 327 games and recorded an unmatched 5,714 strikeouts and seven no-hitters.

Nolan Ryan, P, 1966-1993

G	GS	CG	SHO	GF	SV	IP	H	BFP	HR	R	ER	BB	IB	SO	SH	SF	WP	HBP	BK	2B	3B	GDP	ROE	W	L	ERA	RS	PW
807	773	222	61	13	3	5386	3923	22575	321	2178	1911	2795	78	5714	205	146	277	158	33	649	106	314	274	324	292	3.19	3.80	22.2

Mike Schmidt

Although he was baseball's best all-around third baseman during the peak of his career, Mike Schmidt ended pretty much the way he started. He batted .206 as a rookie in 1972 and .203 as a veteran in 1989. But in between: Hoo, boy! He crushed 548 homers, drove in 1,595 runs and stole 174 bases, an extraordinary number for a third baseman. In his last at-bat, on May 23 at Candlestick Park, he drew a walk from the San Francisco Giants' Mike LaCoss.

Despite his down numbers in 1989, fans honored him by voting the aging star onto the All-Star team. He did not play, but he did take part in the opening ceremonies.

Mike Schmidt, 3B, 1972-1989

G	AB	R	H	2B	3B	HR	RBI	BB	IBB	SO	HBP	SH	SF	XI	ROE	GDP	SB	CS	AVG	OBP	SLG	BFW
2404	8352	1506	2234	408	59	548	1595	1507	201	1883	79	16	108	0	118	156	174	92	.267	.380	.527	77.3

Tom Seaver

Like many members of the Hall of Fame, Tom Seaver was a bench-riding spectator in his final game. Dividing his 1986 season between the Chicago White Sox and the Boston Red Sox, he went 7-13. In his last appearance, pitching for the Red Sox on September 19, he strained his knee after walking Willie Upshaw to open the fifth inning at Toronto's Exhibition Stadium. He left the game trailing, 3-2. The Blue Jays won 6-4, and Seaver took the loss. When the Red Sox went to the World Series, he was still injured…and unavailable to pitch.

Tom Seaver, P, 1967-1986

G	GS	CG	SHO	GF	SV	IP	H	BFP	HR	R	ER	BB	IB	SO	SH	SF	WP	HBP	BK	2B	3B	GDP	ROE	W	L	ERA	RS	PW
656	647	231	61	6	1	4782.2	3971	19369	380	1674	1521	1390	116	3640	187	111	126	76	8	675	120	315	221	311	205	2.86	3.94	49.5

George Sisler

George Sisler played the final game of his career as a member of the Boston Braves on September 22, 1930, retiring with an astounding .340 career batting average. But at one time Sisler was just regarded as a good-hitting pitcher. He finished his pitching career with a lifetime 5-6 record; on September 17, 1916, Sisler picked up his last win by defeating Walter Johnson, 1-0.

Following his major league career, Sisler played in the minors for two seasons in what was his first minor league experience—he had gone directly to the majors from college.

George Sisler, 1B, 1915-1930

G	AB	R	H	2B	3B	HR	RBI	BB	SO	HBP	SH	SB	CS	AVG	OBP	SLG	BFW
2055	8267	1284	2812	425	164	102	1175	472	327	48	226	375	127i	.340	.379	.468	24.8

Warren Spahn

Warren Spahn made his final major league start as a San Francisco Giant on September 27, 1965, carrying his 363 career wins against the St. Louis Cardinals' Tracy Stallard, who had 28 at the time. Spahn went 4⅓ innings but did not qualify for the win. Stallard lasted long enough to take the 8-4 loss.

In Spahn's last major league appearance on October 1, 1965, he pitched one third of an inning against the Cincinnati Reds, giving up one hit, one walk, and one unearned run in relief of Gaylord Perry. All in all, it wasn't that bad a performance, given that the Giants lost, 17-2. Sammy Ellis, the last batter Spahn faced, singled.

Warren Spahn, P, 1942-1965

G	GS	CG	SHO	GF	SV	IP	H	BFP	HR	R	ER	BB	IB	SO	SH	SF	WP	HBP	BK	2B	3B	GDP	ROE	W	L	ERA	RS	PW
750	665	382	63	67	29	5243.2	4830	21547	434	2016	1798	1434	68i	2583	218	73i	81	42	5	336i	73i	221i	136i	363	245	3.09	4.47	51.4

Willie Stargell

The beloved Pops of the "We Are Family" Pittsburgh Pirates, Willie Stargell bid the Steel City adieu in customary style. He had been battling painful arthritis in his knees, having said, "I found myself in a race with Mother Nature to play as much baseball as I could before she forced me to stop." On October 3, 1982, he singled in the first inning against the Montreal Expos' Steve Rogers. When pinch runner Doug Frobel arrived to replace him, Pops waved goodbye to the 14,948 fans at Three Rivers Stadium.

On July 9, 1967, Stargell homered over the right field roof at Forbes Field, breaking a 1-1 tie to beat Jim Maloney and the Reds 2-1 in the bottom of the ninth inning. Only 18 home runs were ever hit over the right field roof at Forbes, and this was one of seven by Pops. None of the other nine batters who accomplished this feat hit more than two. He is the only player to hit two home runs completely out of Dodger Stadium, in 1969 and 1973.

Willie Stargell, OF, 1962-1982

G	AB	R	H	2B	3B	HR	RBI	BB	IBB	SO	HBP	SH	SF	XI	ROE	GDP	SB	CS	AVG	OBP	SLG	BFW
2360	7927	1195	2232	423	55	475	1540	937	227	1936	78	9	75	0	85i	143	17	16	.282	.360	.529	29.5

Casey Stengel

The only person to wear the uniform of all four New York teams, Casey Stengel played for the Brooklyn Dodgers (1912-1917) and the New York Giants (1921-1923) before managing the New York Yankees (1949-1960) and the New York Mets (1962-1965).

As the first manager of the Mets, Stengel's number 37 was officially retired on September 2, 1965.

Casey Stengel, Manager, 1912-1925

G	W	L	PCT	RS	RA	EJ
3765	1905	1841	.509	16694	16303	41

Bruce Sutter

The closer's job is to record last licks. Bruce Sutter, the first Hall of Fame reliever to make all of his appearances from the bullpen, recorded 300 last licks, earning his 300th save in his final appearance. It would be wrong, however, to assume he hung on just to reach the 300-save plateau.

As far back as 1972, when Sutter had an operation on a pinched nerve in his elbow that he didn't tell his employer about, he had a problematic right arm. Returning from surgery, he discovered the doctors had left his fastball on the operating table. But, he said later, that was the best thing that ever happened to his career.

Fred Martin, the Chicago Cubs' roving minor league pitching instructor, convinced Sutter to try the split-fingered fastball, a pitch that resembles a fastball but drops off quickly when it approaches the plate. Sutter said, "Without [the split-finger fastball], I would've been, at best, a Double-A player. If they told me it would hurt my arm if I threw it, I'd do it all over again."

Opposing hitters and managers were astounded by his splitter. "It's unhittable," said Montreal Expos manager Dick Williams, "unless he hangs it, and he never does." On one occasion against the Expos, Sutter struck out the last six batters of the game and fanned the side (Ellis Valentine, Gary Carter and Larry Parrish) on nine pitches in the ninth inning.

After the 1984 season, Sutter signed a six-year, ten-million dollar free-agent contract with the Atlanta Braves, but his shoulder began acting up. He missed the last five months of 1986 and the entire 1987 season with a partial rotator-cuff tear. With 286 saves to his credit, he made one final effort in 1988, not so much to reach 300 as to revive his pitching career.

Sutter had 12 saves by the All-Star Break. Then shoulder pain held him to one more save through August. On September 9, Sutter pitched the 11th inning with the Braves holding a 5-4 lead at San Diego's Jack Murphy Stadium. He got Tim Flannery on a fly to left and Dickie Thon on a grounder to short. Only Roberto Alomar separated Sutter from the save. It was fitting that Sutter struck him out with a split-fingered fastball; Sutter's 861st career strikeout was the last pitch he ever threw. When a full rotator-cuff tear was uncovered the following March, he retired with 300 saves in just 12 seasons.

Bruce Sutter, P, 1976-1988

G	GS	CG	SHO	GF	SV	IP	H	BFP	HR	R	ER	BB	IB	SO	SH	SF	WP	HBP	BK	2B	3B	GDP	ROE	W	L	ERA	RS	PW
661	0	0	0	512	300	1042.1	879	4251	77	370	328	309	83	861	75	25	37	13	8	138	27	85	68	68	71	2.83	-	18.5

The Pittsburgh Pirates' shortstop had nothing left to prove by the 1917 season and was reluctant to play. Honus Wagner had already recorded his 3,000th hit in 1914, and he became the oldest player to hit a grand slam as a forty-one-year-old in 1915. But then his average dropped to .287 in 1916, and the sixth-place Pirates didn't appear to have much of a future. Besides, Wagner married Bessie Baine Smith on December 31, 1916, and grew portly on her cooking.

But play Wagner did in 1917. After a decent start he slumped, and he mostly benched himself after being spiked by Casey Stengel on July 14. The Pirates dropped into the cellar, and manager Jimmy Callahan was fired. Wagner became acting manager but quit after one win followed by four losses. Baseball's best all-around shortstop played one game at the position during his tenure as manager. In his last appearance, at Braves Field on September 17, he played three innings at second before Bill Wanger pinch hit for him and struck out. The Braves won, 4-1. Wagner batted .265 for the season, but he retired with a lifetime average of .327, with 1,732 RBI and 722 stolen bases.

Honus Wagner, SS, 1897-1917

G	AB	R	H	2B	3B	HR	RBI	BB	IBB	SO	HBP	SH	XI	ROE	GDP	SB	CS	AVG	OBP	SLG	BFW
2792	10430	1736	3415	640	252	101	1732	963	5i	327i	125	221	0i	16i	8i	722	37i	.327	.391	.466	82.2

Ted Williams

Ted Williams homered off Thornton Lee of the Chicago White Sox as a rookie on September 19, 1939. On Sept. 2, 1960, Williams hit a home run off Washington Senator Don Lee, making Williams the only player to homer off a father-son combination.

He made only one appearance on the mound: August 24, 1940, when he pitched the last two innings of a 12–1 loss to the Detroit Tigers. Williams allowed three hits and one run. He did record one strikeout, getting slugger Rudy York, who had driven in five Detroit runs. Joe Glenn, who caught Babe Ruth's last pitching appearance in 1933, was Williams' catcher, which makes Glenn the only player to catch both Williams and Ruth.

The story of Ted Williams' last at-bat has been told and re-told many times. But no account compares with John Updike's *New Yorker* report, "Hub Fans Bid Kid Adieu," which begins with the unforgettable line: "Fenway Park, in Boston, is a lyric little bandbox of a ballpark."

On a cold, wet Sept. 28 in 1960, only 10,454 fans showed up at Fenway to see Williams' final home game. He'd endured a stormy relationship with the local press, and Red Sox followers were divided about the future Hall of Famer they'd watched over the course of four decades—a player who'd once spat at them. If there was any parting shot from Teddy Ballgame, everyone expected it to be verbal.

And Williams delivered. Standing on the pitcher's mound in a pregame ceremony, he said:

In spite of all my differences and disagreements with the knights of the keyboard upstairs, I must say that my stay in Boston has been the most wonderful thing in my life. If I were ever asked what I would do if I had to start my baseball career over again, I'd say I would want to play in Boston for the greatest owner in the game and the greatest fans in America.

Williams was finally courting the fans, even as he kissed off the writers. Reporters and columnists from the seven Boston papers were there, but none of the noted out-of-town columnists were in attendance. No doubt they expected Williams to make his curtain call in the season-ending series at Yankee Stadium. Williams, however, had decided on Fenway, a fact disclosed to only a few insiders, among them radio voice Curt Gowdy, who let his listeners in on the secret during the game. The contest was not televised.

Having begun the season with a home run in his first at-bat off the Washington Senators' Camilo Pascual, Williams wanted to end the same way. He thought he'd connected when he launched a long fly in the fifth inning, but center fielder Al Pilarcik caught it at the 380-foot mark in front of the visiting bullpen.

"Damn, I hit the living hell out of that one," Williams told Baltimore Orioles first baseman Vic Wertz. "If that one didn't go out, nothing is going out today."

By the eighth, Baltimore pitcher Jack Fisher, a

young right-hander, was all but laughing. Williams slowly approached the plate. The crowd stood as one, and not one person booed. After a ball, Fisher threw a fastball by the old man, who lunged at it feebly. Fisher motioned to catcher Gus Triandos to return the ball quickly.

"He laid a ball right there," Williams said later at his Hall of Fame ceremony:

I don't think I ever missed in my life like I missed that one, but I missed it. And for the first time in my life, I said, 'Oh, Jesus, what happened? Why didn't I hit THAT one?' I couldn't believe it. It was straight, not the fastest pitch I'd ever seen, good stuff. I didn't know what to think, because I didn't know what I'd done on that swing. Was I ahead or was I behind? It wasn't a breaking ball and right in a spot that, boy, what a ball to hit. I swung, had a hell of a swing, and I missed it. I'm still there trying to figure out what the hell happened. Then I could see Fisher out there with his glove up to get the ball quickly, as much as saying, "I threw that one by him, I'll throw another by him." And I saw all that and I guess it woke me up, you know. Right away, I assumed, "He thinks he threw it by me." The way he was asking for the ball back quick, right away, I said, "I know he's going to go right back with that pitch."

Fisher threw another fastball, thigh-high, and Williams, ready now, launched a monstrous fly to right-center. "The ball climbed on a diagonal line into the vast volume of air over center field," Updike wrote. "From my angle, behind third base, the ball seemed less an object in flight than the tip of a towering, motionless construct, like the Eiffel Tower or the Tappan Zee Bridge. It was in the books while it was in the sky."

With the blow landing 440 feet from home plate, on top of the Red Sox bullpen roof, Williams passed Tris Speaker as 10th on the all-time batting average list: to be precise, .3444388 to Speaker's .3444322. "He is a sort of supernatural power," Judge Emil Fuchs, the former Boston Braves owner, said of Williams.

Williams circled the bases and disappeared into the Red Sox' dugout. Despite the pleas of everyone— the fans, his teammates, the umpires, even opposing players—he refused to reappear and tip his cap. Nor did he acknowledge the fans in the top of the ninth when Carroll Hardy trotted out to left and Williams trotted in.

"Gods do not answer letters," Updike wrote. The Sox won, 5-4.

To meet Williams in retirement was to encounter a latter-day John Wayne, his voice carrying through the room and bouncing off walls. Williams spoke with such gusto and zeal that it was impossible to disagree with him on any subject, even when he told you that the greatest man he ever met was Richard Nixon.

But how did he feel about his last lick? Williams didn't display the totality of his feelings about the blast for years. Finally, he told television host Bob Costas, "I have to say that was certainly one of the more moving moments, the tingling in my body, that I ever had as a baseball player, that last home run. That it was all over and I did hit the home run."

Note that he said "one of the more moving moments." No reconsideration of Williams would be complete without mention of others, which invariably seemed to involve last licks of one kind or another.

In the 1941 All-Star Game, Williams hit a two-out, three-run homer off Claude Passeau in the ninth inning—"the most thrilling hit of my life," he said at one point—to give the American League a 7-5 win at Detroit's Briggs Stadium. Nor should anyone overlook the final day of the 1941 season, when Williams could have stayed on the bench with a .39955 average that would have rounded off to .400. He insisted on playing, went 6-for-8, and finished the season at .406, the last time anyone cleared .400. Playing in his final game before going off to fight in the Korean War on April 30, 1952, Williams hit a game-winning, two-run homer off Dizzy Trout—"a towering thing of typical Williams majesty," Jerry Nason wrote in the Boston *Evening Globe*—to give the Red Sox a 5-3 win over the Detroit Tigers. And he accomplished this before 24,764 fans, including a sailor who hitchhiked up from Providence, two truant schoolboys, and a businessman on crutches, all there for Ted Williams Day.

Said Williams in *My Turn At-Bat*: "You can't imagine the warm feeling I had, for the very fact that I had done what every ballplayer would want to do on his last time up, having wanted to do it so badly, and knowing how the fans really felt, how happy they were for me. Maybe I should have let them *know* I knew, but I couldn't. It just wouldn't have been me."

There was nothing phony about the way the Thumper orchestrated his exits.

Williams had decided in advance not to join the

Sox when they played their final series in New York, but that's not to say that Williams deprived his rivals of a Williams-esque ending. His homer on Sept. 6, 1960, in his final game at Yankee Stadium, led Boston to a 7–1 win.

Williams managed his final game when his Texas Rangers lost to the Kansas City Royals 4-0, on October 4, 1972. A better hitter than a manager, he finished with a record of 273-364. His winning percentage of .429 was just .022 higher than his 1953 batting average. The Splendid Splinter was replaced by the White Rat, Whitey Herzog.

Ted Williams, OF, 1939-1942, 1946-1960

G	AB	R	H	2B	3B	HR	RBI	BB	IBB	SO	HBP	SH	SF	XI	ROE	GDP	SB	CS	AVG	OBP	SLG	BFW
2292	7706	1798	2654	525	71	521	1839	2021	86i	709	39	5	20i	0i	18i	197	24	17	.344	.482	.634	86.5

LAST LICK

Not surprisingly, Ted Williams was the last member of the Boston Red Sox to wear uniform number 9. The team retired the number in a ceremony in 1984. The last person to wear the number before Williams was Ben Chapman in 1938, the year before Williams joined the club.

Early Wynn

The number 300 has special resonance for baseball players. If one can win 300 games, save 300 games, or bat .300 over a career, one just might win themselves a plaque in Cooperstown. So when a player finishes at precisely 300, it's easy to assume he was hanging on just to get there.

That certainly seemed to be true for Early (Gus) Wynn. After enduring eight seasons with the horrible Washington Senators, somehow winning 18 games in 1943 and 17 in 1947, he was traded to the Cleveland Indians in 1949, and his career took off. He went 11-7 in 1949, then became the most successful pitcher in the American League during the 1950s, winning 188 games and leading the majors with 1,544 strikeouts. He had a league-best 23-11 record in 1954, when Cleveland went to the World Series, and was a 20-game winner four times.

Along the way, Wynn developed a reputation as a head-hunter. When asked if he would throw at his own grandmother, he said, "I'd have to. My grandma could really hit the curveball."

Traded to the Chicago White Sox after the 1957 season, Wynn again led the league in wins with a 22-10 record in Chicago's pennant-winning 1959 season. He slipped to 13 wins in 1960 and eight in 1961. In 1962, he went 7-15, and as the season ended he failed three times to win his 300th game. His ERA ballooned to 4.46. After the season, he was released and re-signed by the Indians for the expressed-purpose of winning number 300. He was forty-two years old. Truly, this was a charity case's charity case.

Cleveland trotted him out to start four times early in 1963, and he failed to win each time, although the record should show he went the distance in his first start and lost to the Baltimore Orioles on Ron Hansen's ninth-inning home run. Seven consecutive starts and no 300th victory; finally on July 13 he went five innings and left with a fragile 5-4 lead over the Kansas City Royals. Thanks to Jerry Walker's four innings of shutout relief, Wynn got the win 7-4, his 300th and last.

And that, surely, would have been the end for him. Except that manager Birdie Tebbetts saw something left in Wynn's raggedy arm. Wynn stuck with the team as a reliever and finished 1-2, with a 2.28 ERA and one save. In his last mano-à-mano against the California Angels at Dodger Stadium on September 13, 1963, Wynn retired Charlie Dees on a liner to short. Released on October 14, he retired with a 300-244 record and a 3.54 ERA. Early Wynn may have started the season as a charity case, but he ended up earning a respected place on the team.

Early Wynn, P, 1939-1944, 1946-1963

G	GS	CG	SHO	GF	SV	IP	H	BFP	HR	R	ER	BB	IB	SO	SH	SF	WP	HBP	BK	2B	3B	GDP	ROE	W	L	ERA	RS	PW
691	612	290	49	66	15	4564	4291	19408	338	2037	1796	1775	36i	2334	246	52i	51	64	2	174i	27i	82i	51i	300	244	3.54	4.50	19.5

Like Ted Williams, his successor in left field at Fenway Park, Carl Yastrzemski is a member of the Hall of Fame. Because he was given the impossible job of replacing baseball's best hitter in the shadow of the Green Monster, the Boston-area media cut Yaz some slack for his general surliness in the clubhouse and his constant worrying about his skills. His image improved when he won the Triple Crown, led the Red Sox into the Impossible Dream World Series, and possibly saved Fenway Park in 1967.

By the time Yaz concluded his last lap around the American League in 1983, he was an object of appreciation for most New Englanders, if not his teammates. A crowd of 33,491 swelled in Fenway for his exit on Sunday afternoon, October 2. The day before, Yastrzemski had impulsively broken off from a pregame ceremony in his honor and trotted along the right field line, slapping the hands of surprised and delighted fans. With Fenway organist John Kiley playing "My Way," then "The Impossible Dream," then "Auld Lange Syne," he kept going, all around the field, a baseball first.

Even the umpires were set to crown him King Carl. On Friday night, two days before his exit, Cleveland Indians pitcher Lary Sorensen and a few of his teammates ran into the umps at a bar. "…Rich Garcia told us, 'Look, fellows, if he doesn't swing, it's a ball,'" Sorensen told the Boston *Globe*.

Evidently spooked by those words, Cleveland starter Dan Spillner tried to steer rather than throw the ball when Yastrzemski came to bat for the last time in the eighth inning. He took three balls. The fourth pitch was up around his eyes, but Yastrzemski couldn't bear to retire with a walk. He tried to "jerk it out," in his words, and lofted a high pop to second baseman Jack Perconte.

Smiling ruefully as he ran toward first thinking about his 1-for-3 in this, his final game, he reflected on the irony of it all. Though he was a fine clutch hitter, he seemed to punctuate endings by hitting the ball unthreateningly in the air, particularly in games that mattered (the Sox won this meaningless game, 3-1).

Concluding Game 7 of the 1967 World Series—a game long since lost, to be sure—Yastrzemski flied out against Bob Gibson. In Game 7 of the 1975 World Series, he did the same against the Cincinnati Reds' Will McEnaney. And in the final out of the climactic one-game playoff against Bucky Dent and the New York Yankees in 1978, the tying run edging off third, Goose Gossage coaxed Yastrzemski to foul out to third baseman Graig Nettles, a denouement so odious that Boston *Globe* columnist Ray Fitzgerald said a director should ask for another take, and *The New Yorker*'s Roger Angell wrote, "I think God was shelling peanuts."

Carl Yastrzemski, OF, 1961-1983

G	AB	R	H	2B	3B	HR	RBI	BB	IBB	SO	HBP	SH	SF	XI	ROE	GDP	SB	CS	AVG	OBP	SLG	BFW
3308	11988	1816	3419	646	59	452	1844	1845	190	1393	40	13	105	1	153	323	168	116	.285	.379	.462	42.7

LAST LICK

Carl Yastrzemski was the last Boston Red Sox to wear number 8. The last prior to him was Ed Sadowski in 1960, the year before Yaz donned the uniform.

The Last...

Tokyo Yomiuri Giants slugger Sadaharu Oh.

...#42

On April 15, 1997, Major League Baseball retired number 42, the same number Jackie Robinson wore, in recognition of his accomplishments on and off the field. Baseball commissioner Bud Selig made the announcement during his remarks at the Jackie Robinson Celebration at Shea Stadium:

The day Jackie Robinson stepped on a major league field will forever be remembered as baseball's proudest moment. Major League Baseball is retiring number 42 in tribute to his great achievements and for the significant contributions he made to society. Number 42 belongs to Jackie Robinson for the ages.

Seven players wearing 42 at the time were grandfathered in and allowed to continue wearing it:

Butch Huskey, New York Mets
Mike Jackson, Cleveland Indians
Scott Karl, Milwaukee Brewers
Jose Lima, Houston Astros
Mariano Rivera, New York Yankees
Mo Vaughn, Boston Red Sox
Lenny Webster, Baltimore Orioles

Robinson's number had been retired by the Dodgers on June 4, 1972.

LAST LICK

The last remaining active player to wear number 42 is Mariano Rivera, the closer for the New York Yankees.

...team to integrate

On July 21, 1959, Pumpsie Green pinch ran in a 2-1 loss to the Chicago White Sox and became the first African-American to ever play for the Boston Red Sox. Boston was the last major league team to field a black player, and Green took his first at-bat the following day when he started at second base against the White Sox and Early Wynn. Green played his last major league game as a New York Met on September 26, 1963, going 1-for-4 against the Los Angeles Dodgers and popping out to shortstop in his final at-bat.

Green, in *Where Have All Our Red Sox Gone?* by Harvey Fromer, said:

People made me aware. They wouldn't let me forget it. I did not think of myself as another Jackie Robinson, as a pioneer with the Red Sox. I just wanted to make the team. As long as I had that chance, I was going to try and do the best I could. It got to be sort of tiring when the media kept asking me questions about being the first black on the Red Sox and what it meant to me, and what was my opinion as to why Boston had never had a black player before.

...National League team to integrate

On April 22, 1957, John Kennedy appeared as a pinch runner for Solly Hemus, and ten years and one week after Jackie Robinson debuted for the Brooklyn Dodgers, the Philadelphia Phillies had their first African-American player. Kennedy took his first at-bat on April 24 after again entering the game as a pinch runner. The Phils batted around against the Pittsburgh Pirates, and Kennedy made the last out of the inning by grounding out to shortstop.

Yet again as a pinch runner, Kennedy made his last major league appearance on May 3, 1957. He was 0-for-2 in his major league career.

...Negro league player to make the major leagues

Ike Brown became the last Negro league player to make it to the major leagues when he joined the Detroit Tigers on June 17, 1969.

...Negro league player to regularly appear in the major leagues

Hank Aaron was the last Negro league player to regularly appear in the major leagues when he bid farewell on October 3, 1976.

...Negro league player to appear in a major league game

As a stunt, at age fifty-four, Minnie Minoso pinch hit for the Chicago White Sox on October 4 and 5, 1980, fouling out to the catcher and grounding out.

...and only player to integrate two teams

Hank Thompson became the first African-American player to take the field for the St. Louis Browns on July 17, 1947. Then he and Monte Irvin became the first black players for the New York Giants on July 8, 1949.

...Chicago Cub to wear #10

Chicago Cubs manager Bruce Kimm wore number 10 only through the 2002 season, because in 2003 the Cubs retired Ron Santo's number.

...New York Met to wear #14

Third baseman Ken Boyer wore number 14 in 1967, but in 1982 the New York Mets retired former-manager Gil Hodges' number.

...New York Met to wear #41

Pitcher Gordie Richardson wore number 41 in 1966. He was the last to do so before the New York Mets made Tom Seaver's number the only player's number they've ever retired, on June 24, 1988.

...Chicago Cub to wear #14

Outfielder Paul Schramka appeared in two games for the 1953 Chicago Cubs. He was the last to wear number 14 before Ernie Banks, in whose honor the uniform was retired.

...Chicago Cub to wear #23

Outfielder Jim Tracy, who played outfield and first base for the Cubs in 1980 and 1981 and later became a manager, wore Ryne Sandberg's number 23 before it was retired in the Hall of Fame second baseman's honor.

...Chicago Cub to wear #26

Fritz Connally went 1-for-10 for the 1983 Chicago Cubs, striking out five times, before number 26 was retired in honor of Billy Williams.

...Chicago Cub to wear #42

Coach Dan Radison wore number 42 in 1995-97. Radison never played in the major leagues and was randomly assigned 42 when he was with the Cubs. He later switched to number 3.

...and only New York Yankee to wear the same numbers as Babe Ruth, Mickey Mantle and Alex Rodriguez

The center of this New York Yankees maelstrom was Cliff Mapes.

In 1948, the rookie Mapes was the last to wear Babe Ruth's number 3 before it was retired on June 13, 1948. He then became the first Yankee to wear Alex Rodriguez' number 13.

In 1949, 1950 and 1951, Mapes wore Mickey Mantle's number 7. Mantle, who originally wore 6, was sent down to Triple-A in July, 1951, because he was slumping. When he returned in August, he was given number 7, which remained his number for the remainder of his career. The Yankees retired number 7 on Mickey Mantle Day, June 8, 1969.

But there's more...

On August 11, 1950, Joe DiMaggio was in a 4-for-38 slump that dropped his average to .279. When he was benched for the first time, his substitute, one Cliff Mapes, homered to give the Yankees a 7–6 win over the Philadelphia Athletics.

...and only player to wear his birthday on his uniform

The younger brother of Lee May, Carlos May batted .274 from 1968-77, primarily with the Chicago White Sox. Carlos May wore number 17 most of his career, and his uniform read "May 17." He was born on May 17, 1948.

...and only player to wear his hometown on his uniform

Pitcher Bill Voiselle, number 96 in your program, lived in Ninety Six, South Carolina. Playing for the New York Giants, Boston Braves and Chicago Cubs between 1942-50, he went 42-50 with a 3.83 ERA.

...and only player to wear a fraction on his uniform

The St. Louis Browns' Eddie Gaedel was 31 inches tall (short?) when he led off the second game of a doubleheader on August 15, 1951, against the Detroit Tigers. In his only major league appearance, Gaedel wore 1/8 on the back of his uniform, which he borrowed from the team's batboy. Not surprisingly, Detroit pitcher Bob Cain issued a four-pitch walk to the tiniest strike zone in baseball history.

...nearly perfect pitcher

John Kull was born John A. Kolonauski on Saturday, June 24, 1882, in Shenandoah, Pennsylvania. Kull was twenty-seven years old when he made his sole major league appearance on October 2, 1909, with the Philadelphia Athletics. Quite a few pitchers have gone 1-0 in their only big league appearance, ending their careers with a winning percentage of 1.000. But Kull is the only one to also boast a batting average of 1.000 (after going 1-for-1 in his only plate appearance) and a fielding percentage of 1.000 (after getting an assist in his only chance). He did give up one run in his three innings of work, ending his career with an ERA of 3.00.

...other nearly "perfect" pitcher

Almost any pitcher who makes it to the big leagues and hangs around for a while will win his share of games. This is particularly true when you appear in 55 games over a four-year period, as Terry Felton did with the Minnesota Twins.

Selected in the second round of the 1976 amateur draft, he won 33 games in the minor leagues before joining the Twins in 1979 and throwing two scoreless innings in his one appearance. Felton was 0-3 over five games in 1980 and gave up six runs in one brief appearance in 1981. In 1982, he made 48 appearances, starting six, finishing twenty, and picking up three saves in three opportunities.

What he didn't pick up was a win. On August 12, 1982, Felton broke the major league record for rookie pitchers by losing his 14th straight game, setting records for most career losses without a victory and most consecutive losses from the beginning of a career. Ironically, this could not be characterized as a slump, because a slump, like a valley in one's career, comes between high points.

There were no high points for Terry Felton, unless you count May 29, 1982, when he started against the New York Yankees. In the top of the second, Bobby Murcer and Graig Nettles singled. With the runners moving, Roy Smalley struck out. Sal Butera's throw to Gary Gaetti at third was so far ahead of Murcer that he stopped and retreated toward second, where Nettles had arrived. Nettles ran back to first. Gaetti threw to Kent Hrbek, who tagged Nettles out. When Murcer broke for third. Hrbek threw to pitcher Felton covering the bag and Murcer was out for a triple play. This event caused Murcer to quip, "We need a second base coach."

Nonetheless, Felton was 0-16 after 1982, and his major league career was over. He was perfectly... winless.

...and only pitchers to strike out the same number of batters in a game as his age

On September 13, 1936, pitching for the Cleveland Indians, seventeen-year-old Bob Feller struck out 17 Philadelphia A's. Then on May 6, 1998, twenty-year-old Kerry Wood of the Chicago Cubs struck out 20 Houston Astros. Wood allowed one hit and walked no one in one of the greatest pitching performances of all-time.

... the last National League pitcher to lose over 25 games in a season

They say you need to be good to lose 20 games in a season. In that case, kudos to Paul Derringer, who in 1933 went 0-2 for the Cardinals before he was traded to the Reds in May and for whom he went 7-25 to end the season 7-27. Don't believe he was that good? His ERA was 3.30 that miserable season.

...the last American League pitcher to lose over 25 games in a season

Happy Townsend went 5-26 for the 1904 Washington Senators. His ERA was 3.58 that season. We just want to know what he was so happy about.

...American League pitcher to hit before the advent of the designated hitter

On October 3, 1972, the day before the end of the regular season, Baltimore Orioles rookie Roric Harrison hit his only home run of the year off Cleveland Indians veteran Ray Lambin in the second game of a doubleheader. Because the designated hitter would be introduced the following season, Harrison hit the last roundtripper by an American

League pitcher until interleague play began.

The Chicago White Sox' Terry Forster (David Letterman's "fat tub of goo") couldn't have been happy with the advent of the DH; in 1972, Forster went 10-for-19 for a resounding .526 batting average. On October 3, he pinch hit for Hank Allen (Dick Allen's brother) against Wayne Granger of the Minnesota Twins, and singled home the go-ahead run. Forster then stole the only base of his career, making him the last AL pitcher to steal a base before interleague play.

Wednesday, October 4, 1972, was the last day of games with American League pitchers coming to the plate. Closing the regular season on the west coast, the first-place Oakland Athletics faced the California Angels and Nolan Ryan, who sought his 20th win of the season. Despite pitching a complete game, striking out 10 and allowing only one earned run, Ryan lost, 2-1. At the plate he was 0-for-3, and when he struck out against Joel Horlen in the bottom of the seventh he was the last pitcher to hit in the pre-designated hitter American League.

…game catching two Hall-of-Famers

On August 24, 1940, catcher Joe Glenn made his last major league appearance. Glenn's Boston Red Sox were losing 12-1 and their left fielder came in to pitch the last two innings. The pitcher was Ted Williams making his only appearance on the mound. On October 1, 1933, Glenn also caught the last pitching appearance of another Hall-of-Famer. This time Glenn was catching for the Yankees and their opponent was the Red Sox; the pitcher was Babe Ruth and he threw a complete game en route to a 6-5 win.

…17

Ed Rommel was baseball's first knuckleball pitcher. Like the knucklers of today, he could throw a lot of innings. From 1921-1925, Rommel averaged more than 283 innings per season as a starter. But even knuckleballers' arms get tired, and by 1927 Connie Mack used Rommel as a reliever except for the occasional spot start.

Being a relief pitcher doesn't always mean pitching fewer innings. In his last season, 1932, he finished a game that ranks as one of the oddest experiences for a relief pitcher.

The date was July 10, but more importantly Sunday, when the Philadelphia Athletics were scheduled to host the start of a five-game series against the Cleveland Indians. In those days, Pennsylvania still had Blue Laws that forbade any baseball being played on Sunday. So the two teams traveled by train to Cleveland for one game and then resumed the series in Philly the next day.

Times were lean for many ballclubs during the Depression. Because Philadelphia owner Connie Mack was in financial difficulty, he took only a partial squad to Cleveland and didn't book hotel rooms, preferring to play the game and return to Philadelphia by train the same day. Mack brought only two pitchers: Lew Krausse to start and Ed Rommel to relieve if necessary. It became apparent to Mack that Krause had little that very hot day. In the first inning he gave up four hits, a walk and three runs. In came Rommel.

The A's had scored a pair in the first, so Rommel trailed, 3-2. Philadelphia tied the score in the third and went ahead 5-3 in the fourth. Cleveland came back with three in the bottom of the fourth to take a 6-5 lead, and then added another run in the bottom of the fifth to make it 7-5. Each team scored in the sixth inning and Cleveland had an 8-6 lead going into the seventh.

In the top of the seventh, the Athletics knocked out starter Clint Brown and reliever Willis Hudlin before reliever Wes Ferrell came in to end the seven-run inning that gave the A's a 13-8 lead. Rommel must have felt great, at least until he gave up six runs of his own in the bottom of the inning and found himself trailing 14-13 going to the eighth.

Both teams were scoreless in the eighth, but all that changed in the ninth…twice. The A's got to Farrell for two runs in the top of the inning to take a 15-14 lead, but Rommel couldn't hold it and gave up the tying run. Probably the last thing that Ed Rommel wanted at this point was what he got: extra innings with the score tied, 15-15.

As hot and tired as Rommel and Ferrell must have been, the batters had nothing left either and the score remained tied for the next six innings. Fortunately for Rommel, the A's scored two runs in the top of the 16th to take a 17-15 lead. Unfortunately for Rommel, the Indians scored two runs in the bottom of the 16th. The game continued deadlocked, 17-17.

In the 18th inning, Jimmie Foxx, who had already

homered three times, got his sixth hit of the day and drove home his eighth run of the game. That proved to be the game-winner as somehow Rommel pitched a scoreless 18th inning and picked up the last major league win of his career. The loss went to Ferrell, who pitched the last 11⅓ innings, allowing 12 hits, four walks, and eight runs.

In this most amazing of all relief appearances, Rommel pitched 17 innings, allowing 29 hits, nine walks and 14 runs for the win. He also went 3-for-7 at the plate, scoring twice and driving home one.

The game only took 4:05 to play. Cleveland shortstop Johnny Burnett set the major league record for hits in a single game, going 9-for-11.

...18⅓

On June 17, 1915, Chicago Cubs pitcher Zip Zabel relieved starter Bert Humphries with two outs in the first inning and pitched the remaining 18⅓ innings to pick up a 4-3 win over the Brooklyn Dodgers. Jeff Pfeffer wasn't impressed. He was the losing pitcher, and he pitched the whole game. Zabel's relief stint set the record for the most relief innings thrown in one game by a single reliever. Zabel's full name was George Washington Zabel.

...pitches of Art Fowler

Art Fowler was 54-51 with a 4.03 ERA and 32 saves over nine major league seasons with the Cincinnati Reds, Los Angeles Dodgers and California Angels (he had a successful career as a pitching coach as well). His active career ended on May 4, 1964, while he was pitching for the Angels against the Kansas City Athletics. On the last two pitches of his career, Fowler threw back-to-back gopher balls to Rocky Colavito and Billy Bryan. Fowler lost the game, 7-4.

...and longest wait for a last lick

How long would you wait for one more shot at the Show? How long would you hang around, pitch batting practice, do a little coaching, with the hope of getting on the mound one more time? For one last lick?

Paul Schreiber pitched briefly for Brooklyn in 1922 and 1923, appearing in 10 games before coming up with a sore arm. He was only twenty years old that last season, and he wanted another shot at the Show so badly he spent the rest of the decade in the minor leagues. After pitching for Allentown in 1931, he gave up.

For most players that would be the end of the story, but it wasn't for Schreiber. By 1945, players were returning to action after World War II. The first-place Detroit Tigers came into Yankee Stadium for a seven-game series on September 4 with a record of 72-54-1. The Yanks were 67-58 and had won 11 of their last 14 games. Figuring he needed every available arm and impressed by the knuckler he'd developed, New York manager Joe McCarthy activated his batting-practice pitcher, Paul Schreiber, when the rosters expanded a few days earlier.

By the sixth inning the Tigers, behind homers from Roger Cramer and Hank Greenberg, who hit his ninth since returning from the war, had a 10-0 lead. This was a perfect time for the forty-two-year-old Schreiber. After nine years as a batting-practice pitcher, fourteen years since his last competitive appearance in a game, and twenty-two years since his last major league game, Schreiber came on to pitch with two outs in the fifth and struck out Paul Richards. In fact, Schreiber went the rest of the way, pitching 4⅓ innings of hitless ball, walking two in the ninth but escaping without a run. He walked back to the dugout to a rousing cheer from the fans.

No one before or since has ever been out of the majors for as long as Schreiber had and then returned to the game. He didn't have to wait long for his second and final appearance. He pitched one more inning on Sept. 8, 1945, again against the Tigers. This time he didn't fare as well. James P. Dawson in the New York *Times* wrote the next day, that the "Forty-three-year-old [sic] Paul Schreiber, late batting practice pitcher, who finished up in a perfect demonstration of his forte, throwing the ball against the clubs of the batters."

In his last appearance, Schreiber gave up four hits and two runs in his one inning of work. The Yankees lost, 11-4. The Tigers took five of seven in the series and went on to win the World Championship.

...and only hitless career

Randy Tate pitched one season in the major leagues, 1975, with the New York Mets. You could say that Tate was not a good pitcher (5-13 with a 4.45 ERA) and you would probably get some arguments that yes, Tate was bad, but he was by no means the worst. There are no arguments, however, that Tate was the worst-hitting pitcher in his only season, because he went 0-for-41 with 22 strikeouts. In one of his rare appearances running the bases, he was caught stealing in his only attempt.

…and only major league pitcher to give up a home run to his first batter…but also homer in his first at-bat

Dave Eiland, who was pitching in Class-A ball the year before, made his major league debut as a starter for the New York Yankees on August 3, 1988, at Milwaukee's County Stadium. On a 1-and-2 count, Eiland hung a slider that Paul Molitor hit over the fence in left-center.

"It was the first batter," Eiland told the New York Times. "'It only counts for one run."

Jump ahead to Friday night, April 10, 1992, at Jack Murphy Stadium in San Diego. After four cups of coffee with the Yankees, Eiland was pitching for the San Diego Padres. With Jack Clark aboard in the second, Eiland had his first major league at-bat. Eiland homered to become the only pitcher to give up a homer to his first batter in the majors and homer his first time at the plate.

…and only time a pitcher hit as many as nine home runs in one season

In 1931, pitcher Wes Ferrell of the Cleveland Indians surrendered nine homers and hit nine homers. Earl Averill led the team with 32, followed by Ed Morgan's 11, and Ferrell's nine. As a pitcher, Ferrell finished the season 22-12 with three saves.

Ferrell's 1931 home runs:
1. April 29 — vs. St. Louis Browns
2. May 17 — vs. Philadelphia Athletics
3. June 4 — vs. Boston Red Sox
4. June 21 — vs. Washington Senators
5. July 17 — vs. New York Yankees
6. Aug. 2 — vs. St. Louis Browns
7. Aug. 31 — vs. Chicago White Sox
8. Aug. 31 — vs. Chicago White Sox
9. Sept. 26 — vs. Detroit Tigers

…and only 20-game season…and career

Henry Schmidt went 22-13 for Brooklyn in 1903. Not being a fan of the East Coast, the Texan retired after the season, becoming the only pitcher to win 20+ games in his only major league season.

…and only (wild) pitch

Dick Hall was a steady big league reliever from 1955 to 1971. At age forty, he was the oldest pitcher in baseball when he made his last appearance with the Baltimore Orioles on September 25, 1971. Hall pitched one inning, allowed no runs, one hit and a hit batsman, leaving two on base. The last batter he faced, Chris Chambliss, flew out to left. But it was his last loss, on August 20, 1971, that won Hall a place in this book.

Hall was struggling, but it wasn't the four runs (three earned) he surrendered in one-third of an inning that was unusual, nor the four hits. It was what happened after he gave up George Mitterwald's double to lead off the ninth inning. The second pitch to Steve Braun was wild, allowing Mitterwald to reach third base. That was hardly newsworthy for some pitchers, but, in sixteen years of pitching, with 495 pitching appearances, 669 total games (Hall started in the majors as an outfielder), and 1,259⅔ innings pitched, it was the only wild pitch of Hall's career.

…and only pitcher to throw shutouts in both ends of a doubleheader

On September 26, 1908, the New York Giants and the Pittsburgh Pirates were half a game behind the Chicago Cubs for the lead in the National League. Cub pitchers were exhausted as they prepared to face the Brooklyn Superbas (soon to be called the Dodgers) in a critical doubleheader at Brooklyn's Ebbets Field.

Chicago's Big Ed Reulbach took the mound in the first game, played in the morning, and allowed just five Dodger hits to beat Kaiser Wilhelm, 5-0. Reulbach pitched the afternoon game too, and halted the Dodgers on three hits and a walk, shutting down Jim Pastorius, 3-0. The second game took just seventy-two minutes to play.

Thanks to Reulbach's 24-7 record (including nine wins against Brooklyn and a 2.03 overall ERA) the Cubs won the pennant after a one-game playoff with the Giants.

...and only perfect hitter

Of the 902 everyday players with just one game's experience from the dawn of baseball until today, only 26 hit safely in all their big league at-bats. Twenty-five went 1-for-1 or 2-for-2. Then there was John Paciorek.

The oldest of eight athletes and brother of former major leaguers Jim and Tom Paciorek, John was born on February 11, 1945, in Detroit, Michigan, where his father worked on a Chrysler-Plymouth assembly line. Paciorek was eighteen when he made his only major league appearance as a right fielder for the Houston Colt .45s, against the New York Mets at Colt Stadium on a hot, humid September 29, 1963. Only 3,899 fans watched Paciorek bat against pitchers Larry Bearnarth, Ed Bauta and Grover Powell. Paciorek went 3-for-3 with four runs, three RBI and two walks to help Houston win, 13-4. He also made two fine catches in right field. Paciorek's batting average, slugging percentage, on-base percentage and fielding percentage were all 1.000. He was Associated Press Player of the Day.

An All-State performer in football, basketball and baseball at St. Ladislaus High School in Hamtramck, Michigan, Paciorek had back problems earlier in the season while his average declined from .326 to .219 at Modesto, California, in Class C. Nonetheless, Houston manager Harry Kraft wanted to use his minor league players. In fact, two days before Paciorek's appearance, Kraft fielded an all-rookie team. On September 29, the last day of the season, his starting lineup consisted of eight rookies, including Joe Morgan, Jim Wynn, Rusty Staub, Chris Zachary and Paciorek.

"I didn't feel any pain during the game," Paciorek says. "It was a great experience." After playing in extreme pain and hitting .155 and .063 for two minor league teams in 1964, however, he underwent spinal fusion and his weight dropped from 210 to 160. Despite missing the entire 1965 season, he hung on in the minors until 1969, when numerous health problems led to his release at age twenty-four.

All in all, it sounds like a sad case of potential greatness thwarted. Not so, says Paciorek's son Pete, who played nine years of professional ball before becoming the baseball coach at Principia College of Illinois. In fact, there was an element of good luck attached. "My father was in Houston to have his back checked. They asked him if he wanted to play, and he said sure." So if his back hadn't been hurting, Paciorek might not have had that one, perfect, major league game.

After being released, Paciorek earned a physical education degree at the University of Houston and was a sports instructor at Houston's Jewish Community Center for six years. Since 1976, he's been a P.E. teacher and sports coach at the Clairbourn School, a nursery-through-junior-high private school in San Gabriel, California.

"Why did I hit so well in my one major league game?" Paciorek asks. "Because I thought I belonged there. I was cocky. That, plus I always could do things in a nothing-to-lose situation. But pitchers would have figured me out in the long run."

Virtually every spring he's sought out by local reporters for his views about the upcoming season. And he's always receiving baseball cards with his incomparable stats to sign. Having the most perfect major league record has its rewards.

"When it happened, I didn't realize that it would make me more popular years later," he says. "At the time, I thought that what I did and a dime would get me a cup of coffee."

...and only hits that were home runs

The Brooklyn Dodgers' Clem Labine was a pretty good pitcher, but a pretty lousy hitter. His thirteen-year career batting average was .075, but in 1955, Labine had a strange season. He hit .097, which wasn't so strange, but his slugging percentage was .387. Labine collected three hits, all of them home runs—the only homers of his career.

...and only persons to appear in a Phillies uniform for games at Connie Mack Stadium, Veterans Stadium and Citizens Bank Park

Larry Bowa and John Vukovich

...and only extra-base hit

There is no standard by which one might call relief pitcher Clay Carroll a good hitter. In fifteen big league seasons, Carroll batted .131, going 27-for-208.

Of his 27 hits, 26 were singles, but that one extra-base hit came on May 30, 1969, while he was pitching for the Cincinnati Reds. That night Carroll threw three innings of hitless relief and won his own game when he homered off Bob Gibson in the 10th inning.

...and only time a team drew 11 walks in one inning

September 11, 1949, saw the New York Yankees (who would win the pennant by one game over the Boston Red Sox) face the Washington Senators (who would finish last, trailing the Yanks by 47 games) in a doubleheader at Yankee Stadium.

When the Yanks came to the plate in the bottom of the third, the game was scoreless. At the end of the inning, fifty minutes later, the Yanks were up, 12-0. Eighteen Yankees came to the plate, and Senator pitchers Paul Calvert (two), Dick Welteroth (four), Enrique Gonzales (four), and Buzz Dozier, who wore sunglasses while pitching (one), walked 11 of them.

The Yankees scored their 12 runs on only four hits, a two-run double by Bobby Brown, a Phil Rizzuto single, a popfly to center field by Yogi Berra—one that numerous Senators watched drop—and another when Senators shortstop Sam Dente and left fielder Bud Stewart collided on a short fly to left field by Yankee pitcher Allie Reynolds. Both were knocked out cold, although neither was seriously injured.

...and only home run

On May 29, 1976, the Houston Astros' Joe Niekro faced his brother, the Atlanta Braves' Phil Niekro. With the Braves up 2-1 and one away in the top of the seventh, Joe hit the only home run of his career (973 at-bats). The Astros went on to win the game 4-3, with Joe the winning pitcher and Phil the loser.

...and only home run that was also the first

In the Montreal Expos' first game on April 8, 1969, Montreal pitcher Dan McGinn hit a home run in the top of the fourth inning off New York Mets ace Tom Seaver. It was the first Expo homer and the only one of McGinn's career.

...bounce home run

In 1926, Major League Baseball Rule 6.09 stated, "It is a ground-rule double instead of a home run if the ball is hit over the fence in fair territory if the fence is less than 250 feet from home plate."

In 1931, Rule 6.09 said, "A fair ball that bounces through or over a fence or into the stands is considered a ground-rule double instead of a home run."

When the Brooklyn Dodgers' Al Lopez drove one over the head of Cincinnati Reds left fielder Bob Meusel, and the ball bounced into the bleachers at Ebbets Field for a home run on September 12, 1930, he hit the last "bounce" homer in baseball history.

And no, Babe Ruth never hit one.

...and only player to hit fewer than 25 home runs in a season, yet still lead his league by more than 10

In 1915, Gavvy Cravath of the Phillies hit 24 homers to lead the National League. The runner-up that season was Cy Williams of the Cubs who hit 13.

...and only pine-tar incident

On July 24, 1983, at Yankee Stadium, the New York Yankees held a 4-3 lead with two outs in the ninth inning and the Kansas City Royals' U.L. Washington on first base. True to his reputation as a clutch performer, George Brett hit a two-run home run off Goose Gossage to give the Royals a 5-4 lead. Yankees manager Billy Martin came out to talk to umpire Tim McClelland, and on the way Martin yelled to his batboy to bring Brett's bat. Martin contended that Brett used pine tar that exceeded the eighteen-inch limit beyond the handle. McClelland laid the bat across the seventeen-inch home plate and ruled that Brett's bat's pine tar exceeded the one-inch border around home plate. As the result of his examination, McClelland ruled "no home run" and called Brett out. When the Yankees were declared the winners by the original 4-3 score, an enraged Brett stormed out of the dugout to argue and was ejected.

The Royals protested the game, and American League president Lee MacPhail upheld the protest by determining that excessive pine tar did not make the ball go farther. The game resumed on August 18 (a scheduled off day for each team), with the Royals leading, 5-4. Now was the time for another Martin hissy fit. The Yankees contended that Brett had not touched all the bases. But crew chief Davey Phillips produced an affidavit signed by the four members of Brinkman's crew stating that Brett and the baserunner in front of him (Washington) had touched all the bases on July 24. Martin was ejected.

The game took four weeks plus twelve minutes and 16 pitches to complete. The Yankees showcased pitcher Ron Guidry in center field and left-handed rookie outfielder/first baseman Don Mattingly in his only game at second base.

Brett sat in the Spanish Tavern in Newark Airport with Don Ameche's son Larry, a TWA rep, and Kansas City officials watching the conclusion of the game while waiting for a flight to Baltimore. Meanwhile, Dan Quisenberry saved the game, and the Royals were 5-4 victors.

…and latest home run hit in any game

The Chicago White Sox and Milwaukee Brewers were tied 3-3 in extra innings on May 8, 1984, when the game at Comiskey Park was suspended by the 1:00 A.M. American League curfew. When play resumed the next afternoon, Ben Oglivie hit a three-run home run to put the Brewers ahead in the 21st inning, but the White Sox somehow got three runs of their own. Finally, on the 753rd pitch of the game, Chicago's Harold Baines won it 7-6 with a 25th-inning dinger. Time elapsed: eight hours and six minutes. Tom Seaver, who pitched the 25th inning, notched the win and racked up another victory later on August 9 in the regularly-scheduled game.

…and longest second game

On May 31, 1964, the New York Mets and San Francisco Giants played a doubleheader before 55,037 fans at the one-month-old Shea Stadium. After the first game started at 1:00 P.M., the Mets jumped to a quick 3-0 lead, but that was all they would get off Juan Marichal. Al Jackson, Tom Sturdivant and Larry Bearnarth couldn't hold off Willie Mays, Orlando Cepeda, Harvey Kuenn, Jesus Alou, et al, and the Giants won 5-3 in a neat two hours and twenty-nine minutes.

The Giants held a 6-1 lead after five innings of Game 2. Then something strange happened to the normally anemic hosts: Both the Mets' bats and bullpen arms came alive. Joe Christopher, who had singled and scored in the sixth on an Eddie Kranepool triple, hit a three-run homer off Willie Mays' glove to tie the score in the seventh. It was a pitcher's duel from that point on…and on…and on.

Sturdivant pitched 2⅔ scoreless innings, and Frank Lary pitched two more. Then Bearnarth pitched

seven scoreless innings, topped only by Galen Cisco's eight. For the Giants, Bob Shaw pitched 1⅓ scoreless innings, and Ron Herbel four more. Then Gaylord Perry threw 10 innings of goose eggs.

In the 23rd inning, with two outs and nobody on base, the Giants' Jim Davenport, who entered the game in the eighth inning, tripled (he went 1-4). Cap Peterson (0-for-4), who had come in for the 13th, was intentionally walked. Del Crandall pinch hit for Perry and doubled off Cisco, driving home Davenport for the first Giant run since the third inning. Jesus Alou (4-for-10) had an infield single to drive home Peterson and complete the scoring. The Mets went down very quietly in the bottom of the 23rd, with Chris Cannizzaro (1-for-9) striking out against Bob Hendley, who was making his only relief appearance of 1964. John Stephenson, pinch hitting for Cisco, fanned as well (22 Met batters struck out). Amado Samuel (1-for-7), who entered the game in the third, flew out to Alou in right and the game was over, probably to the relief of the stragglers left at the park.

The second game took 7:23 to play, and baseball's longest day ended at 11:25 P.M.

> ## LAST LICK
>
> On August 27, 2000, the Philadelphia Phillies played the San Francisco Giants at home. In the bottom of the sixth inning, Bobby Abreu hit a home run to tie the game 1-1. In the bottom of the 10th, Abreu hit a walk-off, inside-the park homer to give the Phils a 2-1 victory—the only inside-the-park, walk-off homer.

…game for Frank Howard

Frank Howard played his final major league game as a Detroit Tiger on September 30, 1973. Serving as the designated hitter, as he had done for 76 of the 85 games he played that year, and facing Fritz Peterson at Yankee Stadium, Howard went 1-for-4 before striking out for the 1,460th strikeout of his career.

Howard already knew his time was up. Reminiscing later to the Washington *Post*, he said:

> Last series in '73 [actually it was the second to the last series], a cold, rainy, sleety night in Detroit, about 5,000 people in the ballpark

[pretty close, there were 10,529 in attendance, but Hondo was probably right there were half that amount when he came to the plate], and [Orioles pitcher] Jimmy Palmer's got us shut out 7-0 on two hits going into the eighth.

[Detroit Manager] Billy Martin says, 'Frank, grab a bat.' . . . I'm up with runners at first and second and nobody out. I hit what I thought was a BB inside the bag at third. And I'm thinking, Jesus Christ, a double and a couple RBIs…

As Howard broke out of the batter's box, he took a peek, figuring the ball was rattling around the left field corner. "Here's that great third baseman, Brooks Robinson, and he backhands me on the line and goes bing, bing and bing. Three outs. Triple play [around the horn, Robinson to Bobby Grich to Boog Powell]. That's when I knew it was over."

Howard batted .256 in 1973, not far removed from his .269 lifetime average, and hit 12 home runs to bring his lifetime total to 382. Trying to extend his career, he signed with Taiheiyo of Japan's Pacific League in 1974. At 6'7", Hondo towered over the American players, and the thought of him playing with much smaller Japanese players was a marketer's dream. In his first time at the plate, Howard took a huge swing and struck out. In the process, he tore something in his back and never played another game in Japan.

…and ultimate walk-off

Sometimes great things happen to not-great players. To be fair, describing someone as a not-great player doesn't make him a bad person, just a run-of-the-mill major leaguer whose greatest achievement was making it to the big leagues.

Take Ron Lolich. Selected by the Chicago White Sox in the 10th round of the 1965 amateur draft, he hit .211 with four home runs and 23 RBI in parts of three seasons. But on April 22, 1973, Mickey Lolich's cousin did something great.

It was the first game of a Sunday doubleheader at Cleveland's Municipal Stadium. The Indians faced the Boston Red Sox. With the score tied 4-4 in the seventh, Lolich pinch hit for Oscar Gamble and ended the inning by lining out.

With the score still 4-4 going into the ninth, Luis Aparicio doubled home one Boston run and Carl

Yastrzemski homered with Aparacio aboard to give the Sox a commanding 7-4 lead. In the bottom of the ninth, Leo Cardenas led off and reached on an error by Aparicio. After Rusty Torres flew out, Tom Ragland singled and Chris Chambliss walked to load the bases. Sonny Siebert came in to replace John Curtis on the mound and struck out Charlie Spikes. That brought up Lolich with the bases loaded, two out and his team down by three runs. Not a bad situation… Lolich hit the ultimate grand slam to give his team an 8-7 victory.

…home run for Chris Jelic

Jelic's career: 11 at-bats with the New York Mets in the last week of the 1990 season. Facing Doug Bair of the Pittsburgh Pirates, who was pitching the last game of his career, Jelic got his only major league hit on October 3—a home run to deep left-center in the last at-bat of his career.

…record-breaking home run for Roger Maris

Roger Maris hit his record-breaking 61st home run of the season in the final game of 1961, teeing off on rookie Boston Red Sox pitcher Tracy Stallard. The fourth-inning shot on October 1 was caught by Sal Durante, a nineteen-year-old truck driver from Coney Island and one of 23,154 fans at Yankee Stadium. The Yankees won the game, 1-0. This was Maris' only home-run crown.

…record-breaking home run for Mark McGwire

Mark McGwire hit his record-breaking 70th home run of the 1998 season on September 27 off the Montreal Expos' Carl Pavano.

…record-breaking home run for Barry Bonds

Barry Bonds hit his record 73rd home run of the 2001 season on October 7 off Los Angeles Dodgers pitcher Dennis Springer. His 50th homer that season was given up by Joe Borowski, currently the Indians closer, who was called up by the Chicago Cubs in 2001. It was Borowski's only start in the big leagues.

…the other record-breaking home run for Barry Bonds

Bonds broke Henry Aaron's all-time home-run record on August 7, 2007, when he hit home run number 756 off Washington Nationals left-hander

Mike Bacsik in the fifth inning. The San Francisco Giants lost to the Nationals, 8-6.

…home run as a Pirate by Barry Bonds

October 4, 1992, against Bret Saberhagen of the New York Mets.

…and only batter to hit a home run in his last at-bat and hit 50 home runs in a season

On October 1, 2000, Albert Belle of the Baltimore Orioles hit a home run off the New York Yankees' Denny Neagle in a 7-3 victory at Camden Yards. It was the last at-bat of Belle's career, making him the only player to hit 50 home runs in one season and homer in his last at-bat. Don't bother looking up Ted Williams; the authors did, and the most homers he ever hit in a season was 43.

…and only bookend home runs

Many players hit home runs in their first at-bat in the big leagues, many homer in their last at-bat, but the only player to do both was John Miller.

On September 11, 1966, the New York Yankees' Miller hit a two-run homer in his first at-bat, against Lee Stange of the Boston Red Sox. After batting .087 for the season, he didn't return to the big leagues until 1969, when he hit .211 in 26 games with the Los Angeles Dodgers. In his last official at-bat (he walked in one additional plate appearance), Miller blasted a pinch-hit home run off the Cincinnati Reds' Jim Merritt on Sept. 23. These were the only home runs of his career.

…and only grand slam

Peter Milne was a seldom-used outfielder for the New York Giants, but on April 27, 1949, his pinch-hit grand slam against the Brooklyn Dodgers—an inside-the-park home run—was the only homer of Milne's career.

…at-bat for Sadaharu Oh

The great home run hitter of the Tokyo Yomiuri Giants wrote a verse to commemorate the final at-bat of his career:

The sound of the crowd.
The clear colors of the sky.
The warmth of the sun.
The light of winter coming.

…and only switch-hitter to lead the National League in home runs and RBI in the same season

New York Mets third baseman Howard Johnson had 38 home runs and 117 RBI in 1991.

…walkoff that didn't happen

Some seasons start better than others. In 1976, the New York Yankees opened in Milwaukee's County Stadium. New York manager Billy Martin protested the Game 1 loss, claiming an improperly sloped pitcher's mound (it wasn't). Game 2 was even more interesting. The Yanks trailed the Brewers 6-0 going into the seventh. But the New Yorkers scored four times in the seventh and then five times in the ninth to take a 9-6 lead.

The Brew Crew had last licks and put their first three baserunners on. Milwaukee first baseman Don Money then hit the ultimate grand slam for a 10-9 Brewer victory.

Well, not exactly.

You see, Martin wanted rookie pitcher Dave Pagan to pitch from the wind-up and signaled that information to first baseman Chris Chambliss, who in turn signaled first base umpire Jim McKean by raising his hand for "time." McKean signified "time out" with his right hand, advancing to the dirt part of the infield when Pagan delivered the ball.

Money said, "I didn't hear nothing. I didn't see nothing...I didn't know what happened until I got back to the dugout."

Billy Martin certainly did. He ran onto the field and started screaming at McKean. After several minutes of histrionics, the homer was disallowed and everybody was called back on the field to finish the game.

The Yanks won, 9-7. Brewers manager Alex Grammas filed a protest, but in the end, this walkoff never happened.

…stolen base

When people discuss great defensive center fielders, invariably the speedy Johnny Mostil comes up. One spring training Mostil reportedly caught a foul ball down the left field line. If true, that's one fast center fielder.

Mostil played seven full seasons with the Chicago White Sox, leading the league in stolen bases twice and finishing second twice. But on May 29, 1929,

Mostil tripped over the front end of home plate on the front end of an uncontested double steal, fell, and broke his leg.

Just thirty-three, he never played in the major leagues again.

...and only American League player to have two World Series RBI without the benefit of a hit

On October 11, 1971, in Game 2 of the World Series, the Baltimore Orioles defeated the Pittsburgh Pirates, 11-3. In the fourth inning, Orioles starting pitcher Jim Palmer drew a walk off Bruce Kison with the bases loaded to drive home a run. In the fifth inning, Palmer came up again with the bases loaded—this time facing Bob Veale. Once again, Palmer walked, driving home a run. Palmer finished his career with a lifetime Series average of .048. Palmer was a career 1-for-21 with his only hit in the World Series on October 14, 1970, a single, against Gary Nolan of the Reds. He scored his only run as a result of that single.

...and only player to hit for the cycle twice for the Browns

George Sisler on August 8, 1920, and then again on Aug. 13, 1921.

...and only time a player drove in all nine of his team's runs

The Seattle Mariners had a pretty good night against the Boston Red Sox on September 2, 1996, playing at home in the Kingdome: They scored eight runs and held all but one of the Red Sox to zero RBI. The only trouble was Boston's Mike (Gator) Greenwell, who drove home nine RBI all by himself.

On Greenwell's first at-bat, against starter Bob Wolcott in the top of the third, he flew out to deep right-center. By the time Greenwell hit again in the top of the fifth, the M's had scored five times off Roger Clemens. With two outs, Tim Naehring walked and Greenwell homered to cut the deficit to 5-2.

The score remained the same until the top of the seventh, when Gator hit a grand slam off Bobby Ayala to give the Sox a 6-5 lead. In the bottom of the inning, the M's retook the lead 8-6 off Reggie Harris, with a two-run home run by Alex Rodriguez and a bases-loaded walk. But in the top of the eighth, Greenwell struck again, dropping a double down the left field line and driving home two runs to tie the game, 8-8.

The game remained tied until the top of the 10th inning when Greenwell singled home Wil Cordero with his ninth RBI of the game to give the Sox the 9-8 victory. Greenwell became the only player to drive home all nine of his club's runs (George Kelly in 1924 and Bob Johnson in 1938 each drove in all of their club's eight runs in nine-inning single games).

Alex Rodriguez summed up the story: "It was Greenwell nine and the Mariners eight."

LAST LICK

The only batter to rack up seven hits in one game was Rennie Stennett of the Pittsburgh Pirates, who went 7-for-7 against the Chicago Cubs on September 16, 1975. Stennett had four singles, two doubles, and a triple. The Pirates won 22-0, racking up 24 hits.

...and only player to earn a hit with two different teams on the same day

Joel Youngblood was the only major league player to hit with two different teams on the same day—the New York Mets in the afternoon, the Montreal Expos in the evening.

On August 4, 1982, Youngblood started in center field for the Mets, who were playing the Chicago Cubs at Wrigley Field. In the third inning, Youngblood broke a 1-1 tie with a two-run, bases-loaded single off Cubs starter Ferguson Jenkins. At the completion of that inning, Youngblood was pulled from the game and told that he had been traded to the Montreal Expos for a player to be named later (it turned out to be pitcher Tom Gorman).

"We hoped to make the deal by game time," Mets general manager Frank Cashen told the New York Times. "But there was a phone circuit problem, and we couldn't complete it. [Mets manager George] Bamberger asked me what to do with Youngblood, and I told him to go ahead and start him, we'd take a chance on his getting hurt."

Youngblood headed to Philadelphia's Veterans Stadium, where his new team, the Expos, was playing the Phillies. He arrived during the third inning. He entered the game in the sixth as a defensive replacement, and in his only at-bat singled off Steve Carlton.

"I heard in the third inning that I was traded," Youngblood said. "I made plane reservations [with] minutes to spare. I had dinner in the plane and caught a cab here. It's funny, I left there in the third and got here in the third."

Not only did Youngblood have two hits for two different teams on the same day...both came off future Hall of Fame pitchers.

....hit for Birdie

On September 14, 1952, the Cleveland Indians' Birdie Tebbetts went 1-for-1 against Allie Reynolds and the New York Yankees. The hit was the 1,000th and last of his fourteen-year major league career.

....and only player to strike out 400 times while collecting fewer than 100 career hits

Dean Chance, a pitcher from 1961-71, was a lifetime .066 hitter with 44 hits in 662 at-bats. Chance struck out 420 times.

...and only time three brothers hit consecutively in the same inning

On September 10, 1963, the miserable New York Mets faced the mediocre San Francisco Giants in New York's Polo Grounds. The youngest of the three Alou brothers, Jesus, made his major league debut pinch hitting for shortstop Jose Pagan in the top of the eighth. Facing Mets starter Carlton Willey, Jesus grounded out to shortstop Al Moran.

Next came the middle Alou, Matty, who pinch hit for pitcher Bob Garibaldi and struck out. Finally, the eldest Alou, Felipe, bounced back to the mound. Three Alous, three outs, no balls hit out of the infield.

...and only game caught by Lenn Sakata

A true utility infielder, Lenn Sakata played games at second, short and third for the Milwaukee Brewers, Baltimore Orioles, Oakland Athletics and New York Yankees over 11 seasons. On August 24, 1983, the Orioles' Sakata entered the game in the eighth inning to play second base against Toronto. The Blue Jays led 3-1 in the bottom of the ninth inning when Sakata drew a two-out walk and eventually came around to score the tying run.

Through a variety of machinations that produced the tying run, Tim Stoddard came into pitch, John Lowenstein moved to second, Gary Roenicke moved to third, Benny Ayala moved to left, and Lenn Sakata moved behind the plate for his only career appearance at catcher.

Stoddard immediately gave up a home run to Cliff Johnson and then a single to Barry Bonnell. That brought in lefty Tippy Martinez. Bonnell took a large lead in preparation for running on Sakata—too large as it turned out, because Martinez picked him off. Dave Collins then drew a walk. He too prepared to run on Sakata, and he too was picked off by Martinez. Willie Upshaw then beat out a single and guess what happened? Upshaw was picked off, again by Martinez.

Sakata's excellent adventure wasn't over. Cal Ripken led off the bottom of the 10th with a game-tying homer. Eddie Murray and John Shelby walked, and with two outs Sakata hit a walk-off three-run homer to give the O's a 7-4 win.

...home run for Pryor

Hall of Fame players have so many stellar moments they can't remember them all. Everyday players have fewer but remember them vividly. Greg Pryor, who played for the Texas Rangers, Chicago White Sox and Kansas City Royals between 1976-86, is a case in point.

Pryor only hit 14 big league home runs (never more than four in a season), but three of them were walkoffs. Pryor describes them:

On the Sunday before the 1980 All-Star break, we were playing Oakland, whose manager Billy Martin had sent me down to the minors three times when I was a rookie with Texas. We were trailing by a run with two out in the ninth, when Todd Cruz hit a grounder that should have ended the game, only Jeff Newman was drawn about six inches off first base to take the throw and he was called safe. They brought in a left-hander named [Bob] Lacey, and our manager, Tony La Russa, said, "Pryor, you're pinch hitting."

I was completely surprised. I hadn't even played for about 10 games and I didn't even have my batting gloves on the bench. I asked [infielder] Jim Morrison if he had any of my bats, and he did have one. Our third base coach, Bobby Winkles, said I'd get a good pitch to hit. I let the first pitch go, and it was right down the middle. I thought I'd blown it. But the next one was a good pitch, too. I hit it deep to left, Rickey Henderson jumped at the wall, and something white came out. I was in a fog, and I missed first base and ran down the right field line. Then an umpire made the home-run call. The ball was two or three rows in the stands, and it was a cup that had fallen out. I rounded third and ran past Martin. I heard later that he threw a clock radio against the wall in the clubhouse.

I was changing my clothes and the clubhouse guy said, "You've got to go out there—they're cheering for you." I put my uniform back on and took the first curtain call of my career. I've always said the White Sox' fans are the best in baseball.

A couple of seasons later, playing for the Royals, I hit another walk-off homer against Tippy Martinez of the Orioles. It's always a pleasure to run by a Hall of Famer like Eddie Murray on your way around the bases.

My last one was in 1984 in Kansas City [against the White Sox]. It was about 120 degrees on the artificial turf, and we went into the ninth inning tied. I turned to the umpire, John Shulock, and said, "If I hit one out, will you buy me a dozen golf balls?"

"Nah," he said. "You make enough money already." I came up again in the 12th, asked him the same question and got the same response. When I returned to the bench, I told our manager, Dick Howser, "I asked Shulock if he'd give me a dozen golf balls if I hit one out."

"Forget about him," Howser said, "I'll give you a dozen golf balls."

In the 16th inning, I came up against a big right-hander named Bert Roberge and hit a deep fly to left. Ron Kittle ran back to the wall, and the ball disappeared in the stands.

The next day a dozen balls were sitting in my locker. "Hey, skip," I said to Howser, "Shulock delivered the balls after all."

"No," said Howser, "I did."

...at-bat for Tony Kubek

Yankee shortstop Tony Kubek was one of those ballplayers, and later broadcasters, who didn't *need* baseball. He was just twenty-nine when he retired and had been suffering from the pain caused by crushed vertebrae. In his last game, on October 3, 1965, at Fenway Park, Kubek went 3-for-4 and in his last at-bat hit a home run to right field off Dick Radatz. Whitey Ford picked up the win.

LAST LICK

What is the connection between a .225 lifetime batter with 17 career home runs in eight seasons, two Hall of Fame outfielders, and the man who broke Babe Ruth's single season home-run record? Carroll Hardy was the only man to pinch hit for all three: Roger Maris on May 18, 1958 (Hardy hit a three-run homer), Ted Williams on September 20, 1960 (Hardy lined into a double play), and Carl Yastrzemski (bunt single) on May 31, 1961.

Oddities

...and only player to play for the Boston and Milwaukee Braves, and the New York and San Francisco Giants

Pitcher Johnny Antonelli, who also played for the Cleveland Indians.

...and only tripleheader

The only tripleheader took place at Pittsburgh's Forbes Field (there were two tripleheaders in the nineteenth century). The Pirates hosted the Cincinnati Reds on Saturday, October 2, 1920, for three very cold games. (The teams already had been scheduled to play a Saturday doubleheader; Sunday games were prohibited in Pittsburgh.)

In 1933, while sitting through a rainout, then-Chicago Cubs manager Charlie Grimm recalled the experience to a New York *Times* columnist. Grimm played for the Pirates in 1920:

It was toward the end of the season. And we could gain third place from Cincinnati if we played all our games and we won them, and at that time the first three teams shared in World Series money. The only way we could fit them all in was if we played three in one day in Pittsburgh.

Talk about the longest day in the year; that was the longest day of any year if you ask me.

The Reds won the first game 13-4, beating Wilbur Cooper and Whitey Glazner—that clinched third place for them and made the remaining games meaningless—and the second game 7-3, beating Guy Zinn. The Pirates won the third game, shortened to six innings by darkness, 6-0, behind Jug Handle Johnny Morrison. Five players appeared in all three games—Clyde Barnhart, Cotton Tierney and Fred Nicholson of the Pirates and Pat Duncan and Morrie Rath of the Reds. Reds catcher Ivey Wingo played the only two games of his career at second base in the nightcaps. Reds pitcher Hod Eller played the only game of his career at second base in Game 2 (he played first in Game 3). Following that afternoon, the National League directors ruled out tripleheaders unless they are necessary to determine a championship.

LAST LICK

Pittsburgh Pirates third baseman Clyde Barnhart collected a hit in each game of the tripleheader on October 2, 1920, going 4-for-11. He was the only player to hit in three games…in one day.

…real way to end a game

On May 7, 1925, the Pittsburgh Pirates played the Cardinals in St. Louis and trailed 9-4 going into the eighth inning. But after scoring six runs in the eighth, they held a precarious one-run lead going into the bottom of the ninth. The Cards put runners on first and second with no one out. Whereupon Jim Bottomley hit a liner that Pittsburgh shortstop Glenn Wright grabbed, stepped on second to double up Jimmy Cooney, and tagged Rogers Hornsby coming from first to complete an unassisted triple play. The Pirates won, 10–9.

On May 31, 1927, the Detroit Tigers led the Cleveland Indians 1-0 in the top of the ninth inning. Glenn Myatt and Charlie Jamieson reached base. Homer Summa hit a line drive to first baseman Johnny Neun, who tagged Jamieson between first and second base for the double play, continued running, and tagged second base for the game-ending triple play.

…not-so-real way to end a game

In the 1968 film *The Odd Couple*, starring Walter Mathau (Oscar) and Jack Lemon (Felix), Oscar misses a game-ending triple play by the New York Mets because he's on the phone with Felix. According to www.IMDb.com, the scene was filmed at Shea Stadium before a regularly-scheduled contest between the Mets and Pittsburgh Pirates on June 27, 1967. Originally, Roberto Clemente was supposed to hit into the triple play. When he refused, Bill Mazeroski took his place, successfully performing his stunt in just two takes.

…and only player with an artificial limb

Minor league pitcher Bert Shepard crashed while flying a fighter during World War II and had his right foot amputated. This didn't stop Shepard from pitching batting practice and exhibition games for the Washington Senators while wearing an artificial leg. He pitched so effectively that the pitching-strapped Senators activated him. While the Senators were playing five doubleheaders in five days, manager Ossie Bluege brought Shepard into the August 4, 1945, game that the Senators would lose to the Boston Red Sox, 15-4.

Shepard pitched 5⅓ innings, giving up just one run on three hits and one walk while striking out two. Shepard went 0-for-3 at the plate in this his only game.

…owner to manage his ballclub

Businessman and visionary Ted Turner has led an exciting life. Philanthropist, CNN founder, once Mr. Jane Fonda, he became the only owner-manager of the Atlanta Braves on May 11, 1977.

To say his Braves were struggling is an understatement: They had lost 16 straight games. Turner sent manager Dave Bristol on a ten-day "scouting trip" and took the reins against the Pittsburgh Pirates wearing uniform number 27.

The Pirates got a run in the first off Phil Niekro and the Braves tied it in the second off John Candelaria before Dave Parker's home run in the third gave the Bucs a 2-1 lead. Turner let coaches Vern Benson and Chris Cannizzaro make the strategic decisions ("I could have made some if I wanted," said Turner), although with two outs in the ninth inning and the score still 2-1, Turner joined Benson for an on-field discussion. With Pat Rockett on first, they decided to bat Darrel Chaney for Niekro against Goose Gossage. "We decided to use Chaney because he was our only left-handed hitter left," Turner explained later.

The move looked brilliant when Chaney lined a tweener to left-center that would have scored the tying run if it hadn't bounced into the stands for a ground-rule double. Rowland Office then struck out to give the Pirates their 11th straight victory and the Braves their 17th straight loss.

In his postgame interview, Turner stated, "Tonight I learned first-hand what's going on with our club. We're snake-bit…I'll be back again tomorrow. I don't want to be remembered as an 0-1 manager."

But that's exactly what happened. While preparing to manage the next day, Turner received word from National League president Chub Feeney that Rule 20, Section E forbids an owner from being a manager or a player without expressed permission from the commissioner. Since Turner and commissioner Bowie Kuhn were involved in a running feud, that wasn't going to happen.

Turner wasn't planning a longterm stint as manager anyway, since he had plans to captain *Courageous* in the America's Cup (which he won) that June. Turner enjoyed his managing experience. "I can spit my tobacco on the floor of the dugout," he said. "You can't do that in the stands." He added, "Managing isn't all that difficult. Just score more runs than the other guy."

…and only games managed

On May 12, 1977, franchise owner Ted Turner watched Vern Benson manage his Atlanta Braves to a 6-1 victory over the Pittsburgh Pirates and end the losing streak. The next day, manager Dave Bristol's "scouting trip" was cut short and he returned to manage the Braves until he was fired on October 24. The Braves finished the season 61-101. It was the only game that Vern Benson managed.

Here are the only games for nine other managers:

Manager	Team	Year	Record
Bibb Falk	Cleveland Indians	1933	1-0
Bill Burwell	Pittsburgh Pirates	1947	1-0
Andy Cohen	Philadelphia Phillies	1960	1-0
Jo-Jo White	Cleveland Indians	1960	1-0
Del Wilber	Texas Rangers	1973	1-0
Roy Johnson	Chicago Cubs	1944	0-1
Rudy York	Boston Red Sox	1959	0-1
Eddie Yost	Washington Senators	1963	0-1
Marty Martinez	Seattle Mariners	1986	0-1

…and only times teams used yellow baseballs

When we think of baseball gimmicks, we think of Charlie Finley and Bill Veeck, but it was the Brooklyn Dodgers' general manager Larry MacPhail who introduced canary-yellow baseballs at Ebbets Field. They were designed to help ballplayers see the ball more clearly in night games, since teams often had only temporary, freestanding lights.

The Dodgers tested the dandelion-dyed balls in an August 2, 1938, game against the St. Louis Cardinals, and the players complained about them. In 1939, the yellow ball was used in three more Dodger games: July 23 and 31 against the Cardinals and September 17 against the Chicago Cubs. Then the balls were put to rest, making these the only times a baseball any color other than white was used in a regular-season game.

…and only (but best?) day of his professional life

Facing the Texas Rangers on April 14, 2002, at the Ballpark in Arlington, twenty-six-year-old Seattle Mariners rookie and designated hitter Ron Wright struck out, hit into a double play, and hit into a triple play.

Wright came to the majors with blockbuster credentials. A three-time minor league All-Star, he hit two home runs that carried more than 500 feet, but Wright had serious back problems. Stretching before a minor league game in 1998, he collapsed and was rushed to the hospital. Wright had a disk removed from his back, but during the operation his sciatic nerve was cut. From that day forward, his right leg would feel numb, and he wouldn't be able to create power with it. At 6'1" and 235 pounds, Wright was suddenly a Punch-and-Judy hitter.

After a four-year marathon that took him from Altoona to Durham to Calgary, he was called up when Edgar Martinez ruptured a hamstring tendon. Following two days on the bench, he won an opportunity when a batting-practice ball ricocheted off the pitcher's screen and smacked into the side of Jeff Cirillo's head, opening a cut. Then Wright was bedeviled three times by Texas pitcher Kenny Rogers.

First, he struck out. Next, he came up with runners on first and third and no outs. Wright hit a chopper up the middle that Rogers fielded and threw to Alex Rodriguez for the force at second. When Ruben Sierra broke from third, Rodriguez threw home. In the ensuing rundown, Sierra was tagged out and Wright, trying to take second, was thrown out.

"I could see it developing," Seattle manager Lou Piniella said of the triple play. "Like a thunderstorm on the gulf."

Wright hit the ball hard on his third at-bat, but Rodriguez fielded it and started a 6-4-3 double play.

After another day on the bench, Wright was sent down when the Mariners needed bullpen help. He retired after re-injuring his bum leg in a collision at home. Married with four children, he is currently studying at the Idaho State University College of Pharmacy. He reviews his lone big league game with a sense of humor.

"Best day of my professional life," he told Lee Jenkins of the New York *Times*.

...and only Latin American All-Star Game

Baseball had its only Latin American All-Star Game on October 12, 1963, at the Polo Grounds. Before the game, Orlando Cepeda was honored as the most popular Latin ballplayer. The only extra-base hits were by Tony Oliva, who doubled, and Al McBean, who tripled but was thrown out trying to stretch the triple into a home run. Reliever McBean was the winner and Pedro Ramos the loser.

...and only time a player hit into a triple play and was not charged with a time at-bat

The Washington Senators' Goose Goslin stood on first and Babe Ganzel on second with no one out in the fifth inning of a Fenway Park game against the Boston Red Sox on September 26, 1927. When Joe Judge hit a long flyball to center fielder Ira Flagstead, Ganzel tagged up and went to third. In those days, that counted as a sacrifice fly, and Judge was not charged with a time at-bat.

Meanwhile, Goslin tried to take second and was thrown out. Then Ganzel decided to try and score, but Bill Regan threw to catcher Grover Hartley, who tagged out Ganzel to complete the triple play.

Flush with their fielding prowess, the Sox dropped the game 4-3, and lost the nightcap 11-1, committing 10 errors.

LAST LICK

On April 10, 1973, Houston Astros pitcher Jim Crawford made a memorable debut. In his first time at-bat he doubled in the 12th inning off George Culver of the Los Angeles Dodgers to score Johnny Edwards with the winning run.

It was the only walk-off hit of his career.

...and only hit in a game

There's a litany of players who broke up no-hitters by getting the sole hit of the game, but Denny Doyle holds a unique place. In eight major league seasons, Doyle hit .250 with just 16 home runs. But that didn't stop him from burdening a fair number of pitchers.

On April 18, 1970, the Philadelphia Phillies' Doyle led off the game with a single off the New York Mets' Nolan Ryan. Six walks and 15 strikeouts later, Nolan had a one-hit shutout. On May 24, 1971, Doyle got the only hit off Gary Nolan of the Cincinnati Reds: a two-run home run to beat Nolan, 2-1. Finally, on July 18, 1972, Steve Arlin of the San Diego Padres had a no-no going with two outs in the ninth inning when Doyle came to the plate. Fearing a bunt or a dribbler, third baseman Dave Roberts crept in close. Doyle blooped the ball over Roberts' head to break up the no-hit bid. Arlin was so shaken that he balked Doyle to second and gave up an RBI single to Tommy Hutton before notching the 5-1 victory.

...and only time Drungo Hazewood didn't strike out

The first time Drungo La Rue Hazewood came to the plate in the major leagues was October 4, 1980, for the Baltimore Orioles. Hazewood had played in four games as a pinch runner. In the bottom of the 11th inning, he pinch hit for Mark Belanger and flew out to center. The Orioles eventually won the game 3-2 in 13 innings, and manager Earl Weaver started Hazewood in right field for the second game.

First time up, Hazewood struck out against Rick Waits.

Next time up, still facing Waits, Hazewood whiffed.

Third time up, Waits struck him out again.

Fourth time up, Waits threw a pitch that Hazewood took for a called third strike. Hazewood walked back to the bench, never to appear in another major league game.

…Chance

On April 12, 1912, Vic Saier took over at first base for the Chicago Cubs, effectively ending the famous Tinker-to-Evers-to-Chance double play combination.

…and only team to win big and then lose big

In 1998, the Florida Marlins became the only team in major league history to lose 100 games the season after winning the World Series.

…and only home run hitter

The Atlanta Braves' Kyle Davies went 1-for-23 in 2006. His only hit was a home run off Randy Wolf.

…and only game not played by Larry Yount

Robin Yount's brother was taking his warm-up pitches on September 15, 1971, preparing to make his major league debut in the ninth inning against the Atlanta Braves, when he felt pain in his elbow and had to leave…never to return to a major league game. Because he was officially announced, he received credit for appearing in the game, but he never threw a pitch. So, let the record show that the Yount brothers played a total of 2,857 games, one for older brother Larry and 2,856 for Robin.

…and only appearance of Jay Dahl

Top winner on the Salisbury (North Carolina) Astros' staff, Jay Dahl was fatally injured in a car crash at the age of nineteen, making him the youngest former major leaguer ever killed. The accident occurred on June 20, 1965.

The Houston Colt .45s utilized him as the starting pitcher specifically to exhibit an all-rookie lineup against the New York Mets on September 27, 1963. Dahl gave up seven runs in three innings and was charged with Houston's 10-3 defeat. The other starters in that lineup included Rusty Staub, Joe Morgan and Jimmy Wynn.

…and only player to be used in more than 100 games without coming to bat or taking the field

From April 4, 1974, to May 4, 1975, Herb Washington of the Oakland A's appeared in 105 games, solely as a pinch runner. He stole 31 bases while being caught 17 times and scored 33 runs.

…and only appearance for Moonlight Graham

On June 29, 1905, the New York Giants were playing their crosstown rival Brooklyn Superbas (eventually to be known and loved as the Dodgers). The Giants held a 10-run lead in the eighth inning when manager John McGraw replaced right fielder George Brown with Archibald Wright Graham. No balls came Graham's way in either the eighth or the ninth. In the bottom of the eighth Claude Elliott flied out to end the inning as Graham waited on deck for his first major league at-bat. After that game, Moonlight Graham retired to pursue a career in medicine.

Doc Graham served the people of Chisholm, Minnesota, for fifty years and was immortalized in the movie *Field of Dreams*.

…player

According to Baseball-Reference.com, without which this book couldn't have been written, the last player alphabetically to play in the major leagues, making his debut on August 14, 1910, for the Chicago White Sox, was outfielder Dutch Zwilling.

Finishing his career with a .284 average in 167 games, Zwilling played his final game for the cross-town Chicago Cubs on July 12, 1916. He's the toughest part of the answer to the question that's been bedeviling you all chapter:

Who were the four players to start and end their careers in the same city, but with different teams?

Hank Aaron, Babe Ruth, Willie Mays and Dutch Zwilling.

Recommended Reading

We were inspired by many wonderful books that have been written about our great sport including:

- Anything and everything written by David Halberstam and Harvey Frommer
- *Baseball in '41: A Documentation of the "Best Baseball Season Ever"—in the Year America Went to War* by Robert W. Creamer (Viking), 1991
- *Baseball: 100 Classic Moments in the History of the Game* by Marty Appel, Neil Hamilton & Joseph Wallace, in Association with the National Baseball Hall of Fame (Dorling Kinderley, 2000)
- *Baseball's Strangest Moments* by Robert Obojski, (Sterling January 1, 1989)
- *Dingers!: A Short History of the Long Ball* by Peter Keating (ESPN Books, 2006)
- *Fall Classics: The Best Writing about the World Series' First 100 Years* edited by Bill Littlefield & Richard A. Johnson (Crown Publishers, 2003)
- *Game of My Life: Boston Red Sox* by Chaz Scoggins (Sports Publishing L.L.C., 2006)
- *Heartbreakers: Baseball's Most Agonizing Defeats* by John Kuenster (Ivan R. Dee, Publisher March 25, 2002)
- *Koppett's Concise History of Major League Baseball* by Leonard Koppett (Carroll & Graf; February 9, 2004)
- *Last Time Out: Big League Farewells of Baseball's Greatest* by John Nogowski (Taylor Trade Publishing; December 25, 2004)
- *Ninety Feet from Fame: Close Calls with Baseball Immortality* by Michael Robbins (Carroll & Graf; February 17, 2004)
- *Once Around the Bases: Bittersweet Memories of Only One Game in the Majors* by Richard Tellis (Triumph Books, 1998)
- *One Hit Wonders: Baseball Stories* by George Rose (iUniverse April 30, 2004)
- *Out of Left Field: Over 1,134 Newly Discovered Amazing Baseball Records, Connections, Coincidences, and More!* by Jeffrey Lyons, Douglas B. Lyons, and Bob Costas; (Three Rivers Press March 3, 1998)
- *That One Glorious Season: Baseball Players with One Spectacular Year, 1950-1961* by Richard H. Letarte (Peter E. Randall Publisher, 2006)
- *The Answer Is Baseball* by Luke Salisbury (Vintage; April 14, 1990)
- *The Baseball Uncyclopedia: A Highly Opinionated, Myth-Busting Guide to the Great American Game* by Michael Kun and Howard Bloom (Emmis Books; January 11, 2006)
- *The Best Baseball Games Ever Played* by John McCollister (Citadel Press, April 2002)
- *The Big Book of Baseball Brainteasers* by Dom Forker, Robert Obojski, and Wayne Stewart (Main Street; March 23, 2004)
- *The New Biographical History of Baseball* by Donald Dewey and Nicholas Acocella (Diane Pub Co; March 2, 2004)
- *The Seventh Game: The 35 World Series that Have Gone the Distance* by Barry Levenson (McGraw Hill, 2004)
- *The Unofficial Guide to Baseball's Most Unusual Records* by Bob Mackin (Greystone Books; (March 2, 2004)
- *The World Series: Complete Play-by-Play of Every Game 1903-1985 Compiled by the Originators of the Baseball Encyclopedia* by Richard M. Cohen & David Neft (Macmillan, 1986)

Index

Index (cont.)

Index (cont.)

Index (cont.)

Index (cont.)

Index (cont.)

Index (cont.)